Georges Bernage

Dominique François
for the iconographical research

Erik Groult
for the reportages in the field

First US Army

HEIMDAL

- Based on an idea and written by Georges Bernage with contributions by Dominique François and Erik Groult.

- Order control: Gabrielle Baqué.

- Maps: Bernard Paich.

- Art work: Erik Groult.

- Graphic art: Christian Caïra, Philippe Gazagne, Christel Lebret.

- Computer graphics: Philippe Gazagne.

- English translation: John Lee.

Left to right: Corporal John Hartlage of Brees (Illinois), Corporal Edward L. Smith of St Paul (Minnesota) and Private George Roberts of Herndon (Virginia) photographed on a half-track prior to D-day. (US Army.)

Editions Heimdal
Château de Damigny - BP 61350 - 14406 BAYEUX Cedex
Tél. : 02.31.51.68.68 - Fax : 02.31.51.68.60 - E-mail : Editions.Heimdal@wanadoo.fr

Copyright Heimdal 2004. La loi du 11 mars 1957 n'autorisant, aux termes des alinéas 2 et 3 de l'article 4, d'une part, que les « copies ou reproductions strictement réservées à l'usage privé du copiste et non destinées à une utilisation collective » et, d'autre part, que les analyses et les courtes citations dans un but d'exemple et d'illustration, « toute reproduction ou représentation intégrale, ou partielle, faite sans le consentement de l'auteur ou de ses ayants droit ou ayants cause, est illicite. Cette représentation, par quelque procédé que ce soit, constituerait donc une contrefaçon sanctionnée par les articles 425 et suivants du code pénal.

ISBN 2 84048 191 X

Foreword

On 6 June 1944 there took place on the coast of Normandy the largest amphibious operation of all time. By the evening of 7 June, the beachhead had been firmly secured, without penetrating far inland however, and after the initial surprise, the Germans were bringing up divisions in reinforcement. They would dig into the thick hedgerow country to fight the terrible Battle of Normandy, which lasted eighty days.

This album is a monument dedicated to the civilians who were also crushed or caught in this hellish battle, and to the veterans whose lives would never be the same again. It starts after the battle for the beaches, in the American First Army sector (1). The fighting on D-day has already been presented in our Utah Beach and Omaha Beach books (2), along with several hundred photographs. The present volume presents the First Army's eighty day battle in Normandy.

It offers a broad synthesis of the battle fought in Normandy by the US armies, and chiefly the First Army. It is the fruit of twenty years of labor and research already carried out on the battle of Cherbourg (3), that crucial initial phase which provided the First Army with a major port and a much bigger lodgement area. And also on Cobra (4), a little known and yet decisive operation which marked the end of the exhausting battle of the hedgerows and the breakout to Coutances and on to Avranches and Brittany within a few days. This body of knowledge, both historical research with our friend the American historian Martin Blumenson, and iconography perused for a quarter of a century, have made it possible to produce this monumental work on the battle fought by the US Army in Normandy. It will remain at once a reference work for researchers and a "memorial" to veterans and Norman civilians.

Alongside the detailed text, offering a clear synthesis, accompanied by 54 maps, we present nearly 1,150 photos taken in 1944 (nearly 200 previously unpublished) – including eighteen in color - and 243 presentday color photos for comparison, in addition to photos of items and badges, making a grand total of over 1,450 photos and maps.

We hope this book will help to gain a better understanding of that tragic summer of 1944 which changed the face of Normandy for ever and marked a decisive turning-point for the outcome of the war. It also shows that the war could have ended sooner had the net been drawn tighter around the retreating German armies in the followup to the brilliant breakout by the US armies. Twenty years after the book on Operation Cobra, this decisive battle again takes center stage.

Georges Bernage

(1) This is the official form. In these pages we shall also be using the form 1st Army.
(2) Editions Heimdal, 2004 and 2002.
(3) G. Bernage, *Cherbourg, première victoire américaine en Normandie*, Heimdal, 1990.
(4) G. Bernage, *Cobra, la bataille décisive*, Heimdal, 1984.

1. Without the war correspondents who covered the battlefield camera in hand, this book could never have been written. Pictured here are six female war correspondents at Cherbourg.
2. This battle ended in defeat for the German Army in Normandy. Pictured here is General Bradley interrogating German prisoners, officers, in August 1944. Here he listens to a Waffen-SS officer.
3. All the units committed to the battlefield suffered very heavy losses. Pictured here is an American medical orderly treating a wounded German. The German Army left behind 210,000 prisoners in Normandy.
4. Medics moving a wounded German.

Contents

Foreword 3

Contents 4

Order of Battle 5

Chapter 1:
The beachhead at Utah Beach (8 to 10 June) .... 6 - 11

Chapter 2:
The Omaha beachhead (7 to 10 June) .... 12 - 23

Chapter 3:
Hedgerow hell (11 June to 11 July) .... 24 - 37

Chapter 4:
Carentan and Saint-Sauveur (10 to 16 June) .... 38 - 61

Chapitre 5:
The battle of Cherbourg (17 to 30 June) .... 62 - 135

Chapitre 6:
Hedgerow hell (1 to 15 July) .... 136 - 191

Chapitre 7:
The battle for Saint-Lô (11 to 18 July) .... 192 - 253

Chapitre 8:
Preparation of Cobra (15 to 23 July) .... 254 - 279

Chapitre 9:
"Cobra" (24 to 30 July) .... 280 - 397

Chapitre 10:
The Pursuit (1 to 30 August) .... 398 - 459

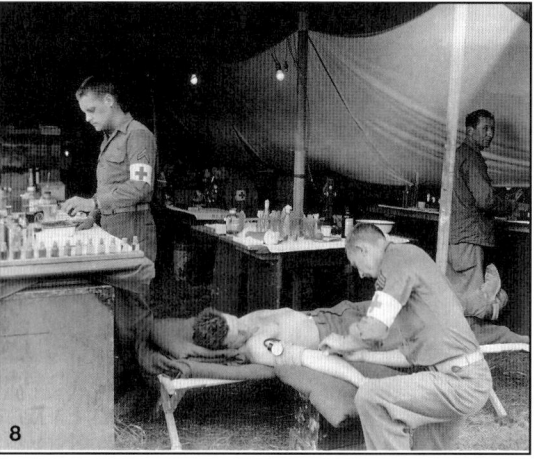

5. A GI examines German paratroopers' graves in the Saint-Lô sector in July 1944. The German Army had 240,000 men killed in Normandy.
6. Another German cemetery is examined by GIs.
7. An American field hospital on 24 July 1944. The US Army medical services took care of a large number of wounded, not just Americans but also Germans and even civilians.
8. Inside the American field hospital in August 1944.
9. In the early days, losses were heavy in the airborne bridgehead around Sainte-Mère-Eglise. Paratroopers killed in the first hours were just covered with parachute canvas. From 6 June to 25 August 1944, American losses totalled 124,394 men.

Ordre de Bataille
Order of Battle

 1st Army
 3rd Army
 V Corps
 VII Corps
 VIII Corps
 XII Corps
 XV Corps
 XIX Corps
 XX Corps
 1st Inf. Div.
 2nd Inf. Div.
 4th Inf. Div.
 5th Inf. Div.
 8th Inf. Div.
 9th Inf. Div.
 28th Inf. Div.
 29th Inf. Div.
 30th Inf. Div.
 35th Inf. Div.
 79th Inf. Div.
 80th Inf. Div.
 83rd Inf. Div.
 90th Inf. Div.
 Armored Divisions
 8nd Air. Div.
101st Air. Div.

10. American graves at the La Cambe cemetery. It was an American military cemetery before it became a German cemetery.

11. Temporary American military cemetery at Isigny in August 1944. Personal nameplates were fixed on the crosses for identification.

12. German tank dump built up by the US Army in the Cherbourg sector on 7 August 1944. Notice how most of the tanks used by the Germans in the Cotentin were salvaged French ones.

13. Here Americans are cutting up steel tetrahedra beach obstacles set up by the Germans. They mounted pieces on the front of their tanks to dig through the hedges during Operation Cobra.

These thirteen photos are all previously unpublished, as are nearly two hundred others in this book. (D.F./Heimdal.)

1 | The beachhead at Utah Beach (8 to 10 June)

The VII Corps' successful drop of two airborne divisions, 82d Airborne in the Sainte-Mère-Eglise sector and 101st Airborne in the Sainte-Marie-du-Mont sector, followed by the landing of the 4th Infantry Division against weak opposition at Utah Beach, enabled a beachhead to be firmly secured on the eastern side of the Cotentin peninsula as of the evening of 7 June.

On **8 June** however, this beachhead was still pinned down to the east of the La Fière marshes. In the south, after mopping up Saint-Côme-du-Mont in the afternoon, Maj.Gen. Collins ordered the 101st Airborne Division to carry on and take Carentan. In the west, on **9 June** the 82d Airborne Division led the attack on the La Fière causeway. Once across the marshlands, its battalions gained a foothold on the west bank. The next objective was Pont-l'Abbé. In the south, the 101st advanced on Carentan, and the 327th Glider Infantry Regiment took up position at the La Barquette lock, in preparation for the final assault.

In the north, the 4th Infantry Division now inched its way forward towards Montebourg, with the 8th Infantry Regiment west and the 12th IR east of Highway 13, and tank support from Company "A" of the 70th Battalion Tank. The advance passed through Ecausseville, past its huge airship hangar on 9 June, arriving on 10 June at Montebourg Station, some way out of town.

Further east, along the coast, the 22nd Infantry Regiment captured the Azeville battery on 9 June but the formidable Saint-Marcouf/Crisbecq battery was not overrun for another three days.

Thus the Utah beachhead had been firmly secured by evening on 10 June. Men and equipment poured in across the beach. Further south, the assault was launched on Carentan (see Chapter 4). In the west, once across the Merderet River, the advance continued towards Pont-l'Abbé and Picauville. But in the north, the attack was held up in front of Montebourg which was to become the cornerstone of the front in this sector until 19 June. The assault was therefore redirected furrther west, towards Pont-l'Abbé, Saint-Sauveur-le-Vicomte and the sea!

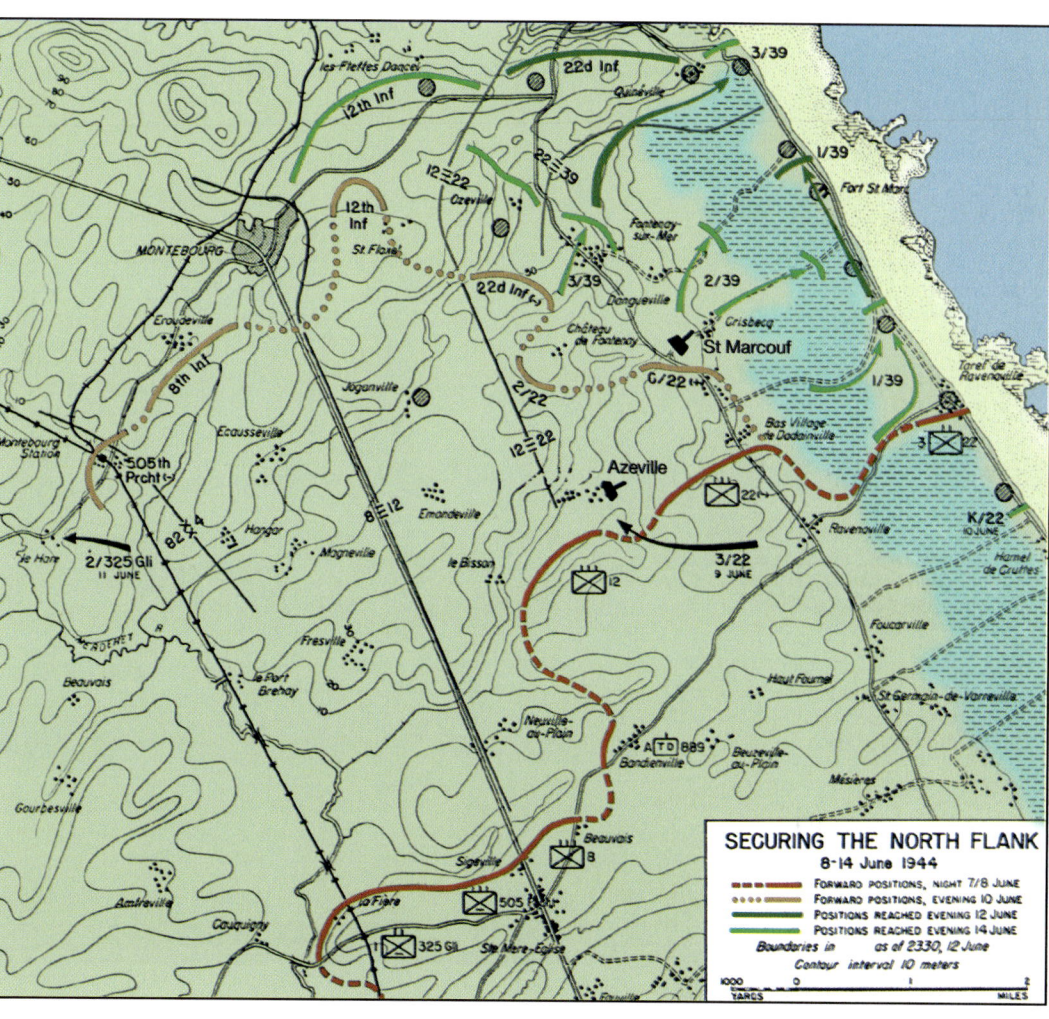

1, 2 and **3**. These three photographs were taken on Red Beach (Uncle Red) at Utah Beach, on the left of the beach sector, the right part being Green Beach (Tare Green). Here the banner marked Red Beach Hq has been censored out and Red Beach masked (there are some prints with the complete text). So this is the beach HQ located near Exit 2 more favorable than Exit 3, which for several days came under fire from the Saint-Marcouf/Crisbecq battery. On this beach, large masses of men and equipment were brought ashore. (D.F./Heimdal.)

4. At the same spot, an infantry column moves up off the beach towards Exit 2.

5. The front line was reinforced north of Sainte-Mère-Eglise. Pictured here is an artillery prime mover bringing up a 155 mm howitzer in the Montebourg sector on 17 June.

6. Supplies were also brought in by glider. Here, the runway at La Londe.

7. The Marcouf Navy-Battery (3./1261), known as "Crisbecq" to the Americans, was armed with powerful 210 mm guns housed in huge casemates. These guns strafed Utah Beach. The battery, defended by *Oberleutnant zur See* Ohmsen, held out until 11 June, before finally wilting under a succession of attacks. Pictured here is one of the Czech-built 210 mm guns after the battery was stormed by a battalion (2/9) of the 9th Division.
(Photographs courtesy D.F./Heimdal.)

8. This map shows us the fighting on the northern flank of the beachhead from 8-14 June, towards Montebourg which was a salient from 14-19 June. Pictured in the center is the advance of the three regiments (8th, 12th and 22nd) of the 4th Infantry Division, later reinforced along the coast by the 9th Infantry Division (39th IR). Covering the left flank was a regiment of the 82d Airborne Division (the 508th). Notice the capture in succession of the Azeville and Saint-Marcouf batteries. (US Army.)

9. On Utah Beach, the Americans temporarily park German prisoners before their transfer to England. (US Army.)

La Londe airfield, starting on 12 June 1944.

On the evening of 7 June, near La Londe Farm, owned by the Mauger family, two kilometers east of the town of Sainte-Mère-Eglise, bulldozers set to work clearing hedges to open the first airstrip in Normandy. The La Londe airfield was up and running inside five days, as a base for the 371st Fighter Group, commanded by Colonel B.T. Kleine from Gonzales (Texas), comprising three Fighter Squadrons flying P-47 Thunderbolts, the 404th (commanded by Major R.E. Gunther), the 405th (commanded by Major H.L. Case) and the 406th (commanded by Major E.D. Taylor). Each squadron had 25 aircraft, 16 operational and 9 held in reserve. The airfield remained operational until 30 Septembrer 1944.

1. Airstrip A-6 under preparation at La Londe. The engineers are rolling out Sommerfield track to make a 1,700 meter long strip which was operational by 12 June.
2. In this photo taken at La Londe on 15 June, the wing of a P-47 is being rearmed. The eight 12.7 mm guns on this fighter provided devastating firepower against unarmored targets. (5322)
3. This contemporary color photo taken at an unspecified airfield, mabybe La Londe, pictures the same operation.
4. One of these aircraft has just crashed at the La Londe airfield.
(US Army, NA and D.F./Heimdal.)

Sainte-Mère-Eglise sector, 11 and 12 June.

1. South-west of Sainte-Mère-Eglise, between the village of Gambosville (to the west) and Highway 13, from the very first days the Americans set up a huge field hospital in tents. The hospital was on a ten hectare plot between the Auvray family farm and the highway, which provided direct access. This photo was taken on 11 June. On the left, lifebelts have been set aside which the men were still wearing when they were wounded.

2. A German pfc is given an intravenous drip. The two American medics belong to the 90th Infantry Division. This photo was taken on 15 June.

3 and **4.** Two more views of the same field hospital. Notice some Germans among the wounded.

5. On 12 June, a captured German truck brings in the bodies of men killed during the battle. A temporary cemetery was set up. The first temporary cemetery was at the sports ground at Sainte-Mère-Eglise. The second temporary cemetery was on the Chef-du-Pont road.

6. The bodies are lined up for burial, wrapped in a shroud.

7. A medic, Sergeant Peter Slusarezyk, performs identifications.

8. This photo of the funeral of Brigadier Roosevelt killed on 12 June was taken a month later on 15 July. The ceremony took place at n° 2 cemetery at Sainte-Mère-Eglise.

9 and **10.** Ceremony at n° 2 cemetery.
(D.F./Heimdal.)

2

The Omaha beachhead (7 to 10 June)

1 and **2**. After seeing action at Pointe du Hoc and on Omaha Beach, the Rangers were again in action in the beachhead sector on 12 June. A liaison officer arrives on horseback with a message. The battalion mascot has a Rangers' badge fastened to its collar. (D.F./Heimdal.)

3. This map shows the rapid advance made from 7-10 June to the south of the Omaha Beach sector, beyond the swamps of the Aure valley, the capture of Isigny and later Trévières then the alignment of the front line as planned along the Elle and Vire valleys. (Heimdal.)

On D-day evening, after the V Corps sustained heavy losses on the beach, the Oma-ha beachhead was very narrow. On the morning of **7 June**, the village of Colleville was mopped up by the 1st Infantry Division which got as far east as Huppain that evening and south to Formigny on a level with Highway 13. To the west, the 29th Infantry Division sent 500 men of 1/116 and the two Ranger battalions to try and pull clear the Rangers pinned down at Pointe du Hoc, but failing in the attempt. On this second evening, the beachhead was still very narrow. On **8 June**, progress was much faster. In the west, in the 29th Division's sector running along the coast, the 116th Infantry Regiment finally cleared Pointe du Hoc and reached Grandcamp and Maisy, against German elements that fell back to Isigny. The 175th Regiment reached Highway 13 just before **La Cambe** and arrived not far from Isigny. To the south, its 115th Regiment took Longueville (on Highway 13) at 09.00 hours. 3/115 was at **Formigny** by noon. The beachhead now extended as far as Highway 13. Next stop: Isigny and across the Aure marshes.

On **9 June**, in the west, the assault was launched against **Isigny** as it burned following a naval bombardment. At 05.00, the infantry of 2/175 and 3/175, with the 747th Tank Battalion in support, captured the ruined town and took 200 German prisoners. The tanks passed through while an infantry company, K/175, attempted to take the bridge over the Vire River, but the bridge was destroyed and the other bank was well defended. South of Isigny, with the 747th Tank Battalion in support, the 175th Regiment advancec to cover V Corps' right flank. Its 1/175 arrived at **Lison** where it had dug in by nightfall. The 3/175 reached **La Fotelaie**, which it took over at 18.00 hours.

To the south, the four bridges across the marshy Aure valley, still wet and muddy at this time of year, were destroyed by the retreating Germans. The previous evening, Lieutenant Miller and his patrol went over to Colombières on the other side. At **08.30 on 9 June**, 3/115 followed the same path but were held up by the deep ditches and had to call in the engineers to throw bridges across them. This battalion finally reached **Colombières** at **10.30**, followed by 2/115. On meeting German resistance, 1/115 passed via **Canchy**. At around 23.00 that evening, 3/115 at last entered **La Folie** while 2/115 repelled a counter-attack from self-propelled Marder guns at **Bricqueville**. That battalion carried on, took a wrong turning and marched for hours, passing through Vouilly and then at Le **Carrefour**, with a fresh Marder attack, amid total confusion, 150 men of 2/115 fell, some of them to friendly fire. To the east, the 2d Infantry Division, having set up its HQ at Formigny, attacked towards Trévières. 2/9 set off at 11.00 hours, reaching Rubercy by midnight, after some heavy fighting. 3/9 was pinned down in front of **Rubercy**. The 38th Infantry Regiment finally reached **Trévières** at around midnight, by which time the place had been evacuated by the elements of Grenadier-Regiment 916 who had pulled out during that night of 9-10 June.

By **10 June**, all objectives had been reached. The 175th Regiment held the Neuilly-la-Forêt and Lison area. The 115th Regiment arrived at **Sainte-Marguerite-d'Elle** after a few skirmishes with retreating German elements, and held onto the north bank of the Elle. The 352. Infanterie-Division formed a new line of resistance along that river. To the east, the 9th IR (2d Division) passed through Cerisy Forest, reaching the sector north-west of **Balleroy** that evening, against elements of the reconnaissance battalion of 17. SS-Panzergrenadier-Division as they came up to the front. The 38th Regiment reached the village of Cerisy-la-Forêt.

By the evening of 10 June, the objectives had been reached. But German reinforcements were moving up to the front line: 17. SS-Pz.Gren.-Div. "Götz von Berlichingen", paratroopers of the 3rd Division, and elements of 353. ID. The hard battle of the hedgerowws was about to begin in this sector (see Chapter 3).

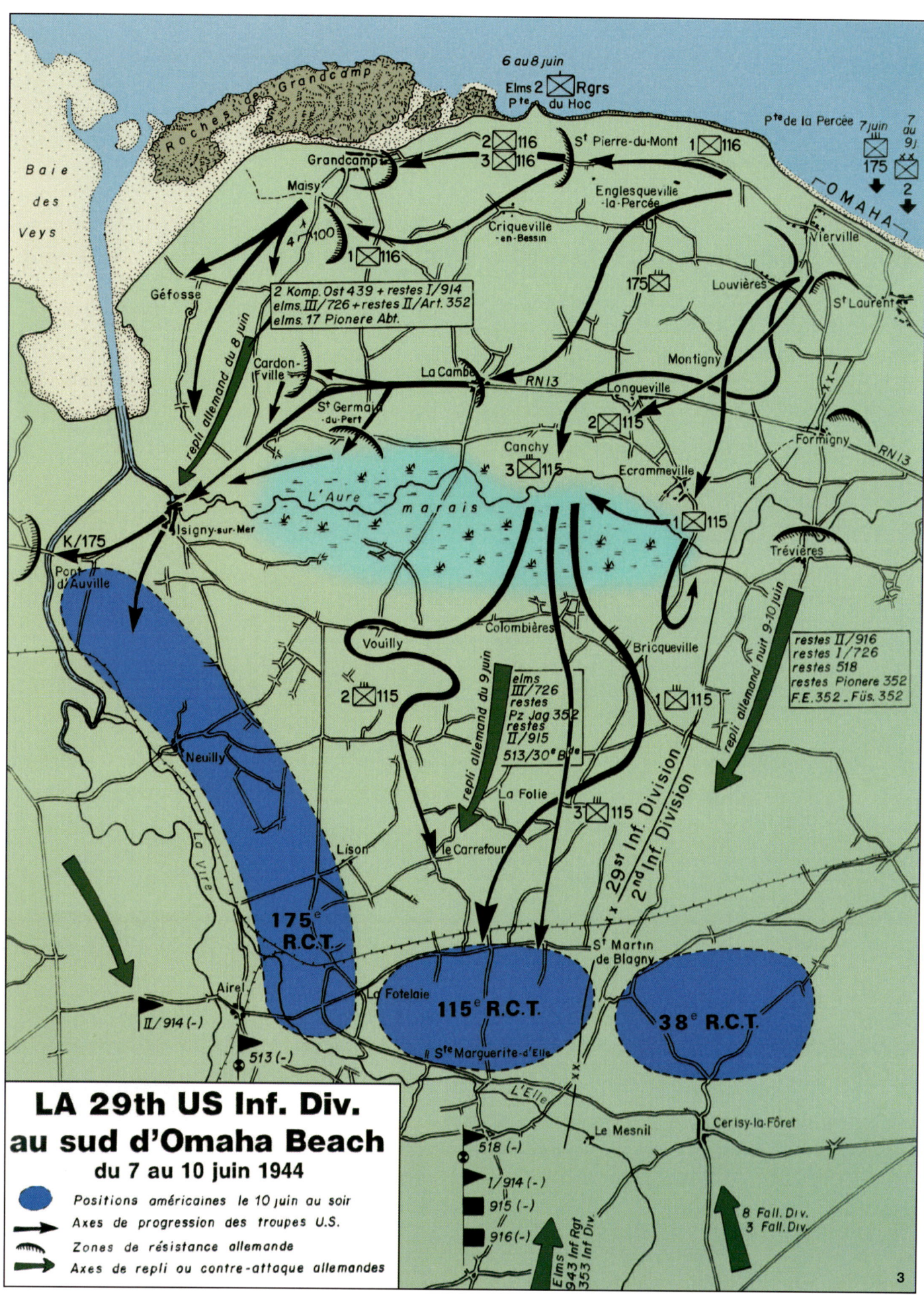

Isigny.

1. On 9 June 1944, 1/175, 29th Infantry Division took Isigny. However it still had to mop up in the small town destroyed by artillery fire and naval shells. Men of the 29th (notice the man in the foreground's divisional badge) patrol the central square.

2. This photo was taken just minutes after the previous one. The church bell-tower cannot be seen through the dust and smoke where its silhouette ought to be, at the back of the central square now covered in rubble.

3. A house in Isigny ripped open by shells. A Russian cannon has been abandoned by the retreating Germans.

4. An American half-track passes in front of the church at Isigny where the bell-tower, occupied according to the caption by German snipers, has received a number of shell hits.

5. Isigny was now firmly in American hands. On 12 June, Carentan was captured and the two US beachheads were linked up. An MP now directs heavy traffic, with columns of vehicles moving up to the front line.

(Photos courtesy Heimdal coll.)

The central square at Isigny.

1 and **2.** The central square at Isigny looking east, in the background is the street leading off towards Bayeux. An MP is directing traffic. The rubble has already been partly cleared away after the civilian population returned home. The hotel pictured here is still there today.

3. The same square seen from the opposite angle, facing west. Notice in the background the church bell-tower pictured on the previous page. Civilians are making their way back to the ravaged town they evacuated.

4. In the same direction, photo taken from the middle of the square. The vehicle convoys pass in both directions through the ruins.

5. On **15 June 1944**, civilians just arriving in Isigny where they found their homes destroyed following artillery duels between the Allies and the withdrawing Germans. They gathered in small groups to talk over what was to be done.

6. Discussion between an American soldier and some civilians. We recognize in the background the ruins pictured on the right in photo n° 1, on the south side of the square.

(Photos courtesy Heimdal coll.)

17

17-19 June. Isigny.

1. An American convoy crosses the main square heading west on 19 June.

2, 3, 4 and **5.** More photos of the same square in the same direction, 17 June.

6. A telephone exchange at Isigny used first by the Germans (with signs written in German still visible) and later by the US Signal Corps, photo taken on 19 June.

7. Photo taken the same day at Brévands, near Isigny, picturing a German telephone exchange linked up to the various coastal defenses. It was sabotaged by the Germans before they left.

8. Anothere shot of the central square at Isigny this tame taken facing east; notice the parish priest among the returning inhabitants.

9. The civilians have come home with their horsedrawn vehicles to be confronted with destruction on a vast scale, photo taken on 19 June.

10. They set to work to clear the rubble, 17 June.

(Photos courtesy Heimdal coll.)

Trévières, 10-15 June 1944.

1. This small locality was to the south of Highway 13 and the Omaha Beach sector. The 38th Infantry Regiment (2d Infantry Division) fought a hard battle all day on 9 June to take the village, only reaching it that evening. The Germans fell back overnight and on the morning of 10 June the Americans entered Trévières; pictured here is the central square facing north-eastwards.

2 and **3.** This photo was taken on 15 June in the market-place opposite the Hôtel Saint-Aignan, which escaped destruction. The body of a German soldier has been lying there abandoned for five days.

4 and **5.** This photo was taken from a little further back and pictures destroyed buildings (since rebuilt), to the right of the hotel.

6. The butcher's store seen on the left in the previous photo was badly damaged.

7. The mutilated war memorial testifies to the destruction.

8. This plaque recalls the four days of fighting needed to reach this village just a few kilometers of Omaha Beach.

(D.F. and E.G./Heimdal.)

5. On 17 June, a bulldozer at work to begin clearing rubble from the ruined buildings on the west side of the marketplace.

Trévières, 10-17 June 1944.

1 and **2.** Houses ripped apart by bombs could be tempting for looters, and the American authorities posted placards warning that looting was punishable by death.

3 and **4.** And the village soon became a hub of traffic heading for the front: Pvt William H. Brennan of Kingston, Pennsylvania, on point duty among the ruins.

6. The 2d Infantry Division pursues its southward advance to Le Molay-Littry, and now arrives in Balleroy Forest on this 17 June. Notice the wrecked German vehicles on the roadside. The men of this division came up against German paratroopers under these dense fronds. (5394)

(NA and E.G./Heimdal.)

3

Hedgerow hell
(11 June to 11 July)

On the evening of 10 June, the line of the Elle river was reached and it now remained for the beachhead to be deepened inland as far as the major strategic crossroads of Saint-Lô, a town that fell prey to the flames four days earlier, carrying off about a thousand of the local people (1). At La Fotelaie, on the Isigny/Saint-Lô road, the latter town was only fifteen kilometers away. Also, at a time when Isigny had just been taken, the two US beachheads still had to be linked up.

Up to **Caumont-l'Eventé** – on the left flank, the two V Corps divisions, 1st and 2nd Infantry, made fairly rapid progress against a crumbling German front. The deepest inroads were made by the **1st Infantry Division**. Field Order n° 37 of 11 June instructed it to race to Caumont-l'Eventé with the 18th IR and 26th IR, while the 16th IR was held back in reserve. The attack was launched at 06.00 hours on **11 June**, against slight resistance that only stiffened on arriving at Caumont. Company F, 26th IR entered the town where the Germans still had something like two infantry companies, an 88 mm gun and five or six self-propelled guns; it was repulsed. Reinforcements were required, particularly from the 743rd Tank Battalion, to capture Caumont on **13 June**. On a mound, the town, fittingly nicknamed the "Bare Mountain", was strategically an excellent point dominating the whole area. Here the V Corps had reached the southernmost sector of the entire First Army front, on a ridge, only to stay put for another month and a half! This was because on this 13 June, after being blown away, the German front was reformed and once more very strong. A fresh armored division had just moved up to this sector; the first prisoners of the 2. Panzer-Division were rounded up by the 1st Infantry Division.

On its right flank, the **2d Infantry Division** advanced as far as **Saint-Georges-d'Elle** but came under German counter-attack on **15 June** by elements of Fallschirmjäger-Regiment 8 and the engineeer battalion of 2. Panzer-Division freshly moved up to the front line. The American divisions had made rapid progress against a handful of retreating units. The arrival of German reinforcements – 2. Panzer-Division in the east, opposite the Caumont and Livry sectors, 3. Fallschirmjäger-Division north-east of Saint-Lô – would now hold up the front until mid-July, including further west.

In the west, let's come back to the **29th Infantry Division** which arrived on the Elle and Vire rivers on 10 June. On **12 June**, it had to cross the Elle to launch its offensive on Saint-Lô. The 115th Infantry Regiment crossed the river with three artillery battalions in support. However on reaching Les Fresnes (north of Couvains), 3/115 was encircled at around 11.00 hours by elements of Grenadier-Regiment 916 with a few self-propelled guns; this battalion had to fall back, and at 19.00 hours it crossed back over the Elle, having lost 66 killed and 164 wounded. 1/115 was unable to cross the river and so the 116th IR was committed at around 16.30; it crossed the Elle, reaching **Saint-Clair** at around midnight. This regiment continued advancing on **13 June**. With Sherman tanks in support, 1/116 took **Couvains** at around

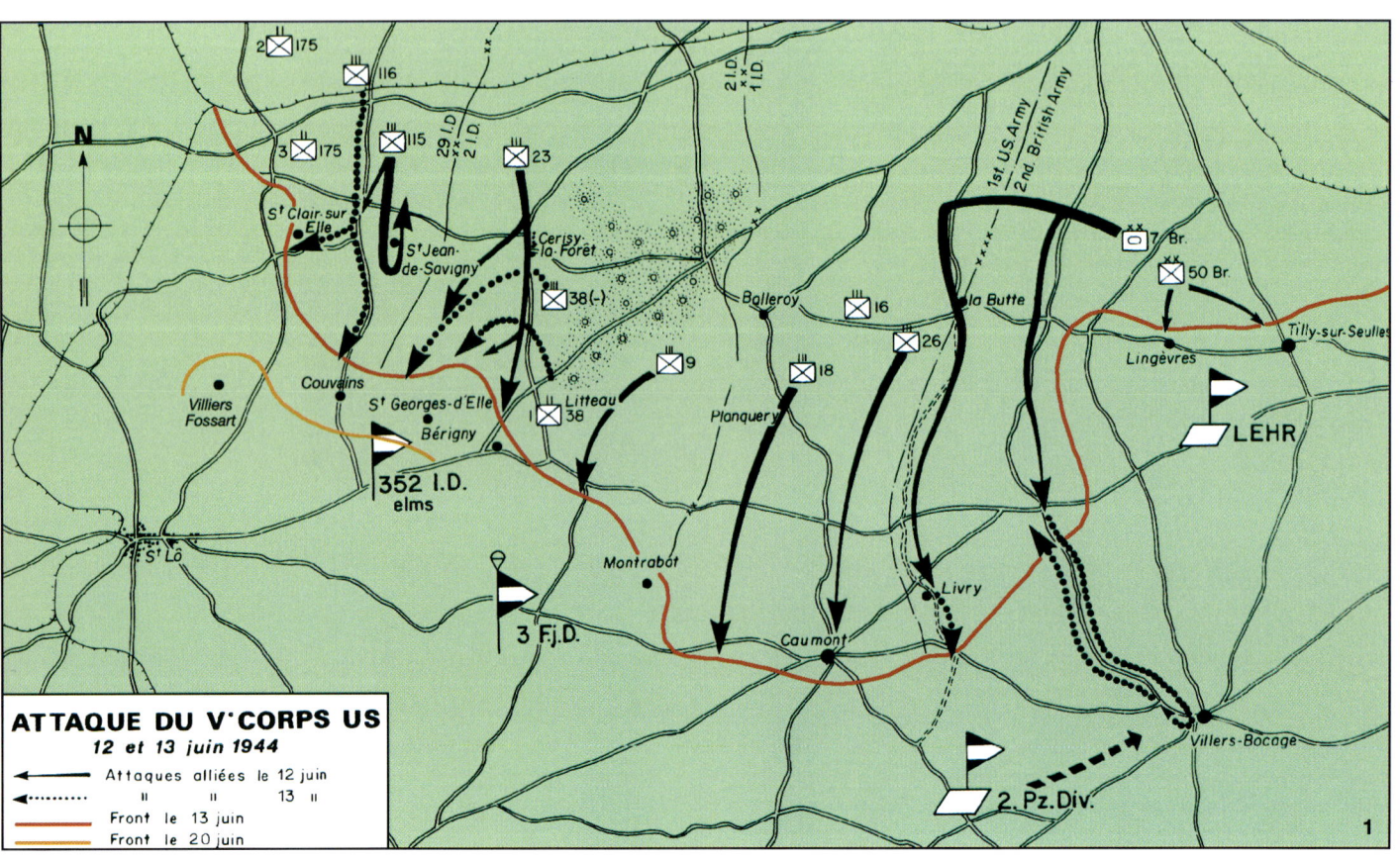

24

10.45, followed by 3/116. But this crossing of the Elle cost 547 losses among Maj.Gen. Gerhardt's men, and from then on the front stiffened. Despite the death of General der Artillerie Erich Marcks, the LXXXIV. (r. 84) AK commander killed by a fighter-bomber on 12 June, the arrival of German reinforcements enabled a firm front line to reform. Despite seven days of hard fighting, on **20 June**, the 29th Infantry Division was still pinned down south-west of Couvains, about six kilometers outside Saint-Lô, facing the Villiers-Fossard salient where in what came to be known as "hedgerow hell" capturing a single hedgerow was turned into a costly battle. There began a month of hard static fighting, with things only made worse after the terrible equinoctial storm of 19-21 June, destroying the artificial harbor at Omaha, substantially slowed down the influx of reinforcements and equipment for several days, and interrupting any offensive.

(1) The exact numbers are not known, around 500 recognized killed and 500 missing in the blaze.

1. The attack by the V Corps on 12 and 13 June 1944. The 1st Infantry Division managed the deepest penetration, as far as Caumont-l'Eventé which dominated the whole area, but the front stayed pinned down until early August. The 2d Infantry Division and 29th Infantry Division crossed the line of the Elle and covered a few kilometers before coming up against freshly arriving reinforcements, notably the paratroopers of 3. Fallschirmjäger-Division who got dug into the thick hedgerow country, stoutly defending every yard of ground. (Heimdal.)
2. The temporary grave of General der Artillerie Erich Marcks, commander of the LXXXIV. (r. 84) Armee-Korps controlling all German troops in the sector where the Allies landed. He was killed on 12 June 1944 by a fighter-bomber near Hébécrevon.
3. Sketch showing a typical German position set up through a hedge in the Saint-Lô sector. The right flank was held by the Germans, the left by the attacking Americans. An access is dug in the ground, then an underground corridor with a chicane passes through to the other side (part of this corridor is not shown in the sketch). On the other side, a trench is protected by a firing step. (Drawing by Heimdal after Albert Pipet.)
4. This GI comfortably ensconced in a shelter captured from the Germans. He even has a Norman cider jug close to hand. The Germans made a remarkable job of occupying the bocage. (D.F./Heimdal.)

Airfields in the American beachhead.

1. This reportage made at an unspecified airfield shows the successive operations needed to build runways at high speed, in just a few days. In this first photo, we see a truck automatically rolling out two hundred yards of Hessian mat, reinforced canvas on the future landing strip.

2. Engineers of the 9th US Air Force tarmac together two ends of Hessian mat.

3. A vehicle rolls out strips of Hessian mat.

4. In this photo, taken at the Grandcamp airfield on 16 June, the men are laying Sommerfield track. Pictured here, from left to right, are Pvt. Nick Sardella of Syracuse (N.Y.), Pvt. Lewis Wood of Mars (Pa.) and Cpl. Andrew Sotak of Munchall (Pa.). (5435).

5. A Lightning lands at an airfield in the Omaha sector.

6. This contemporary color photo, taken at an unspecified airfield, pictures ground crews coming to refuel some P-51 Mustangs.

(NA and D.F./Heimdal.)

4

5

6

12-20 June.

1. The 2nd Battalion, 116th Infantry Regiment, 29th Division, captured Saint-Clair-sur-Elle on 12 June. This is an aerial photo of that village which has taken some artillery fire. The Isigny road is on the right and the Saint-Lô road on the left alongside the church. This photo was taken by Carolan at an altitude of 400 feet on 7 July. (9536)

2. The church today, taken from a similar angle but on the ground. These houses can be seen on the right in the aerial photo.

3. The bar was already there in 1944, at the far end of the square at the top of the aerial photo.

4. At Saint-Clair-sur-Elle (photo taken on 21 June), an MP, Pvt. John Walters, inspects an office evacuated by the Germans of the 352. Infanterie-Division. The guard rota is still

sentday photo was taken by Bernard Paich in February 2004. (NA and D.F./Heimdal - presentday photos: St-Clair (E.G.) and Littry (B.P.)

marked on the board: - at Pont-Hébert, Sergeant Maurer, Staff Sergeants Bäck, Bauer, Netzel, Liebig, Himal, Weinzierl; at Saint-Clair, Staff Sergeant Graf ; - at Saint-Martin-des-Besaces, Staff Sergeants Bernsen, Dingel, Ernig, Fischer, Lauger; - at Roucamp, Staff Sergeants Engelhardt and Pfeifer, Corporal Berger. - Staff Sergeants Sendler and Lattwein are hostages. We were able to read off all this information with a magnifying glass from the unusually clear original photo. Hitler's portrait is still in place nine days after the village was liberated. (5648).

5. Saint-Clair-sur-Elle, memorial to the 29th Infantry Division.

6. At Sainte-Marguerite-d'Elle, north of Saint-Clair (the Elle river runs between the two villages), two GIs of the 29th Division (probably the 115th Infantry Regiment) read The Stars and Stripes and a letter from home in a trench on 16 June 1944. Notice the foxhole in the background.

7 and **8.** Less than fifteen kilometers from the above two places, west of Littry, near the oratory, a 4.7 cm Pak (t) Panzer-Kampfwagen 35 R (f) has been abandoned. This was a Czech antitank gun mounted on a French Renault tank chassis, a remarkable piece of DIY. It belonged to Schnelle-Abteilung 517. This photo was taken by Moran on 20 June 1944. The place has remained the same, the pre-

12 June 1944, visit by General Marshall

That day the top Army and Naval commanders came to take stock of the progress of the bridgehead in Europe. On Omaha Beach **(photo 4)**, First U.S. Army commander Lt. Gen. Omar N. Bradley (left), Gen. George C. Marshall (center), U.S. Army chief of staff, and Gen. Henry H. Arnold, general of the U.S. Army Air Force. Pictured again here **(photo 5)** are Gen. Henry H. Arnold and Lt. Gen. Omar N. Bradley along with (left), Major General Ralph Royce, deputy chief-of-staff who came over to supervise activity on the front. The official visit continued with an inspection of the Omaha Beach artificial harbor under construction. DUKW X32 was used for this tour of inspection. Aboard are Gen. Dwight D. Eisenhower, Lt. Gen. Omar N. Bradley, Gen. George C. Marshall, Gen. Henry H. Arnold and Admiral Ernest King. The visit then moved inland, with the same men plus Maj. Gen. Gerhardt in the background **(photo 6)**. Then we see **(photo 7)** General George C. Marshall and Admiral Ernest King.

(Photo courtesy D.F./Heimdal.)

15-23 June, reinforcements arrive

1. In England, these women of the Women's Auxiliary Corps (WAC) prepare to go to Normandy where they were assigned to services behind the lines. This photo was taken on 23 June and their crossing was held up by the storm. They fill in the time practising their French from a phrasebook.

2. These women embarked at Southampton on 15 June.

3. Pfc. Rocco Festa was a member of the Military Police of the 2nd Infantry Division. On 15 June 1944, he too made the crossing over to Normandy learning a smattering of French. The leading elements of his division landed on D-day evening.

4. These members of the First U.S. Army services pose under Normandy apple-trees on 15 June 1944.

5. Two days later, these others enjoy the delicious Normandy milk.

6. On 21 June, the mail reaches the front.

(Photos courtesy D.F./Heimdal.)

Lison station, on 17 June 1944.

Lison station, between Isigny and Saint-Lô, was a major rail junction where trains from Paris, via Caen and Bayeux, either continued northwards to Valognes and Cherbourg, or turned south to Saint-Lô, Coutances, Avranches and on to Brittany. Prior to D-day, the Allied air force had bombed such rail junctions. Pictured here is the outcome of the planned destruction: bomb craters, ripped-up rails, and burnt-out wagons. Several shots were taken facing west coming in to Lison station **(1, 2, 3)**. One locomotive has been spectacularly ripped open.

However, in order to move their vast quantities of supplies, the Allies were going to need the railroad network and so immediately set about making repairs. Thus in the Allied beachhead it was possible to go from Bayeux to Cherbourg via Lison station, until such time as further rail links were opened as the front advanced. On 12 July 1944, as we shall see later, the first locomotive set off from Lison on its way to Bayeux station.

(Photos courtesy D.F./Heimdal and DR.)

Captured German weaponry and equipment.

1. Pictured here are samples of weaponry captured on the battlefield from the Germans by the Americans. In this yard are eight 75 mm Pak 40s. Notice too the searchlight, the remains of two 88 mm guns and a 20 mm antiaircraft gun. The Pak 40 was a formidable German antitank gun firing a 75 mm shell capable of piercing 98 mm of armor at 2,000 meters and with a maximum range of 7,680 meters.

2. The famous German MG 42 machine-gun here mounted on a tripod ("s.MG" as opposed to the "l. MG" model with no tripod).

3. German 80 mm mortar, the Granatwerfer 34 which had a maximum range of 2,400 meters.

4. S/Sgt. John O'Brien of Hyattsville (Md.), shows how the anti-aircraft range-finder was used; behind him are some artillery observation binoculars.

5. Various weapons and other items of equipment: - a range-finder, - a Panzerschreck (German bazooka), - several rifles.

6. This GI is holding a rare weapon, a Fallschirmgewehr 42, specially issued to the German paratroops.

7. Examples of German mines and grenades. All these weapons were brought together for the photographer on 23 June 1944 at Saint-Clair-sur-Elle (where the 29th had its command post), except the guns in photo n° 1, which were photographed on 13 July.

(Photos courtesy Heimdal coll.)

4 — Carentan and Saint-Sauveur (10 to 16 June)

1. The attack on Carentan, on 10 and 11 June, involved a great sweeping movement by the 327th Glider Infantry Regiment which crossed the Douve near the river mouth. One of its companies (A/401) even linked up with the 29th Division (K/175) at Auville-sur-le-Vey. The two bridgeheads were now joined together. The final assault came from the west (2/502 at Pommenauque – the "cabbage patch") and especially from the north, via the wet dock with G/327 and A/401. (Heimdal after US Army.)

2. The attack launched west of the Merderet from 10 to 13 June involved first the 90th Infantry Division which launched its three infantry regiments in line. But it was an inexperienced division, and its advance was disastrously slow and costly in men; its commander was sacked, even though Pont-L'Abbé was taken at midnight on 13 June. (US Army.)

To deal once and for all with Carentan, a two-pronged attack was launched by the 101st Airborne Division during the night of 9-10 June. It lasted three days. The 327th Glider Infantry Regiment (with Colonel Joseph H. Harper in command) crossed the Douve near the river mouth, to the north-east, arriving east of Carentan with two of its battalions (1/327 and 2/327) while its third battalion (1/401 – a battalion detached from another regiment to make up numbers) approached from the north via the wet dock. Meanwhile, the 502d Parachute Infantry Regiment (then commanded by Lt.Col. John H. Michaelis, standing in for Colonel Moseley who broke a leg on D-day) led a frontal attack along the causeway through the inundated area. This unprotected causeway came under German machine-gun fire and on reaching "dry land", Lieutenant-Colonel Robert G. Cole, commanding 3/502, led a bayonet charge against the now famous "cabbage patch", a feat for which he was awarded the Medal of Honor. Thus on the evening of **11 June**, in the north-west, 2/502 was in front of Carentan. Elements of the 327th Glider Infantry Regiment (G/327, A/401, 2/327 and 1/327) were north and east of the little town. Also A/401 was at Auville-sur-le-Vey where it linked up with K/175. **The linkup had been established** between the Utah and Omaha beachheads!

Having run out of ammunition, Major von der Heydte, in command of the German paratroops of Fallschirmjäger-Regiment 6, evacuated Carentan late in the afternoon of 11 June. The battle for Carentan was thus fought between paratroops on both sides. The Americans bombarded the town during the **night of 11-12 June**, a pointless exercise as Carentan had just been evacuated by the defending Germans. Then the final thrust was made by the 327th GIR which entered Carentan unopposed from the north on this **12 June**. All the photographs shown in the following pages were taken on that day. On **13 June**, the 17. SS-Panzergrenadier-Division "Götz von Berlichingen", which had only just arrived in the German front line, launched a counterattack from the Périers/Carentan road. The assault destabilized the defending Americans, the Germans reached the outskirts of Carentan, in the station quarter (see pages 48-49). However the situation was restored with the help of reinforcements from the 2d Armored Division, brought in from the Omaha beachhead. The German attack was repelled. Carentan now became a vital communications center between the two beachheads. However, in the south, the German front was still close, hanging on in front of Sainteny where it put up some stout resistance.

In the west, the bridgehead secured on the west bank of the flooded Merderet valley would be used as a basis for the main offensive. The 90th Infantry Division under Maj. Gen. Jay W. McKelvie in turn crossed the Merderet and relieved the 82d Airborne Division, which had already sustained heavy losses since the night of 5-6 June. The 90th's three infantry regiments attacked in line (from north to south, 357th, 359th and 358th). The 358th IR took Picauville on **10 June**, its first objective. But, despite support from tanks and 155 mm guns, the offensive soon got bogged down.

On **12 and 13 June**, again little progress was made. Each day of fighting, the totally inexperienced 357th

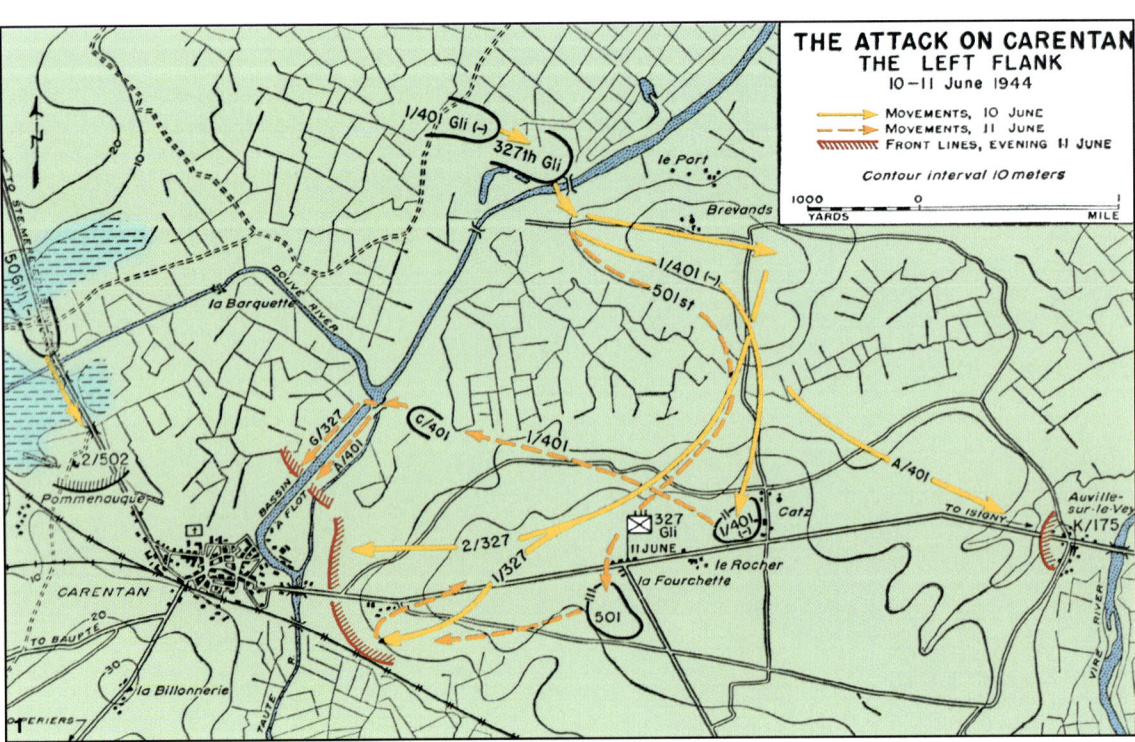

38

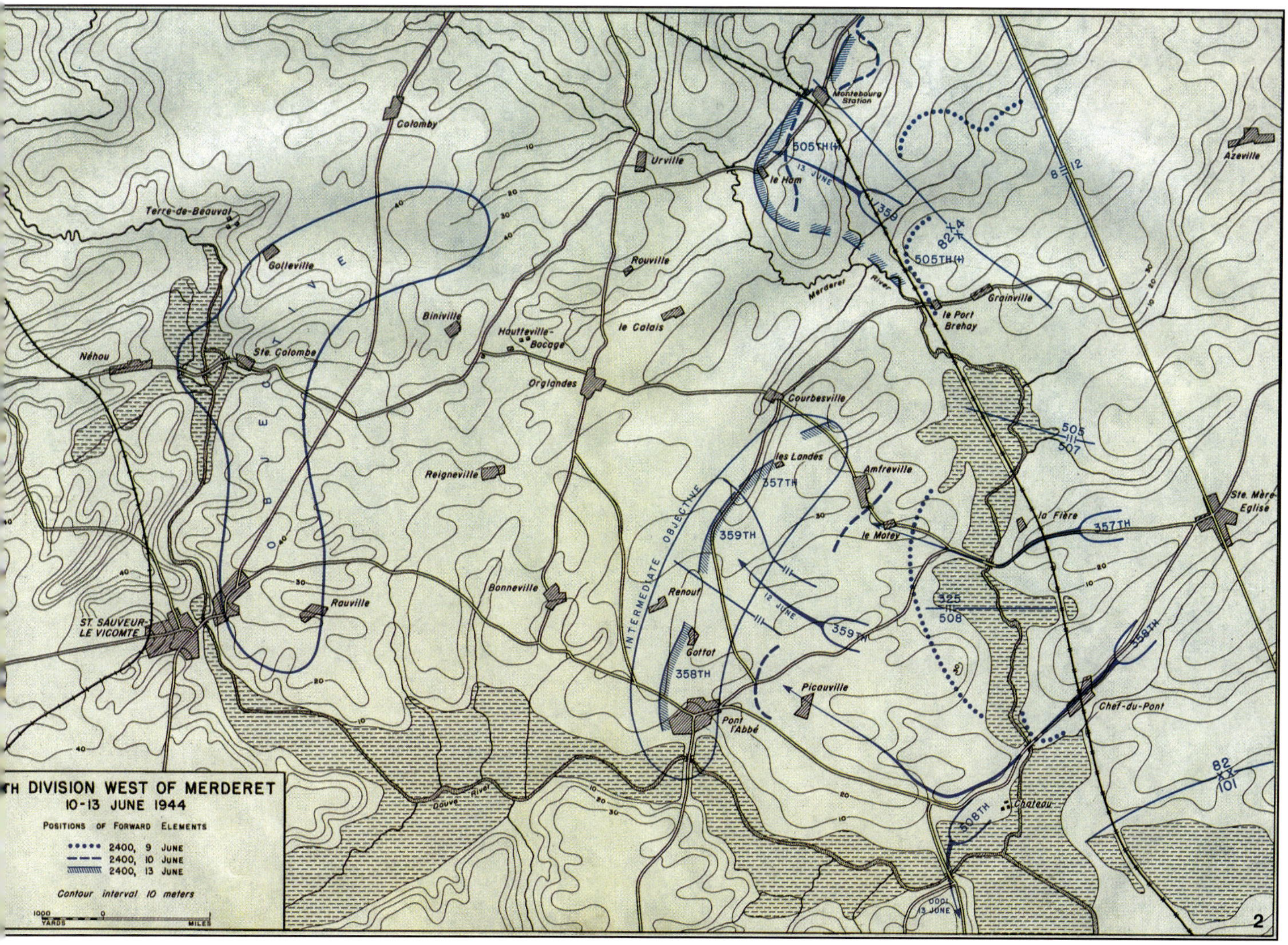

Infantry Regiment was losing 150 men! Against the stubborn Germans, the Americans bombarded Pont-l'Abbé at around 17.00 hours on 12 June. During the night of 12-13 June, the Americans finally reached the empty, ruined town. Foolowing the failure of the offensive, Maj. Gen. McKelvie was relieved of his command and replaced as 90th Infantry Division commander by Maj. Gen. Eugene M. Landrum. Also that same day, Maj. Gen. Collins brought the 82d Airborne Division back into the line to help the rookies of the 90th.

At dawn on **14 June,** the airborne troops of the 82d advanced west of Pont-l'Abbé, as far as the Bonneville sector. On **15 June**, the 82d Abn. Div. pursued its advance on either side of the road to Saint-Sauveur-le-Vicomte (see map on page 54). The assault on the town started at first light on **16 June**, with the Americans facing the locality dominated by its powerful medieval castle; they held the east bank of the Douve. Immediately at nightfall, they crossed the river and entered Saint-Sauveur. Further north, on the right flank, the 9th Infantry Division broke through the German lines in the Orglandes sector, advancing during the day further west on Sainte-Colombe and Néhou. By now everything was in place for a race westwards to the sea!

3. During the final assault towards the sea, the 9th Infantry Division covered the right flank. Pictured here are two men of one of the division's infantry regiments, the 39th IR, manning a mortar. They are recognizable from the letters stencilled on their helmets: AAAO (Anytime, Anything, Anywhere, Nothing. (D.F./Hemdal.)

39

Carentan, 12 June 1944.

1 and **2.** On 12 June, leading elements of the 101st Airborne Division entered Carentan along the wet dock. All hell was then let loose on the town and Major von der Heydte's German paratroops were forced to leave. In the Rue Holgate, leading from the downtown area to the level crossing (visible in the background), a house is still burning as the paratroopers of the 101st Airborne Division arrive.

3. Carentan firefighters, assisted by the civil defense, clear the ruins over a cellar.

4. Pictured here are firemen fighting a blaze in the Rue Holgate in the house seen burning in photo n° 1. This other shot was taken from the opposite angle, facing towards the town center.

5. Men of the 101st examine the destroyed house next to the one burning down in the previous photo. Most of the American soldiers pictured in these photos belong to the 327th Glider Infantry Regiment.

6. Another shot from inside the store.

7. Still in the same spot looking towards the town center (notice the church steeple in the background), men of the 101st survey the destruction. (D.F./Heimdal and US Army.)

41

Carentan, 12-14 June.

1. This particular photo was taken in the Rue Holgate on 12 June (the house on the left is still smouldering) facing towards the level crossing.

2. This photo was taken at the same spot two days later, on 14 June. But although the rubble has not been cleared away, the hospital units' jeeps could still get through.

3. This presentday photo was taken at the same spot from a slightly different angle, showing the 17th century stone and brick house (the former Augustine convent, now the Town Hall) and the modern buildings built where the houses destroyed by fire used to stand.

4. Another view of the town center, the hospital units continue moving towards the level crossing and the road to Périers where the front line is. Pictured here is a German ambulance captured by US paratroops.

5 and **6.** More shots picturing troops and medics moving down the Rue Holgate towards the level crossing and the Périers road. The destruction is worse on the left, east side of the street.

7. We now come close to the level crossing and Désiré Ingouf's restaurant (since destroyed), which became famous through these photos. A jeep moves up the front line with an antitank gun in tow. The German signs are still in place on Désiré Ingouf's house.

42

8. A little further on, rounding the street corner, we come to the street leading to Sainte-Mère-Eglise and Cherbourg. The GIs have captured a German Kübelwagen previously used by the German paratroopers - the "W L" is a Luftwaffe registration.
(Photos D.F. and E.G./Heimdal, US Army.)

1 and **2.** Another photo taken on the morning of 12 June as smoke from the fires rises up over the town. This is again the Rue Holgate, south of the railroad, at the junction of the roads to Périers (now the D 871 road), along which the 501st PIR is advancing, and to Baupte and La Haye-du-Puits (now the D 903 road), along which the 506th PIR is advancing. Notice the ambulance abandoned by Fallschirmjäger-Regiment 6. The present-day photo shows how little the spot has changed. The house in ruins has been replaced by a new, traditional-style building.

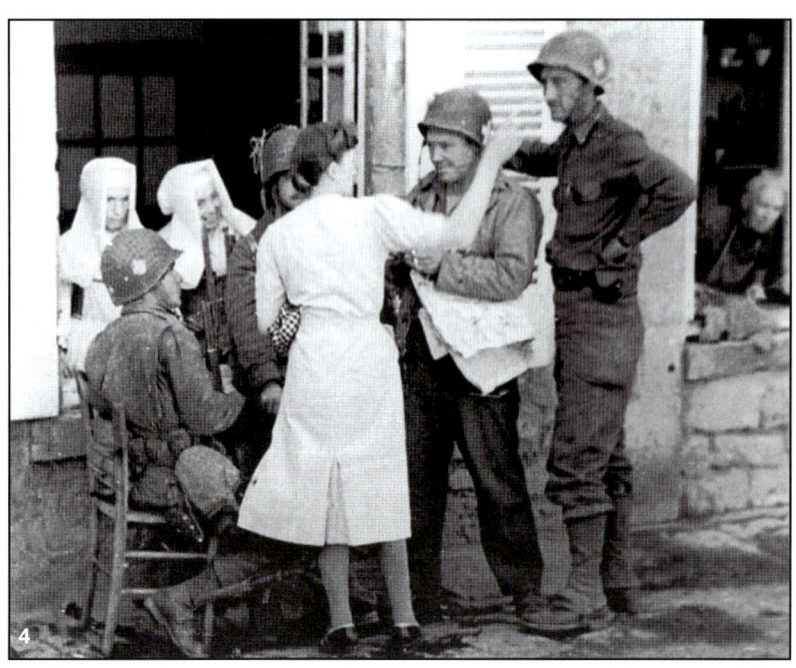

3. In the same neighborhood, men of the Glider Infantry Regiment take a break in front of the house opposite Désiré Ingouf's restaurant on the Cherbourg road (see the photo with the Kübelwagen, on the right of the page 43).

4. Men of the 327th Gliders with civilians, including some nuns.

5. But the men of the 101st Airborne Division would find more vehicles abandoned by von der Heydte's paratroopers, tracked motorcycles in particular. The Kettenkrad, here in a shelter dug in a schoolyard (photo taken on 14 June), was their favorite vehicle, owing to its great mobility on even the hilliest terrain. This one was christened "Julitta" by the German paratroopers.
6. It could carry two passengers.

7, 8 and **9.** It could also be loaded with equipment and tow a trailer.
10. Some were covered in camouflage paint.
11. Others were heavily laden.
(D.F./Heimdal and US Army.)

Carentan, downtown area, 14-16 June.

1. In the Place Vauban, men of the 327th Glider Infantry Regiment (recognizable from the cloverleaf of the regimental crest stencilled on their helmets) show directions that appear to bring them closer to victory: Cherbourg, Saint-Lô and even Paris. These are still distant objectives however. This square is between the Rue Holgate and the downtown area with the Place de la République. The Rue Holgate is on the left, the old Cherbourg road is straight ahead, with the Place de la République on the right.

2 and **3.** A little later, Pvt. Willie Hinesy, of the same regiment, mounting guard at the same spot.

4. We now come to the Place de la République where a jeep has stopped, on its way from the Place Vauban. Here too there is destruction. Notice the road to Isigny in the background.

5. Again in the Place de la République, where men of the 327th GIR have gathered round the war memorial.

6 and **7.** At the same spot two days later, 16 June. A 101st Airborne Division chaplain blesses the paratroopers gathered round the memorial, which has been draped with parachutes.

8. The war memorial from an angle similar to the one in photo n° 4 (again notice the destroyed house near the Café du Progrès). Pictured are Pvt. Charles E. Rinehart (506th), Sgt. James V. Longane (327th) and Pvt. Charles A. West (506th).

9. The south side of the memorial, towards the church visible in the background.

10 and **11.** A first ceremony was held in the Place de la République on 16 June, photo taken facing the Place du Valnoble with the medieval arcaded houses on the right.

(D.F./Heimdal and US Army.)

47

Carentan, 13 June 1944, the German counterattack.

1 and **2.** On 13 June, 17. SS-Panzergrenadier-Division "Götz von Berlichingen" counter-attacked along the line of the Périers-Carentan road. It launched its SS-Panzer-Abteilung 17's 37 assault guns on Carentan, approaching from the south to within about 500 yards. These elements had support from von der Heydte's paratroopers of FJR6 who took on their American counterparts around Carentan station. The American paratroops were thoroughly trounced and sometimes pushed back from their positions south-west of Carentan (Hill 30). However reinforcements were soon at hand to save the day before things got too dangerous. arrivent The US 2d Armored Division had already landed on Omaha Beach and its CCA arrived to bolster the paratroopers of the 101st, by now in serious trouble. The leading tanks were reported at 10.30. An all-out attack was launched at 14.00 hours on the western flank by the paratroops of the 501st PIR with support from the 66th Armored Regiment's tanks, the guns of the 14th Armored Field Artillery Battalion and P-47s of the 9th US Air Force. Under this deluge of fire, the Germans fell back, leaving behind in the field assault guns and over 500 bodies of Waffen-SS and troopers of II./FJR6. Pictured in this photo taken five days later, on 18 June, at the Carentan level crossing, is a 105 mm self-propelled howitzer of the 14th F.A.B., 2d Armored Division crossing the railroad on its way back from the Périers road where it helped to crush the German attack. In the present-day photo, the half-timbered gable wall of the house has been rebuilt, and the level crossing has gone, replaced by a bridge a little further west.

3 and **4.** Near one of SS-Pz.-Abt. 17's destroyed assault guns, an American antitank gun has been set up facing south towards Périers aimed at the "Götz von Berlichin-

gen" Division. On the left (to the west), the road from Baupte and La Haye-du-Puits comes to an end.

5. An American howitzer in action in the Carentan sector; the artillery helped to crush the German counter-attacks.

6. An Sd.Kfz 222 armored reconnaissance vehicle with a 20 mm gun was destroyed in the Carentan sector. It probably belonged to the Götz's reconnaissance battalion, SS-Pz.-Aufkl.-Abt. 17.

7. A dump for destroyed German equipment was set up near Carentan. Pictured here is an ambulance with a "WL" registration, maybe the one we saw in Carentan.

(Photos DAVA, D.F. and E.G./Heimdal.)

Carentan, 15-20 July.

1 and **2.** On 17 June, chaplain Francis L. Sampson blesses the bodies of troopers killed in the Carentan sector. The bodies were wrapped in parachutes.

3. Two women put flowers on a paratrooper's grave.

4. After the fighting and once the threat of a counterattack had been removed, these men of the 101st Airborne Division can at last take a rest and relieve the stress. One has put an airborne trooper's cap on a local kid's head.

5. On 15 June, these civilians are flying a French flag and the Stars and Stripes on the balcony of their house in the Place de la République, next to the Café du Progrès.

6. Another ceremony was held in the Place de la République on the evening of 20 June. Silver Stars were awarded to officers and men of the 101st Airborne Division. Colonel Johnson (501st), Lieutenant-Colonel Michaelis (502d), Colonel Sink (506th) and Colonel Harper (327th/401st) received the Distinguished Service Cross.

7 and **8.** Coming from downtown and heading for Isigny, this jeep of 1/401 takes what was still Highway 13 and has since been downgraded to the Rue de l'Isle.

(US Army and D.F./Heimdal.)

Carentan, behind the front line

1. Following the German counterstroke of 13 June, the immediate threat had been removed but the German front line was still close, north of Sainteny, and the German artillery threatened this vital passing point between the Omaha beachhead to the east and the Utah beachhead to the west. Here again, elements of the 101st Airborne Division have salvaged some German vehicles. One has been converted into an ambulance.

2. Here again, the fighting has caused devastation and ruin. Two men of the 101st Airborne Division survey a small house half-destroyed on the edge of the marshes pictured in the background.

3 and **4.** The 327th Glider Infantry Regiment was ordered to capture the railroad passing through Carentan, the Paris-Cherbourg line. But, here as elsewhere, it had been destroyed by the strategic air force, as we shall be seeing later at Lison, a rail junction located between Carentan and Bayeux. It all had to be put back in working order as there would be very heavy rail traffic to bring up Allied supplies, especially when the front line began to advance quickly towards the end of July.

5, 6 and **7.** A month later, life goes on and Bastille Day is celebrated at Carentan where the houses are draped with flags and a ceremony is held at the war memorial.

8. North of Carentan, the church was damaged at Brévands.

(US Army and D.F./Heimdal.)

From Pont-l'Abbé to Saint-Sauveur-le-Vicomte, 14-16 June.

1. Starting on 14 June, flanked on its right wing by the 9th Infantry Division, the 82d Airborne Division advanced westwards from Pont-l'Abbé in front of which the 90th Infantry Division had sustained heavy losses. Pictured here are men of the 82d Airborne Division amid the ruined town.

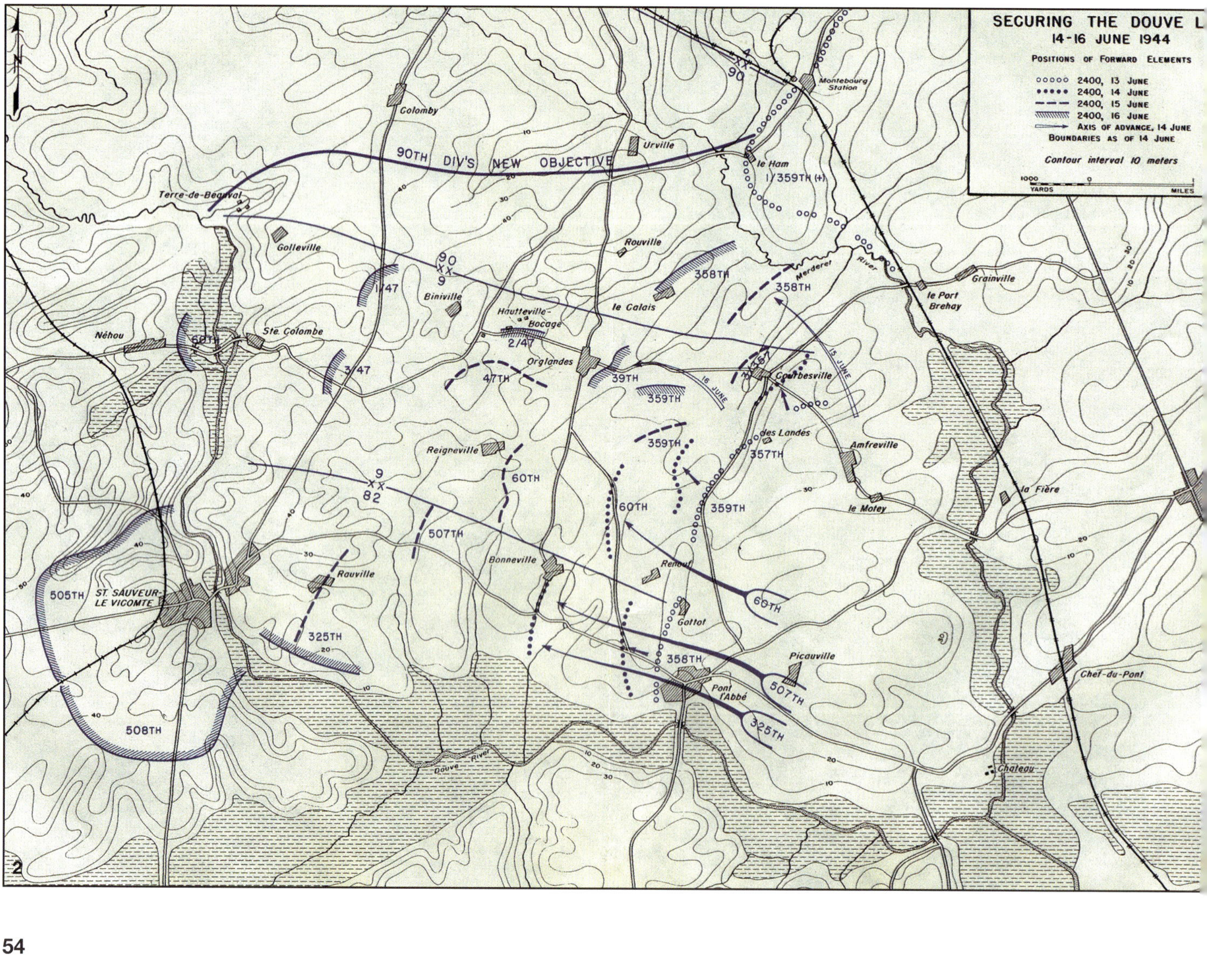

4. Advancing on Saint-Sauveur, a platoon of troopers has taken shelter in a ditch, ready to open fire. Notice in the background a German truck covered in camouflage paint, blocking the road.

5 and **6.** Two oldish German soldiers have surrendered and are led away by a paratrooper as some civilians look on.

(NA/Heimdal and US Army - map: US Army history department.)

2. Map showing the three American divisions' advance towards the Douve, its next obstacle, from 14 to 16 June. On 15 June, as German resistance weakened, the 505th PIR relieved the 507th PIR and took up position south of Reigneville while the 325th Glider Infantry approached Saint-Sauveur-le-Vicomte. At noon on 16 June 1944, three regiments of the 82d Airborne Division (505th Parachute Infantry, 508th Parachute Infantry and 325th Glider Infantry) were pinned down on the east bank of the Douve, facing the town of Saint-Sauveur-le-Vicomte. The Germans were in the process of withdrawing and VII Corps headquarters then allowed Major General Ridgway to make the most of the situation; he immediately launched a bridgehead on the other side of the river, established with the 505th PIR and 508th PIR, with elements (A Company) of the 746th Tank Battalion in support.

3. Lieutenant Kelso C. Horne (1st Platoon, I Company, 508th PIR) puts down his Garand. Although sorely tested in a hardfought ten-day battle, the US paratroopers proved their outstanding mettle.

Saint-Sauveur-le-Vicomte, 16 June.

1. This aerial photo, taken facing east, is of Saint-Sauveur-le-Vicomte in ruins, where the main feature is the medieval castle with its powerful keep (top left). In the background is the road from Pont-L'Abbé and the Douve river (most clearly visible behind the castle). In the top right is the crossroads pictured on following pages.

2 and **3.** Paratroopers of the 505th PIR advance down the Rue Bottin-Desylles towards the station, still in German hands.

4 and **5.** These photos complete the previous reportage. Already photo n° 2 pictured the wing of the front-wheel drive and the house seen throughout the reportage. This platoon leader sitting on the wing of the front-wheel drive with his FM BAR on his shoulder is listening to one of his men reporting on the enemy positions.

6 and **7**, then **8** and **9.** Still in the Rue Bottin-Desylles but further back on the opposite sidewalk, we see the antitank gun (one in photo n° 2) and the front-wheel drive in the background. The house at n° 50 (now n° 56) was still dilapidated in 1984 but has since been renovated. Its late 17th century doors and windows have been renewed (the small panes have gone and a replica of the door has been made with no knocker).

(NA/Heimdal.)

Saint-Sauveur-le-Vicomte, 16-20 June 1944.

1. Pictured in this familiar photo is Lieutenant-Colonel Vandervoort leaning on his crutch amid the ruins of Saint-Sauveur-le-Vicomte. Notice in the background the road sign to La Haye-du-Puits on the right. It was still a month away. Photo taken facing east. (D.F./Heimdal.)

2. The same spot in the Rue du Vieux Château, as it looks today. (E.G./Heimdal.)

3. Lieutenant-Colonel Ben Vandervoort in his M 43 raincoat.

4. This second photo taken at the same spot on 16 June, this time facing west; notice on the left the house seen on the right in photo 1. Lieutenant-Colonel Vandervoort has continued advancing on his crutch, his jeep has stayed put. (D.F./Heimdal.)

5. The same spot from a slightly different angle. GIs clear the ruins. (D.F./Heimdal.)

6. The same spot **(photos 4** and **5)** today. Notice on the right part of the forward castle enclosure cleared of the houses that masked it up until 1944. (E.G./Heimdal.)

7. Near Saint-Sauveur-le-Vicomte on this 16 June, the Americans have recovered a German Borgward vehicle and turned it into an ambulance. (D.F/Heimdal.)

8. Four days later, on 20 June, US Engineers have constructed a bridge over the Ouve at Saint-Sauveur-le-Vicomte to enable vehicles to move up to Bricquebec and the northwest of the Cotentin peninsula. (D.F./Heimdal.)

9. Today. (E.G./Heimdal.)

59

Saint-Sauveur-le-Vicomte, after the figthing.

1. After the battle, these men of the 82d Airborne Division rest under a school blackboard where they have chalked up the words "The town (or remains) of St. Sauveur Le Vicomte is hereby liberated as of now by US soldiers". The trooper in the foreground has the 508th PIR's winged foot painted on his helmet.

2. Here again, however, the civilian population paid a heavy price in the bombing and fighting. A small truck requisitioned for use as an ambulance takes a young wounded boy to the medical unit. He is ten-year-old Jean-Louis, with injured arm and legs.

3 and **4.** Young Jean-Louis is now being treated by military surgeons.

5. A little further on, medics treat the wound.

6. The horror of a little girl who was less fortunate than Jean-Louis being pulled out of the rubble by a paratrooper.

(Photos US Army.)

5 | The Battle of Cherbourg (17 to 30 June)

After his success at Saint-Sauveur-le-Vicomte, Maj. Gen. Collins had reached the heart of the Cotentin, and more precisely the center of the base of the peninsula, this belt of marshlands barring the greater part of it. And, in the midst of this watery trap where the paratroops and the GIs had been literally bogged down since D-day, the last pocket of resistance was defeated at Saint-Sauveur; the Douve was crossed, the last river of any size from here to the ocean, in the west.

On **17 June**, the advance was resumed, this time decisively. It was entrusted to just the **9th Infantry Division** which carried on westwards. To the south, the 47th Infantry Regiment advanced on Saint-Lô d'Ourville and Portbail. To the north, the 60th Infantry Regiment already in Néhou raced to its objective, Barneville sur Mer.

At **22.10**, Eddy in his jeep overtook the leading elements of the 60th Inf. Rgt., ordering them to advance throughout the night. The coast roads were cut off by the now rapidly advancing battalions. At dawn on **18 June**, at five in the morning, Company K, 3./60th secured a plateau overlooking Barneville; the sea was close and the **peninsula was cut off**.

To avoid being encircled, the Germans counter-attacked against the flanks of the American breakthrough. This daring move had cut in two several divisions holding the sector, notably the 77. Infanterie-Division which had only just arrived in Brittany. Various elements tried to escape encirclement by driving southwards. Thus, a column of the 77. ID took to the Bricquebec to Barneville road. The batteries of the 60th Field Artillery Battalion then opened fire, strafing along eight kilometers of road and destroying thirty-five German vehicles, ten guns and some light vehicles. Several 77. ID staff officers were taken prisoner. But part of this division lived to fight another day in the south of the peninsula under the name of Kampfgruppe Bacherer (named for its commander Colonel Bacherer). Two other divisions fighting in the peninsula also had some elements slip through the net; they were KG 243. ID and KG 91. ID.

Thus on 18 June, the trap was closed. Elements of four German infantry divisions, the 24th, 77th, 91st and 709th, were captured in the pocket or Kessel. The commander of the 709th, General von Schlieben, took over command of all these elements: an easy choice, for the three other generals were all dead! General Falley (91. LL. Division) was killed in the early hours of 6 June. General Hellmich (243. ID) was killed on 17 June, as was General Rudolf Stegmann (77. ID), while preparing his division's retreat.

For the final attack, Collins lined up four infantry divisions, from west to east: the 9th Infantry Division (Maj. Gen. Eddy), the 90th Infantry Division (Maj. Gen. Landrum), the 79th Infantry Division (Maj. Gen. Wyche) and the 4th Infantry Division (Maj. Gen. Barton). In the end, having proved less than brilliant, the 90th Inf. Div. was withdrawn. The already sorely tried 82d Airborne Division took no part in the attack. So the 9th Inf. Div. advanced in the west, along the coast to La Hague, with the 4th Cavalry Group in support. They faced no more than a few elements of IR 920 and 921 (243. ID) and elements of the 77. ID. The **79th Inf. Div.** advanced on Cherbourg in the center, between the Douve and Merderet rivers, against elements of IR 1049 (77. ID) and IR 1057 (91. LL.Div.). To the east, the **4th Inf. Div.** advanced towards the Saire Valley, encountering opposition mainly from KG Keil and in KG Müller.

The attack started at **05.00 on 19 June** in the west and center. In the west, the 9th Infantry Division's objectives were Saint-Germain-le-Gaillard and Rauville-la-Bigot. The 79th Infantry Division was to take the high ground to the west and north-west of Valognes but its ultimate objective remained Cherbourg. In the east, the 4th Infantry Division prepared for the final assault on Montebourg, a salient that had had held out against every attack.

Major General Barton brought in two of his infantry regiments for this final attack: the 8th Infantry Regiment west of the railway, and the 12th Infantry Regiment on the east side. With no preliminary artillery fire, the attack was launched at **03.00 hours** that morning, with the two regiments to skirt round the locality. If necessary, the 183rd Field Artillery Battalion was ready to act with its 155 mm howitzers and the 801st Battalion with its tank-destroyers. In the east, the 12th IR opened a salient in the German front, a favorable position from which to take Hills 100 and 119 dominating the entire sector north of Montebourg. At first it came under German artillery and rocket fire but pressed on regardless, and at 10.00 hours, Keil (the German commander in the sector) was told that a few American tanks were approaching the high ground north of Montebourg; the 2/12 had just captured Hill 100. Meantime however, further east, the 3rd Battalion was stopped in its tracks, unable to take Hill 119 until around 16.00 hours, after tanks were sent up in support.

To the west, the 8th IR under Colonel Van Fleet was faced with a more difficult situation as German grenadiers had dug in along the Montebourg/le-Ham railroad. It was **02.50** in the morning and it was raining. Captain John A. Kulp thought that if the weather failed to improve, they would have to do without tactical air support. He started out from the highway with his men of Company F (2nd Battalion - 2/8). He had ten minutes to reach his starting position and came in as close as possible behind the mortar fire unleashed by Colonel Van Fleet ahead of his men's attack. The heat of the explosions burnt him in the face. Under cover of night, he passed through the German front line and without much of a fight reached his objective 900 meters north-west of Montebourg. But he only had around forty-five men with him - two thirds of his company had been left behind. Company E commander, Lieutenant John C Rebarckek, advanced along a sunken lane where he met head on one of Kulp's platoons, pinned down in the battle raging fiercely throughout the sector, and tanks were needed to force a decision. But all that was to change late that morning.

General withdrawal

Since 17 June, after the American breakthrough to the west coast, the German command had been considering having units in danger of encirclement fall back on Festung Cherbourg where they would have a good line of resistance. **At noon** on this 19 June, the German units were ordered to fall back to the fortress. This was a planned withdrawal. In this sector, it was first of all to be done along the Valognes-Quettehou line, and this new line of resistance had to be held until 23.00 hours, an operation made easier by the rainy weather. This withdrawal went ahead unbeknown to the Americans, although there were a few skirmishes. In his book Utah Beach to Cherbourg, Major Roland G. Ruppenthal describes how in the afternoon, German resistance dropped off in the Montebourg area and the retreat began. In actual fact, the Germans stood up to the American attack from their positions almost until midday. But then they followed instructions to retire and did so in orderly fashion. Apart from a few skirmishes with delaying forces, the Americans found themselves unopposed and so were able without a fight to capture **Montebourg**, the hinge on which revolved both the front and the entire sector located north of the town. Two weeks after D-day and after ten days of hard fighting, Montebourg was at last in the hands of the 4th Division.

In all parts, the Germans methodically followed orders for a general withdrawal to Festung Cherbourg. The 9th and 79th Infantry Divisions advanced rapidly, slowed down only by the destruction caused by engineer units or rearguard elements. That evening, the 9th Infantry Division arrived before Valognes. Progress was again slowest in the Montebourg sector, opposite the 4th Infantry Division's front. But now the Battle of Cherbourg was about to commence.

The battle before Festung Cherbourg (20-23 June)

The Germans thus had no trouble falling back on Festung Cherbourg with all the trapped units brought together in one place. The only problems were due to the congestion caused by retreating columns passing each other on the small lanes leading to the basin in which the town of Cherbourg lies. This operation was facilitated by poor weather and the cautious approach of the American units, which failed to realize the scale of the withdrawal.

On **20 June**, to the west, the **9th Infantry Division** was to reach the high ground above and to the west of Cherbourg and cut off the La Hague peninsula by taking Hill 170 east of the top of Biville. It would then advance across a stretch of more rugged country, with deeper valleys carved into it, but also a barer landscape of moorland and rocky outcrops, and not so many hedgerows. Hill 170 was attained but the 60th Infantry Regiment (Colonel de Rohan) came under an artillery bombardment on its way up the hill. The 1st and 2nd Battalions, 47th Infantry Regiment reached the crossroads on Hill 114 south-east of Acqueville. The two battalions were stopped by artillery and light arms fire from the high ground to the east. The 2nd Battalion sustained losses to 88 mm and 20 mm shells and also MG bullets. An 88 mm shell fell on an HQ unit, killing the battalion commander and two other officers. But despite these two setbacks, overall this division had a good day. It reached the

On 19 June the attack started at five in the morning with the 9th Division in the west and the 79th Division in the center. To the east, the 4th Division launched its attack at three in the morning. (US Army history dept.)

THE ADVANCE NORTH 19 – 21 June 1944

On this map showing the VII Corps's advance from 19 to 21 June, we see that the advance was much quicker at first in the west on 19 June and the 4th Division was held up before making up ground the next day to reach contact as well with the Festung positions by the evening of 20 June, to which the Germans had withdrawn. (US Army history dept.)

Courbesville - Acqueville - Sideville line, facing the west side of the Festung.

In the center, the **79th Infantry Division** began moving forward at **06.00 hours** that morning. Bypassing Valognes, it advanced as far as Delasse, encountering German outposts at the Delasse crossroads. The 313th Infantry Regiment passed by the vast Brix building site of bunkers to house the "special weapons". The 314th Infantry Regiment came up against the German front lines near Saint-Martin-le-Gréard. The two regiments then moved up into contact with the Festung.

The **4th Infantry Division** finally realized that the Germans were withdrawing, and the division pressed on quickly to re-establish contact. The Bocage was so dense in this sector approaching the Saire Valley that you could never be sure that there were no German delaying forces still lying in ambush behind this or that hedgerow. This area of Normandy was a veritable "hedgerow hell" for the American infantry and progress was difficult. However, at **09.15**, Colonel Foster, acting commander of the 22d Infantry Regiment, sent a message to boost his units to the effect that he had heard that the 9th Division was threatening Cherbourg with its guns and that Major General Barton would not be pleased to see the 4th Division beaten to Cherbourg by another division. So, for extra speed, from noon the 8th and 22d Regiments took to the roads.

In fact the Germans facing Maj. Gen. Barton's division beat a double retreat. Units coming up from the south (Montebourg and Valognes sectors), including KG Keil, headed north towards Festung Cherbourg. But the Saire Valley (east of Cherbourg) was also mostly evacuated. Lieutenant Krausshar, commanding the Luftwaffe transmitter at Teurthéville-Bocage, withdrew with his men the day before. So did an 88 mm gun battery at Ourville (between Le Vast and Le Theil) and the artillerymen manning the Gatteville battery. The previous night, the Germans sabotaged and abandoned the guns of the Pernelle battery. Quettehou, Saint-Vast and the entire east coast of the Saire Valley were evacuated. This area east of Cherbourg is low-lying, mostly rocky, coastline. Carved into it, from west to east, is a steep-sided valley through which flows the Saire river. The valley slopes were partly wooded, making it quite an obstacle to overcome. Apart from the strip of open country along the coast, the Saire Valley was also covered with thick hedgerows where it was easy to dig in, but here too the Germans withdrew. They used the entrenchment of the east wing of Fortress Cherbourg, the Osteck position ("the eastern corner"). In this sector, the defensive line followed the course of the Saire north of Le Theil, moving north through Gonneville to east of Cap Le Vi.

Accordingly, in the afternoon, the 22d Inf. Rgt. arrived at last in the Le Theil sector, with the German positions north of the Saire towering above. The Germans then unleashed their devastating firepower; the 1st Battalion (1/22) suffered heavy losses. At nightfall the 8th Regiment came into contact with German outposts south-east and east of Ruffosses. The men dug in 550 meters from the crossroads. The 4th Division was now in contact with Fortress Cherbourg; during the day its 8th Regiment had covered over ten kilometers, and the 22d Regiment over thirteen. A fierce battle awaited them on the morrow.

Wednesday 21 June

The Germans were now in place in their Festung positions, ready waiting for the enemy, but with no illusions. The fortress was fearsome for an enemy coming from the sea, with all the forts and batteries facing seaward. But, apart from two fortifications, Westeck and Osteck, the landward line of defense was no more than a rough string of small strongpoints, some of which were not even protected behind barbed wire entanglements. There were very few concrete defensive works. In addition to the two abovementioned fortifications, just two sets of pillboxes defending Cherbourg on Highway 13 had concrete positions. Also, the quality of the troops occupying this line of defense was uneven. Lastly, most of the available guns were locked up in bunkers facing out to sea. Thus, in a few days, the formidable Fort du Roule dominating the port of Cherbourg from the rocky clifftop, for all its bunkers and artillery guns, was quite simply taken from the rear, across the lightly defended plateau on the blind side of the clifftop artillery. The Germans now knew that they had their backs to the sea behind a pretty weak line of defense, with just a few field artillery batteries and rocket launchers in support. Although they could not hold out for more than a few days, they were ordered to do so for as long as possible while the engineers methodically destroyed the Cherbourg port installations. The Allies desperately needed the port to bring in supplies and fresh divisions. They had to be deprived of this prize for as long as possible, with the Germans still hoping to bring reinforcements up to the front line before the Allies could. Indeed II.SS-Panzerkorps was coming into line in the Caen sector.

The Festung defenses - As of 20 June, von Schlieben, commanding the Festung, disposed his available units along the defensive perimeter from west to east as follows:

- **Kampfgruppe Müller**, commanded by Lieutenant-Colonel Müller who came from Lestre with his Regiment 922 (originally assigned to the 243. ID), it held positions at La Hague and in front of the Westeck defensive fortification.

- **Kampfgruppe Keil**, commanded by Lieutenant-Colonel Günther Keil, who set up his HQ in a gallery carved out of the rock near Querqueville where there was already a heavy artillery battery command post (Major Quittnat). Here Keil had his regiment's 2nd and 3rd Battalions (II./919 and III./919), with companies down to thirty or fifty men. It also had part of MG-Battalion 17, elements of a battalion of obsolete tanks (Wenk - Pz.Ers.A.Abt. 101), young people on "National Labor Service" (RAD) with no proper military training, and naval marching companies with no military background to speak of or fighting spirit. As von Schlieben told Keil at the time, when put in the front line the men of the services behind the lines "do not have a good attitude and show little stomach to fight". From west to east, Keil disposed his II./919, III./919, Mg-Batl. 17, along fifteen kilometers in front of fifteen token "pockets of resistance" (some had no wire). - Then (in the center) came **Kampfgruppe Köhn** under Colonel Köhn with his Jäger-Regiment 739. - **Kampfgruppe Rohrbach** with various elements including Infanterie-Regiment 729 (also originally with 709. ID). These odds and ends had barely the total strength of a division. The bulk of these forces were non-combatant personnel.

To the west, the **9th Infantry Division** was detailed to cut off Fortress La Hague. In this sector, the 4th Calvary Group (Colonel J.M. Tuly) was to relieve the 60th Infantry Regiment (Colonel Frederick J. de Rohan) and reconnoiter towards La Hague. The regiment's 2nd battalion failed in an attempt to enter Sainte-Croix-Hague. Also, the 3rd Battalion, 47th Infantry Regiment (Colonel George W. Smythe) advanced cautiously, avoiding combat, to gain information on the enemy's positions. It sent out patrols to find out more about German positions on Hill 171. Lastly, the 39th Infantry Regiment (Colonel Harry A. Flint) relieved the 4th Calvary Group.

In the center, the **79th Infantry Division** tried to move forward into contact with the German line but everywhere the patrols came under fire from German machine-guns and canons. The 313th Infantry Regiment tried to advance on Saint-Martin-le-Gréard.

Meanwhile the most significant progress came in the **4th Infantry Division's** sector. That division initially

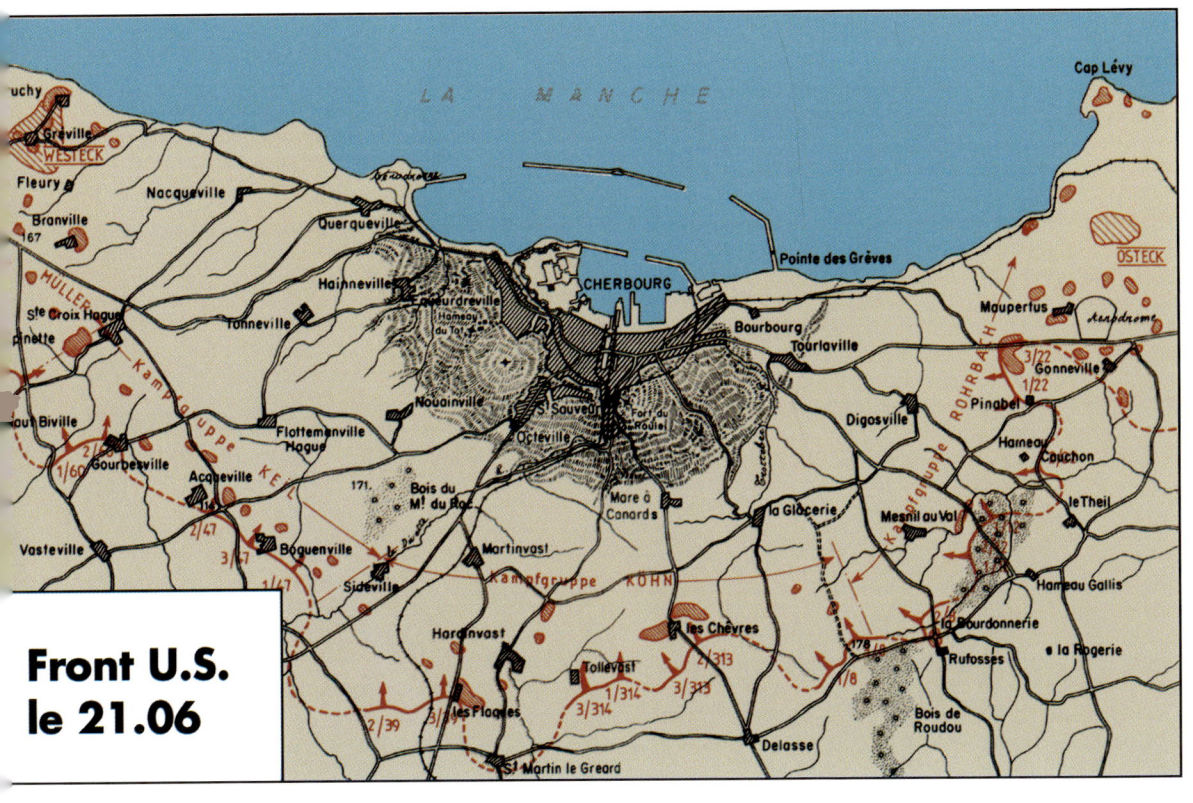

Front U.S. le 21.06

On 21 June, in the east, the 22d Regiment advanced on Gonneville. (Heimdal.)

made rapid progress owing to its not having been everywhere in contact with the main line of German resistance (Hauptkampflinie) the day before. Maj. Gen. Barton issued his division's infantry regiments three objectives:

- to the west of the division's sector, the 8th Infantry Regiment (Colonel Van Fleet) was to take Hill 178 (actually Hill 177 on current IGN maps) west of Ruffosses. The previous day the regiment had attacked this objective without success.

- the 12th Infantry Regiment was to establish the exact position of the German line of defense beyond the Bois du Coudray.

- The 22d Infantry Regiment was to cross the Saire and attack due north to hold the Saint-Pierre-Eglise - Cherbourg road west of Gonneville.

The 1st and 3rd Battalions started out at 10.00 hours, the 3rd Battalion advancing east of the Bois du Roudou and mopping up the last German pockets of resistance at Ruffosses with the aid of the 70th Tank Battalion's tanks. But these two battalions were stopped by artillery fire from the wood where the V1 rocket base was. The 2nd Battalion then attacked, its Company E passing through the German lines, only to be cut off in the middle of the enemy. Company F in turn attacked behind a screen of tanks, successfully. The tanks of the 70th Tank Battalion smashed through the hedges, which were low and not too thick here, and Company F linked up with Company E. But the Germans still held the crossroads and cut off the American companies in the rear, leaving them encircled to spend the night surrounded by Germans.

The 12th Infantry Regiment attacked that evening opposite the Bois du Coudray. The 2nd Battalion launched its attack at 17.30 and came into contact with the German positions at around 18.00 hours. At first it advanced rapidly through the undergrowth until it came under mortar and MG fire in front of the – destroyed – bridge over the Saire, at the Desplanques crossroads.

Further east, the 22d Infantry Regiment had a particularly important mission. It had to cross the Saire river and advance northwards to take Hill 158 dominating the sector west of Gonneville on the Saint-Pierre-Eglise - Cherbourg road. If successful, the operation would cut off the eastern section of the Festung, and more specifically Osteck, which would then be encircled. A wise choice indeed. It was a major objective for the entire VII Corps and its commander, Maj. Gen. Collins.

The 1st and 2nd Battalions started out from Le Theil with Company B of the 70th Tank Battalion in support. The companies advanced behind an artillery barrage. This was at 16.00 hours. The units progressed under heavy artillery fire coming from Maupertus, advancing as far as the Hameau Pinabel when the artillery fire stopped them in their tracks. The regiment requested support from P-47s which proceeded to bombard the German positions. They resumed their advance up to Hill 158 and Hameau Bellevue, reaching the road at last. The young seventeen and eighteen year-old "National Labor Service" recruits put up a stout defense, using their personal shovels when they ran out of ammunition. The Americans even lost three tanks behind the burning outbuildings of Bellevue Farm. But they had conquered this vital strategic point dominating Cherbourg. The regiment's three battalions stopped there but the Germans infiltrated their rear on a level with Gonneville, with the 22d Infantry Regiment cut off from the rest of the division. For four days, supplies came in with the aid of tanks along several lines through some dangerous terrain, and there were a few losses.

That evening marked the end of Phase One of the Cherbourg offensive. After coming everywhere in contact with the German positions, three American divisions now braced themselves for the final assault. But the Germans put the rugged terrain to good use, hanging on along the steep slopes dominating the enemy positions. The Americans now had to score a very quick victory as the solstice storm had been raging since 19 June. It lasted until the 22nd, by which time three days of severe gales had completely destroyed the American artificial harbor at Saint-Laurent and badly damaged the one at Arromanches as well. Supplies were considerably down, offering the Germans a fresh chance. Ammunition supplies were cut by a third in the Cherbourg sector.

Thursday 22 June

During the night of 21 to 22 June, Lt. Gen. Collins issued General von Schlieben with an ultimatum, explaining to him the desperate nature of his position and demanding that Cherbourg be surrendered to him. The ultimatum expired at 09.00 hours on 22 June. Maj. Gen. Collins however had his doubts as to how his proposal would be received and made preparations anyway for the final assault. It was to receive massive air support. The first wave was to be provided by the RAF with four squadrons of Typhoons followed by six squadrons of Mustangs, elements of the 2d Tactical Air Force. They would be followed by the bombers of the 9th US Air Force commanded by General Quesada, a force of 562 P-47, P-38 and P-51 bombers. The ultimatum having still received no reply by 09.40, Maj. Gen. Collins issued the order to attack.

Maj. Gen. Collins shared the objectives among his three divisions:

- To the west, the 9th Infantry Division was to seize the strongpoints to the north and east of Flottemanville-La Hague and Martinvast, in particular the Bois du Mont Roc positions, then push on to Octeville and take the high ground above Cherbourg.

- In the center, the 79th Infantry Division was to take the two lines of concrete obstacles on Highway 13 then seize the spur on which stood the Fort du Roule.

- To the east, the 4th Infantry Division would pursue its assignment, especially the 12th Infantry Regiment which had a major role to play in the drive towards Tourlaville.

At the time of the bombardment, the troops were to move back 900 meters, the artillery would come into action and then the regiments would launch the assault. The weather was favorable, and following the order given at 09.40, the fighter-bombers of the 2d Tactical Air Force would operate at 12.40. Then, at around 13.00 hours, it would be the turn of General Quesada's 562 bombers to appear overhead.

But the American bombardments also hit the American front lines, with losses to several infantry regiments (47th, 60th and 22d). The 9th Infantry Division and the 79th Infantry Division attacked at 14.00 hours. The 4th Infantry Division followed at 14.30. But the bombing did little damage apart from cutting lines of communications and battering the troops' morale. For all the resources made available, precision was lacking. The best results were reported on the west side of the Festung, facing the 9th Infantry Division in KG Keil's sector.

To the west, in this the **9th Infantry Division's** sector, the assault was launched on the Acqueville-Sideville line. The Germans were cut off from Bois du Mont Roc (Hill 171, north of Sideville). Units of the

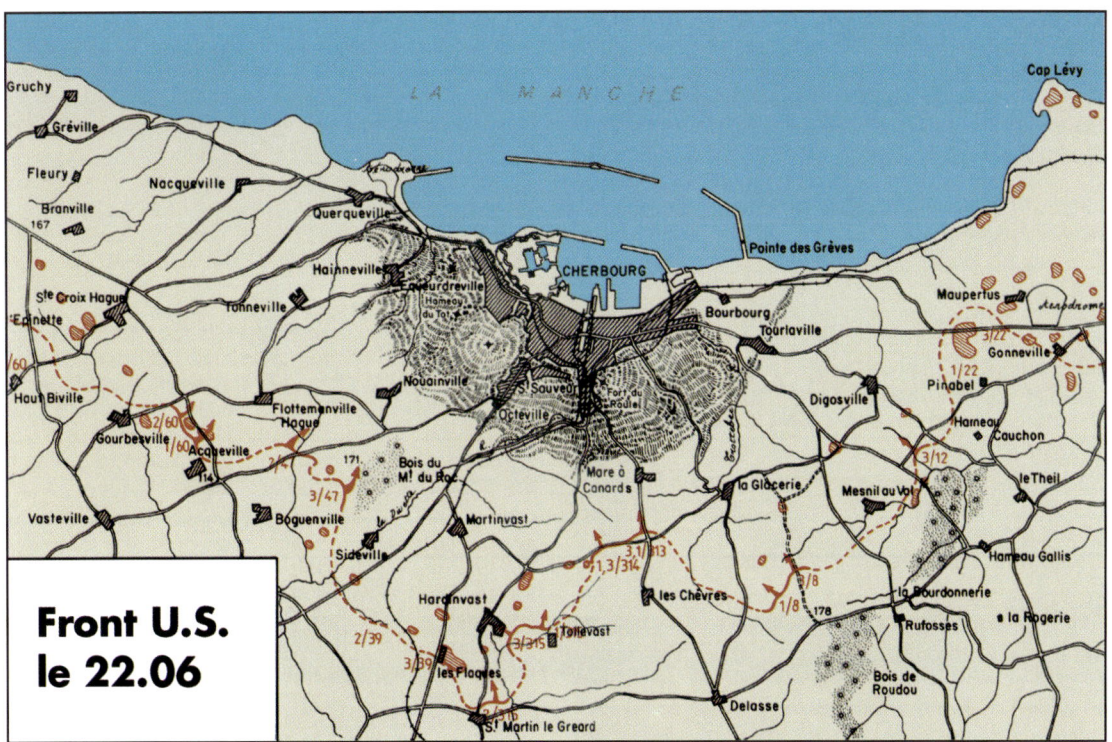

Front U.S. le 22.06

On the 22nd, the whole army was advancing. (Heimdal.)

9th Division initially made good progress thanks to the bombardments. The 60th Infantry Regiment took Acqueville thirty minutes after departure. But the drive was cut short as it came up against German positions south-west of Flottemanville-La Hague, somewhat inconclusively. As for the 47th Infantry Regiment, its 2nd Battalion finally captured the Carrefour des Pelles crossroads after several grenade attacks. The regiment's 3rd Battalion slipped south of Baudienville on its way up for the assault on the Bois du Mont Roc but came under artillery fire. During the night, some German elements infiltrated. Although progress was made, Hill 171 remained an objective to be seized the next day.

In the center, the **79th Infantry Division** had to break through three lines of defense:

- Near Les Chèvres (north of Delasse), there were concrete positions controlling Highway 13. This strongpoint linked up to the valley of the Douve (in the west) and the Trottebec (in the east). In front of the strongpoint lay a zigzagging anti-tank ditch. Here the ground was bare.

- Four kilometers further north was the Mare aux Canards strongpoint, by the roadside.

- Further north was the Fort du Roule.

- The division also had to deal with the fortified perimeter of the plateau taking the road north of Hardinvast.

A frontal attack was launched with the division's three regiments. The main thrust was required from the 313th, up against the Les Chèvres position. The attack started at 14.00 hours, after the bombardment, but progress remained difficult. The Les Chèvres position was reduced by an encircling movement. The battle continued everywhere until 2 in the morning, the front line was broken through and the 1st and 3rd Battalions of the 313th reached Pierre Butée.

To the east, the **4th Infantry Division** had to advance against Kampfgruppe Rohrbach (elements of the 729. IR, the 739 IR, naval marching companies, Flak or coastal artillery personnel).

On the division's left wing, the 8th Infantry Regiment under Colonel Van Fleet was to take Le Mesnil-au-Val and reach the day's objective: the high ground east of La Glacerie. But crossroads 148 (the Brisquet crossroads north of Ruffosses) was still in German hands. During the night, the Germans encircled the leading companies and even carried out a raid on 2nd Battalion HQ. They could not be allowed to go on like this! A heavy concentration of artillery (guns and mortars) lasting eight minutes was aimed at the copse where the Germans had dug in. Seventy-five shell-happy Germans waved white flags in surrender, but a large number of their comrades held out. The bombardment was resumed and another hundred surrendered. There were many casualties, with over a hundred wounded picked up on the ground. Altogether, nearly three hundred Germans were put out of action.

At 14.30, the battalions could at last get going again, passing the old V1 rocket base as they moved up north. The 3rd Battalion advanced 900 meters, coming to a new German position. It was pinned down by enemy fire. Company I lost fifty men in a flanking attack. Finally, the battalion took the position at nightfall having lost thirty-one killed and ninety-two wounded.

Near Cherbourg, men of the 359th Infantry Regiment, the 9th Division (the unit's marking has been censored out) observe German positions. One of them is ready to fire a rifle grenade. (NA/Heimdal.)

67

In the center of the 4th Division, the 12th Infantry Regiment (Colonel S.J. Luckett) was to take Tourlaville. On the division's right flank, the 22d Infantry Regiment would cover the 12th to its right and rear. So the 12th Regiment was in the Bois du Coudray, facing the destroyed bridge over the Saire. The 3rd Battalion attempted a sweeping movement but was located by the Germans, who opened fire and the Americans returned fire. At 14.30, Companies I and L managed to charge up the other side of the slope; the Germans were taken by surprise and fell back, leaving twenty prisoners. Gradually and with difficulty, the various companies of this battalion secured positions on the north bank of the Saire. At nightfall, the battalion fell back slightly to occupy more favorable ground but was cut off in the rear by infiltrating Germans.

The situation was now confused and the two American regiments (the 12th and 22d) had failed inasmuch as they only achieved their intermediate objectives, with Tourlaville still out of reach.

Friday 23 June

Three divisions continued to fight on this day to achieve their objectives of the previous day. Let us go back to where we were on the evening of 22 June, with the 22d Infantry Regiment, on the right wing of the 4th Infantry Division. Progress was hard and confused, and it was to be another poor day.

In the center, the 79th Infantry Division continued its drive towards the Fort du Roule. The Germans infiltrated the Americans' rear overnight. Two battalions (1st and 3rd) of the 314th Infantry Regiment were cut off in the rear, as was the 313th. Today, the division continued to go for the second line of defense. After an initial attack by the tactical air force, the 3rd Battalion of the 314th captured some of its objectives but heavy German artillery fire caused it heavy losses. A later attack by the 1st Battalion yielded better results. But the 314th moved back to make space for more decisive action by the air force on these positions the following day.

On the left of the front, south of La Hague, the 9th Infantry Division prepared for the final offensive during the night of 22-23 June. The Bois du Mont Roc and the entrenchment at Flottemanville-La Hague were surrounded on at least three sides while remaining in the hands of the men of KG Keil.

On this day, the 39th Infantry Regiment, 9th Division took part in the attack with the aid of tank-destroyers north-west of Beaudienville. On its right, the 47th Infantry Regiment attacked Hill 171 (Bois du Mont Roc), but the attack by its 1st Battalion was strafed by Flak guns. Finally, the 2nd Battalion attained its objectives at day's end. The GIs took four hundred prisoners. The regiment now pressed on to Nouainville, west of Octeville. On the division's left wing, near La Hague, the 60th Infantry Regiment waited all day for the Flottemanville-La Hague positions to be bombed. In the end however, artillery fire crushed the positions, which the GIs seized.

On this day, General Karl Wilhelm von Schlieben was appointed commander-in-chief of all the forces of the Festung in place of General Robert Sattler the former Stadtkommandant, who now became his subordinate. Until then, Von Schlieben had only commanded the ground forces. Now the naval units also came under his command. But von Schlieben was in a serious predicament. His four Kampfgruppen were still holding out, but for how much longer? Their sectors had been broken through at many different points. The first line of defense had been breached in several places, some local offensives by American divisions had even broken through the second line of defense and Cherbourg would then come under direct fire from these American units. The situation was as follows, from west to east, the front of the Festung can be divided into four sectors:

- To the west, Lieutenant-Colonel Müller held the La Hague sector with what remained of his Infanterie-Regiment 922 (originally assigned to the 243. ID) and other elements. This sector still remained outside the battlefield.

- To the south-west (i.e. east of La Hague), on the road to Les Pieux (to the east), was Günther Keil's sector with what remained of Infanterie-Regiment

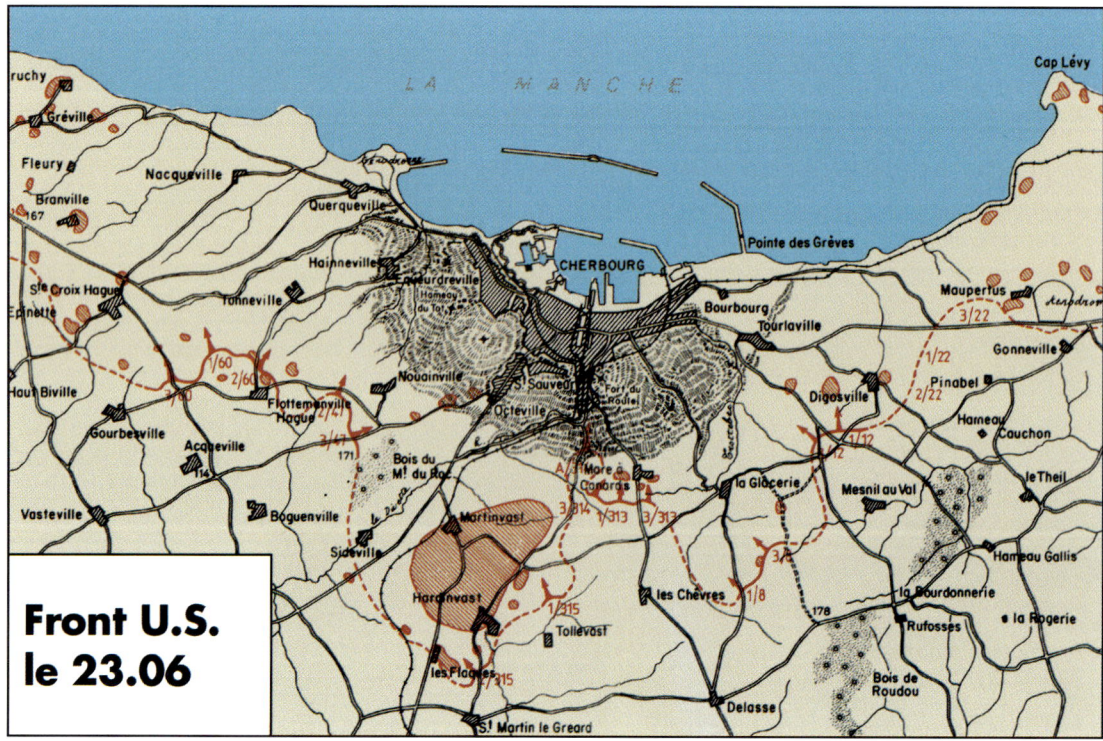

On the 23rd, in the middle the 314th Regiment advances on Fort du Roule. (Heimdal.)

919 (originally assigned to the 709. ID) and various elements, including a company of Panzer-Ersatz-Abteilung 101.

- To the east (facing the Saire Valley), Lieutenant-Colonel Rohrbach formed a fresh Kampfgruppe from various elements, including Infanterie-Regiment 729 (originally assigned to the 709. ID). In the east of this sector a pocket had now closed around the Osteck fortified camp. The troops there were commanded by Major Küppers.

Numerically, the forces under General von Schlieben were slightly lower than the strength of the three American divisions they had to face. But on the military level, the men of no fighting value did not count. In the front line, only fragments remained of the infantry regiments that had fought for two weeks. These were chiefly the four Kampfgruppen, plus the garrisons of the two fortified camps, Westeck and Osteck. Each Kampfgruppe had the strength of an infantry regiment (often with composite personnel) facing an American division with a strength of three infantry regiments, each with an artillery regiment in support. On the front line, American superiority was around three to four to one, with clear superiority in terms of artillery and total superiority in terms of aircraft. This American superiority had further increased over the last two days with the loss of strongpoints crushed by bombs or shellfire, and positions outflanked and encircled.

General von Schlieben fought this final battle from his HQ at Villa Maurice, near the Rue Waldeck-Rousseau and the Rue Président Loubert at Octeville. Here there was an underground command post consisting of four crossing galleries. At the time it housed over a thousand men! A completely disillusioned Von Schlieben had just issued orders to "fight to the death". It that remained to do was to hold out for a few more hours, or even days, to delay the moment when the Allies took possession of this major port.

The final assault on Cherbourg Saturday 24 June

All day long, the P-47 fighter-bombers lent decisive support, particularly in the sectors of the 4th Infantry Division (Digosville, Tourlaville, La Glacerie) and of the 79th Infantry Division (La Mare aux Canards). Resistance broke down everywhere under their aerial attacks using napalm bombs, and the three divisions took direct control of Cherbourg.

To the east, in the Saire Valley, the **4th Infantry Division** was to advance and veer off towards Cherbourg and have its share, with the others, in the capture of that city. On the Saire Valley side, the 22d Infantry Regiment committed two of its regiments to protect the VII Corps' right flank against the Germans who had dug in at Maupertus and Gonneville. The sector was still dangerous and there were still Germans in among the American lines south of Hill 158. So the 22d would have to secure the supply route from Le Theil.

On the 22d's left wing, the 12th Infantry Regiment (Colonel Luckett) was to spearhead the division's attack. For this assignment, it was reinforced by the 2nd Battalion, 22d Infantry Regiment. It gradually drove towards Tourlaville. Facing it were the fortified positions established west of Digosville, still a tough nut to crack. It attacked west of Digosville and outflanked the strongpoint on the left. It took many prisoners but came under artillery fire and lost its new commander, Lieutenant-Colonel Merril. On the right, the attack by the 2/22d was poorly coordinated. The infantrymen drove forward through some thick hedgerow country. Suddenly, when they were just 200 meters from the enemy positions, the Germans opened fire. Four tanks of the 70th Tank Battalion came to their aid and opened fire, overshooting the German line which continued to fire at the infantry in spite of this breakthrough! After the tanks, it was the air force's turn to join in; twelve P-47s came and pounded the German positions. The tanks and GIs then finished the job after a short battle. A few Germans withdrew, leaving a hundred and fifty prisoners in the GIs' hands. Disgoville had finally been taken.

On the left, the 2/12th, which was committed in turn, seized the concrete position of the Saint-Gabriel fortification (including a bunker on two levels) and took three hundred prisoners. That evening, Colonel Luckett's regiment arrived on the high ground above Tourlaville. Cherbourg was now clearly visible, and directly in the artillery's firing line. Maj. Gen. Barton wanted to take advantage of this and resumed the attack although night was beginning to fall. George Prével, a Free French soldier, contacted the Americans offering to guide them into **Tourlaville**. The 3/12th, which had been kept in reserve on Hill 140, was launched against that locality along with a few tank-destroyers. The battalion encountered no resistance and came to the main square at Tourlaville. In the middle of the night, Colonel Luckett organized his defenses around the town. At two in the morning came the rumble of the tank-destroyers pulling out. He could be well satisfied with the task accomplished, as his regiment had taken eight hundred prisoners during the day. But he wanted to build as much as possible on this success, and so, in the middle of the night, he ordered the 2/22d to move on from Digosville towards the sea.

On the 4th Infantry Division's left wing, Colonel Van Fleet was to attack and take one of the last strongpoints east of La Glacerie. This was a powerful position astride a crossroads. The assault was allotted to the 2nd Battalion of the 8th Infantry Regiment, with 1/8th in support on its left. Here again, the air force attacked the German position, twelve P-47s successfully bombarding it.

Out of eighty 500-pound bombs dropped, twenty-three landed on target! Then the artillery took over… The battalion then set off, preceded by a barrage of artillery and mortar fire. It advanced along a front two companies wide. But despite the precision bombing, the German positions were not destroyed and the personnel of these two companies in turn came under artillery fire. They were forced to withdraw, with Company E down to forty men, having suffered the most casualties! They now had to wait for two hours while tanks were brought up to support a fresh attack. The position was outflanked on the right. The Germans withdrew hurriedly, abandoning their parts guns without having time to sabotage them. The Americans took a hundred prisoners, however a German pocket held out for another seventy-two hours in this sector, pinning down several companies. But Colonel Van Fleet's 8th Infantry Regiment sustained heavy losses, with thirty-seven killed during the day, including 1st Battalion commander Lieutenant-Colonel Simmons. The regiment was relieved the next day and taken out of the front line. The 3rd Battalion, on the other hand, reached "Hauts-des-Bois" encountering next to no opposition.

In the center, the **79th Infantry Division** continued its advance on the Fort du Roule. On the right, the 313th Infantry Regiment veered slightly eastwards to capture the strongpoints west of La Glacerie and towards Hameau Gringor. The regiment fought all the way to Gringor, on the boundary with Tourlaville, taking two hundred and fifty prisoners.

On the 313th's left, at around 08.00 hours, twelve P-47s bombarded the Mare aux Canards strongpoints. Colonel Robinson then sent his 314th Infantry Regiment onto the attack. By ten, the 2nd and 3rd Battalions had gained nine hundred meters. They now controlled the Fort du Roule but came under German artillery fire from Octeville. The two battalions met on a level with the Rouges Terres wireless station.

In the west, in the La Hague sector, the **9th Infantry Division's** assignment involved taking out the last strongpoints and entering Cherbourg. The 47th IR and the 39th IR took part in the attack, with the 60th IR covering the left flank against KG Müller, which had formed a ring round La Hague. The Martinvast and Hardinvast sectors, still held by the Germans, were to be bypassed. The 47th Infantry Regiment was to advance on the left (west) and the 39th Infantry Regiment on the right (east).

The 47th had to knock out three strongpoints. The regiment's 2nd and 3rd Battalions passed through Nouainville. The attack started at 08.00 hours and the first two "W"s were early that afternoon. But both regiments were held up in front of the third pocket of resistance. They were in front of the slope leading to Octeville. The artillery lent a hand, but to no avail. That evening, Company E, 2/39th IR took out the position. The 39th Infantry Regiment was at last at the foot of Octeville. On the left, 2/47th took the Fort du Tot and attacked from the rear of the Couplets fortification.

For Günther **Keil**, this day marked the high point of the battle. He found out that the enemy had broken through the sectors held by Colonels Köhn and Rohrbach. In his own sector, Mg-Battalion 17 was the hardest hit. The 9th Company was driven back and the Americans reached the battalion HQ. The remains of the battalion and 10./919 were driven back to Cherbourg by the 39th Infantry Regiment's attack. 10./919 was committed near Octeville. The company commander fell back to Cherbourg. Given the situation, General von Schlieben felt it would be extremely foolish to bring back KG Keil's two other battalions into the city. During the afternoon, he ordered Keil to withdraw into the La Hague peninsula. Keil was to dig in there and take over command of KG Müller which had not yet borne the brunt of the American troops in the battle for Cherbourg. Keil suggested to von Schlieben that the withdrawal should take place during the night of 24-25 June while the Americans were concentrating on Cherbourg and while most of Keil's front was still intact, except for the left wing. Von Schlieben assented.

Keil managed to establish a decisive front on a level with La Traisnetterie, ahead of Tonneville. Here the new front line joined Hill 179 there (178). At nightfall, Keil's left wing was pushed back to Hainneville. Hill 179, which had already cost a great deal of bloodshed, now became the cornerstone of the new front held by Keil. At 23.00 hours, unbeknownst to the Americans, the withdrawal was completed with no problems. Keil then moved on to the Westeck fortified camp. He established himself at Gréville from where he set up his units.

That evening, three American divisions now held Cherbourg in the jaws of a vice. Maj. Gen. Barton's 4th ID covered the city from Tourlaville. Maj. Gen. Wyche's 79th ID was near the Fort du Roule. Maj. Gen. Eddy's 9th ID was at the foot of Octeville where General von Schlieben had his underground HQ. The situation was hopeless for von Schlieben.

Sunday 25 June

General von Schlieben had a dramatic night. He knew that he could not hold out for much longer, with the Americans likely to enter the city within a few hours. A thousand men were piled up in the underground galleries of his command post. There were wounded and demoralized men, casualties to napalm bombs or unceasing artillery fire. Many were dazed or deafened, in a state of shellshock. Von Schlieben had another look at the map of Festung Cherbourg. Everywhere arrows had been inserted amid the German defenses, showing the penetration of three American divisions now approaching the city center. In the center and south of the peninsula, the land is no more than thirty meters or so above sea level. Then this rocky mass appears, rising northwards towards Cherbourg and the sea. This rocky base with deep valleys cutting into had allowed him to establish the Festung defenses. But, as it comes to Cherbourg, this solid mass rises to over a hundred meters, with

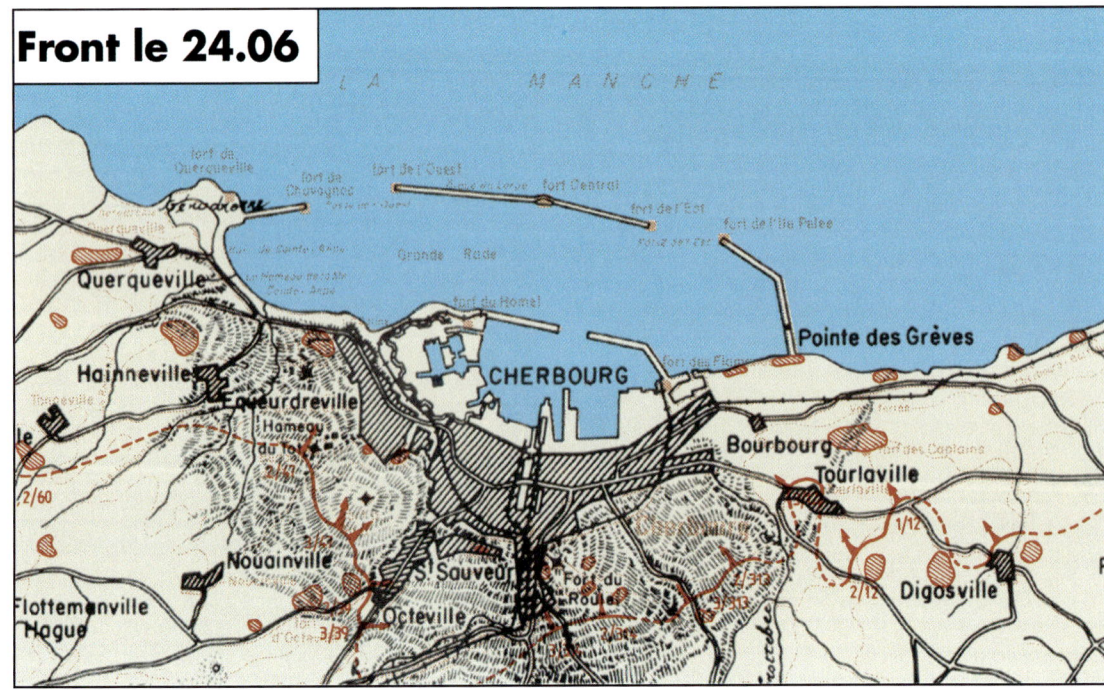

On the 24th, the various regiments approach the high ground overlooking the town. (Heimdal.)

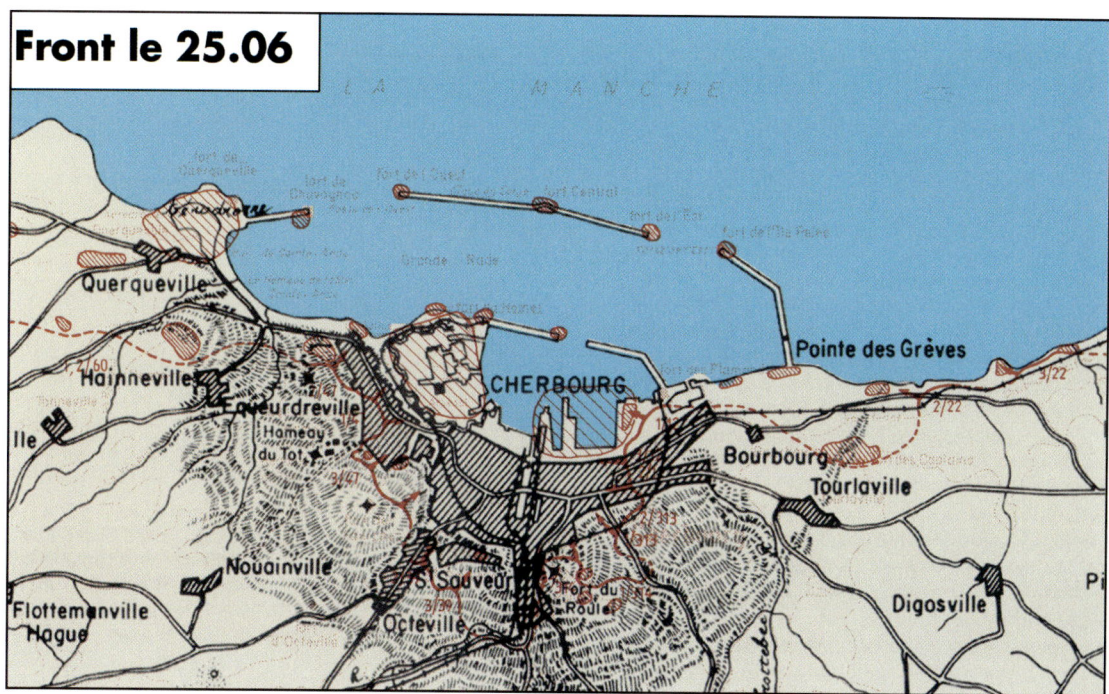

On the 25th, the 314th Regiment was at Fort du Roule, and the 12th Regiment was in Tourlaville. By day's end, it had secured the east bank of the Divette. (Heimdal.)

summits at 170 meters (Hill 179 near Flottemanville-La Hague, Hill 171 at Bois du Mont du Roc, and Hill 178 (177) near Ruffosses). Up there is a commanding view over the port and city from Les Rouges Terres or Octeville. The city is set at the foot of a large rocky circus, with a hundred meter drop into the downtown area. Whoever holds the high ground holds everything. In the middle of this rocky circus a narrow ridge ends in a 104 meter high rocky cliff. This is where the Fort du Roule was built, commanding the whole area. But most of all it commanded the sea front with its casemates armed with four 105 mm guns set in the cliff face! Cherbourg was a fortress turned towards the sea... The Americans were now within hand's reach of the two observatories overlooking the city, Octeville and Le Roule. Also, they were in Tourlaville, where a small coastal plain leads due west to the city center. Von Schlieben suspected that this was going to be the day the Americans would make an allout attempt to capture the two final obstacles and obtain the city's surrender.

At 7 in the morning, a German medical officer, the deputy chief surgeon at the naval hospital, came with an American pilot officer. Together they crossed the 9th ID's lines near Octeville to request that the hospital should not be bombarded and to obtain blood plasma and with a demand for immediate surrender saying: "The Fortress Cherbourg is now surrounded and its defenses have been breached. The city is now isolated... You are tremendously outnumbered and it is merely a question of time when Cherbourg must be captured. The immediate unconditional surrender of Cherbourg is demanded". At the same moment, **4th ID** commander Maj. Gen. Barton attacked from the east, from Tourlaville. The 12th Infantry Regiment advanced towards the coast. Tourlaville is set in a valley bordered on the north side by a plateau overlooking the sea. On this plateau, the Caplains battery (Brommy) contained four 150 mm SKC/28 guns. In a few hours, the Allied fleet would be coming into action against Cherbourg and so it was thought wiser to silence this casemated battery. First aircraft were called in to help the regiment's advance, but the men of the 1/12th came under fire from the 20 mm Flak guns in the fort. So now tanks were called to the rescue. Before following the 12th Infantry Regiment's battle on the afternoon of the 25th, let us see what was going on in the Fort du Roule sector.

It was here, facing this fort, that the major battle of the day was fought. At 08.00 hours, a flight of P-47s bombarded the fort. The weather was fine and the bombing accurate but the guns came through intact, especially of course, the ones set in the cliffside. Meanwhile, twenty-one civilians were killed in a shelter in the Rue Ludé. The sector was so narrow that only the 314th Infantry Regiment took part in the attack and the advance, and only its 2nd and 3rd Battalions at that.

That morning, two men of the 314th Infantry Regiment went on the assault along with the rest of their comrades in the regiment: Corporal John D. Kelly of Company E, 2nd Battalion, Lieutenant Carlos C. Ogden of Company K, 3rd Battalion. Kelly's company was one of the two leading companies. The 2/314th led the assault with the 3/314th providing cover. The 2nd Battalion Companies E and F spearheaded the drive. These companies advanced through the north-west of the plateau and came under artillery fire from both Octeville and the fort, and the attack lost momentum. They came to the last few positions that had to be taken in order to approach the fort. Some Bangalore torpedoes, three meter-long barrels filled with fifteen kilos of TNT, were used to breach the barbed wire entanglement. Corporal Kelly's company took part in the assault. His platoon set off up the slope when machine-guns opened fire from a pillbox. Kelly's comrades were pinned down but Kelly bravely volunteered to take a Bangalore torpedo. He slowly climbed up to the base of the bunker and placed his pole charge, but the blast was ineffective. He came back down, took another torpedo and started up again. This time, the blast hit the embrasure and the ends of the machine-guns were blown off. But Kelly went back down again to fetch yet another charge. This he placed at the rear of the bunker, and this third blast blew off the door. He tossed some grenades inside the bunker. The Germans surrendered. The way now lay open for Company E, but Kelly was badly wounded. He died of his wounds in November 1944. He was nominated for the Congressional Medal of Honor, and the award was made posthumously.

71

On the left of the 2nd Battalion leading the assault, the 3rd Battalion knocked out a number of strongpoints, but Company K of the 3/314th was stopped by fire from an 88 mm gun aided by two machine-guns controlling the anti-tank ditch. Company K had already sustained heavy losses after first being caught in the line of fire of some Germans on the edge of the plateau. Captain Oberman, the company commander, was badly wounded. Then the second-in-command, Lieutenant Orton, fell in turn. Lieutenant Carlos C Ogden then took over command of the company. His men were now locked in battle with this lousy 88! Ogden armed himself with an M1 rifle and a grenade launcher and climbed the slope on his own. He was wounded in the head and legs, but carried on regardless. He then fired a rifle grenade at the gun, destroying it. It was silenced but he was again wounded in the legs. What was to be done? Ogden was now close to his goal. He carried on alone and knocked out the two machine-guns with grenades. Ogden was joined by his men; once victorious, he at last had his wounds attended to. He too was awarded the Congressional Medal of Honor, on 2 April 1945.

Meanwhile, the 313th Infantry Regiment drove forward on the 314th's right, with its 2nd Battalion leading the way down to Hameau Gringor, racing down the slope to Louguemare, south-east of Cherbourg and under the right flank of the Fort du Roule. But it was forced to halt, under threat from the fort's guns.

In the meantime however, the Allies also attacked Cherbourg on the other front. At around ten that morning, a fleet of warships appeared off Cherbourg, battleships, cruisers and destroyers, the fleet commanded by Admiral Morton L. Deyo and his second-in-command, Admiral Bryant. In the center of the German defenses was the Hafenkommandant (the port commander), Fregattenkapitän Witt. He was at the Fort du Homet observing the by now obsolete American vessels. He noticed that some of them were of the Gittermast type. But the ships fired salvo after salvo, crushing certain German positions.

Direct hits were scored on the Fort des Flamands, ammunition dumps were blown up, and fires broke out. But the powerful fleet kept out of range of some of the guns. However, it came closer to the port, moving eastwards. Witt thought that it would soon come into the range of his heavy batteries, the York battery (8./MAA 260 near Amfreville, south of Querqueville, four 170 mm guns) and especially the Hamburg battery (in the Osteck fortification, with its four powerful 240 mm guns commanded by Oberleutnant zur See Gelbhaar). The York battery immediately hit the Texas, then a light cruiser and a destroyer. The Hamburg battery fired its 240 mm shells at two Cumberland class cruisers. The US admiralty admitted that the following units were hit by the German batteries: USS Texas, USS Brien, USS Bardon, USS Laffey and HMS Glasgow. Then at about noon the Allied fleet retired out of the German batteries' range. But these batteries now came under a massive attack by Lightning bombers. Paul Carell states that eighty of these aircraft were shot down by a concentrated barrage from all the Flak guns.

As for the Caplains battery (Brommy), according to Fregattenkapitän Witt it was silenced. As we have seen, it was under siege by men of the 12th IR coming from Tourlaville. The battery was captured at 16.00 hours. The 3rd Battalion seized two coastal casemates mounted with 105 mm guns. The regiment now came to the eastern outskirts of Cherbourg.

At **Fort du Roule**, Lieutenant Ogden's action made it possible to remove the final obstacles, and the fort was finally **taken at around 22.00 hours**. But the Americans only held the upper section. Oberleutnant zur See Rose was still in command of his battery of 105 mm guns left intact in the Roule mountainside. The lower floor of the fort was still in German hands. However, the Americans had control of the city from the upper floor.

On the left flank, the **9th Infantry Division** made little progress that day, with the 2nd Battalion of its 39th IR pinned down by 20 mm guns near Octeville. On the positive side, the 47th IR entered Equeurdreville. That morning, it had to tackle the fort surrounded by a ditch. Aircraft bombarded the position at 09.30, and the artillery took over at 10.45. Then the tank-destroyers opened the way and the drive went ahead behind a rolling barrage of mortar fire.

Behind this tremendous pounding, the infantry had no trouble entering the fort and taking eighty prisoners. **Equeurdreville** was captured. 3/47th took the Redoute des Fourches.

Thus, the Americans of the 9th Infantry Division approached General von Schlieben's underground HQ where the situation was even more dramatic. In his book, Paul Carell reports how Admiral Hennecke's aide-de-camp Lieutenant Blume described the situation, with the hill under which their shelter was built also encircled. The Americans were blowing up the south entrance and drilling over their heads after previously sending explosive charges down the ventilating shafts. They did not do too much damage, but, with the ventilation out of order, the gases from the explosions would build up and soon the air would become unbreathable.

To come back to the east of the city, in the sector where Maj. Gen. Barton's **4th ID** was advancing. The 12th Infantry Regiment was approaching the center of Cherbourg. The 3/12th went down the Rue Carnot and the harbor boulevard. There, Company K reached the Rue Jules-Ferry and came under heavy artillery fire. Meanwhile, the 1st Battalion was committed in front of the Fort des Flamands and the artillery bombarded the position. At 23.23, an ammunition dump was blown up inside the fort, lighting up the night sky. At 23.40, the final artillery barrage began. However, the American infantry was held up by fires from pillboxes. The Germans put up a stout defense, sending up flares to open fire on the Americans as they drove forward. The GIs were forced back by machine-gun fire. All hell was let loose that night as the Germans destroyed the Fort des Flamands installations, the Amiot factories and the harbor station. At **05.30** in the morning, tanks appeared in front of the fort and the Germans finally surrendered. That night, the 4th Infantry Division attained all its objectives, reaching the limit of its sector, the Rue de la Bretonnière. **The Americans secured the downtown area on the east bank of the Divette.**

General von Schlieben had gained another day. But the Americans were already in Cherbourg and attacking his HQ. He knew now that he was close to surrendering.

The final battle of Cherbourg at La Hague Monday 26 June

Cherbourg was now caught in an inexorable pincer movement, on one side Tourlaville, the Montagne du Roule mountain, the high ground at Octeville and the Fort des Fourches. The 47th Infantry Regiment commanded by Colonel G.W. Smythe (assigned to Maj. Gen. Eddy's 9th ID) was there. This regiment came down from the fort and was stopped at the level of the Rue de la Polle. The sector was mined and came under fire from German artillery guns positioned at the municipal soccer stadium. The time was **10.00 hours**.

On the right, the 79th Infantry Division, which had taken the upper section of the Fort du Roule, advanced towards the coast with the 313th Infantry Regiment on the right (east) and the 314th Infantry Regiment on the left (west). These two regiments reached the foot of the Montagne du Roule. The 315th advanced even further to the right in its drive west of the Divette. But the Quincampoix valley railway tunnel had been destroyed and it pursued its advance by moving up on Octeville. The GIs of the 313th advanced in a column up the Rue du Val du Saire. They knocked out a light gun on the corner with the Rue d'Inkermann.

On the high ground at Octeville, Maj. Gen. Eddy set up his combat command post near the church. A few hundred meters away, under ground, life was becoming increasingly precarious at General von Schlieben's HQ. In the crammed corridors, there were numerous casualties "dying like flies". In Invasion: They're Coming!, Paul Carell recounts a conversation between Admiral Hennecke's aide-de-camp, Lieutenant Blume, and a medical sergeant. Blume asked the sergeant why the men were dying so fast and the sergeant replied, because the ventilation system had stopped working. The wounded were slowly being asphyxiated and dying from lack of oxygen in the air, and from the foul air from the explosions in the ventilating shafts penetrating right into the hospital cells. Blume reported these remarks to the admiral. A discussion then took place between Admiral Hennecke and General von Schlieben, who realized the tragic plight of this underground hospital. With the American troops close at hand, he knew that the coming surrender would save these men's lives.

Maj. Gen. Eddy advanced two of his regiments, the 39th IR and the 47th IR. They fought in the still stoutly defended western part of Cherbourg. The 39th Infantry Regiment drove into Octeville in the vicinity of General von Schlieben's HQ. The march up to the objective proved difficult, and the infantrymen of the 39th IR advanced under the low-angle fire of the 88 mm Flak guns and under waves of howling Nebelwerfer rockets. They finally arrived at the tunnel entrance. First they opened fire on this entrance, to no avail. Then a man appeared brandishing a white flag, soon followed by the tall figure of General von Schlieben, wearing his helmet and coat. Behind him came Admiral Hennecke, wearing coat and cap. The time was **14.00 hours**. With them, the Americans took eight hundred prisoners, many of them wounded. The two general officers were taken to the high ground at Octeville, near the church where Maj. Gen. Eddy was waiting for them. The 9th ID commander demanded total surrender, but von Schlieben was still playing for time. He had his wounded brought out of the smoke-filled bunker, hoping now that some of the strongpoints might further delay the American victory. He was thinking of officers like Oberstleutnant Keil, Fregattenkapitän Witt, Major Küppers, who might still prove nasty thorns in the side of the American corps. So von Schlieben answered that he was no longer in touch with most of his units. Later, Maj. Gen. Collins offered to let him use his own wireless equipment. Von Schlieben refused. More fighting went on in the city until evening. The surrender only involved eight hundred men and the two general officers. However, it did have an unquestionable effect undermining morale among those troops still committed. General von Schlieben and Admiral Hennecke were then led off to Maj. Gen. Collins's command post established at Château de Servigny at Yvetot-Bocage, near Valognes. They were received by Maj. Gen. Collins in an upstairs reception room, where they signed the capitulation of the Festung.

Meantime, in the center, the 79th Infantry Division continued to push forward the 313th and 314th IR. That afternoon, the two regiments came under fire from the 105 mm guns of the Fort du Roule battery. But the 2nd Battalion, 314th stayed on the top of the fort. It had the difficult assignment of destroying the battery. Explosive charges were dropped down the ventilation shafts. Also TNT charges were passed down the cliff face on the end of ropes. They were to explode on a level with the embrasures, but proved ineffective. The walls of the fort were skirted and the entrance to the underground battery was reached. Sergeant Paul A. Hurst destroyed the machine-guns covering the entrance with a bazooka. The entrance defenses were silenced. An explosive charge was placed at the base of the armor-plated door, blowing it down. The GIs then entered the tunnel carved out of the cliff face. At **17.00 hours**, the crew manning the first gun surrendered. At **17.30** the other naval artillerymen did likewise. Meanwhile, the 3rd Battalion of the 314th had gone down via the Rue Levéel where it attacked the navy tunnel carved out of the foot of the Montagne du Roule. Over three hundred Germans then surrendered. Thus, by day's end on 26 June, the entire **Fort du Roule** was in American hands.

To the south-west, the 315th IR mopped up the whole Martinvast sector, all resistance collapsed and two thousand two hundred Germans surrendered to Colonel Bernard B. McMahon.

To the west, in the 9th Infantry Division's sector, the 47th IR and the 39th IR pressed on. Two battalions of the 47th Infantry Regiment arrived at the heavily fortified Arsenal. The GIs were at the naval hospital where they found a hundred and fifty wounded Americans being cared for by the Germans. But they could get no further than that, and were halted by light arms fire from the arsenal's Bastion III. The attack was pinned to the ground by fast low-angle 20 mm Flak.

On the 47th IR's right, the 39th IR spent part of the day taking on the fortified City Hall defended by a German colonel. After a siege lasting several hours, he finally capitulated along with four hundred men, surrendering to Lieutenant-Colonel Frank L. Gunn at **20.07**. At the same moment, the 47th IR and the 39th IR linked up on a level with the Rue Hélain. The day ended with Germans surrendering in all parts of Cherbourg. Only the arsenal still held out and so the attack was postponed until the following day.

So Maj. Gen. Collins now had just three pockets of resistance: the arsenal and the forts along the roadstead north of Cherbourg, the fortified Osteck camp to the east, and the fortified camp at La Hague relying on Westeck, to the west.

While preparations went ahead for the assault on the arsenal, the threat took shape against the enclave still held by Major Küppers in the **Saire Valley**. Until 25 June, one of the three infantry regiments of Maj. Gen. Barton's division, the 22d IR, had the sole task of covering the whole VII Corps' right flank, ensuring communications and holding the Germans in Maupertus. The day before, Maj. Gen. Barton ordered Colonel Foster (22d IR) to capture the Osteck fortification up to Cap Le Vi. The attack was launched on this morning at **11.00 hours** towards Maupertus airfield with a front of three battalions and cavalry elements on the wings. But heavy artillery fire stalled the attack for several hours. 1/22 had support from the howitzers of the 44th Field Artillery Battalion, it took Gonneville and positions south of the airfield. Meanwhile, 3/22 took Maupertus and positions north of the airfield, the airfield however remaining in German hands. Captain Katzmann and his men wilted under the American assault but Major Küppers still had the situation under control. He observed the American drive from his observation post near the Hamburg battery.

During the night, Witt took steps to evacuate the **arsenal** which was on fire. He thought General Sattler was going to surrender. As "port commander", Fregattenkapitän Hermann Witt took the matter in hand. He conferred with several officers at the Fort du Homet. Korvettenkapitän Wist and Oberleutnant Franz would cover the retreat of a group of officers and men led by Hermann Witt. At **03.30** in the morning, he left the Fort du Homet aboard a yacht he had had made ready. The rest of the group followed in a whale-boat. The two boats slipped unnoticed to the Fort de l'Ouest, from where Witt intended to carry on fighting by blocking the entries to the outer roads!

Tuesday 27 June

In **Cherbourg**, the arsenal bastions still afforded a degree of protection to the few hundred Germans still fit to fight. But General Sattler, responsible for defending the **arsenal**, is thought to have been accused of seeking to turn over to the enemy (hence his "disgrace", according to Witt's account). He had no intention of fighting it out. At dawn, Colonel Smythe's 47th IR launched its assault on the arsenal. At **08.00 hours**, a section of Company A supported by a tank-destroyer set off to reconnoiter the German defenses. The infantry advanced, the TD staying under cover. Then it opened fire, destroying two 20 mm guns with direct hits. At **08.30**, an ultimatum was sent out to the German defenders and was eagerly accepted by General Robert Sattler who had decided to surrender. Unarmed Germans appeared on the ramparts and white flags could be seen. General Sattler then led out four hundred completely demoralized men. At **10.00 hours**, all resistance officially ended in Cherbourg.

Maj. Gen. Collins, accompanied by several of his generals (Maj. Gen. Barton, Maj. Gen. Eddy...) arrived at the City Hall in an armored command car at around **16.00 hours**. Maj. Gen. Collins came to meet the mayor of Cherbourg, Dr Renault to hand over the civil administration to him on behalf of the US Army. By way of a gift, he presented him with a French flag cut out of American parachute silk. Cherbourg was the first large city where the Allies took control. It marked a significant watershed in the Battle of Normandy. On this occasion, Lt. Gen. Bradley made a speech expressing his pleasure at being able to tell the people of France that their first major town was being handed back to them.

Wednesday 28 June

Fregattenkapitän Witt was now settled with his men at the Fort de l'Ouest and the Fort du Centre. Thus holding the Digue du Large outer pier, he hoped to block all access to Allied shipping. But the Americans had not forgotten about him and, since the evening before, the Fort du Centre commanded by Lieutenant Reinelt came in for bombardment by the Americans. Witt's yacht was in fact located in the port of this fort, which became a prime target. An American vedette boat even hit a mine while trying to close in. At around **10.50**, nine Thunderbolts attacked the fort, causing heavy damage. Further west, marines reported to Witt that the Americans had advanced along the seawall at Querqueville and seized Fort Chavaignac. They were now on the other side of the fairway, opposite the Fort de l'Ouest where Witt was. An American vehicle stopped near Fort Chavaignac. Admiral Sullivan, accompanied by two other US Navy officers, observed the fort that would not surrender to him. The Americans lined up two 20 mm Flak guns found intact on the seawall at Querqueville and opened fire on the Fort de l'Ouest.

In the Saire Valley, Maj. Gen. Barton decided to get it all over with. He placed an artillery battery of the 44th Artillery Battalion on the road from Carneville to Fermanville, at a place named Le Sapin, near the Hamburg battery. He lined up the 22d Infantry Regiment supported by a battalion of Rangers and two tank battalions (the 24th and the 7th). At **03.00 in the morning**, a jeep entered the perimeter fortified by an unmined sector. An emissary came down. Küppers refused the surrender offer proposed to him but was willing to receive Maj. Gen. Barton to talk the matter over. At **08.00 hours**, Barton arrived along with some of his staff officers. A discussion ensued, during which Maj. Gen. Barton negligently left lying on the table a detailed map of Küppers' positions (a scene described by Paul Carell). Küppers realized that it was pointless continuing to hold out when the enemy knew so much about his situation, and signed the surrender shortly before noon. Late that afternoon, what remained of the Osteck and Hamburg garrison – 990 men – headed off into captivity. All German resistance now ceased in east Cherbourg.

Apart from the two forts off Cherbourg where Witt and its men were still dug in, all that was left were Lieutenant-Colonel Keil and 6,000 men in the La Hague peninsula. The American disposition was reorganized, with the 4th Infantry Division to take control of Cherbourg while the 79th Infantry Division left the VII Corps and set off southwards to join the VIII Corps, in the marshland area. There it confronted elements of the 77. ID that had escaped encirclement. The 9th Infantry Division was ordered to close the La Hague pocket, with the 4th Cavalry Group in support. The units began to regroup the day before. The 47th IR took up position in the Hainneville sector, the 39th IR west of Octeville and the 60th IR west of Sainte-Croix-Hague. This was all done under fire from the German batteries at La Hague.

Thursday 29 June

Things were beginning to look bleak for Hafenkommandant Witt. Various artillery batteries, including four 155 mm guns near the Fort du Homet, opened up on the Fort de l'Ouest. The air force also joined in and the navy prepared to follow suit. Witt and his 186 men were powerless to act, and could only hope that the large circular fort would protect them. At **10.00 hours**, the Petit Pierre, a large boat with Paul Sébire, one of the harbor pilots, at the helm, brought in two US Navy messengers. At around **10.30** it came into view of the port of the Fort de l'Ouest raising a white flag. There was a ceasefire. Then some Germans appeared carrying a white flag. Fregattenkapitän Witt had to believe the evidence of his own eyes. The Fort du Centre had been destroyed, and the mine control panel had been destroyed. Lieutenant Reinelt had abandoned the fort with some men and gone to the Fort de l'Ouest. A few men were evacuated aboard the Petit Pierre. Then the shooting started up again. At **16.45**, the Petit Pierre came back. Hermann Witt received a chest wound. He had the surrender signalled by flag. A total ceasefire ensued.

There would now be one last stand at **La Hague**. The previous day, at 3 in the morning, the Seventh Army command announced to Keil that distinctions had been awarded to some of the Germans fighting in such a "God-forsaken place". Günther Keil received a well-earned Knight's Cross of the Iron Cross. Some German gold crosses were also distributed.

La Hague became the target of the air force. Querqueville, Gruchy, Nacqueville and Jobourg were bombarded by P-47s on the 27th. Then the following day, heavy Marauder bombers dropped their bombs on the Laye and La Roche batteries and also on the "W" strongpoints in the Rue de Beaumont and at Beaumont-La Hague. On this day, P-47s again attacked Beaumont-La Hague with heavy American artillery fire. In the center, the 60th IR attacked towards Branville-La Hague. The advance took an hour, with nothing to report until it came up against the first position on a level with Hill 167, where two roads

This aerial photo of Cherbourg and the roadstead, taken from the south-west, pictures, in the foreground, the road leading from Les Pieux to Octeville, a locality overlooking Cherbourg where Major-General Eddy set up his divisional HQ. The arsenal, and the roadstead can be seen in the background. (D.F./Heimdal.)

The plane now shows the town from the west with its arsenal and vast roadstead. (D.F./Heimdal.)

The "York" Battery's control bunker (8./MAA 260). From this range-finding post guided the battery's four 170 mm SKL/40 guns were trained on the Allied fleet on 25 June. (D.F./Heimdal.)

1. Aerial shot of one of the 240 mm SKL/40 guns of the Hamburg battery. The casemate is unfinished. One of the concrete walls has been cut into to give the gun extra clearance to the west. It did a good job in fact against the Allied fleet on 25 June. (NA/Heimdal.)

2. One of the "York" Battery's four casemates housing a 170 mm gun. (D.F./Heimdal.)

3. View of the "York" Battery site at Amfreville, west Cherbourg. (D.F./Heimdal.)

4. The Couplets Battery's control bunker (8./HKAR 1261) with four 155 mm guns. (D.F./Heimdal.)

5. 4.7 cm Pak (t) Skoda gun chamber in one casemate of the battery (3./MAA 260) at Cherbourg harbor station. (D.F./Heimdal.)

6. B26 Marauders bomb strongpoints at La Hague on 28 June 1944. They have just hit the Auderville-la-Roche battery at the end of the La Hague peninsula. (USAF/B. Paich coll.)

meet (one coming from Les Pieux, to the south, the other coming from the east). There was an anti-tank ditch on either side of the road, and also machine-guns and anti-tank guns. But on the right, with tanks and TDs in support, 2/60th outflanked the position on a level with Fleury and came to the crossroads leading to Gréville. UKG Hadenfeldt had been breached. Meantime, Major Quittnat's artillery had survived the air raids and continued to fire at the Americans although shell supplies were dwindling fast.

On the right, the 47th IR advanced from Querqueville until noon. But later, 3/47th encountered positions in the Gréville sector in front of Westeck; these did not fall until around 22.00 hours. That evening, Keil took stock of the situation. His men knew that the struggle was hopeless, and morale was not good. The first position was submerged. Keil sent a mes-

sage to the Channel Islands to ask for his men to be evacuated in fast patrol boats. To boost his men's morale, he also asked for his unit to get a mention in the Wehrmacht's daily dispatch. Both his requests were granted. But the fast patrol boats were spotted by the Allies and failed to get through. However, the following day, Kampfgruppe Keil was mentioned over the radio.

Friday 30 June

On the left, the attack by the 4th Cavalry Group proceeded fairly uneventfully. It started out at **07.00 hours** in a stark landscape and compartmentalized between valleys. The armor crushed Lieutenant-Colonel Müller's positions, and at **09.00 hours**, Keil was informed that the front had been breached in this sector. However until **16.00 hours**, Major Quittnat forbade any advance on Jobourg owing to his artillery running short of ammunition. The 4th Cavalry Group then resumed the advance.

In the center, the Hill 167 position was outflanked by the tanks the previous day but remained an obstacle in front of Beaumont. Artillery preparation from **08.05** to **08.15** knocked out all the 88 mm guns. 2/60th then launched an assault on the position. Captain Stephen W. Sprindis led his Company E in a remarkable infantry charge with three platoons in line against the German machine-guns. He had Company F supporting his right flank with tanks advancing along the road. Morale among the Germans holding the sector collapsed and Sprindis won the day. The two companies entered Beaumont-La Hague. At **10.00 hours**, Major Hadenfeldt reported to Keil that the front of II./919 and III./919 had been breached. It was now encircled in the Westeck fortification.

A terrific concentration of artillery fell upon Gréville as the tank guns neutralized the bunkers of the Westeck defensive works. Then 2/47th seized the positions in this sector but had more trouble in the Gruchy sector where the German positions backed onto a small ridge. The Americans came under German mortar fire. Early in the **afternoon**, two US artillery battalions shelled the sector. Keil watched through binoculars as shells hit the bunker occupied by Major Hadenfeldt, with whom he remained in telephone contact until **16.00 hours**. The tanks surrounded the position. However, Hadenfeldt held out until around 11.00 hours the next day in one last sector of Westeck. Meanwhile Müller was captured at around 16.00 hours.

At **18.00 hours**, Keil watched as the two companies of the 60th IR advanced on Jobourg with the aid of tanks. He then requested support from a heavy Alderney battery. Shells whistled over the sea to slow down the American advance. Keil was now at the second position but had no wireless. His aide-de-camp went out to reconnoiter and reported back to him that the veterinary company had not been attacked and that the parachute company still held out, but had lost contact with the Georgians. Meanwhile, Captain Kaldanke was encircled on Mont Pali with the remnants of Sturm-Batl. AOK 7. He further announced to him that assault craft had just landed in his rear! The second position was already collapsing; the battle was almost over. At around **19.00 hours**, the Alderney battery (three 170 mm guns from the Elsass battery) stopped firing. The veterinarians were submerged by tanks entering Jobourg. At around **20.00 hours**, Keil wanted to withdraw and leave his control bunker, which was under fire. In the next bunker, they thought that Keil had been killed and some old sailors had already hoisted the white flag and sabotaged their rifles. He left along a sunken lane with his driver, Voss, to get to his vehicle, when they encountered about twenty American soldiers. He then entertained thoughts of suicide but such a gesture might be wrongly interpreted and his driver would be in danger. He was taken prisoner although he had hoped to go down fighting. It was **23.00 hours**. The Americans had reached Cap de La Hague at last.

Saturday 1 July

The last German pockets of resistance collapsed. It was all over at around **11.00 hours**. Major Hadenfeldt in turn surrendered. The Americans took stock of their victory. At La Hague, they took some 6,000 prisoners. After the final battle in Cherbourg, 10,000 prisoners (including 2,600 sick and wounded) had been rounded up. Altogether, during the Battle of the Cotentin, the Americans took **39,000 prisoners**. But the exact number of killed and wounded is unknown. There must have been many killed. Keil reported that of the forty-nine officers at his disposal on 6 June, eight had been killed and fifteen wounded. There must have been comparable losses in rank and file. III./919 had 780 men (not including those who were captured). The percentage losses of human lives were obviously much higher for the infantry than for the navy. The total of German losses must be in the region of 50,000 men (taking into account evacuated casualties and elements of three divisions that evaded encirclement). There was nothing else on the scale of the "Cotentin Pocket", apart from the "Falaise Pocket", with even heavier losses in terms of num-

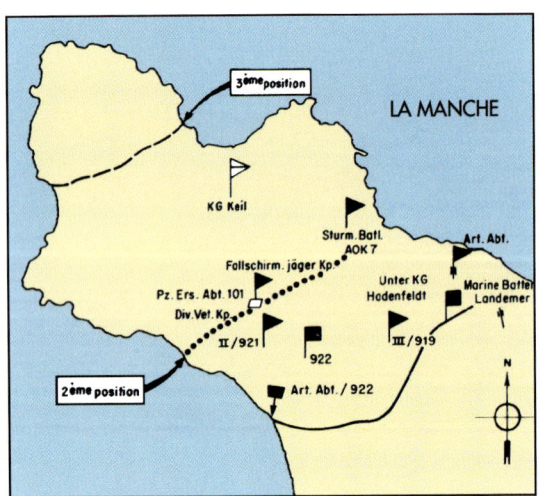

Last German positions at La Hague, 29 June. (Heimdal.)

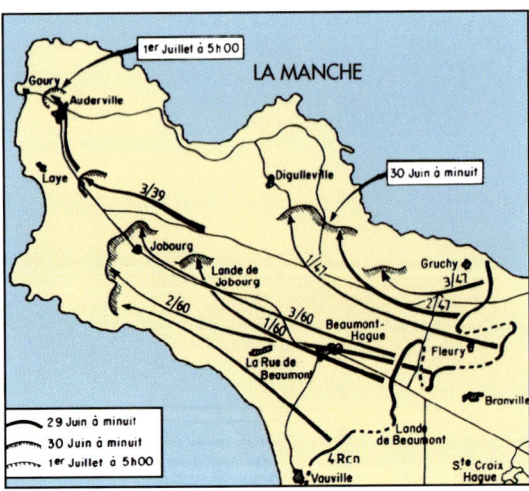

The final battle at La Hague, 29 June to 1 July. (Heimdal.)

bers for the German army. This was indeed the first great American victory in Normandy.

But the cost of this victory was relatively high. VII Corps lost 22,119 men, including 2,811 killed and 13,564 wounded. The 4th Infantry Division suffered the heaviest losses, 5,452 including 844 killed, heavier than those sustained by the airborne divisions (4,670 for the 101st Airborne Division, 4,430 for the 82d Airborne Division). This division had been in the front line since 6 June and fought successively in the difficult Montebourg and Saire Valley sectors. The other three infantry divisions each had under 2,500 casualties. Remember that the 8th Infantry Regiment (Colonel Van Fleet), 4th ID suffered such heavy losses that the regiment was withdrawn from the front at the end of the assault on Cherbourg.

Epilogue

For the Germans, this was a crucial battle. It naturally blocked this major port but it also kept busy three good American infantry divisions sorely needed elsewhere. The offensive southwards, beyond the marshes, towards La Haye-du-Puits and Coutances, only got underway in the early days of July. The capture of Cherbourg was initially planned by D + 8 then, with improved intelligence, postponed to D + 15. In the end, it occurred on D + 21 with the end of the fighting on D + 25. These delays fell in with the Germans' plans for an offensive by six Panzer divisions on the Balleroy-Bayeux line on 20 June, with the summer storm raging, in order to divide the two sectors into two separate beachheads and then mop up the sector east of the Orne RIver. Cherbourg would then have made an excellent focal point for grievances. Also, a long drawn-out battle left time to go about the methodical destruction of the port of Cherbourg, viewed as something "unprecedented in the annals of coastal defenses" by Hitler who even awarded a Knight's Cross of the Iron Cross to Admiral Hennecke to thank him for the success of this assignment.

But despite the scale of the destruction, the Americans in turn accomplished another feat. Following the example of what had been achieved at Naples, the Americans thought they could reopen the port within three days. In view of the damage - destroyed quays, mined docks, sunken ships, destroyed harbor station - the deadline was increased to three weeks. Mine clearance operations went on until 14 July. The last of the wrecks was not cleared until the end of September. But, as of 27 June, at a time when Witt still held two of the forts of the Outer Roadstead, the 1056th Engineer Port Construction and Repair Group arrived in Cherbourg and immediately got down to business. Its work first of all involved opening a hole in the anti-tank wall facing the Place de la République (near the City Hall) and clearing access to the New Beach (Nouvelle Plage). Here on 16 July the first DUKWs unloaded a cargo ship at anchor in the harbor. This work progressed at great speed. On 9 August the first Liberty Ship berthed at the Homet pier. Assembly of the Pluto pipeline at Querqueville was completed on 12 August. Laid across from the south coast of the Isle of Wight, this was a Hais type pipeline with a flow rate of 250 tons per day. That same day, thirty-two goods trains left Cherbourg for Le Mans.

By the end of August, the port of Cherbourg was taking in 10,000 tons of supplies a day. By November, its daily capacity had risen to 14,500 tons with a total of 433,201 tons unloaded in that month alone, a huge figure when compared with the total activity for the whole year of 1937 which stood at 325,100 tons, or with pre-D-day forecasts of 8,500 tons a day.

Thus, Cherbourg was a double victory - the first American military victory in Normandy – and a great success in terms of getting through supplies to the Allied armies. If we stop to consider that an American division then had a daily consumption of 1,600 tons of supplies, we understand the full importance of General Eisenhower's comment to the effect that without the splendid work carried out by the personnel of the non-combatant services in the rear, by solving the difficult logistical problem of bringing up supplies, the victory that liberated France would not have been possible. Cherbourg was the key to final victory for the Allies in Normandy.

June 1944 : objective Barneville-sur-mer.

On 17 June, with Saint-Sauveur-le-Vicomte in the Americans' hands, they now needed to carry on westwards and cut off the Cotentin peninsula. The 9th Infantry Division was to pursue this breakout westwards alone. In the south, from Saint-Sauveur-le-Vicomte, the 47th Infantry Regiment continued down the road to Saint-Lô-d'Ourville and Portbail. This regiment overtook the troopers of the 82d Airborne Division who stayed behind in the Saint-Sauveur sector.

Further north, the 60th Infantry Regiment, with the 3rd Battalion leading the way, continued to advance out from the small bridgehead, it was now at Néhou. Its objective: Barneville-sur-Mer! The regiment made excellent progress all day. Seeing the results, General Collins ordered it to carry on as far as possible, even after sundown. It was 22.10, Maj.Gen. Eddy jumped into his jeep and overtook the 60th's staff group, and shouted to them: "We're going to advance all night!"

In the south, the 47th Infantry Regiment was also making satisfactory progress. Its 3rd battalion's K company was near Saint-Sauveur-de-Pierrepont. Meanwhile, the regiment's 1st Battalion cut off the Barneville–La Haye-du-Puits road. This was the link road between the Cotentin peninsula and the southern Cotentin; the Germans now had no exit route and were virtually encircled. At five in the morning of the 18th, K Company of 3/60th IR secured a plateau overlooking Barneville, with the sea close by. The peninsula had officially been cut off.

Faced with this new situation the Germans counter-attacked on the flank of the American breakout. The now encircled units in the north were doomed.Those with a chance of breaking out were able to carry on fighting in the south of the peninsula.

1. A column of the 60th Infantry Regiment, the 9th Infantry Division, cross Saint-Jacques-de-Néhou, west of Saint-Sauveur-le-Vicomte on their way to their objective Barneville-sur-Mer. This was a town of potters - the Néhou potteries were well-known at the time - and the house on the left is that of Alphonse Hamel, a potter who was then a prisoner-of-war in Germany. (NA/Heimdal).

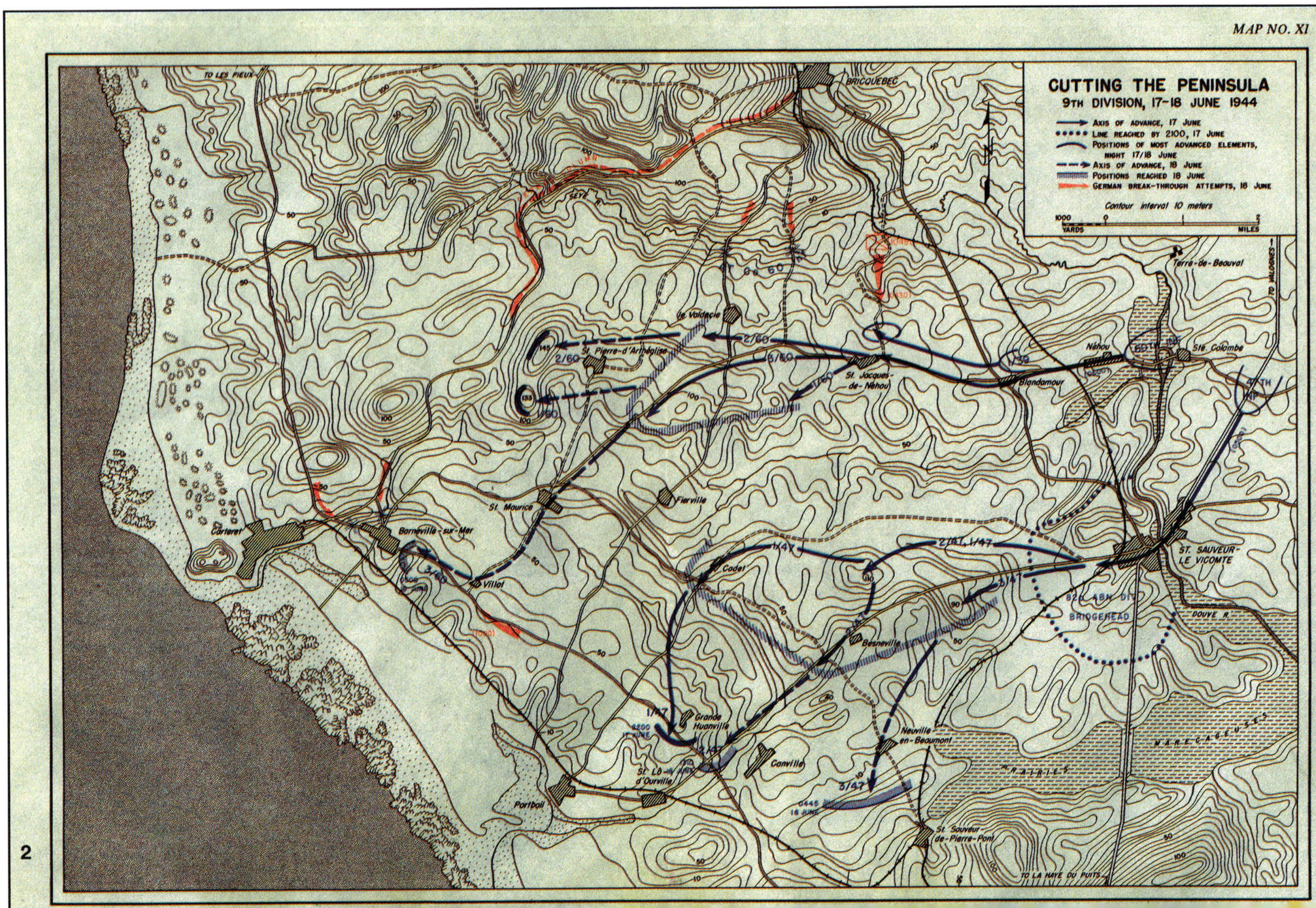

2. This map of the US army history department shows how the Cotentin peninsula was cut off by the 9th Infantry Division on 17 and 18 June, starting from the Sainte-Colombe and Saint-Sauveur-le-Vicomte sector. In the north, the 60th Regiment reached Barneville after passing through Saint-Jacques de Néhou. In the south, the 47th Regiment was approaching Portbail. In the north, we see retreating German elements blocked by the anti-tank elements of the 80th Regiment and by the 1st Battalion, the 39th Regiment.

3. This aerial photograph shows Barneville-sur-Mer taken facing eastwards, from where the American soldiers arrived, the aircraft have just flown over the sea behind the photographer. The town stretches along the coast road from Les Pieux in the north to La Haye-du-Puits in the south. (D.F./Heimdal.)

4. This map shows the new front line on 18 June 1944. The 9th Infantry Division cut off the Cotentin peninsula when it reached Barneville. Elements of four German divisions (24th, 77th, 91st, 709th) were thus cut off and encircled to the north. Other elements of these divisions contrived to withdraw southwards and evade encirclement. Four American infantry divisions (9th, 90th, 79th, 4th) now advanced on Cherbourg against elements of four German divisions which withdrew to Festung Cherbourg. (Heimdal.)

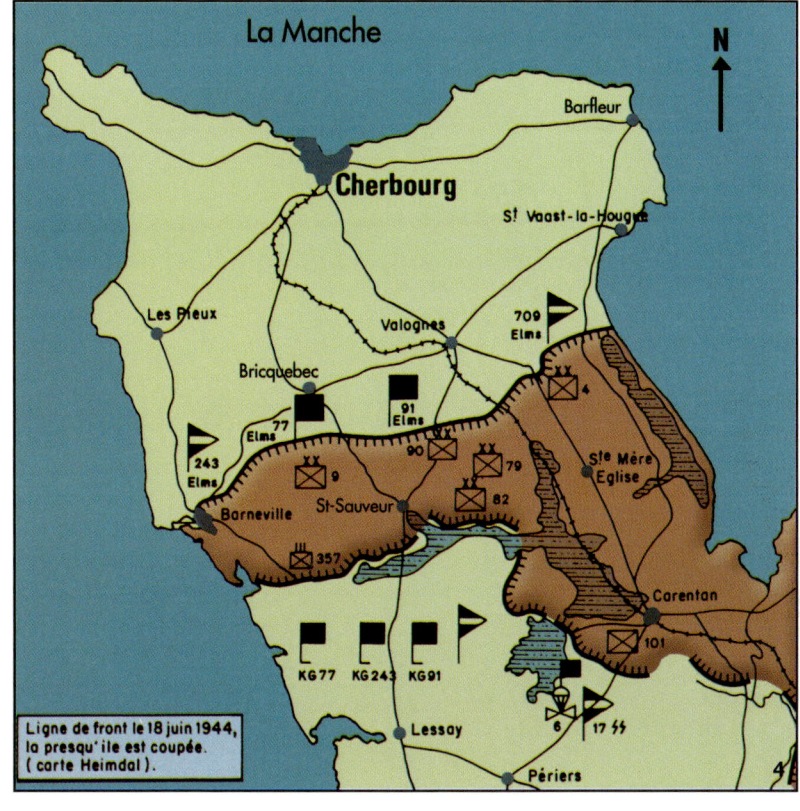

1. Aerial photo of Bricquebec, nestling up around its medieval castle, from the south.
2. Another photograph taken from the north with the Château des Galleries in the foreground.

Bricquebec, 21 June.

On June 18, when the peninsula was cut off, German units attempted to extricate themselves from encirclement. Thus a German column took to the road from Bricquebec to Barneville. It was spotted by the Americans on Hill 45 who brought the 60th Field Artillery Battalion into action. The American artillery enfiladed five miles (eight kilometers) of road, destroying thirty-five German vehicles, ten guns and some light vehicles. These were elements of the 77. Infanterie-Division (on this occasion, several staff officers of that division were captured). But despite this local disaster, other elements of the division managed to break out towards the south. From then on 77. ID was cut in two; those that broke out in the south were gathered together to form Kampfgruppe Bacherer (named for the colonel who took over command).

9th ID

3. Near Bricquebec, medical officers of the 39th I.R., the 9th Infantry Division serve a glass of wine to a German soldier who has been wounded in the nape of the neck. This must be a man belonging to the 77. ID which came under fire from the American guns of the 60th Field Artillery Battalion on the Barneville - Bricquebec road. Notice on one of the medical officers' helmet, a stencilled inscription specific to the men of the 39th Infantry Regiment, 9th ID: AAAO which means Anytime, Anything, Anywhere, Nothing.

4. The Place des Buttes at Bricquebec. Some MPs and GIs with the medieval castle in the background, dominated by its keep and, giving onto the square, J Feuardent's bar-restaurant and A. Touquet's "Rising Sun" coffee-ciderhouse, "Au Soleil Levant".

5. The same square as it is today, the restaurant is still there, but with a covered terrace.

6 and **7.** On 22 June, two GIs pass in front of A. Durels butcher's shop. There is no more opposition but damage in the Rue Saint-Roch, near the bridge, the only place to have been bombarded and to have suffered destruction. The houses on this spot were rebuilt.

8. This other presentday view shows where the destruction occurred around the bridge. The castle can be seen in the background, facing south-east.

(D.F., NA and E.G./Heimdal.)

83

Montebourg from 17 to 20 June.

1 and **2.** This photograph was taken south of Montebourg, near the front line that held until 19 June in the morning. An American vehicle has been smashed by a German shell, and the trailer tipped over. Lieutenant-Colonel Keil's Kampfgruppe (mostly III./919) firmly held this cornerstone of the German front. But on this day, 17 June the Americans broke out westwards as far as Carteret and from there, swung round northwards, heading for Cherbourg. The Germans were thus forced to withdraw and abandon Montebourg. We see the locality's strategically dominant position overlooking the entire sector. (D.F.and E.G./Heimdal.)

3 and **4.** On this 20 June, the American troops were in Montebourg, which was evacuated. Here we see some of the 4th Infantry Division's jeeps.

5. The church at Montebourg, a fine medieval building, dominates the locality.

6. Still on 20 June, T/5 Walter Halloran of the 4th Infantry Division examines an 88 mm flak gun, sabotaged and given up by Flak-Regiment Hermann which had no artillery prime movers to withdraw all its ordnance.

(D.F and E.G./Heimdal.)

Montebourg, 20 June 1944.

On 18 June, KG Keil was issued orders to fall back from Montebourg during the night of 18 to 19 June, and withdraw to Valognes. This Cotentin town had been the cornerstone of German resistance outside Cherbourg for some twelve days.

1. In this aerial photograph, we see the scale of the destruction; Montebourg was severely pounded by Allied naval artillery on 11 June. The main square where the market was held can be seen, and also another smaller square dominated by the massive outline of the church.

2. American troops entered the locality on 19 June, after the Germans withdrew. This picture was taken on 20 June, in the high street, coming from Carentan and heading north towards Valognes, at the entrance to the main square. A civilian, one of nearly three hundred civilians who had survived amid the ruins, tries to pass by a destroyed vehicle. (5639)

3 and **4.** In this photograph, war correspondent Franklin has moved on a few yards and turned round to take a new shot facing south. We recognize the destroyed vehicle in the previous photograph. Notice the badly damaged covered market on the left; it was rebuilt a little further back. (5642)

5 and **6.** And carrying on round the square, it is a sorry sight indeed, with some goats wandering about.
(Photographs D.F. and E.G./Heimdal.)

Montebourg, 20 June 1944.

1. The houses are still smouldering after the fierce blaze.

2. In the Place A. Pélerin, the Hôtel-Restaurant du Midi has been rebuilt. In this square, Nos 12, 14, 16, 18, 20 and 22 came through more or less intact.

4. Here we see the same square, with the Hôtel du Midi in 1944 and as rebuilt.

3 and **5.** The statue which used to stand there was later moved.

6. Horses were used for transport. These GIs have recovered a horse-drawn cart the German army had used to bring water and supplies up to their colleagues in the front line. (5742)

7. Another view of the place, this time with a jeep.

8. A convoy on its way up to the front line amid the ruins.

9 and 10. Commemorative monuments. (D.F. and E.G./Heimdal.)

Montebourg.

1 and **2.** From a distance, the church steeple at Montebourg dominates the whole area. In June 1944, it was toppled by shellfire but the damaged church survived.

3. Its walls still bear the marks of the impacts.

4. Inside the church on 21 June.

5. A child mends a bicycle by a destroyed vehicle, 23 June.

6. War correspondent Collier wrote "saved for the toast" as a comment on the strange fate of these fragile glasses preserved in a house destroyed at Montebourg, on 28 June. (6053)

7 and **8.** "Requisition". The American infantry used German army wagons and horses, on 21 June, to move supplies. Photograph taken by Runyan in front of n° 40 Rue Verblay (then n° 32) still standing here. On the other hand, further down, everything from numbers 5 and 18 onwards had to be rebuilt. (5686).

9 and **10.** Further on, a new house has replaced the ruins.
(D.F. and E.G./Heimdal.)

Valognes, 20 and 21 June 1944.

1. After the American breakout in the west Cotentin and the German retreat from Montebourg during the night of 19-20 June, in the heart of the Cotentin, the historic town of Valognes, known as the "little Versailles of Normandy", was also abandoned without a fight by the Germans who had planned a withdrawal to Festung Cherbourg as early as 17 June. On this 20 June, the 4th Infantry Division finally realized that the Germans had withdrawn. Colonel Van Fleet dispatched patrols of the 1st Battalion of his 8th Infantry Regiment as far as Valognes; his men reported to him that the place had been evacuated. But the bombing had reduced the historic town center to a pile of rubble, the streets were blocked by debris and the division's advance fell behind schedule as it skirted the town. In this aerial photograph, we see the western part of the town comparatively spared by the bombardments. The columns and pediment of the law courts are recognizable on the right.

2. An American engineers excavator clears rubble from the main street of Valognes near the Place Vicq d'Azir. The same place is also pictured in the next two photographs.

(Photographs courtesy NA and D.F./Heimdal.)

3 and **4.** Passing through Valognes was tough going even for a jeep. Burst water mains flooded the streets quickly cleared by the machine seen in photograph n° 2. A small Goliath can be seen on the right, it has tipped over amid the debris.

Valognes, 20 to 22 June 1944.

1. This photo taken on 20 June pictures, sticking up out of the pile of rubble, the ruins of one of the many private mansions (notice the triangular pediment) which earned Valognes the nickname of "little Versailles of Normandy".

2. On 22 June, civilians pull down a swastika from a portico where the two letters OT stand for "Organisation Todt".

3. There was total devastation in the Place Vicq d'Azir where the church of Saint Malo whose semi-collapsed steeple might prove dangerous. American engineers use T.N.T. to bring it down altogether.

4. A bulldozer sets to work at once to clear the rubble resulting from the destruction of the steeple. (Photograph taken by George Greb.)

5. And here a pan shot of the same spot, showing the Place Vicq d'Azir, surrounded by ruins, and the gutted church of Saint-Malo.

(Photo NA and D.F./Heimdal.)

Valognes, the church of Saint-Malo ruined.

1. The church of Saint-Malo was one of Valognes' medieval jewels; it was very badly hit, gutted in fact. A woman in traditional Cotentin costume passes in front of the choir and what is left of a chapel, opening up into empty space.

2. Inside the ruins of the church, we see two arcades of the choir, the large arcade of the south transept and, in the background, one of the nave arcades.

3. The ruins of the church from the west with, on the right, the remains seen in photograph 2. What is left of the choir is in the background. This church was rebuilt after the war by architect J.Y. Froidevaux, restoring the choir and transept. The nave was rebuilt in a cold, modern style.

4 and **5.** These two rare color photographs taken in 1944 picture some nuns, a woman and some children examining the ruins of the church. This is the south side already seen in photograph 2, on a level with the last remaining bay of the nave.

6. This photograph of the Place Vicq d'Azir was taken a year later, on 6 June 1945. The stones from the rubble were sorted and neatly lined up. The church of Saint-Malo awaits restoration work.

(NA/Heimdal.)

Cloth patch of the 9th Infantry Division.

The Battle of the Cotentin

The American infantry fought some tough battles amid the thick hedgerows of the Cotentin as they advanced on Cherbourg.

1. Some infantrymen listen to their latest exploits over the wireless; they have just cut off the Cotentin Peninsula. (PL/Heimdal.)

2. Lieutenant George Mutter (a name of German origin) guides artillery fire against Cherbourg's external defenses. (AP/Heimdal.)

3. As his platoons forge ahead, the captain commanding a company maintains contact with his leading elements through radio sets carried in backpacks. (PL/Heimdal.)

4. Two men of the 39th Infantry Regiment, 9th Infantry Division tossing grenades over a wall. There was a great deal of close combat on this highly partitioned battlefield. (NA/Heimdal.)

5. Helmet with the markings of the 39th Infantry Regiment. (coll leaves.)

6. On the ground, living conditions were rudimentary. Here Private John Wilczewski shaves without leaving his foxhole. (DAVA 6110/Heimdal.)

7. The American artillery put up a barrage in front of the infantry; here the GIs advance through a field littered with cows and dead Germans. (NA/Heimdal.)

Russians before Cherbourg on 23 June 1944.

1. On 23 June, two Soviet prisoners of war, Dimitri Yerschoff and Alexandre Rebuklin, had worked on construction of the German batteries. They have just surrendered to the Americans to whom they later passed on information. One of them is still wearing his Red Army uniform, including a padded jacket. (DAVA 5745/Heimdal.)

2. However, other former Soviet prisoners of war had been enlisted in the Wehrmacht. Several battalions of Osttruppen made up of former Soviet soldiers were committed in the Cotentin on the Germans' side. Some of these have just surrendered to a unit of the 90th Infantry Division. One of the Russians explains to M/Sgt Ted Henning from Newark (New Jersey) and to S/Sgt Walt Strauss from Jamaica, L.I. (New York) that they hail from the Smolensk area. This photograph is by war correspondent Kenny. (DAVA/Heimdal)

3. One of the Russians, Corporal Sansjiar Waliulin, writes a tract urging his other comrades to surrender. He is being helped by an American intelligence officer with the 90th Division, Captain Herbert Oehmichen, himself of German extraction. (DAVA/Heimdal.)

4. The Russian corporal and Captain Oehmichen from Keokuk in Iowa. (DAVA/Heimdal.)

5. Four of the surrendering Russians look over a copy of the "Yank" newspaper. They were "returned" by an over naive President Roosevelt to Stalin who either liquidated these trusting Russians or packed them off to Siberia … (DAVA/Heimdal.)

The final battle to take Cherbourg was especially hard-fought. Colonel Van Fleet's 8th Infantry Regiment (4th Infantry Division) sustained so many losses that it was detached from the division and sent home to rest.

1. Here we see an American infantryman digging a foxhole before Cherbourg. This was no idle precaution, as the German mortars were particularly effective. Exhaustion and discouragement can be read all over this GI's face. His comrades are scattered in the vicinity. (USIS/Heimdal.) **2.** However, while the German mortars and cannon were fearsome enough, the American artillery was even more so because it could line up a great many more gun barrels. This photo was taken on 25 June 1944 south of Cherbourg, near La Pierre Butée (the 9th Infantry Division's sector). Officers from three divisions, artillery observers, are there to guide the fire of the artillery regiments of their respective divisions, and also range-finding for the Allied navy which opened up on the German positions at Cherbourg on this 25 June. (DF/Heimdal.)

3 and **4.** These two photographs, taken by war correspondents Petrony and Collier on 28 June, show US 155 millimeter howitzers in action. A round has just been fired and they are in full recoil. Many rounds have already been fired. The howitzers have been placed under camouflage nets and one of them under a tree. (DAVA - 6054 and 6055/Heimdal.)

Bunkers

On 24 June 1944, the 79th Infantry Division captured the last of the strongpoints on the Cherbourg road. To reach the Fort du Roule, infantrymen of the 79th Infantry Division (in particular those of the 313th and 314th Infantry Regiments), with the help of the air force, were to take by storm the concrete "Goats" and "Duck pond" strongpoints. Here they blow open a bunker door as they mop up the positions. A GI examines the body of a German corporal. Further on, more GIs occupy some German Tobruks. On the last photograph, a tracked vehicle towing a trailer passes a sign marked Umgehungs-Strasse Cherbourg Ost, "Diversion Cherbourg East". (D.F. and A.P./Heimdal.)

The Fort du Roule, 25 and 26 June 1944

On 25 June, the 314th Infantry Regiment, 79th ID captured the flat land leading up to the Fort du Roule then on to the upper section of the fort, thanks especially to the heroic deeds of Corporal John D. Kelly and Lieutenant Carlos C Ogden. The lower section of the fort (chiefly the underground battery facing out to sea) was taken the next day. These three aerial photographs of the fort were taken by war correspondent Zwick on 8 July and give a good view of the site and its defenses. (Eto-hq-44-7120/24/27)

1. This photo was taken from the south, flying over the flat land leading to the fort. On it can be seen three concrete Flak Tobruks, with the harbor and the station on the left.

2. This photograph was taken from a little further away to the south-west. We see the bomb-cratered west side of the flat land, and a little further on, the part of Tourlaville

next to the center of Cherbourg, and still further on, the succession of two piers, lining the inner and outer harbor. The Fort des Flamands can be seen at the start of the first pier.

3. This last photograph was taken from the north-east. In the cliffside two of the four casemates can be seen (the others are on the other side) and control bunker. The flat land leading to the fort is pictured in the background.

4. At the foot of the Fort du Roule, today. (E.G./Heimdal.)

5. Site plan of the underground battery carved into the Montagne du Roule with its control bunker (3) in the center and the four gun apertures.

(Photographs courtesy DAVA/Heimdal – site plan by Heimdal.)

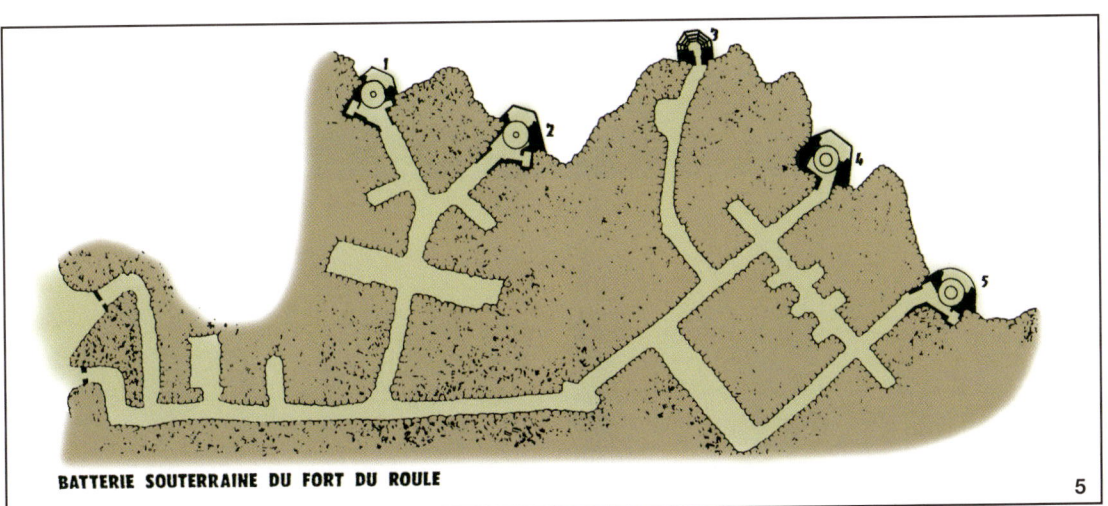

BATTERIE SOUTERRAINE DU FORT DU ROULE

The Fort du Roule, 26 June 1944

1. After the upper section of the Fort du Roule was captured, American soldiers of the 313th IR go round its bastioned walls to try and hit the gun slits of the battery located in the cliffside where guns were still firing on advancing American units at the foot of the fort. Explosive charges were even hoisted with ropes up to the level of the casemate apertures, to little avail. The Amiot factories can be seen on fire in the background on the right. (NA/Heimdal.)

2. The entrance to the Navy tunnel bored into the foot of the Montagne du Roule; this photo alongside a presentday photograph was taken after its capture by the Americans. (DAVA/Heimdal.)

3. A German soldier has been just captured. He has come out of the Navy tunnel (already seen on the preceding photo), near the Avenue de Paris. Three hundred German soldiers were captured here. (NA/Heimdal.)

4. From the Fort du Roule, the Cherbourg Arsenal can be seen on fire. The city center can be seen with its landmark square bell-tower of the church of the Trinity. (NA/Heimdal.)

5. Vestiges at the top of the Fort du Roule. (E.G./Heimdal.)

6. On this other view taken from the Fort du Roule, almost from the same angle, the Arsenal can be seen in the top left. In the center is the fishing port. On the right, the western section of Tourlaville where stood elements of the 4th Infantry Division. In the background is the harbor station. (NA/Heimdal.)

7. The scene today. (E.G./Heimdal.)

General von Schlieben surrenders

1 and **2.** At around 14 hours on 26 June 1944, the 39th IR, 9th Infantry Division open fire on the entrance to General von Schlieben's underground command post. A soldier waves a white flag in surrender **(1).** A helmeted General von Schlieben then emerges from the underground, followed by Admiral Hennecke (wearing a cap and coat) **(2).** Photographs by war correspondent Spangle. (DAVA - 5994 and 6049/Heimdal.)

3. The two general officers are taken to General Eddy (9th Division) at his combat CP near the church at Octeville. They were then taken to Major General J Lawton Collins's CP at Château de Servigny near Yvetot-Bocage. They arrived soaking wet at the château to sign the deed of surrender. (NA/Heimdal.)

4 and **5.** The deed of surrender was signed on the second floor of the château in the presence of Maj. Gen. J Lawton Collins. Photographs by war correspondent Petrony. (DAVA - 5962 and 5948/Heimdal.)

6. The two enemy commanders, and Admiral Hennecke, pose for posterity in front of Château de Servigny. (NA/Heimdal.)

7. After the surrender. (A.P./Heimdal.)

1. After the fall of the Fort du Roule, infantry advance west of the fort. Here they pass by the Park in the Avenue de Paris on their way to the harbor station. (NA/Heimdal.)

2. Today, these impacts recall the battle. (E.G/Heimdal.)

3. The victors dominate Cherbourg from the Fort du Roule. From left to right: General Ira T

Wyche (79th ID commander), Staff Sergeant Paul A. Hwiss, Staff Sergeant Charles Gass and Lieutenant-Colonel Gilman A. Huff. (USIS/Heimdal.)

4 and **5.** Major General Collins and Captain Kirkpatrick (of 79th ID) also came to visit this key site of the battle. (NA/Heimdal.)

6. Today. (E.G./Heimdal.)

7. These soldiers are on their way back from the harbor station. They come to the junction with the Rue du Val de Saire to take the Avenue de Paris on the other side, to the south.

A U.S. 57 mm anti-tank gun can be seen unlimbered on the left and the Café du Rond-Point, which we shall come back to later. (KY/Heimdal.)

8. Today. (E.G./Heimdal.)

9. This photo was taken in the Rue Dom Pedro near the Hôtel Atlantique, in the harbor station district. The German pocket of resistance at the harbor station and the Mielles terreplein has just been reduced. American soldiers survey a German casualty. (NA/Heimdal.)

10. At the same spot, a little later, American soldiers pose with civilians on a French tracked vehicle used by the Germans and now recovered by the Americans. (NA/Heimdal.)

11. Today. (E.G./Heimdal.)

The Americans enter Cherbourg, 26 June 1944

1, 2 and **3.** While advancing towards the center of Cherbourg, the Americans have come up against a street blocked by a concrete wall with a firing slit. They have opened a breach in the wall. In front of this obstacle are the remains of a light gun that armed the firing slit. Behind, a 20 mm Flak gun can be seen, positioned at the corner of two streets so as to enfilade both possible lines of advance. The corner house has burned down after being hit by shellfire. (P.L./Heimdal.)

4. Someplace downtown, an German anti-tank cannon on a tracked gun carriage controlled a crossroads. It has been destroyed and is still smoking. Two American soldiers examine the places. (USIS/Heimdal.)

5. The infantry advance towards the city center. (D.F./Heimdal.)
6. The Americans advance through Cherbourg. (Heimdal.)

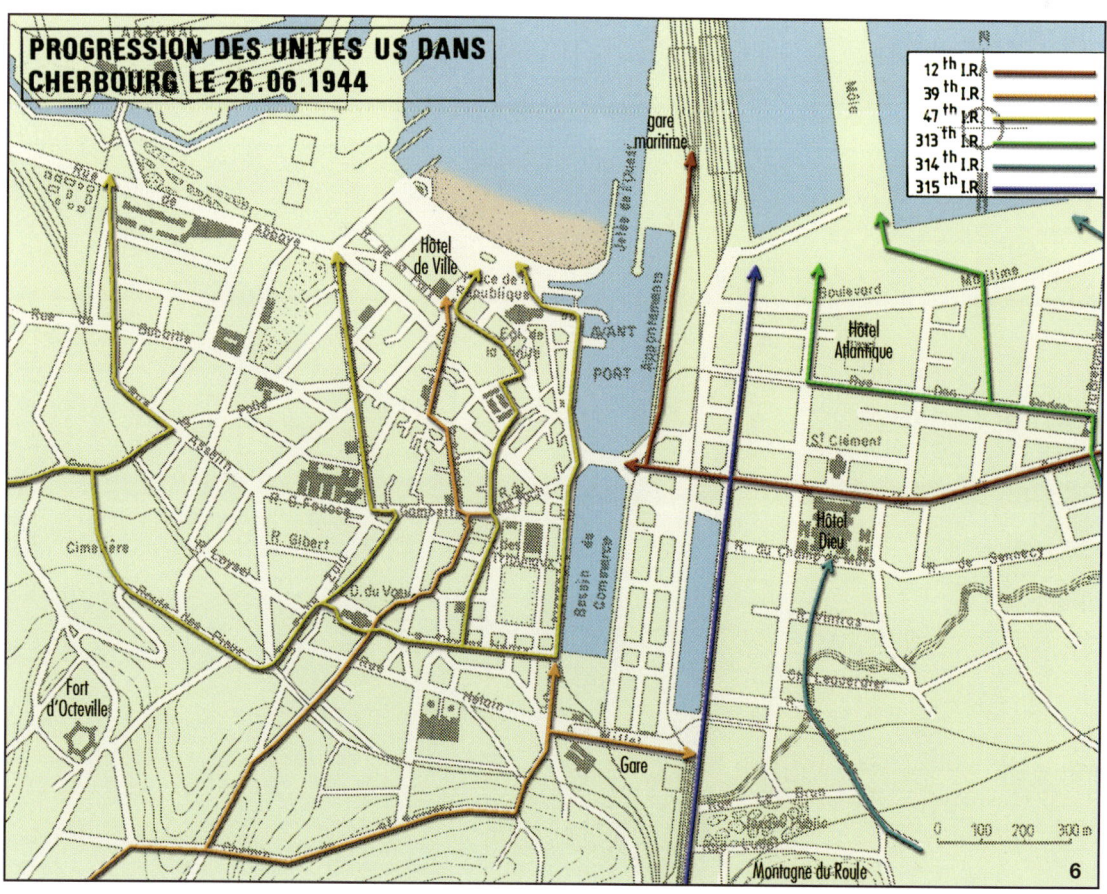

1 and **3.** On 26 June 1944, U.S. tanks advance into Tourlaville. Men of the 1st and 3rd Battalions, 313th Infantry Regiment, coming from Tourlaville, came up against the bunkers of the harbor station and vicinity. They called upon the tanks. These two photographs were taken from the same spot in the Rue du Val de Saire, a little way past the entrance to the Hôtel-Dieu (renamed Pasteur Hospital), the tanks came from the east, from the center of Tourlaville. The shells that missed the Fort du Roule, and particularly the harbor station, hit several houses when elements of the 313th IR had to deal with the bunkers in the harbor station sector, sometimes misaiming… (DAVA - 6041/Heimdal.)

2 and **4.** Today. (E.G./Heimdal.)

5. American tanks advance along what is now the Rue Pierre de Coubertin round the back of the Army hospital the grounds of which are behind the wall seen on the left. Some Germans come up to surrender to the tanks, waving a Red Cross flag. (NA/Heimdal.)

6. Today. (E.G./Heimdal.)

7. Rare color photograph taken in 1944, in the streets of Cherbourg, once the fighting was over. (DAVA.)

The harbor station

Cherbourg's harbor station was one of the city's landmarks. Trains came as far as this station in the back of beyond, right up alongside the ocean-going liners. It was recognizable from afar from its tall marker lamp which has fallen onto the ground. The station was methodically destroyed and rendered unusable by the Germans: 35 tons of explosives were used.

Two bunkers were built at the end of the harbor station pier. They are clearly visible in the aerial photograph. Two photographs show the outside and inside of one of the two casemates. It is armed with a 105 cm gun and surmounted by a flak gun tobruk. The harbor station battery belongs to the last artillery belt, comprising the light batteries. It then included the Bastion II battery and the Fort du Roule battery as well as this one. (NA/Heimdal.)

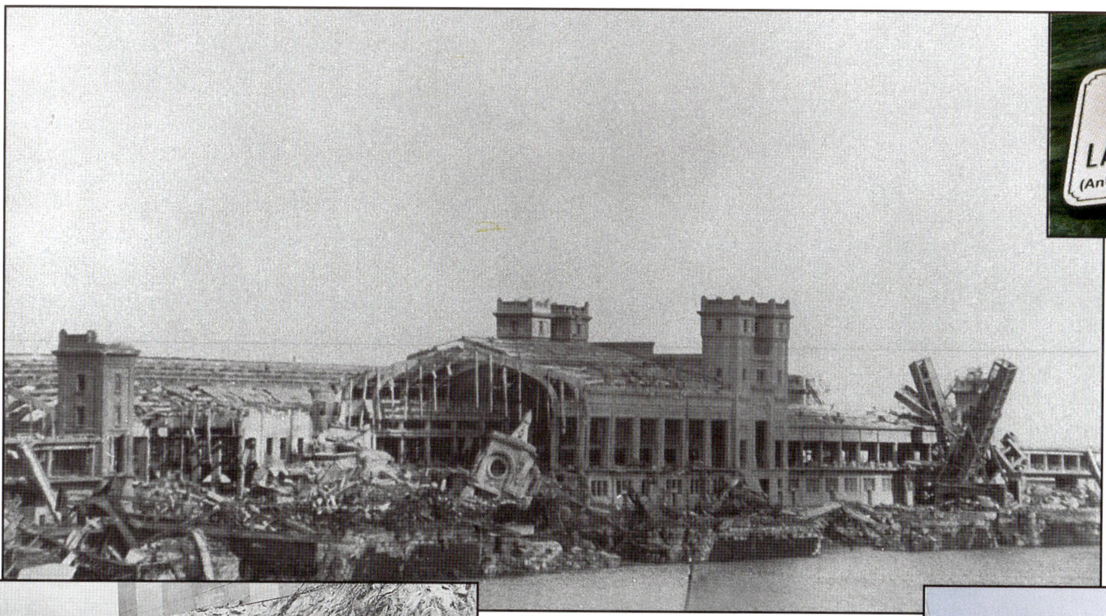

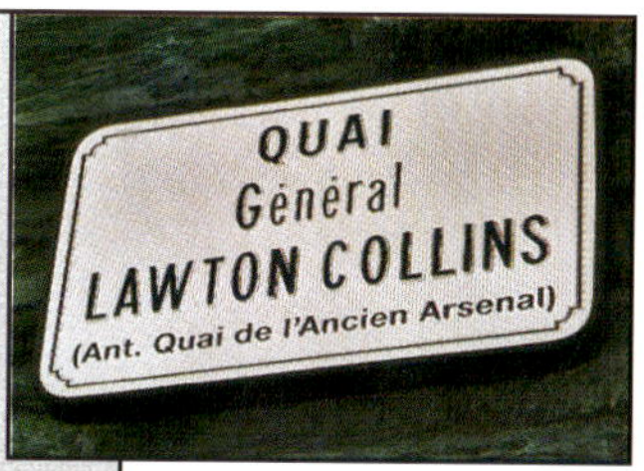
QUAI
Général
LAWTON COLLINS
(Ant. Quai de l'Ancien Arsenal)

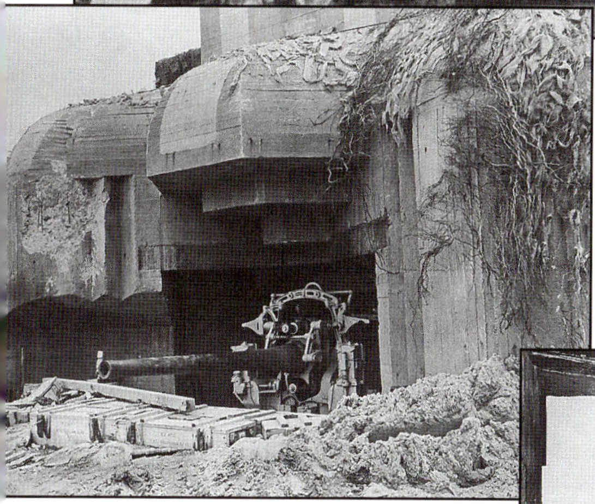

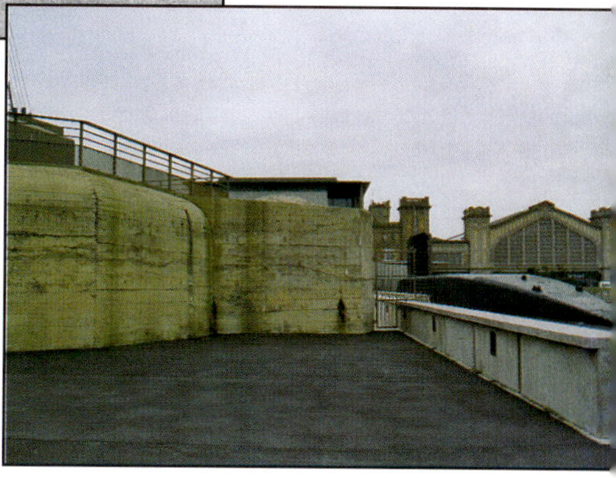

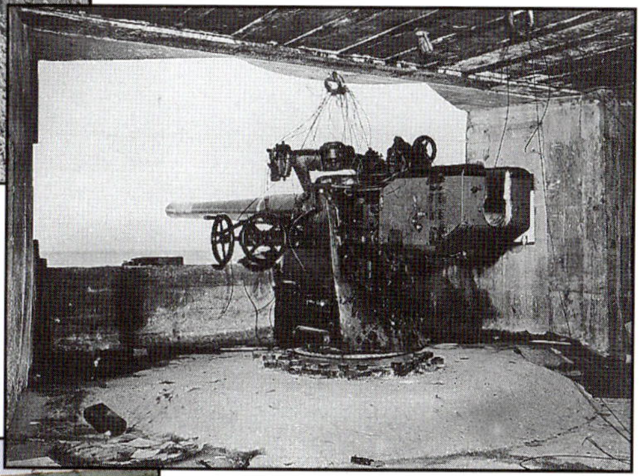

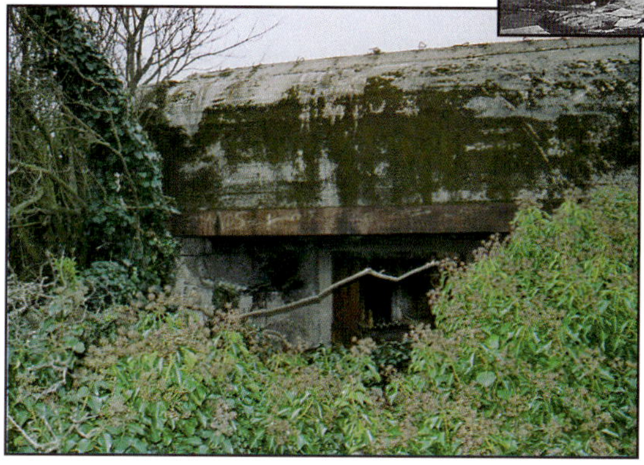

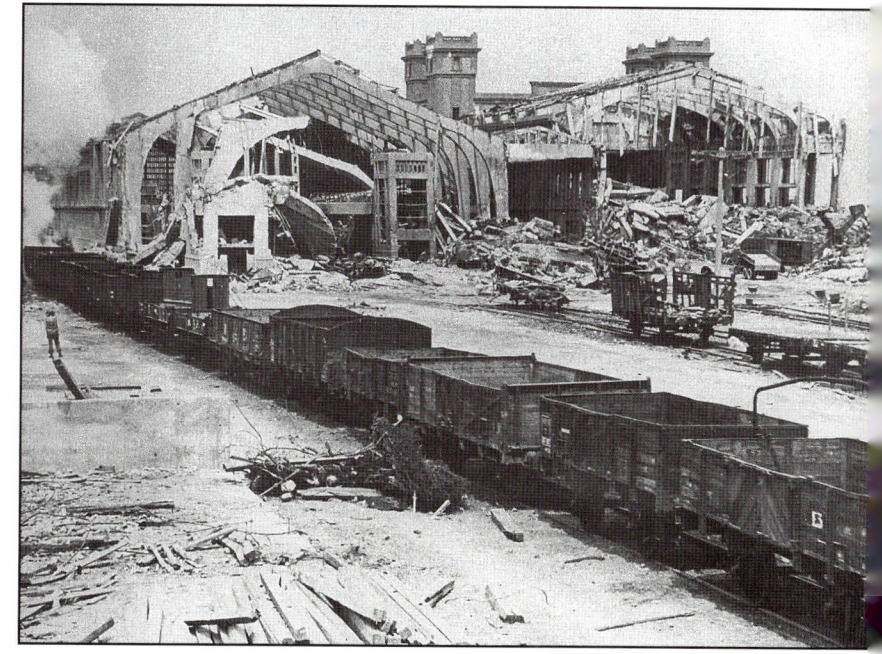

Cherbourg City Hall, 27 June 1944

The day after General von Schlieben surrendered, VII Corps commander Major General Collins came to Cherbourg City Hall on 27 June, for an official reception at 16.00 hours.

1. He arrives in his armored command vehicle (bearing his Major General's insignia); he is accompanied by several of his Generals. (NA/Heimdal.)

2. Today, while the City Hall porch has survived untouched, the frontage has been substantially "modernized". (E.G./Heimdal.)

3. Maj. Gen. Collins was then received officially at the City Hall and the mayor, Dr. Renault, gave him the freedom of the city. Collins for his part came, in the name of the United States, to hand over the conquered city to the administration of its mayor and city council. Lt. Gen. Barton is on the left. (NA/Heimdal.)

4. A ceremony then took place in front of the City Hall, and as the Marseillaise was played, Dr. Renault stood to attention while the Generals around him saluted. Notice 4th ID commander Lt. Gen. Barton (on the left, with the moustache), Maj. Gen. Collins, Lt. Gen. Eddy (wearing spectacles, behind Collins) and a paratroop officer whose faces were always censored on photographs (it has got to be 82nd Airborne Division commander Lt. Gen. Ridgway). Dr.

Renault is holding a flag, a gift from Maj. Gen. Collins, a French flag cut out of American parachutes. (NA/Heimdal.)

5. Ceremony in front of the City Hall. (NA/Heimdal.)

6. Opposite the City Hall, the Americans laid out a guard of honor, here presenting arms, probably at the time of the Marseillaise. (NA/Heimdal.)

7. Photo taken shortly afterwards. The soldiers are now standing at ease. On this occasion, Maj. Gen. Bradley sent a message to the French people expressing his pleasure at being able to tell the people of France that their first major town was being handed back to them. (NA/Heimdal.)

7. The station, of which here is a general view with its equipment, was attached to a unit of the PWD (Psychological Warfare Division). (OWI/HA/Heimdal.)

"Radio Cherbourg" first went on the air on 27 June

1. On the high ground at La Fauconnière, at Beaumont-La Hague, by the city reservoirs, American specialist engineers set up a radio station, the first Allied radio station in France since 1940. **2.** A technician, Sergeant Baranowski, sets up an antenna in a tree, next to a searchlight abandoned by the Germans, while the others stretch cables up to the building which was to house "Radio Cherbourg". **3** and **4**. Some curious civilians watch them at work. (OWI/NA/Heimdal.)

5. This was 27 June 1944, the station is about to go on the air for the first time. Some civilians await the event at the foot of the building.

6. The station was headed by a former American journalist from New York, Bravig Imbs, and by Englishman Imlay Walts, a director of the BBC. The latter (on the left in the photograph) gives the signal. A text is read by Andre Marchese, a civilian who for a year and a half had been a prisoner of the Germans. On the right, Lieutenant Daniel Overton, an officer with the Engineers, monitors broadcasting quality.

123

5. Today. (E.G./Heimdal.)

6 and 7. Old and wounded prisoners pass through Cherbourg. (DAVA - 6041 and OWI/Heimdal.)

8. Some German prisoners have been rounded up. In the front rows are some members of the Todt Organization who are no longer young men. Men like these made up numbers in a besieged fortress but had no fighting value. (NY/Heimdal.)

3. A TD-crew speaks with an old French.

27 June, end of the fighting in Cherbourg

1. On 27 June, the fighting in Cherbourg was over and the Americans began rounding up prisoners. Captain Earl J Topley of St Paul in Minnesota, examines the body of a German who was killed after shooting three of his GIs at the time of the initial fighting in the city. (DAVA-5941/Heimdal.)

2. Two German soldiers were killed by soldiers of the 313th IR, 79th ID after abandoning the Peugeot 202 (taken over by the Wehrmacht) pictured in the photograph. (DAVA - 6018/Heimdal.)

4. Captain W.H. Hooper, commander of I Company, 314th IR, 79th ID (who was killed early in July at the time of the battle for La Haye-du-Puits) and some of his men escorts a column of German prisoners, with the officers leading the way. They are walking up Cherbourg's Avenue de Paris, passing in front of the "Cherbourg" sign marking the old city toll at the foot of the Montagne du Roule. The column is heading south on its way to the POW camps set up on the Montagne du Roule plateau, close to the farm of La Fieffe. (DAVA-6048/Heimdal.)

124

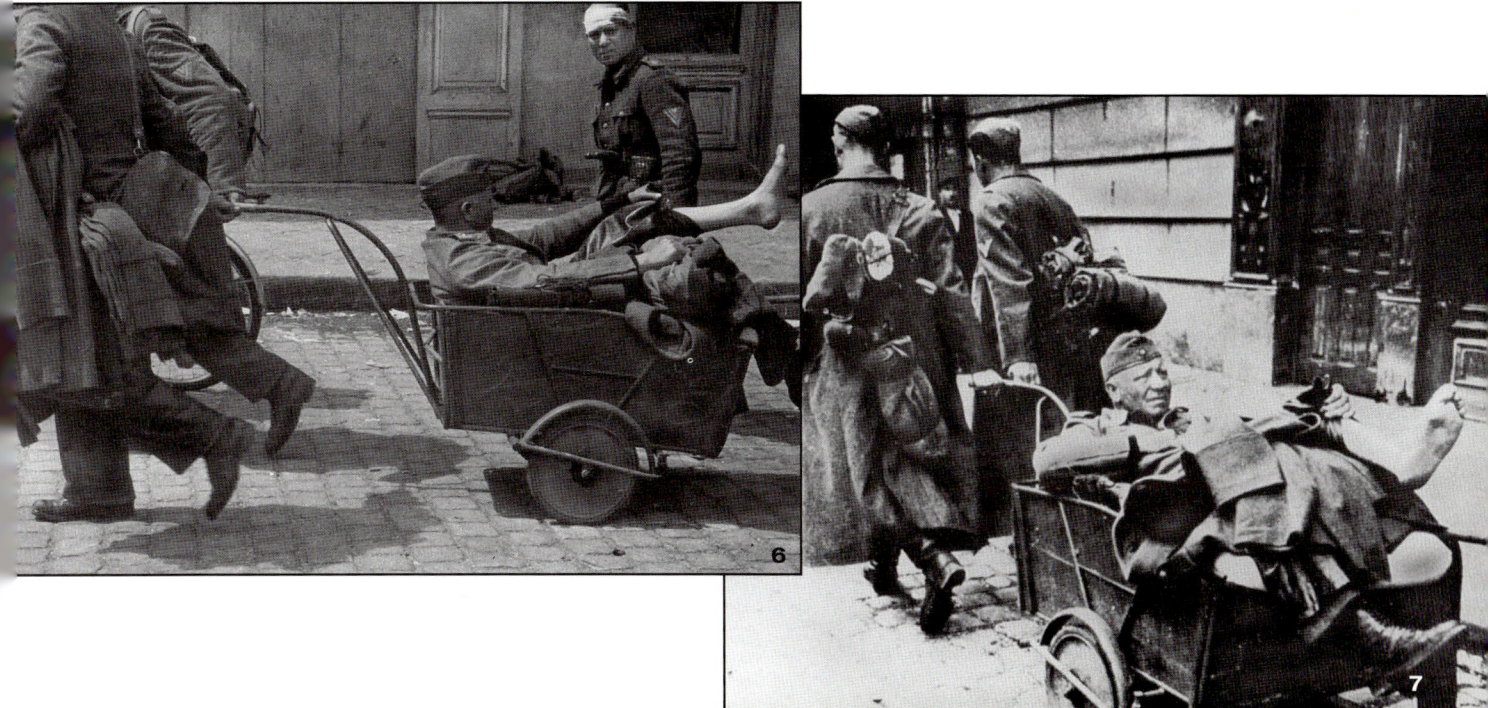

Cherbourg, 28 June

1 and **2.** The Americans were by now established in Cherbourg and Tourlaville. These three soldiers of the 4th Infantry Division are in their sector; the part of Tourlaville next to Cherbourg, east of the Divette and at the foot of the Fort du Roule. They are sitting on the corner of Avenue Aristide Briand and the Rue du Val de Saire in the Place Marie-Ravenel. They are holding the crossroads with a machine-gun… but there are no more German counter-attacks to fear. The bullet marks show just how hard progress was in this part. Notice the 4th Division's badge these three men are wearing on their sleeves. Notice too all the German signposts still in place. The H.V.P. Mar. Laz. sign (main treatment post - Naval Hospital) is to Pasteur Hospital. Raebel Werke probably means the

Amiot factory. OT Micheels Collignon (Todt Organization "Micheels" Unit) tells us that that unit was near the beach at Collignon, in Tourlaville. Here we are at the junction of the road from Valognes to the harbor station and the road into the city center from the Saire Valley. Today: again facing towards Barfleur and Pasteur Hospital…

3. The Sergeants J. Sagert and Spiker guard a former German OT post.

4 and **5.** Here is the Café du Rond-Point again, in the Place Marie-Ravenel, near the house in photograph 1. Like their comrades, these soldiers have an American 30 caliber (7,62 mm) machine-gun. From left to right: Pvt. Daniel B Wassie, Corporal Burd E Showalter, Pvt.P John J Langan and Pvt. Roger E Houle. They are resting near an artillery gun and caisson abandoned by the Germans. Today there is no longer a cafe here. (DAVA - 5985/Heimdal and E.G./Heimdal.)

6 and **7.** A little further on, in the Rue Dom Pedro, helped by American soldiers, civilians tear down the signpost to the Todt Organization's head office in Cherbourg, this was the building that housed the O.B.L. (Oberbauleitung Cherbourg). This building, the Atlantic Hotel, was built at the end of the First World War to lodge emigrants on their way to the United States. It later became an annex of the Amiot factories, before being taken over by the T.O. (NA - 5983 and E.G. Heimdal.)

8. A German officers' mess left untouched when American troops arrived. The table is still set with cups and bottles. (NA/Heimdal.)

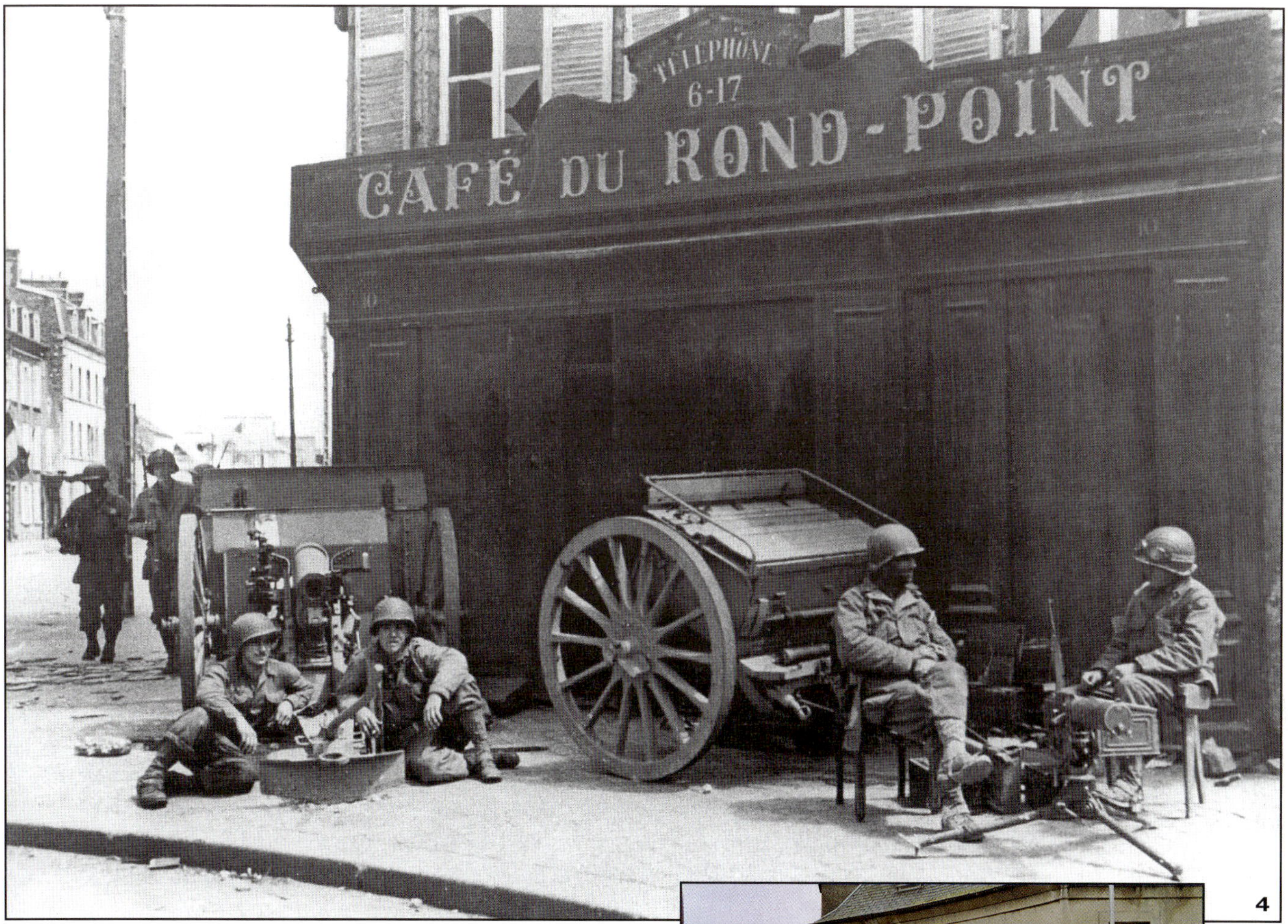
TÉLÉPHONE
6-17
CAFÉ DU ROND-POINT
4

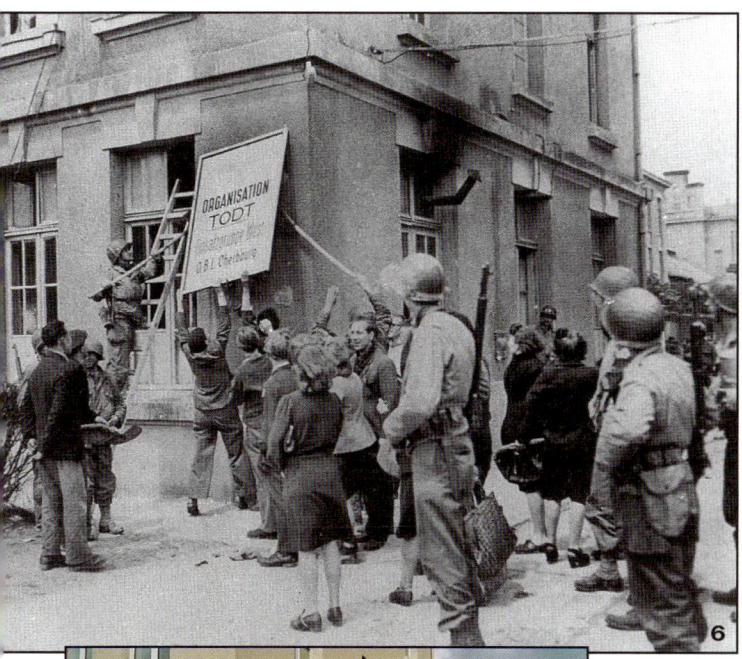

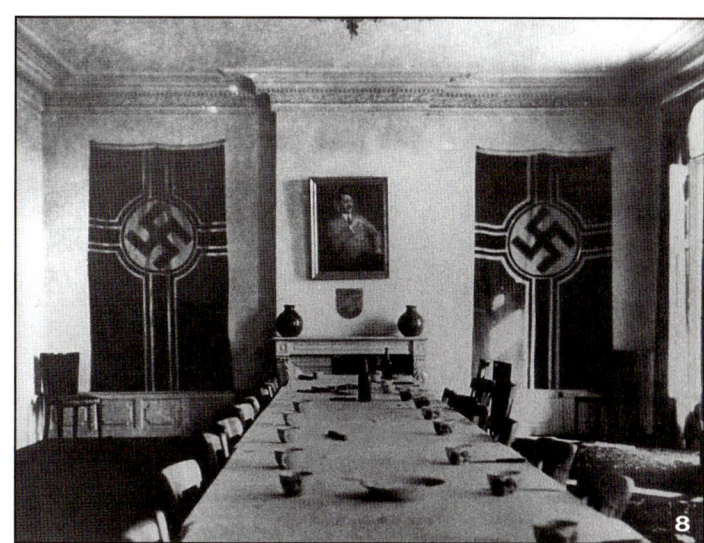

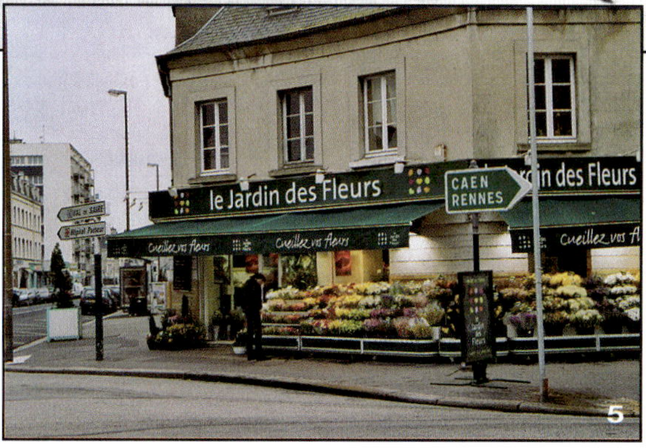
le Jardin des Fleurs
CAEN
RENNES
Cueillez vos fleurs
5

ORGANISATION
TODT
6

7

8

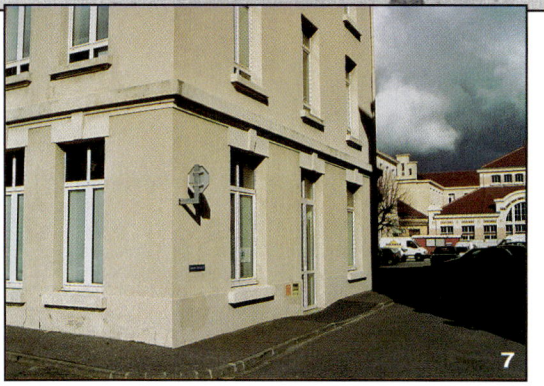

Tuesday 27 June, the Arsenal surrenders

1. Tuesday 27 June, the time 8.30, an ultimatum was sent to the Germans defending the Arsenal. General Robert Sattler, who was a Stadtkommandant, as fortress commander, had the job of defending the Arsenal. But he put up a purely symbolic resistance, and at 10 o'clock, after eagerly accepting the American ultimatum, General Sattler, pictured here, put an end to any resistance in the Arsenal. (D.F./Heimdal.)

2. General Sattler has just surrendered. (NA/Heimdal.)

3. A view of the navy tunnel dug into the Montagne du Roule after the German surrender there on the 26th. There are objects scattered around the tunnel which was used as a barrack room. The bodies have still to be collected. (DAVA/Heimdal.)

4. On this 27 June, Master Sergeant Max Oppenheiwer announces over the radio General von Schlieben's surrender and the capture of Cherbourg. On his helmet is a "VII" for VII Corps. (NA/Heimdal.)

5. Infantrymen of the 79th ID, their helmets covered with characteristic netting, stop for a break in a Cherbourg street to talk to a "French Mademoiselle". Photo taken as of the 26th by Weintraub. (DAVA - 5980/Heimdal.)

6. Local civilians fire questions at the GIs. (OWI.)

129

27 and 28 June, the Arsenal

When the Americans entered Cherbourg Arsenal on 27 June, it had suffered major damage.

1. They also came upon a large bunker for fast patrol boats which the Germans had begun to build. Here we see the rear of this as yet to be completed base. Photo taken on 30 June 1944. (DAVA - 63 96/Heimdal.)

2. The access to the concrete shelter of this base gives onto the Arsenal's outer harbor. Here we see the huge entrance and the as yet unfinished round arch. (NA/Heimdal.)

3. Interior of this shelter with its characteristic vault. While the entrance is reminiscent of a submarine base, the vault, on the other hand, is different from those of the U-Boote bases. (NA/Heimdal.)

4. The same shelter, today. (B. Paich.)

5. A pile of torpedoes. They were photographed not inside the Arsenal but in the Navy tunnel carved into the foot of the Montagne du Roule. (DAVA/Heimdal.)

6. One of the devastated workshops looking out onto the outer harbor. (NA - 6388/Heimdal.)

7. General view showing the fast patrol boat (Schnellboote) base and the ruined buildings looking onto the outer harbor. The dock is mined and strewn with wrecks. The American troops had their work cut out making repairs. (NA - 6397/Heimdal.)

8. Another view of the devastated Arsenal, Rochambeau district. (DAVA - 6871/Heimdal.)

28 and 29 June, forts of Cherbourg

On 28 June, all resistance had not ceased in Cherbourg. Fregattenkapitän Witt and his men still held the Fort de l'Ouest and the Fort du Centre. Towards 10.50, it came under violent aerial attack and the Americans moving up from Querqueville took Fort Chavaignac. On 29 June, the American artillery opened fire on both forts. The Fort du Centre was destroyed and had to be abandoned. Witt was wounded and surrendered at 16.45.

1. The Fort de l'Ouest seen from a plane. On

4. The Americans set up an AA position of DCA against a possible German air attack. It is made up of a 37 mm gun and two 12,7 mm machine-guns, lending it tremendous firepower. (US Army/Heimdal.)

this enormous circular mass, notice the control bunker, various tobruks and searchlight. (NA/Heimdal.)

2. The searchlight mounted on top of the Fort de l'Ouest. (NA/Heimdal.)

3. The Fort de l'Ile Pelée was huge, with a barracks and a port, and it was reinforced by the Germans with three artillery casemates and numerous flak tobruks. It closed off the eastern end of the Grande Digue du Large. This photograph was taken from the north-west. (DAVA-7114/Heimdal.)

5. Photo taken in the Arsenal port, with the entrance to the air and sea base. Notice the destroyed hangars in the background. (NA/Heimdal.)

6. Aerial view taken from over the base. The destroyed hangars are clearly visible. A crane for seaplanes has collapsed into the sea. (NA/Heimdal.)

7. The damaged Amiot factories, photo taken on 29 June. (DAVA - 6332/Heimdal.)

8 and **9.** 28 June. Russian workers released from the Arsenal by the Americans dance while awaiting transfer. On their return, Stalin packed them off to Siberia: they had seen what living conditions were like in the West. (DAVA - 6051 - 9 and 14/Heimdal.)

Cherbourg, from 28 to 30 June 1944

1 and **2.** After the battle, some soldiers were decorated. On that particular day, Major General Raymond C Barton, commander of the 4th Infantry Division, decorated some of his men with Silver Stars for bravery at the time of the battle for Cherbourg. This photograph was taken on 30 June, in the Place de la République in front of the City Hall, visible on the left. Today, the destroyed houses have been rebuilt to match their neighbor which survived intact. The City Hall frontage has been "modernized" and the monument to Deportees and Resistance figh-

ters now stands in this square. (DAVA - 6238 and E.G./Heimdal.)

3. That same day, 1st Army commander Lieutenant-General Omar Bradley (left) met VII Corps commander Major General J Lawton Collins. They look out over Cherbourg from the Fort du Roule. Collins explains to Bradley how his troops seized Cherbourg. (DAVA - 6248/Heimdal.)

4. Two days earlier, on 28 June, a GI examining a German ammunition dump in a ruined house. (D.F./Heimdal.)

5. After the battle was over, civilians evacuated before it commenced show an American officer the homes they are now going back to. (NA - 6032/Heimdal.)

6. Local people crating German propaganda publications later sent off into storage. (OWI/Heimdal.)

7 and **8.** Just off the swing bridge, on 30 June, in the Quai Alexandre III and the entrance to the Rue Maréchal Foch, men and equipment of an AA unit are "on their way to a new position". The place has changed very little. (DAVA and E.G./Heimdal.)

9 and **10.** While Cherbourg had fallen, the havoc left behind by the Germans left the port temporarily unusable. (AP/Heimdal.)

135

6

Hedgerow hell (1 to 15 July)

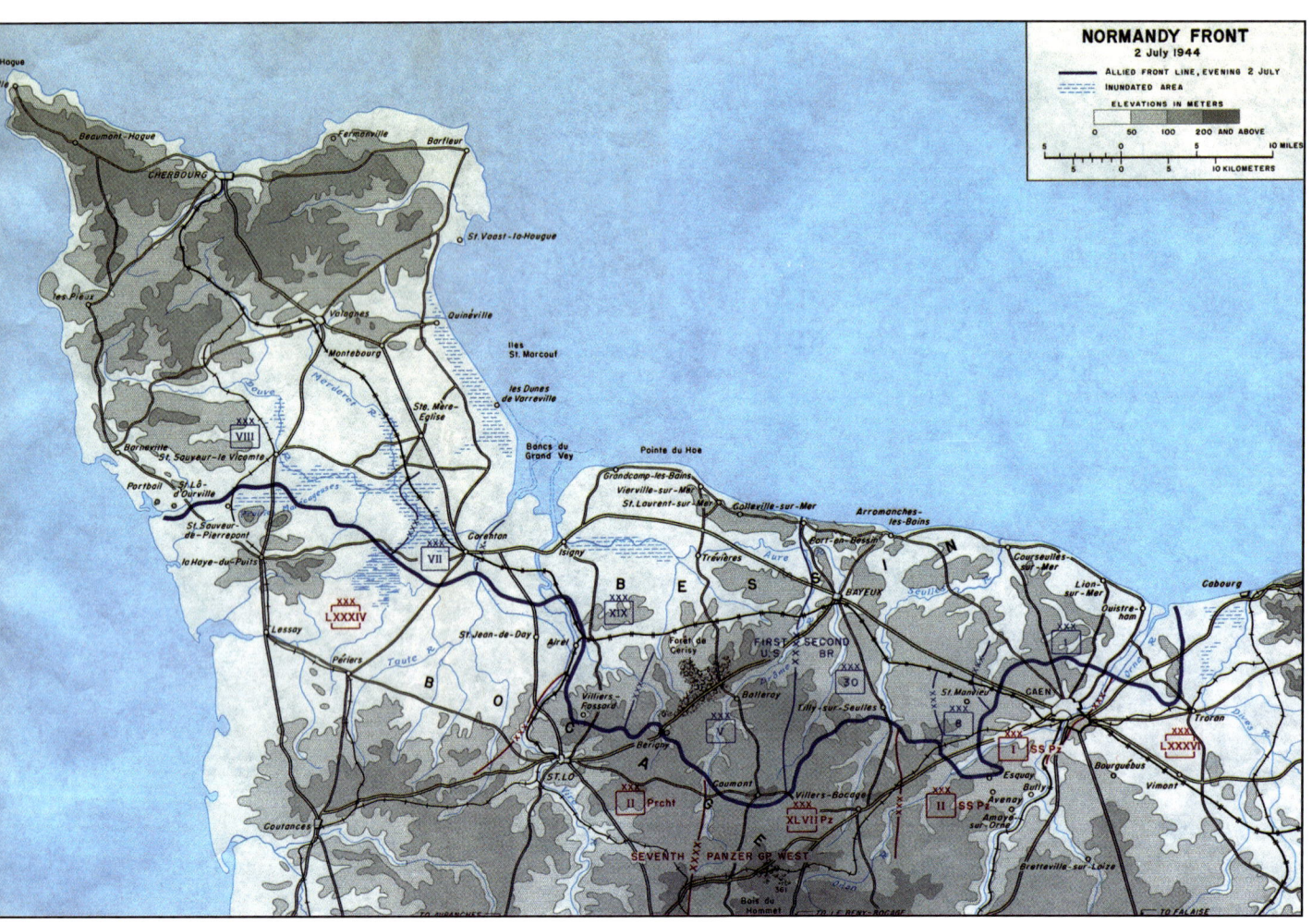

Here we see the Allied front line in Normandy on 2 July 1944. The 1st US Army then lined up four corps. In the west, the VIII Corps facing La Haye-du-Puits, in the middle the VII Corps facing Périers, in the east the XIX Corps facing Saint-Lô and the V Corps in the Caumont sector. In the east, the 2d British Army made much slower progress, on a narrow bridgehead, pinned down in front of Villers-Bocage, Hill 112 and Caen. The American bridgehead was much broader, especially with the Cotentin peninsula, but their path was now blocked by the marshy areas and the stoutly defended bocage. (US Army History Department.)

The battle of the marshes

Situation on the front on 2 July

Once the battle for Cherbourg was over, the American command divided up its forces into four corps and wheeled them all round to advance southwards. They were: - *VIII Corps* (just arrived), - *VII Corps* (which took part in the Battle of the Cotentin with Maj. Gen. Collins in command), *XIX Corps* (just arrived), and lastly V Corps (which landed on Omaha Beach and had been fighting for nearly a month in the western part of the Calvados). The fact that the staff of VIII and XIX Corps had only recently arrived on the scene does not mean that the same was true of all the divisions they had under them. What happened was that the divisions brought in as reinforcements at the end of June were slipped between units already in action to bolster the disposition, and so we find units that had taken part in the early weeks of the battle (4th, 9th, 79th, 90th, 1st, 2nd, 29th Infantry Divisions) alternating along the front line with "fresh" troops. The four corps commanders thus each had at their disposal units that were already battle-hardened and others that were not.

Faced with this new development in the campaign, the German command failed to regain the initiative. On 18 June, following operations in the Cotentin Peninsula, most of the infantry units found themselves encircled in the north outside Cherbourg, with their backs to the sea. But a number of German infantry divisions had been broken up in the American breakout in the west and had several regiments and battalions repulsed northwards into the "Cherbourg Pocket" while others contrived in dire circumstances to fall back southwards. Among these were *243., 91.* and *77. Infanterie-Divisionen*. Their elements that managed to make their way to the south of the peninsula were no bigger than battlegroups; these three divisions lost their generals, either killed or captured. Colonel Bacherer was in command of what was left of *77. I.D.*, which became *Kampfgruppe Bacherer*. Colonel Koenig commanded the remnants of *91. I.D*, and Colonel Klosterkemperer those of *243. I.D.* But these three battlegroups were now reinforced by two fresh divisions: - *353.*

Infanterie-division, commanding officer *Gen. Lt.* Mahlmann, put on the alert in Brittany on 6 June, and which got moving on the 10th, advancing by night, on foot, its leading elements reaching the Saint-Lô sector on 13 and 14 June, while the bulk of the division was held up by Resistance operations. The *353. I.D.* did not muster until 18 June in the Périers sector after suffering losses on the way; it could only line up 11,500 men. The *17. SS-Panzergrenadier-Division "Götz von Berlichingen"* had greater strength, it was a motorized division with armored vehicles including an assault gun section. Its *Kommandeur*, Werner Ostendorff, was wounded and the division came under *Standartenführer* Otto Baum. - *Kampfgruppe Heintz* was a battlegroup with the strength of a regiment under Colonel Heintz; it was detached from *275. I.D.* to bolster the disposition. – The remnants of *Major* von de Heydte's *Fallschirmjäger-Regiment 6* remained a fighting force. All these units were attached to *LXXXIV. (84th) Armee-Korps* with General Fahrmbacher taking over command on a temporary basis after the death of General Marcks on 12 June. General von Choltitz assumed command at the head of this corps on 18 June.

The Germans lost precious time in the early hours of the landings trying to work out the scale of the Allied operation and what to to do about it. Most time was lost through the slowness in getting reinforcements up to the front line, as we saw with the *353. I.D.* German hopes of "throwing the Allies back into the sea" were dashed. This mission of the *"Götz von Berlichingen"* Division was a failure from 13 June onwards, and since then the 1st US Army had been substantially reinforced, and the American breakout of 18 June proved decisive in the battle to follow. It removed from the battlefield nearly 40,000 Germans caught in the "Cherbourg pocket", losses which two fresh divisions brought up in reinforcement hardly made up for, as they should have been employed for an offensive, but were given a defensive role south of the American disposition in the Cotentin. From 18 June, von Choltitz tried to save the situation. He issued instructions (1). Concentrating on the capture of Cherbourg, apart from the odd patrol the Americans took no action in the south. This enabled him to build up a defensive front at the base of the Cotentin Peninsula. *LXXXIV. AK* slowly fell back onto several defensive lines. The remnants of *243. ID* and *91. ID* established **a first line of** defense on the edge of the marshy meadows, aligning no more than about 3,500 fighting men in addition to *Kampfgruppe Heintz* and some *Osttruppen*. **The second line**, resting on La Haye-du-Puits and the swampy meadows of Gorges (the *Mahlmann Linie*), was defended from west to east by *Kampfgruppe Bacherer (77. ID)*, *353. Infanterie-Division* with *Grenadier-Regiment 941* and *Gren.-Regt. 942* up to the Gorges marshes, and *17. SS-Panzergrenadier-Division* beyond them. A third line called *Wasserstellung* ("position of the water"), had its springboard at Lessay towards three rivers, the Ay, the Sèves and the Taute. It was to be prepared by the services in the rear along a route passing through Lessay, Raids and Champs-de-Losque.

The US command had just squandered a chance for an easy victory. Already, on 6 June 1944, the overcautious British command failed to capture Caen, withdrawing its spearhead elements that had pushed ahead that far, meeting practically no further opposition. Once German reinforcements had arrived it would take a month of fierce fighting to capture Caen. Another opportunity was lost here, where the American command gathered the bulk of its forces to close the Cherbourg pocket. In the southern sector of the peninsula, it had only two airborne divisions to provide cover against the weak German elements of Colonel Koenig *(91. ID)*: the 101st stood before Carentan and the 8th between Baupte and Portbail. Facing the last-named, on about 20 June, there were just 3,000 tired, demoralized Germans. This all changed with the arrival of *353. ID* and the reorganization carried out by von Choltitz. As Martin Blumenson observes (2), *"combat patrols noted that the Germans had set up an exceptionally strong outpost screen, replenished their supplies, reorganized their forces (…).intelligence officers judged that enemy morale and combat efficiency had risen only from poor to fair"*. The Germans capitalized on a couple of weeks respite, from having practically nothing left to building up a three-tiered front line that was much harder to break through than it would have been around 20 June. The battle then became very tough, particularly on terrain so favorable to the Germans: very dense hedgerow country, marshy areas, and three hills dominating the landscape. Thousands of GIs fell in action. The offensive by VIII Corps to take La Haye-du-Puits and Lessay was planned for 3 July.

The battle of La Haye-du-Puits (3 – 9 July 1944)

Starting on **20 June,** American troops mounted a small local attack on Colonel Koenig's forward positions, breaking out at Prétot and at Limors Wood. This attack brought on the arrival of elements of *353. Infanterie-Division* to the north-eastern slopes of Mont Castre and Montgardon ridge to form the *Mahlmann Linie*.

On 2 July, VIII Corps, under the command of Maj.Gen. Troy Middleton, was ready at last to move onto the offensive. It comprised three divisions that had seen action in June: the 79th Infantry Division, the 82d Airborne Division and the 90th Infantry Division.

Under its commander Maj.Gen. Ira T. Wyche, the **79th Infantry Division** had three infantry regiments:

(1) See on this subject MS/A-983 kept with the American archives and concerning the 353. ID.
(2) M. Blumenson, Breakout and pursuit, OCMH, Washington, 1961, p. 57.

Major General Troy H. Middleton, commander of the VIII Corps. A hero of the 1914-18 war, he fought with distinction in command of the 45th Infantry Division in Sicily and Italy.

VIII Corps

Here we see the three lines of defense set up by the Germans in the La Haye-du-Puits sector: - a screen of outposts, - the Mahlmann Line, the main line of resistance built around the high ground at Montgardon and Mont Castre, - the position of the water, the line of retreat. (Heimdal map based on American documents concerning the 353. ID.)

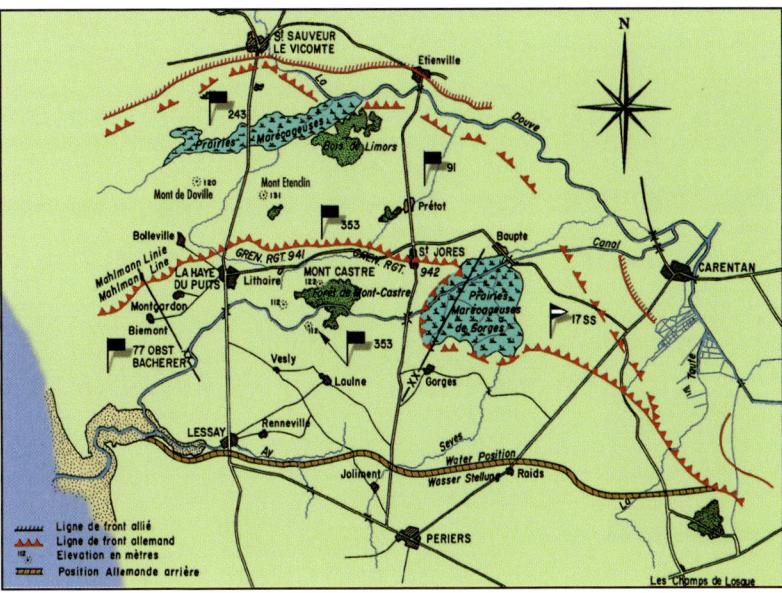

Major General Ira T. Wyche, commander of the 79th Infantry Division.

79th Infantry Division

Major General Matthew B. Ridgway, commander of the 82d Airborne Division.

82d Airborne Division

Major General Eugene M. Landrum, commander of the 90th Infantry Division.

90th Infantry Division

the 313th (Col. Sterling A. Wood), the 314th (Col. Warren A. Robinson) and the 315th (Col. Bernard B. McMahon). It also had four artillery battalions, an engineer battalion and *headquarters* units. It had fought outstandingly in the battle to capture Cherbourg.

The **82d Airborne Division** commander Maj.Gen. Matthew B. Ridgway, lined up three parachute regiments, the 505th (Lt.-Col. William Ekman), the 507th (Col. Edson D. Raff) and the 508th (Col. Roy E Lindquist) and the 325th Glider Infantry Regiment (Col. Harry L. Lewis), also two artillery battalions, an engineer battalion and service units. This crack division fought outstandingly well, as we saw earlier in the Sainte-Mère-Eglise sector, at the time of the crossing of the Merderet and the capture of Saint-Sauveur-le-Vicomte. It had lost half of its strength in these engagements and here took part in its final battle on Norman soil before returning England to refit.

The **90th Infantry Division** was under Maj.Gen. Eugene M. Landrum (who replaced General McKelvie, dismissed after the division's failure at Pont-l'Abbé). It was composed of three infantry regiments: the 357th (Col. George H. Barth), the 358th (Col. Richard C. Partridge) and the 359th (Col. Clark K. Fales). The division's first taste of action was disastrous, this unit of raw recruits lacking cohesion and experience. But it went on to learn the hard way in battle.

For its 3 July offensive, VIII Corps had support from the air and substantial support from the artillery. Maj.Gen. Troy H. Middleton, commanding the operation, had been a soldier since 1910 and had proven his mettle as a divisional commander in Sicily and Italy. Once the operation was over, the 82d Airborne Division was replaced within the corps by the freshly landed 8th Infantry Division.

The objective. The Cotentin peninsula was cut off at the base by marshy pastureland. There was an isthmus of firm soil to the west on the high ground around Portbail. Beyond, in the east, the Gorges Marshes formed another waterlogged obstacle. Between these marshes and the Atlantic Ocean, the small town of La Haye-du-Puits formed a strategically important crossroads where four roads came together. But the town was surrounded by high hills which served as natural defenses. Mont de Doville (121 meters) and Mont Etendin (131 meters) stood to the north of the town over which towered the huge mass of Mont Castre (122 meters) in the east, and, in the west, by the Montgardon ridge (84 meters). These four hills were not only difficult obstacles to capture but most of all wonderful observation posts for the German artillery. From the top of Mont Castre, the Germans could survey the landing beaches in the Utah Beach sector.

As we have seen, the **German defense** was tiered along several lines. The first was a screen of scattered outposts, designed merely to slow down the offensive so as to give to the main line of defense *(Mahlmann Linie)* time to ready itself to meet the attack. West of Limors Wood, facing the 79th Infantry Division's sector, were the remnants of *243. Infanterie-Division* (Colonel Klosterkemperer), then, between Limors Wood and Baupte (either side of Prétot), the remnants of *91. ID* (Colonel Koenig); this unit comprised in the center companies of *Osttruppen*, mostly Russians of little military value. This front line of some 3,500 men facing three American divisions, soon crumbled and had to be withdrawn to the main line, which it joined in reinforcement.

This *Mahlmann Linie* was held, in the far west, by the remnants of *77. ID* (Colonel Bacherer) then by *353. ID* (General Mahlmann) who lined up *Grenadier-Regiment 941* to face Montgardon, La Haye-du-Puits and Lithaire, then *Grenadier-Regiment 942* on the east side of Mont Castre and behind St-Jores. These two regiments' commanding officers were Colonel Schmitz (941st) and Colonel Cordes (942nd).

The 353rd's two grenadier regiments each had just one battalion, the other being held in reserve. The 353rd Engineer Battalion *(Pi.Btl. 353)* under Captain Pillmann reinforced the 941st just outside La Haye-du-Puits and was assigned to defend the town against frontal attack. *353. ID* at this time had a fighting force totalling 6,000 men with 4,500 were in the line, plus a marching battalion of some 1,500 men (3). The defensive hinge was undoubtedly Mont Castre dominated by a medieval ruin and the remains of a Roman camp evidencing the fact that the place had been a strategic site of the utmost importance from time immemorial. It was here in 57 BC that the leader of the Gauls Viridorix and the Unelli were crushed by the Roman legions of one of Julius Caesar's lieutenants, Sabinus.

For Major General Middleton, this was a crucial offensive. The American troops were pinned down in the Cotentin peninsula and needed to escape from the trap of the marshes to reach flatter, firmer ground where their tanks would at last be able to move around properly and build up the offensive.

The main objective was indeed the Lessay/Périers/St-Lô road. To reach it, General Bradley had first to take Saint-Lô in the east, push (in the center) past Carentan to free himself from the narrow isthmus wedged between the Gorges Marshes the Vire-Taute Canal and (in the west) capture La Haye-du-Puits and Lessay on the way. South of Lessay lay some flat moorland almost all the way to Coutances. This made Coutances a possible short-term objective for VIII Corps which could deliver a right hook enabling the entire American army to break out of Normandy. For the time being however, Middleton decided to go for his first two *objectives* - La Haye-du-Puits and Lessay - by mounting an attack in "V" formation. Middleton's decision in fact was mostly about skilfully taking advantage of the terrain. His start line was squeezed in between the Gorges Marshes (in the east) and by the Sensurière Marshes (in the center, north of Mont Doville and Mont Etenclin). Thus the **82d Airborne Division** would attack along a diagonal starting from the Prétot sector towards La Haye-du-Puits and passing through the hamlet of La Poterie (north of Mont Castre). The 82d was flanked on its left by the **90th Inf. Div.** which was to attack alongside it and take Mont Castre from the north-east and then drive round it on the south side through the hamlet of Beaucoudray and the village of Lastelle. In the west, the **79th Inf._Div.** was to launch its attack from the Portbail sector, the Barneville/La Haye-du-Puits road, capture La Haye-du-Puits (an assignment entrusted to the 314th Infantry Regiment and the Montgardon ridge (assigned to the 315th with support from the 313th).

Intelligence gathered in previous weeks indicated a degree of demoralization among the German troops which made the Americans a little too cocksure. Exaggerated reports (4) came in about how scattered the German units were, and they also underestimated their surprising ability to reorganize and their flexibility. These reports failed to take into account the fact that, despite the great shock the Allied landings

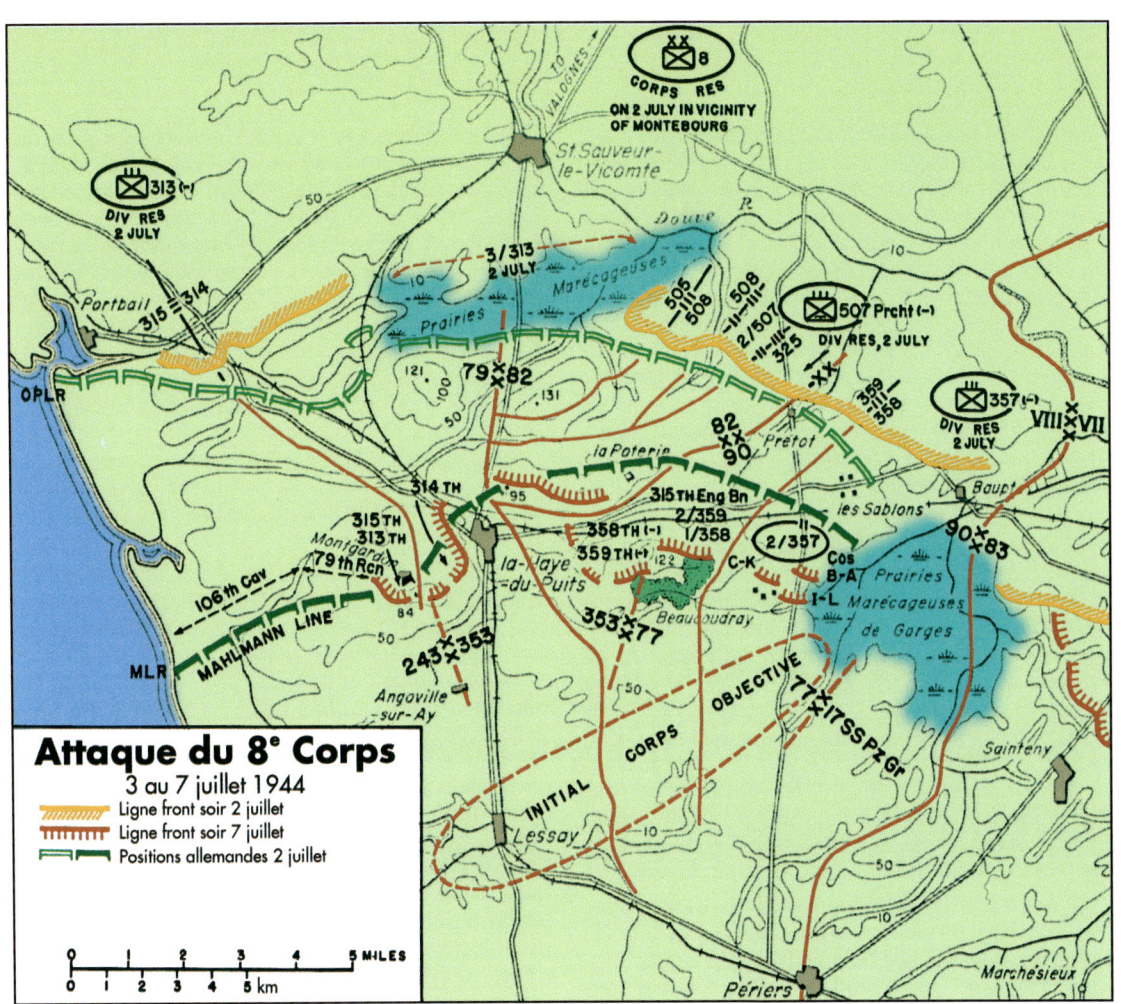

Evolution of the front line in the La Haye-du-Puits sector from 3-7 July 1944 north of La Haye-du-Puits. The Germans' first two defensive lines are marked but not the third, the Wasserstellung. (US Army History Department.)

had been to the German disposition, the German fighter was still the world's best operating under the best staff of officers and NCOs, which more than made up for their serious inferiority in equipment and numbers. Underestimating the enemy in this way (in this sector where the American infantry were about to attack with superior odds of around three to one) the VIII Corps went onto the attack confident in the outcome the battle.

3 July

At first light on 3 July, the whole sector came under a cloud of drizzle. This unpleasant surprise deprived the VIII Corps of the advantage of air support. The Germans knew that something was brewing from the preliminary artillery fire. Von Choltitz ordered the 77th to come over from the left flank (west of Montgardon) to reinforce the positions east of Mont Castre, the small sector thus given up was later retaken by the 243rd after it withdrew.

The **82d Airborne Division** now launched its attack. Before dawn and the start of the softening-up operation by the artillery, a patrol guided by a young Frenchman led an above-strength company of 505th PIR along past the Sensurière Marshes (at the foot of Limors Wood, north of Varenguebec) to the north side of Hill 131, Mont de Doville. At dawn, the company was in the middle of a German outpost held by some *Osttruppen*. The surprised outpost soon fell back. At about midday, the bulk of the 505th Parachute Regiment under Lieutenant-Colonel Ekman joined them and occupied the northern and eastern slopes of Mont Etenclin. Four hours later, the regiment seized the northern half of the stretch of the Saint-Sauveur-le-Vicomte road from the Sensurière Marshes to La Haye-du-Puits. Losses were relatively slight: 4 killed, 25 wounded, 5 missing. 146 prisoners were taken, including some Russians serving in the German army.

In the center of the 82nd's array, the 508th Parachute Regiment (Col. Roy E. Lindquist), reinforced by the 507th, advanced south of the 505th along an east-west line; it took the southern flanks of Mont Etenclin, on the way flushing out some small groups of Germans surprised to see Americans arriving from the east. On the other hand, the 325th Glider Infantry Regiment under Colonel Harry L. Lewis, advancing further south, failed to achieve similar success. This was because, in their "sweeping scythe" attack, the 508th and 505th only encountered feeble opposition from Colonel Koenig's outposts, whereas the 325th, operating further south, came up against the main defensive line. After an initial delay passing through a minefield it advanced fairly quickly on the hamlet of La Poterie for about a mile. But the advance was then held up, with a tank blown up by a mine and three more getting stuck in the mud, depriving the infantry of effective support as they came under German shellfire from Mont Castre. Worse still, this east-west advance came under German fire on its flank coming from the main line of defense running along the foot of Mont Castre.

On the evening of this first day of the offensive, Maj.Gen. Ridgway took into account the easy success in a slightly defended sector around Mont Etenclin and not the attack merely inching forward in the La Poterie sector against the Germans' main line of defense firmly holding its ground.

South-east of the 82nd, in the eastern fork of the "V", the **90th Infantry Regiment** also mounted an

(3) MS/A-983 on the German 353rd ID, p. 14.
(4) M. Blumenson, *op. cit.*, p. 57.

attack from the east in a south-westerly direction, with the exceedingly difficult task of taking Mont Castre from the east and south. This assignment soon turned into tragedy for the 90th. The attack was launched in front of Prétot and Baupte. General Landrum, divisional commander since 12 June, when his predecessor was relieved, had seen action in the Aleutian Islands. But in three weeks he had failed to pull together his new division and give it some much-needed bite. Another two regiments had also received new colonels to replace predecessors dismissed after the failed operation at Pont-L'Abbé. These handicaps did nothing to make the current assignment any easier.

Wedged between the 82nd's sector of attack and the Gorges Marshes, the short start line covered difficult terrain: a dense network of hedgerows and sunken lanes under threat from Mont Castre which dominated the whole area. Maj.Gen. Landrum however decided to split his forces by attacking the hill from the east with one regiment (the 359th - Colonel Clarck K. Fales) and outflanking it on the south with another regiment, the 358th - Colonel Richard C Partridge). The 357th was held in reserve to be unleashed on the assigned objective (the Prétot/Périers road below Plessis-Lastelle) once the 358th had cleared the way south of the hill. This ambitious plan underestimated the then state of the German forces.

The attack started in the rain at 05.30 (British time). Progress was satisfactory against the feeble German outposts. But after two hours advancing a good kilometer, the 90th was halted in front of the main line of defense by the Germans who held out skilfully. The 90th lost 600 men. The advance that day was made with poor coordination between the infantry and the tanks. One of Colonel Partridge's battalions was held up on its start line all day by German assault gun fire. Another of the 358th's battalions advanced very cautiously on the hamlet of Les Sablons. The battalion's command post came under German machine-gun and artillery fire and all its signals personnel were killed or wounded. No further communications were possible. The colonel then pulled out of Les Sablons to obtain a barrage of phosphorus shells on the hamlet, but some German tracked vehicles created panic stations among the GIs. To avoid a rout, Partridge sent in his reserve, which only helped to cause congestion and further chaos. To prevent the Germans from gaining any advantage from the situation and counter-attacking, he sent three TD tanks in cover and the regiment's anti-tank company beyond Les Sablons. Twelve engineers (belonging to the 315th Engineer Combat Battalion) were released by these reinforcements. Colonel Partridge then realized that just a German assault gun and two tracked vehicles had been enough to halt his regiment's advance. The hamlet of Les Sablons came in for a pounding by American artillery fire and the men of the 90th captured the place at nightfall; no further progress was possible that day, and the Germans launched a small counter-attack. Having located the positions reached by the Americans from the observation posts on Mont Castre, under cover of night the German artillery rained shells on the 90th's recognized positions.

In the west of the VIII Corps disposition, the **79th Infantry Division** under Maj.Gen. Wyche was to push out from the Portbail sector to reach its final *objective*: Lessay and the Ay valley. On the way this good division had to capture La Haye-du-Puits and the Montgardon ridge. Maj.Gen. Wyche launched two infantry regiments into the attack: - the 314th (Colonel Warren A. Robinson) on the left, following the line of the Barneville/La Haye-du-Puits highway, taking the Mont de Taillepied (121 meters) on the left for a frontal attack on La Haye-du-Puits; - the 315th (Colonel Bernard McMahon) on the right, along the coast, was to take the western part of the Montgardon ridge (the eastern part to be captured by the 314th along with the attack on the La Haye-du-Puits) before going down to the mouth of the Ay.

At dawn on 3 July, in the rain, Colonel Robinson launched two companies against La Haye-du-Puits, one on either side of the main highway. After advancing for seven hundred meters, the companies were pinned down by machine-gun fire coming from the railroad embankment running parallel to the road. This was the German 24th Division's outposts. Pfc. William Thurston saved the day, charging on his own and dislodging the German position with his rifle; Thurston received a DSC for this heroic action. The GIs followed their comrade, covering over four kilometers by late afternoon. This rapid advance which captured the German outposts and covered about half the distance to La Haye-du-Puits was followed by a halt. The advance enabled Colonel Robinson to dispatch the battalion eastwards behind the leading companies for the purpose of capturing the Mont de Doville topped by a chapel on a bare hilltop rising to 121 meters and a good place from which to survey La Haye-du-Puits. A patrol of twelve men arrived at the foot of the hill at nightfall and disappeared into the darkness, with all contact lost with them for the time being.

4 July

The night of 3-4 July was a busy one for the men of the **79th**. At 02.30 (British time) an artillery liaison officer managed to establish radio contact with Colonel Robinson's men who had set off on the assault of Mont de Doville. They reported that they had a good foothold and encountered just one very light German outpost, and that the battalion had now reached the position. Robinson sent up his reserve battalion and, at dawn, the hill was completely cleared. The rest of the 314th advanced rapidly on La Haye-du-Puits before being stopped outside the town by the German artillery fire. To the east, contact was established with General Ridgway's 82nd Airborne Division. Also, after initially making good progress starting

On 4 July, General Dwight D. Eisenhower, Supreme Allied Expeditionary Force Commander, on the right, in discussion with Major General Ira T. Wyche, commander of the 79th Infantry Division. That day, one of the division's regiments, the 314th Infantry Regiment, made progress but La Haye-du-Puits remained out of reach. (NA/Heimdal - 6707-7.)

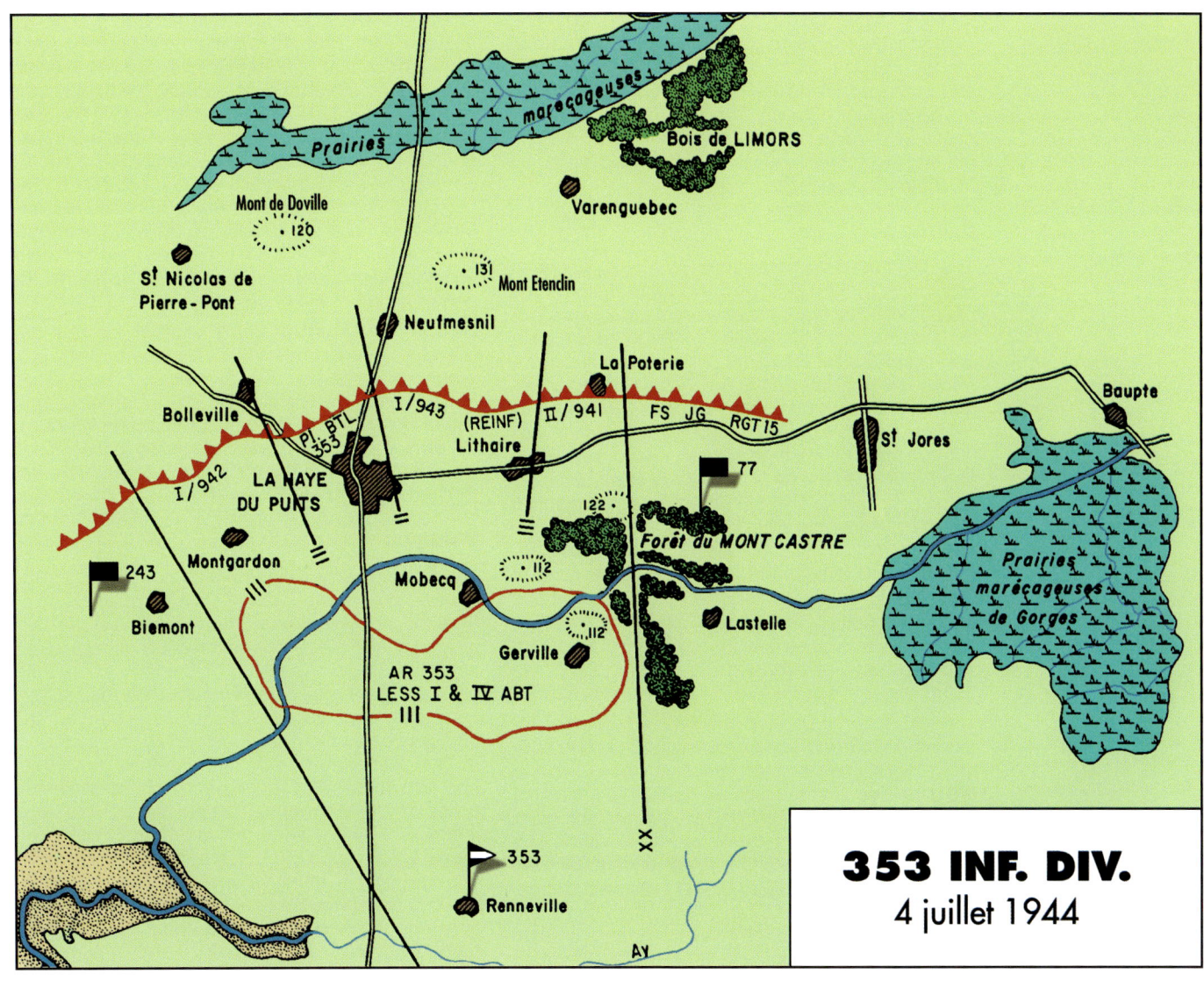

The German front before La Haye-du-Puits during the night of 4-5 July 1944. (Heimdal map based on a German document concerning the 353. ID.)

on the morning of the 3rd, General McMahon's 315th Regiment was soon slowed down in the hedgerow country, especially on encountering a number of German tanks. These opened fire on the American escort tanks, causing the GIs to panic for a time; the infantry slipped back towards the rear amid the confusion. The situation was brought under control but progress continued to be slow, and by the evening of the 4th, three kilometers from the Montgardon ridge, the American infantry were again surprised by a German infantry attack with tanks in support. Two infantry companies resting along a sunken lane were encircled. Four officers and fifty men put up some initial resistance which was soon reinforced and, now under proper control from the Mont de Doville, the artillery joined in. The Americans held out and the Germans lost 64 prisoners.

East of the 79th, the paratroops of the **82d Airborne Division** were now at the foot of the main line of German resistance dominated by the Mont Castre. Progress proved difficult and disorganized. The paratroops attacked La Poterie ridge rising to 85 meters. This line of hills was part of the German defenses and the advance passed through the hedgerows. Several battalions of various regiments took part in the operation. They linked up at dawn the following day. Under cover of darkness Maj.Gen. Ridgway launched a successful attack on La Poterie without coming under German artillery fire. The next morning, the paratroops held onto this salient in the German defensive line. The enemy infantry pulled back in the face of this attack in force by the paratroopers.

In the **90th Infantry Division**'s sector, this fresh day of fighting was again rather confused and costly in men. At dawn, the artillery of the 90th launched a barrage lasting ten minutes. This was followed by the Germans returning fire, and fears of a German attack. It did not materialize but the American infantrymen were tied to the spot for close on an hour. The attack continued all day without really getting anywhere. A single German gun pinned down Colonel Partridge's 358th, firing just ten well-aimed shells, killing and wounding 60 men of one company. Another company was down to its commander and 65 men. 90% of losses were to mortar and artillery shells (on this subject see M. Blumenson, op. cit. p. 67). Soaking in the rain, the men of the 90th were crushed by shellfire from the "Terrible Mount" towering above them. The attack finally got underway at dusk. The Germans also suffered losses. American artillery fire rained down on the Mont Castre, the Germans had no reserve (they were still waiting for the 15th Parachute Regiment in reinforcement) and, after the success of the 82d at La Poterie, they decided to shorten their lines. The 90th took advantage of this withdrawal to advance. The American advance by the men of the 90th proved more effective in the

141

south, in the sector of Colonel Partridge's regiment, in the corridor passing round the south side of the mount. At about midnight, with the GIs exhausted and scattered, Partridge ordered a halt in order to set up a line of defense. This new day proved very costly for the division. The 90th had lost 600 men on the 3rd, but on this day losses were even higher (cf M. Blumenson, p. 67).

5 July

The German front was held chiefly by General Mahlmann's 353rd Division: - the 1st Battalion of the 942nd Regiment (the battalion commander was *Major* Ibe) was outside Montgardon, - the 353rd Engineer battalion (Captain Pillmann) defended La Haye-du-Puits, - the 1st Battalion of the 943rd Grenadier Regiment (battalion commander *Major* Dickertmann) held the front line outside Lithaire, this battalion was reinforced by Russian and Polish *Osttruppen*, - the 2nd Battalion of the 941st Grenadier Regiment (battalion commander Captain Vogel) was in position in the La Poterie sector. The 353rd had on its left (western) flank the remnants of the 243rd (between Montgardon and the sea) and on its right flank (east of Mont Castre) the remnants of the 77th now reinforced by the 15th Parachute Regiment. Notice how the 79th Infantry Division faced only the remnants of the 243rd and two battalions *(I./942* and *Pi.Btl. 353)* of the 353rd.

The 82d Airborne Division only had to face two battalions *(I./943* and *II./941)* of the 353rd. The 90th Inf.Div. was up against the remnants of the 77th and the paratroops of the 15th Regiment. The artillery of the 353rd was in position in the Mobecq sector, guided by observers placed around Mont Castre. The remnants of *77. Infanterie-division* were reinforced by a battalion of the 353rd (*I./941* - Captain Rogge) and those of the 243rd by an infantry battalion of the 353rd (*II./942* - Captain Rosenow) and an artillery battalion of that same unit (*I./AR 353* - Captain Tschirmer).

For this new day, the weather was more favorable for the American army. The weather was fine and so the air force was able to lend its support to the ground operations. To the east **(90th Inf.-Div.)** Maj.Gen. Landrum persisted in his attempt to open up a corridor south of Mont Castre. He dispatched his reserve regiment, the 357th, there to take over from the 358th which had already sustained too many casualties. It failed to make any headway at all to speak of. Meanwhile, to its right, the 359th did manage to advance along the eastern flank of Mont Castre and halfway up the hill. But these were precarious positions up there.

In the center, the **82d Airborne Division** dug in on the hill of La Poterie and mopped a few small pockets of German resistance.

In the west, after making fairly deep and rapid inroads over the previous two days, Maj.Gen. Wyche **(79th Inf.-Div.)** was hoping to reach his objectives again today: to take La Haye-du-Puits and reach the mouth of the Ay by breaking out west of Montgardon, which would make it possible to encircle the Germans in position at Montgardon and La Haye-du-Puits from the south. So he decided to launch his reserve regiment, the 313th (Colonel Sterling A. Wood). This regiment did not set out until noon and was slowed down considerably by some swampy ground crisscrossed by an inextricable maze of hedgerows. It did not reach the foot of Montgardon ridge until late that afternoon. The men then emerged into a huge flat meadow with a stream running through it. They then came under heavy German artillery fire which effectively stalled the attack. At nightfall, the 313th came under two successive counter-attacks by the German infantry of the 243rd who in the confusion pushed the Americans back several kilometers. As soon as news of this failure began to reach him, Maj.Gen. Wyche launched the 315th (Col. Bernard McMahon) head on, directly on the main feature of Montgardon ridge (Hill 84) with the support of tanks and tank-destroyers, and managed to storm the northern side of the ridge.

Despite the return of good weather, on this day Maj.Gen. Middleton's VIII Corps gained very little ground after the first two days of the offensive had gone so well. The GIs now faced the Germans' main line of defense skilfully entrenched there. While the US army had already sustained heavy losses, it had reserves when the Germans did not, although they too had suffered heavy casualties.

6 July

The **82d Airborne Division** was now waiting to be relieved by the 8th Infantry Division for a return to England. It consolidated its positions on the high ground at La Poterie and counted its successes and its losses. It had captured 772 Germans and counted 500 Germans killed and wounded in the sector it had conquered since 3 July. It also destroyed and captured seven German guns: two 75 mm guns, two 88 mm guns and one 37 mm anti-tank gun. But it had also sustained very heavy losses, equivalent to those of the Germans. To take the 325th Glider Infantry Regiment alone, which prior to D-day numbered 2,973 men (135 officers and 2,838 men), by the start of the offensive on 2 July it was down to 1,300 fit men (55 officers and 1,245 men). Four days later, the figure had dropped under the thousand mark (41 officers and 956 men), barely a third of its initial strength! The largest company of the regiment was down to 57 men, the leanest just 12 men... This regiment suffered the heaviest losses of the entire 82d, but the other regiments of the division did not fare very much better.

In the west, **(79th Inf.-Div.)** to consolidate his success of the previous day on the Montgardon ridge, Maj.Gen. Wyche fell back on a less ambitious plan: Hill 84 had to be taken so as to dominate La Haye-du-Puits from the west. He launched two regiments on this single objective: - the 314th, committed opposite La Haye, veered right to take the eastern flank of the Mount, - the 315th made a frontal attack on the north side. The 313th was held in reserve in rear. The attack started in the morning, and by noon the 314th had attained its objectives. In the afternoon, the three regiments launched an all-out attack. While the 313th ran up against minefields and barbed wire to the right (western flank), the 315th (in the center) captured the summit and the 314th consolidated its positions on the eastern flank. This promised Maj.Gen. Wyche a view from above over La Haye-du-Puits for the morrow and his thoughts turned to capturing that locality while the going was good. So optimism was very much the order of the day at 79th *headquarters* on that evening of 6 July.

The **90th Inf.-Div.** had mixed results in the field on this 6 July. It met with success on the northern flank of Mont Castre and failure on the south side. One battalion of the 359th, with aircraft and artillery support, climbed up the northern flank of Mont Castre.

Attacked from all sides, the Germans had to shorten their front line. When night came, there were four US battalions clinging to the top of Mont Castre. But this success also stretched the 90th's own front line as it came under German rocket fire. This stretching, further complicated by the hilly terrain, caused the American positions to become spread out, opening up gaps that made any movement difficult. There were problems evacuating the wounded. The Germans infiltrated between American strongpoints, and it was a daunting business bringing up supplies to them. At day's end, Maj.Gen. Landrum was forced to relieve his physically and mentally exhausted battalion. The rain started to fall again late in the afternoon. At dusk, the Germans regained the initiative, making the most of the dark, rainy night. Unlike the Americans they were perfectly familiar with the terrain, and for the Germans the best form of defense was offense, namely a counter-attack. On the other hand, the results of the attack were more alarming in the "corridor", south-east of Mont Castre. The assault was mounted at dawn, and three companies of the 357th (Colonel Barth) captured the hamlet of Beaucoudray (near Plessis-Lastelle) and made some headway southwards. But the position was vulnerable, and at 23.15 (British time), German artillery and mortars plastered the "corridor", to soften it up for a counter-attack. Two companies of the 357th were encircled by the Germans at Beaucoudray.

7 July

At dawn on the 7th, Colonel Barth (**90th Inf. Div.**) launched a company supported by two troops of medium tanks on Beaucoudray to release his men of the 357th who had been encircled. But they came under fire from German mortars and a counter-attack. The GIs lost all their officers and NCOs, killed or wounded. With no-one in command, the survivors beat a retreat in the afternoon. One of the encircled companies surrendered and the news was brought through by a man who managed to escape via the Gorges Marshes.

But it was again to the north of Mont Castre that the **90th** won further successes on this new day. At dawn, it held the entire summit, particularly the highest point (Hill 122) and the entire north-eastern flank of the hill. But the sky was heavy with rain and the men had great difficulty avoiding getting bogged down in the mud. The Germans barred any further progress on Mont Castre and Maj.Gen. Landrum brought up everything he had to hand, keeping back just one company in reserve. **On the German side**, the main defense of Mont Castre was now provided by the 15th Parachute Regiment *(Fallschirmjäger-Regiment 15)*, under Colonel Gröschke and consisting of young recruits who had barely completed their training.

But the Germans received valuable reinforcements as *2. SS-Panzer-Division "Das Reich"* arriving from the south-west and joining the front in Normandy in stages. On the 5th, it sent a *Kampfgruppe* (battle-group) up to the La Haye-du-Puits sector. This was *Kampfgruppe Weidinger* (named for its commander Otto Weidinger), which comprised a staff regiment *(Rgt. Stab "DF" with 14./DF and 15./DF in support)*, a grenadier battalion *(III./DF)*, a reconnaissance Battalion *(Pz. Aufkl. Abt./DR)*, an assault gun battalion *(Stu.Gesch. Abt./DR)* and an artillery battalion *(III./Art. Rgt. DR.)* The initials "DR." and "DF" mean *"Das Reich"* and *"Der Führer"* respectively, which correspond to the division's own name and that of one of its grenadier regiments. Another grenadier regiment,

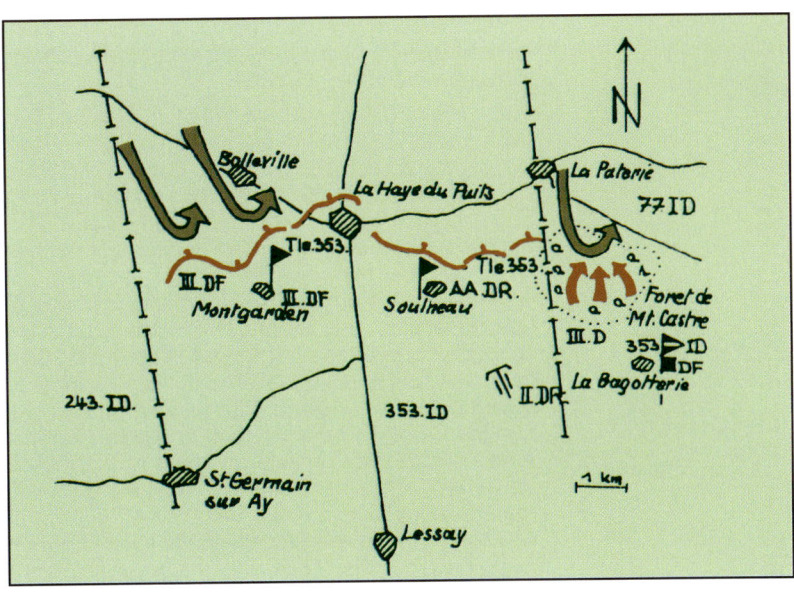

Kampfgruppe Weidinger counter-attacks on either side of La Haye-du-Puits on 8-9 July. (Heimdal after map by Munin Verlag.)

the *"Deutschland"*, was indicated by the letter "D". This tactical force numbered some 4,000 men and combined light infantry, tanks, assault guns and artillery; so it was a particularly belligerent unit, served by aggressive, determined men, some of whom were battle-hardened after seeing action on the Russian Front. The Division set out on 8 June and took only six days to move up from the Toulouse area; it began arriving in the Saint-Lô area on 14 June into the army group reserve. After being somewhat slowed down at first owing to ambushes laid by the Resistance and the summary execution of men in the unit, it reacted vigorously with the bloody repression of Oradour, which opened up the road to the front (as British historian Max Hastings notes in his book). Men of the engineer platoon of the reconnaissance battalion and the 3rd company of the *"Der Führer"* Regiment's 3rd Battalion took part in these acts of repression (Tulle and Oradour).

Kampfgruppe Weidinger had already been committed to the front in Normandy, on 27 and 28 June, to take part in the German counter-attack in the Odon sector, west of Caen. After the arrival of II SS Tank Corps, the *Kampfgruppe* was brought back to the Saint-Lô sector and thrown into the battle for La Haye-du-Puits. At first light on 6 July, *Kampfgruppe Weidinger* was in Périers and moved to Lessay. The grenadier battalion *(III./DF)* was committed at Montgardon in support of *353. ID*'s left flank facing the GIs of the 79th. The reconnaissance battalion *(A.A./DR)* came in support of the right flank of the 353rd opposite Lithaire and on the western side of Mont Castre. The artillery units *(II. Abt./Art. Rgt. 2 DR)* were placed between Laulne and Vesly (southwest of Mont Castre). The assault gun battalion was held in reserve at Mobecq. Another battalion of the *"Das Reich"* Division was committed as reinforcement on the Mont Castre; this was the 3rd Battalion of the *"Deutschland"* Regiment *(III./D)*. However, on the very first day of the battle, the *Das Reich* units came in for a full-blooded fighter-bomber attack (before it started raining again late in the afternoon of 6 July). The commander of the assault gun battalion, Captain Rhöder, was wounded. The counter-attack on Mont Castre by the men of the *Deutschland* Regiment was pinned down. On this **7 July**, the *III./D* attached to *Kampfgruppe 77. ID* (remnants of the 77th), renewed its attack in the Mont Castre sector at 17 hours (German/local time) with the assault

143

guns in support; by dusk, the Americans had been pushed back north of the Carentan/La Haye-du-Puits railroad, west of Mont Castre.

In the western sector of the front, at **79th Inf. Div.** *headquarters*, the optimism of the day before had gone. The men of the 3rd Battalion of the *"Der Führer"* Regiment attacked the Montgardon ridge that afternoon; this particularly fierce attack had support from tracked vehicles and the artillery and the summit was won back. But two regiments of the 79th held out with the support of tanks and thanks to their numerical superiority (two regiments against a battalion, i.e. odds of six to one - or three to one if the 243rd did indeed commit a battalion as it would appear to have done). Three German tanks were destroyed, and the Germans were stopped at nightfall but the Americans had been unable, on this new day, to race down the Montgardon ridge. The situation was even more disappointing for Maj.Gen. Wyche in front of La Haye-du-Puits, which could not be taken by storm as planned on this 7 July, with the engineer battalion under Captain Pillmann still holding out in the town.

The unit was drained, but hung on, trusting in the counter-attack by the grenadiers of *Kampfgruppe Weidinger*. This new day had proved costly for the 79th Inf. Div. which had just lost 1,000 men! The division now totalled over 2,000 casualties in five days of combat.

8 July

Maj.Gen. Middleton now took stock of operations carried out by VIII Corps over the last five jours or more. Overall losses for the corps were around 15%. The initial objective - the Lessay sector - was still a long way off as the offensive had only covered half of the distance. It would however be inaccurate to take the view that the assignment was only half achieved; the ground already conquered included the most difficult obstacles. All that remained to be done was to capture La Haye-du-Puits, drive down Mont Castre and the Montgardon ridge towards easier terrain north of Lessay. It is also quite clear that, in addition to the difficult terrain, the German troops facing them showed great skill and determination. Most of the prisoners taken by VIII Corps (543 on 3 July, 314 on the 4th, 422 on the 5th, 203 on the 6th, cf. M. Blumenson, *op. cit.* p. 76) were "eastern Europeans" not Germans. In this operation, the **82d Airborne Division**, a crack unit, lived up to its reputation but did not have as difficult a sector as the 79th and 90th, which both fought less skilfully than the 82d. They nevertheless managed to break through almost the entire length of the "Mahlmann Line", in itself no mean achievement, holding great promise for subsequent operations. The rain was another serious handicap for Maj.Gen. Middleton. However, casualties were too high for him to follow up this effort along the entire front today or the following day. While total losses for the corps stood at 15%, the infantry regiments had lost around 40%! The picture was even bleaker for the 90th Inf. Div. which, in five days of combat (losses up to the evening of the 7th), already registered 2,000 casualties for six kilometers of ground gained (one man every three meters).

The 82d was now withdrawn from the front to be replaced by the **8th Infantry Division**. The 79th and 90th being exhausted as well, the brunt of the effort in the days to come fell to this fresh and inexperienced division.

For the time being, the corps placed all its ambitions on just one objective: La Haye-du-Puits. The "deathblow" was delivered by the **79th Inf.-Div.** which knew the sector well whereas the **8th Inf.-Div.** had only just come up to the front line. On the **German side,** a fresh attempt at a counter-attack against Montgardon by the men of *"Das Reich"* failed. At La Haye-du-Puits, the engineer battalion of the 353rd was down to 30 or 40 men having suffered 90% losses! Its commanding officer, Captain Pillmann, was reported missing. The unit completely wilted under air and artillery fire, in both defense and counter-attack. All that remained to be done was for the few survivors to make one last stand before falling back. The access roads into town were mined by the Germans. The **79th Inf. Div.** launched an infantry battalion onto the attack with the artillery, mortars and tanks in support. On reaching the minefields, the GIs came under mortar and machine-gun fire from the German lines, late that afternoon. The German machine gunners were camouflaged in trenches that the American had failed to locate. The US infantry sustained heavy losses but managed to infiltrate the town from the northwest. The night was lit up by the fires sweeping through the houses of this Norman town. A decimated company of GIs cut paths through the minefields while others mopped up the houses of any remaining snipers. During this night of 8-9 July, the Americans finally reached the center of La Haye-du-Puits.

9 July

Mopping up of the town was completed on this day and at noon the 79th Inf.-Div. handed over the sector to the men of the 8th Inf.-Div. The Germans now tried to establish a new line of defense south of Montgardon and Mont Castre, by mounting further attacks on those two points. But the "Battle of La Haye-du-Puits" was now over.

To die for Sainteny (4 to 11 July 1944)

While Maj.Gen. Middleton's VIII Corps was mounting its offensive against La Haye-du-Puits on 3 July, Maj.Gen. Collins and his VII Corps were attacking in the center, with Périers their objective. This was the most vulnerable sector of the American front, just 3.5 kilometers outside the center of Carentan - the German counter-attack carried out by *Götz von Berlichingen* on 14 June had in fact arrived just a few hundred meters short of that locality. Also passing through Carentan was Highway N13, which supplied the entire Allied front from Cherbourg to Bayeux. In the vicinity of this Norman town, it came under German artillery fire. This was an uncomfortable situation that required immediate action, especially as a German counter-attack against Carentan could not be ruled out, and that might cut the American beachhead in two.

As of 6 June, Maj.Gen. J. Lawton Collins led VII Corps into action and to victory in the Cotentin peninsula. "Lightnin' Joe" as General Collins was nicknamed now proceeded to attack from Carentan along the road to Périers. His corps' objective was to take the village of Sainteny on the very first day of the offensive, building up enough momentum to carry them on to Périers and the Saint-Lô/Lessay road. But Maj.Gen. Collins faced three problems. - **The terrain**: VII Corps' start line was very short, just a small bridgehead around Carentan, not big enough to build up with many units. The assault zone was extremely narrow; hemmed in between the Gorges Marshes to the west and the Taute marshes to the east. Carentan was no more than an isthmus amid these swamps, but it did widen out however south-west of the town into a kind of peninsula where the village of Auvers was located. But south of the road to Baupte (and on to La Haye-du-Puits), this spit of land again narrowing down to no more than about 3 kilometers wide. Here, at the narrowest point, was where the German front had dug in. Also, this firm ground was covered with a dense maze of hedgerows, definitely not ideal terrain for tanks. **Resources**: given the narrowness of the initial restricted troop sector, the sector was initially held by paratroops of the 101st Airborne Division who were relieved at the end of June by the 83rd Infantry Division.

In addition to the newly arrived **83rd ID**, Maj.Gen. Collins had two other infantry divisions, **4th ID** and **9th ID**. These units took part in the Battle of the Cotentin as part of VII Corps and so were battle-hardened troops who reacted extremely well under fire. But they could only join battle once the bottleneck had been removed and VII Corps advanced south on a broader front along which to deploy these divisions. For the time being, only 83rd ID could enter the fray and then with only two of its three infantry regiments (the 330th and 331st, the 329th being held in reserve). So although a corps commander, Maj.Gen. Collins had just two regiments of one division to carry out the offensive.

The enemy: the Americans were taking on two crack German units. The **6th Parachute Regiment** *(Fallschirmjäger-Regiment 6)* under *Major* von der Heydte was a good unit but had been fighting since D-day and was by now well under-strength, having been reduced almost to the size of a battalion. The **17. SS-Panzer-Grenadier-Division "Götz von Berlichingen"** on the Normandy front had been in action since 12 June and had so far sustained limited losses (chiefly in the counter-attack on Carentan of 12-14 June): 233 killed (including 4 officers), 777 wounded (including 17 officers), 86 missing (including 4 officers), a total of 1,096 casualties up to 28 June. On 30 June, the *"Götz"* numbered 16,976 men (see p. 118 of *"Die Sturmflut und das Ende"* by Hans Stöber). It was a motorized infantry division with two "grenadier" (infantry) regiments, supported by an armored artillery regiment, a tank battalion (with about twenty assault guns), and an anti-tank battalion. In theory the division had 42 assault guns but lost about half of them in the first weeks (some were at the repair shop). So in material terms, it was a division rather less well equipped than the 83rd ID which it faced directly. However the individual worth of each fighting man and the staff came down clearly in favor of the German division. It was a battle-hardened unit with experienced commanders; it fought with great determination and took very few prisoners in combat.

Despite these three handicaps, Maj.Gen. Collins was temperamentally inclined to just go for it, hoping to cover the 14 kilometers from where he was to Périers in two days.

Forces committed by the evening of 3 July

On the American side.

The **83rd Infantry Division** was commanded by Maj.Gen. Robert C Macon, assisted by Brigadier-General Claude B. Ferenbaugh. It had three infantry regiments: - the 329th (Col. Edwin B. Crabill), - the 330th (Col. Ernest L. McLendon), - the 331st (Col. Martin D. Barndollar Jr.). As we have seen, two of these infantry regiments were the only VII Corps units in the front line. They were the 330th, located east of the line of the Périers road, and the 331st, in the west, in the Auvers and Méautis sector, facing marshes and hilly terrain. The 83rd was a unit of rookies who had not yet seen action. It had support from the 746th Tank Battalion, the 802nd Tank Destroyer Battalion, two 4.2 inch mortar companies (87th Chemical Battalion) and the machine-guns of an AA unit (453rd Antiaircraft Artillery).

The **4th Infantry Division** was commanded by Maj.Gen. Raymond O. Barton. It had three infantry regiments: - the 8th (Col. James S. Rodwell), - the 12th (Col. James S. Luckett), - the 22nd (Col. Charles T. Lanham). This unit landed on Utah Beach on 6 June and fought well in the Battle of the Cotentin. But a month of constant fighting had thinned its ranks, with the loss of 5,400 men who were replaced by 4,400 rookies. As Maj.Gen. Barton, the divisional commander since 1942, put it: "We no longer have the division we brought ashore". The 4th ID was temporarily kept in reserve. It had the 801st Tank Destroyer Battalion and the 377th Antiaircraft Artillery in support.

The **9th Infantry Division** commanded by Maj.Gen. Manton S. Eddy was the corps' second reserve. It comprised the 39th, 47th and 60th infantry regiments. It too had fought well in the Battle of the Cotentin, notably during the capture of Cherbourg where it invested the city from the west.

On the German side

The remnants of the **6th Parachute Regiment** were commanded by *Major* von der Heydte. They were in position near Raffoville, on the edge of the Gorges Marshes, facing the 331th IR, 83rd ID.

The **17. SS-Pz.-Gren.-Div. "Götz von Berlichingen"** was commanded by Colonel Otto Baum after General Ostendorff was wounded on 19 June. The unit comprised two infantry regiments: - *SS-Pz.-Gren. Rgt 37* (commanded by Lieutenant-Colonel Fick) with three battalions, *I./37* (Commander Reinhardt), *II./37* (Commander Opificius), *III./37* (Captain Zorn); - *SS-Pz.-Gren. Rgt 38* (commanded by Lieutenant-Colonel Horstmann) with three battalions, *I./38* (Captain Ertl), *II./38* (Commander Nieschlag), *III./38* (Commander Bolte). These grenadier regiments were supported by a tank battalion *(SS-Pz.-Abt. 17,* Commander Kepplinger), a recce battalion *(SS-Aufkl.Abt. 17* - Commander Holzapfel), an anti-tank battalion *(SS-Pz.Jg.Abt. 17* - Commander Schuster), an engineer battalion *(SS-Pi.btl. 17* - commander Kurt Fleischer) and the artillery regiment *(SS-Art.Rgt. 17* - Colonel Binge). The strip of ground stretching between Carentan and Sainteny was held by Lieutenant-Colonel Fick's 37th Regiment, namely, from west to east: *III./37* (Zorn), *I./37* (Reinhardt), *I./37* (Opificius). *I./38* (Ertl) was in the east of the sector held by the division, east of the Taute River on the Graignes peninsula. *III./38* (Bolte) and *II./38* (Nieschlag) were held in reserve, near Tribehou and Pont-Hébert respectively. The most sensitive position was that of *I./37* blocking the Sainteny road. Anyone going anywhere would have to pass here and so the place was given extra cover by the 2nd Company under Second-Lieutenant Hüner, with strongpoints of two or three men.

Beyond, further east, were (along the Vire-Taute Canal): **Kampfgruppe Heintz** (elements of *275. ID*) and **Pi.Batl. Angers** (engineers school of Angers).

Major General Robert C. Macon, commander of the 83rd Infantry Division.

83rd Infantry Division

Major General Raymond O. Barton commander of the 4th Infantry Division, about to examine new positions before the offensive.

4th Infantry Division ("Ivy Division")

Major General Manton S. Eddy, commander of the 9th Infantry Division.

9th Infantry Division

4 July

The sun rose to greet a special day for Americans, "Independence Day", marking the nation's birthday. Maj.Gen. Collins hoped that the day would bring a fresh victory. Dawn broke, the preliminary artillery barrage lasted ten minutes, with metal raining down on the German lines. These were ten minutes of sheer hell for the grenadiers of the *"Götz"*. However the 83rd Inf.-Div.'s inexperience was painfully obvious from the outset with hesitancy and lack of coordination. In the front line, Colonel Barndollar led his regiment, the 331st, into the attack. Two hours later, he died from a bullet wound close to the heart. The 331st was supported by the 329th Battalion which had been detailed to cover it along the Gorges Marshes. This battalion managed to cross a small swampy valley. But as the heavy company was waiting its turn to pass through, von der Heydte's paratroops counter-attacked to close the breach threatening Raffoville and Mesnil. The troopers' mortars and machine-guns rained down on the 329th Battalion which beat a hasty retreat. Losses were heavy, with a whole company reported missing, and another down to a third of its strength. The battalion lost most of its heavy weapons and stayed to cover its start line. That evening, without the general's permission, the battalion commander arranged a truce with the Germans, to go and pick up their dead and wounded. On the left flank, the 330th Regiment (Colonel McLendon) managed to push nearly a kilometer forward. The breakthrough took shape along the line of the road. The *"Götz"* 37th Regiment took the brunt of this thrust. The 6th Company disintegrated *(II./37)*; its commander, Lieutenant Tetzmann, was wounded, leaving just fifty survivors. The breach was filled by the regimental recce company led by Captain Gröner. Things were also looking dire for the 10th Company *(III./37)* under Lieutenant Thomas, down to thirty fighting men. But this wedge that the 83rd Inf. Div. had knocked into the German lines was not the lightning advance that Maj.Gen Collins had in mind.. When one battalion stood waiting for another to catch up before advancing in turn, Collins grabbed a telephone and barked a warning to General Macon: That's exactly what I don't want. Don't ever let me hear of that again!". He wanted battalions breaking through the German lines to forge on ahead without waiting, so as to force the Germans to fall back, while threatening them in rear. Despite some local successes, Sainteny (which was the objective of this first day of the battle) was at best still three kilometers away, and at worst the front line had not moved at all. More worryingly for VII Corps, the 83rd ID had 1,400 or 10% losses. At that rate, there would be nothing left of the division in under a week. A thousand men fell to von der Heydte's paratroops (the failure of the 329th IR battalion being partly to blame) and another four hundred to Lieutenant-Colonel Fick's grenadiers. Meanwhile the Germans suffered heavy losses as well, but not nearly as bad: 450 men, three times less. The troopers lost 50 dead and 250 wounded, the 37th Grenadier Regiment lost 30 killed and 120 wounded were evacuated. The Germans lost only six prisoners taken by the Americans.

5 July

Maj.Gen. Collins, who had been planning to launch this new day of the offensive from Sainteny with two divisions in the line, had no alternative but to carry on advancing with just the 83rd. He made some slight adjustments by putting on the left the 329th which had been in reserve (this regiment's 3rd Battalion remained in support on the right) in order to relieve McLendon's 330th which suffered heavy losses; Lieutenant-Colonel William E. Long took over command of the 331st (replacing Barndollar who had been killed the day before). Another dawn and another ten-minute artillery barrage. Maj.Gen. Macon kept behind his battalion commanders all the time, pressing them on by every means and with repeated telephone messages: "To hell witth the [enemy] fire, to hell with what's on your flank, get down there and take the area. You don't need any recon", "Do not pay any attention to [the enemy counter-attack]; you must go on down", etc. But little fresh ground was gained. On this new day, the Germans noted: "the Americans are bravely launching attack after attack but the fighting will not bring much success for either side". In his official history (op. cit., p. 85), Martin Blumenson writes: "In two days, the 83d Division had dis-

Two days into the VII Corps offensive which was pinned down before Sainteny, Maj. Gen. Collins (notice the VII Corps insignia on his sleeve) takes stock of the situation with General Eisenhower (left), Supreme Allied Commander in Europe, and Lt. Gen. Bradley (center), commander of the 1st Army combining all the US forces that had landed by this time. This photo was taken on 5 July at Château de Franquetot at Carquebut where the 1st Army was then headquartered. (DAVA/Heimdal.)

Major General Barton had led his 4th Division in action since D-day, when it landed on Utah Beach. There followed the fierce battle for Cherbourg. His division had lost 5,400 men, replaced by 4,400 "rookies" (recruits). This led him to say: "We no longer have the division we brought ashore". And yet, the fight was still on. Here we see Maj. Gen. Barton (left), with one of his staff officers, who have come to inspect the front line units prior to the fresh offensive. (NA/Heimdal.)

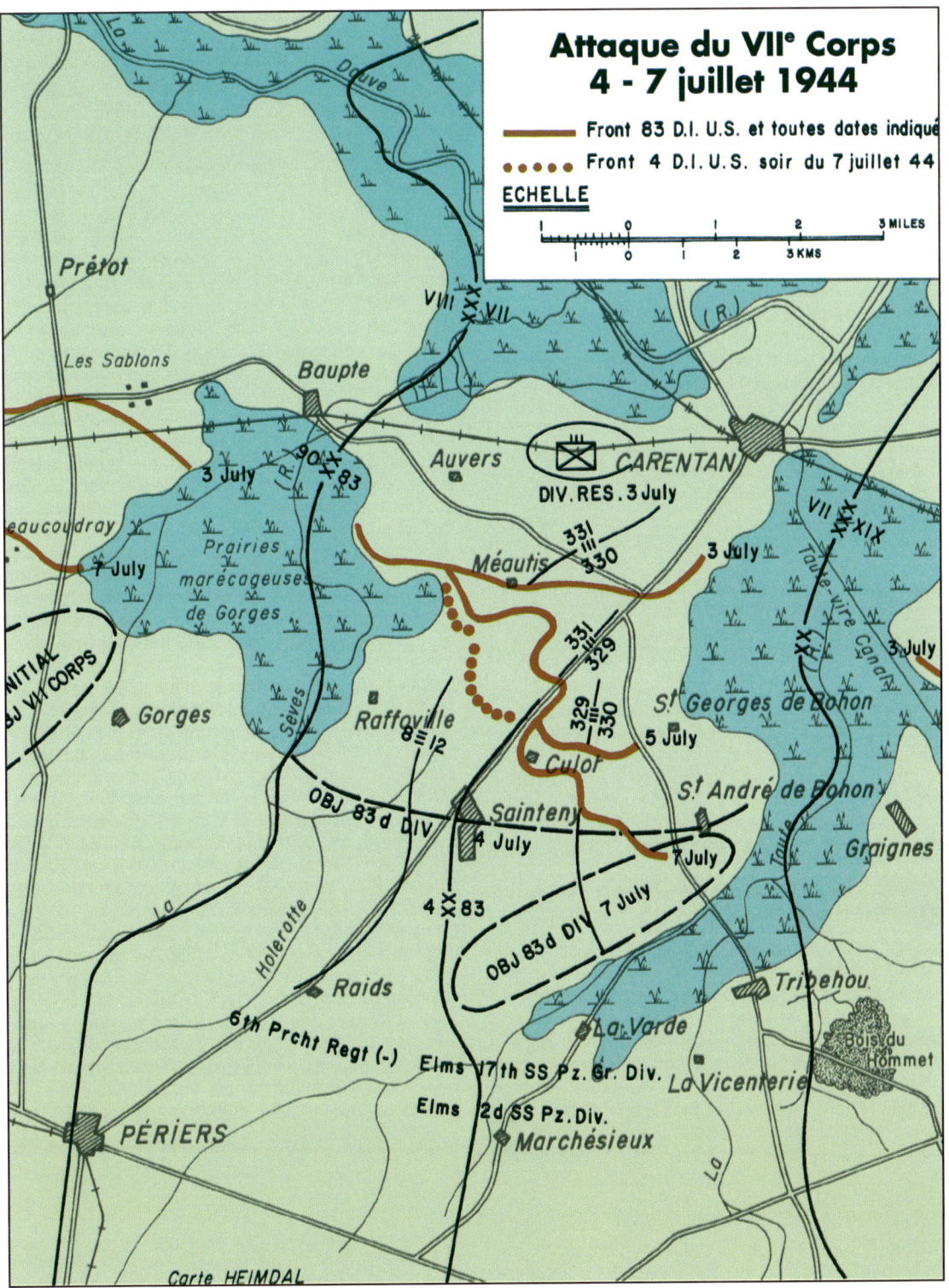

This map shows the sector of the VII Corps' attack, between the Gorges and Taute Marshes against Fallschirmjäger-Regiment 6 (6th Prcht. Regt. on the map) and elements of the "Götz von Berlichingen" Division (17th SS-Pz.Gr.Div. on the map) and elements of the "Das Reich" Division (2d SS-Pz.Div. on the map). Here we see how the front line progressed from 3-7 July, with the assault at first spearheaded by the 83rd Division on a narrow isthmus between the two swamps. The 4th Infantry Division then took over.

played almost all the weaknesses and made virtually all the mistakes of a unit new to combat. Poor reports from subordinate units, incorrect map locations and weak communications made accurate artillery support almost impossible [...]. Lax command control and discipline resulted in an inordinately large number of stragglers. Regimental and battalion commanders did not seem able to coordinate their attached units, institute reconnaissance in time, or press their attacks with vigor." Cooperation between infantry and tanks was especially poor.

Finally this new day brought another 750 casualties among the divisional staff, with significant losses especially among the leadership.

6 July

Not enough ground had been gained the previous day to enable Maj.Gen. Collins to commit a second division. However, to relieve the 83rd ID, seriously weakened after losing 2,200 killed and wounded, he halved its front line sector and committed elements of the 4th ID under Maj.Gen. Barton. The **83rd ID** left behind on its left in the front line the 329th and 330th RI. The overstrained 331st was replaced by 8th and 12th IR, **4th ID**. Colonel Luckett's 12th IR had support from tanks (70th Tanks), tank destroyers (801st TD Bn) and heavy mortars. The 8th IR relieved the remnants of the 3rd Battalion of the 329th along the Gorges Marshes. Despite these rearrangements, the

147

XIX Corps

30th ID

Major General Leland S. Hobbs, commander of the 30th Division.

Colonel Henry E. Kelly, commander of the 117th Infantry Regiment.

Colonel Hamond D. Birks, commander of the 120th Infantry Regiment.

new day failed to produce further gains. The 4th ID was unable to advance. The 83rd ID lost 700 men in repulsing sporadic counter-attacks. The failure of the 4th ID, a well-tried unit, proved to Maj.Gen. Collins that the 83rd ID's setback was not so much a question of experience as fighting on difficult terrain against a formidable opponent. But for the Germans it was nonetheless a terrible day too. This time it was *I./37* (Reinhardt) that took the brunt of the attack. There were few survivors in any of the three companies: 1st (Captain Schlebes), 2nd (Second-Lieutenant Hüner), 3rd (Lieutenant Wagner). Commander Reinhardt went missing in the confusion. The entire battalion was blown to bits. *I./37* and *III./37* were merged under the command of Captain Zorn. *II./37* (Opificius) was also sorely tested in the battle. So it was a very bad day all round for Lieutenant-Colonel Fick's 37th Grenadier Regiment. One of the two reserve battalions was called up to reinforce the battered front line; *III./38* (Commander Bolte), which was at Tribehou, formed a second line in front of Sainteny. This reserve battalion mounted a counter-attack forthwith; Bolte was killed and replaced by Captain Schwiekert. Colonel Otto Baum was pessimistic for the *"Götz"* had just lost two battalion commanders, Bolte killed in the counter-attack and Reinhardt reported missing. Another reserve battalion was called to the front line: the reconnaissance troop *(SS-Aufkl. Abt. 17)* under Commander Holzapfel, after resting in the Lessay moors.

The outcome appeared negative on both sides. In VII Corps, Maj.Gen. Collins registered further losses for the gain of negligible ground, while on the staff of the *"Götz"*, Colonel Baum had to bring in his reserves in view of the scale of his losses. So the balance now favored the Americans whose tremendous thrusts were taking their toll on the German lines.

7 July, the 30rd Infantry Division crosses the River Vire

It was 3 in the morning (British time) early on 7 July. Low cloud hid the full moon as, with their bayonets mounted on their guns, the infantrymen of the 2nd Battalion, the 17th Infantry Regiment reached the banks of Vire made slippery by the rain of the last few days. Silently, the first wave boarded assault craft operated by sappers of the 247th Engineer Combat Battalion. Thirty-two rubber craft carried across two companies of the 2nd Battalion along a front 400 meters wide in a bend of the Vire a few hundred meters north of Airel, where the river was only 9 meters (70 feet) wide. At 03.30 (04.30 German/local time), the artillery of the 30th Inf.-Div. set its guns blazing against the German positions on the left bank held by the infantrymen of *Kampfgruppe Heintz*. XIX Corps commander Maj.Gen. Corlett, had just launched an offensive on the west bank of the Vire. The 30th Inf.-Div. was crossing the river in these early hours with the 117th Inf. Regt. In the leading wave. It received support from the 3rd Armored Division as soon as the bridgehead was secured. The sector held by XIX Corps extended east from the Vire and a good way down south, as far as north of Saint-Lô, and still further south as far as Caumont-L'Eventé. This sector dug deeply into the Normandy Bocage and an attack due west would take the German front line from the rear, as it stubbornly clung on in front of Sainteny against Maj.Gen. Collins' VII Corps. Thus at dawn on 7 July, Corlett came to Lightnin' Joe's rescue.

The XIX Corps then launched two divisions into this new offensive:

- **the 30th Infantry Division** had been commanded since 1942 by General Leland S. Hobbs, assisted by William K. Harrisson. It had three infantry regiments: the 117th (Colonel Henry E. Kelly), the 119th (Colonel Alfred V. Ednie), the 120th (Colonel Hammond D. Birks). This division was named after Andrew Jackson, born on the border between North Carolina and South Carolina and who followed a military career in Tennessee.

The divisional patch, with its blue "O" and "H" on a red oval, recalls this name; three blue crosses in the "H" recall the division's belonging to XXX Corps during the First World War.

- **The 3rd Armored Division** was commanded by Major General Leroy H. Watson who would be transferred to 12th Army Group on 6 August when he was replaced by Maj.Gen. Maurice Rose, who commanded the tank arm of the 2d Arm. Div. Energetic, firm and quick to make up his mind, Rose was a man who led from the front, which is precisely what he was doing late in March 1945 when he was killed in the front line with some of his tank crews. The 3rd Arm. Div., the "Spearhead Division", was an armored force divided, following the American principle, into two tactical groups (Combat Command A and Combat Command B). **Combat Command A** took its orders from Brig.Gen. Doyle O Hickey and included the 32nd Tank Regiment (Col. Leander L. Doan - minus one battalion), the 67th Arm. Field-Art.Batt., a battalion of the 36th Arm.Inf.Regt., a battery of the 486th Arm.AA.Bat., a company of the 703rd TD Bat. (tank destroyer), a medical company and a maintenance company. **Combat Command B** came under Brig.Gen. Truman E Boudinot and included the 33rd Armored Regiment (Colonel Dorrance S. Roysden - minus one battalion), the 391st Arm.Field.Art.Bat., a battalion of the 36th Arm.Inf.Regt, a battery of the 486th Arm.AA.Bat., a company of the 703rd TD Bat, a medical company and a maintenance company. These Combat Commands thus combined the various types of units of a division: tanks, artillery (one battery), infantry (one battalion), TD tanks (one company), AA (one battery), a medical company and a maintenance company. This Spearhead Division gives us a good idea of how American armored divisions operated at the time, divisions that were to prove so decisive in Operation Cobra, a little over two weeks later. Notice how certain units were split between the Combat Commands, as was the case with the division's infantry regiment, the 36th Armored Infantry Regiment (commanded by Colonel Parks; he was replaced on 18 July by Colonel William W. Cornog, Jr.) was divided into three. One battalion was attached to Combat Command A, another to Combat Command B, the third was held at the division's disposal. These infantrymen took the nickname of Blitz Doughs. In addition to its two Combat Commands, the division had a third artillery battalion, the 54th (all the divisional artillery being coordinated by Colonel Frederick Brown), a reconnaissance battalion (the 83rd, Lt.-Col. Prentice E. Yeomans), an engineer battalion (the 23rd, Lt.-Col. Lawrence G. Foster, soon to develop the "hedgecutter" mounted on the front of a tank), various units including the rest of the TD tanks, the AA distributed between the Combat Commands. This was a rather complex organization but which gave the division great flexibility in their use so as to conduct the offensive along two armored lines; we shall shortly be providing an illustration of this. The American armored units' badge aptly reflects this integration of the units: it is triangular with three sections, blue for the infantry, yellow for the cavalry, red for the artillery, black tracks

148

and gun (symbolizing the tanks and firepower) surmounted by a red flash of lightning ("shock action"). The figure in the top third is the division's serial number. The 3rd Armored Division had already been committed at Villiers-Fossard on 29 June to support the 29th Inf.Div..

The previous day, the 30th Infantry Division was deployed in an arc along the Vire and the Taute Canal. From north to south: - the 120th IR (Birks) along the north bank of the canal, - the 117th (Kelly) and 119th (Ednie) east of Vire near Airel (right bank) and Saint-Fromond (left bank, in the west, on the bank held by the Germans) for the firm soil on both banks the better to link up. At Saint-Fromond, the firm ground was 400 yards (c. 65 meters) wide and enabled the deployment of two battalions side by side. Also, the presence of a bridge which was only slightly damaged made it easy for the armored columns to get cross.

Thus, on this **7 July at 03.30** (British time), four artillery battalions opened fire and hit the west bank of the Vire. At 04.20, the infantry of the **2nd Battalion of the 117th IR** crossed the river. The 32 assault craft went back for the second wave but the first German 88 mm shells began to rain down. The second wave crossed the Vire half an hour later amid exploding 88 mm and mortar shells. The men however made progress across the river, although a few had to jump overboard to push some overloaded craft on either side. As soon as the first wave set off, the 3rd troop of B Company, 105th Engineer Combat Battalion, began to bring up the prefabricated elements of the Bailey bridge. to support this major crossing operation, the 30th Infantry Division had all of three engineer battalions: - the 105th Engineer Combat Battalion, the divisional battalion, with special responsibility for setting up the Bailey bridge over the remains of the Saint-Fromond bridge, commanded by Lieutenant-Colonel Caroll H. Dunn; - two units were attached to provide the division with temporary support, the 247th Engineer Combat Battalion and the 503rd Light Pontoon Company. The river banks were scaled with metal ladders, and the infantrymen of the 117th were by now in the ruins of Saint-Fromond at the western end of the bridge, clearing the way with rifle grenades and with bazooka fire. At 08.00 hours, E Company was on its objective, but F Company came up against opposition from a German *Kampfgruppe Heintz* strongpoint, with 14 of the company's men facing 30 Germans, until the support platoon arrived and saved the day with machine-gunfire. Saint-Fromond was now in the hands of the 2nd Battalion of the 117th. The **3rd Battalion** then began to cross while the engineers worked on the bridge, under artillery fire all the time. At 08.00 hours, an infantry footbridge was in place, at the cost of 15 engineers killed or wounded. At 12.30 the Bailey bridge was ready to let vehicles across. The Saint-Fromond bridgehead and the crossing were now secure. The 117th IR advanced nearly 4 kilometers west, reaching the junction with the road running north-south from Saint-Jean-de-Daye to Pont-Hébert. German resistance was stepped up late that morning. Further north, early in the afternoon, the **120th IR** under Colonel Birks forded the river near the destroyed bridge over the Vire-Taute Canal, leading to Saint-Jean-de-Daye from the north.

Following on their heel came Colonel William S. Biddle's **113th Cavalry Group** which immediately veered west to cover the right flank of 30th Infantry's front on the bridgehead. Meanwhile, the remains of the stone bridge at Saint-Fromond were reinforced with metal elements for the purpose of passing heavy vehicles (tanks and artillery) while a floating bridge was built at the foot of the stone bridge for lighter vehicles. So far so good, XIX Corps' bridgehead west of the Vire had achieved total success with only weak opposition from **Kampfgruppe Heintz**, as the German divisions in the sector were pinned down on their respective fronts.

Although *II./38* (Commander Nieschlag) of *Götz von Berlichingen* was in reserve not far from Pont-Hébert and could have taken effective action against the Saint-Fromond bridgehead, the grenadier division had suffered so many casualties that it was needed up in the division's front line.

It was caught in a counter-attack a kilometer southeast of Saint-George-de-Bohon, and lost many officers to American snipers; Lieutenant Baldauf (5th Co) was killed and Lieutenant Tramontana (6th Company) was badly wounded. East of the Carentan/Sainteny road, *III./38* continued to disintegrate in front of the village of Culot. It lost its new commander, Captain Schwiekert, its last surviving officer! The remains of this battalion were commanded by *Oberscharführer* (WO junior grade) Schöpflin, who held out in Sainteny until 11 July with less than a hundred grenadiers. On either side of the road, the men of the recce battalion under their commander Holzapfel died along with those of *Oberscharführer* Schöpflin, defending Sainteny, the last line of defense this side of Périers. This day saw a further hard blow dealt to the 38th SS Regiment. The "suicide attacks" of two of the regiment's grenadier battalions, *II./38* commanded by Nieschlag and *III./38* commanded by Bolte (who was killed), were not to the liking of Colonel Baum who found that the attacks launched overhastily by Lieutenant-Colonel Horstmann were too costly in men at a time when the division could ill afford to lose them. To account for this "wastage", Horstmann was summoned before a council of war, but preferred suicide. His regiment was now leaderless; the remnants of *II./38* and *III./38* were merged into a *Kampfgruppe* and placed under Captain Wahl. A brilliant feat of arms by Second-Lieutenant Hoffmann, an officer with the 38th Grenadier Regiment, lifted the morale of this extremely demoralized unit. Hoffmann received orders to blow up a small bridge at Port-Saint-Pierre, near Taute and north-west of Graignes. For this coup de main he picked forty grenadiers of *II./38* and some engineers to actually blow up the bridge. But the the objective was about ten kilometers behind the American lines… The small party took along four assault guns, seeting off in the morning fog. In its first engagement, the column came under a barrage of fire for ten minutes, losing 11 men but passed on until it came to Rougeville. Hoffmann reached his objective another two and half kilometers down the road. The bridge was blown up. The column got back having captured many American vehicles and even a lieutenant-colonel with a briefcase full of maps and invaluable documents…

While the Germans of *Götz von Berlichingen* sustained further losses that wiped out all their reserves, neither did the situation seem any too encouraging, at the start of this new day, at Maj.Gen. **Collins**'s command post. Collins was hoping that this would be the day Sainteny was captured by the **83rd Inf.Div.** with the **4th Inf.Div.** advancing to Périers, thus enabling him to commit the **9th Inf.Div.** then in the process of assembling around Carentan. This fresh day of operations and offensive was to be supported by the artillery and 100 bombers. The supporting aircraft however were cancelled owing to drizzle that morning (it became more effective during the afternoon as the weather cleared). The day brought little to cheer about for the 83rd, a few hundred meters

Badge of the 3rd Armored Division "Spearhead Division".

Major General Leroy H. Watson commander of the 3rd Armored Division.

Brigadier General Doyle O. Hickey, commander of Combat Command A, the 3rd Armored Division. (DAVA/Heimdal.)

Brigadier General Truman S. Boudinot, commander of CCB, the 3rd AD. (DAVA/Heimdal.)

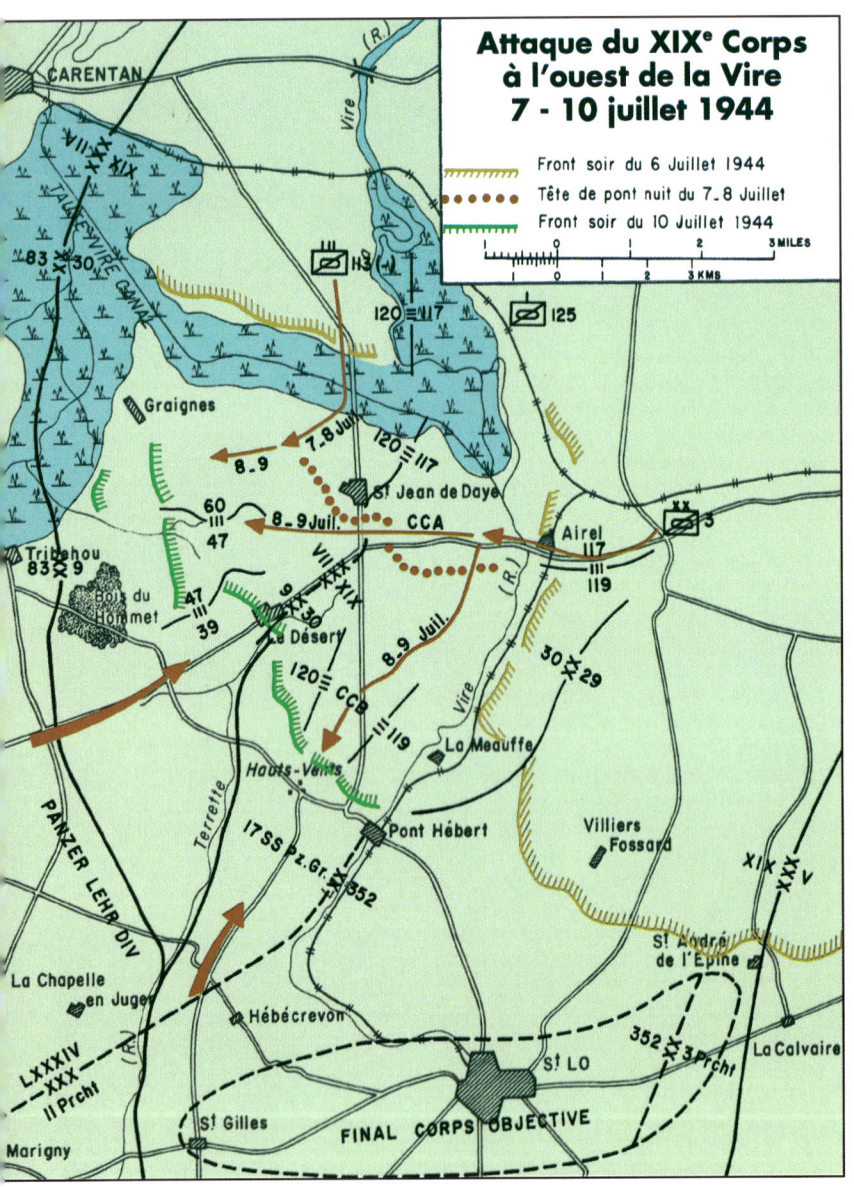

Map showing the sector of the offensive of Maj. Gen. Corlett's XIX Corps and the Saint-Fromond/Saint-Jean-de-Daye bridgehead west of the Vire. Notice the size of the marshlands which considerably hampered the American thrust and made the area easier to defend for the Germans. (Heimdal map based on Martin Blumenson.)

General von Choltitz's German LXXXIV (84th) corps of all its reserves, including its armored reserves (the *Das Reich* Division was committed in the form of *Kampfgruppen*, one, *Kampfgruppe Weidinger*, in the La Haye-du-Puits sector and the other, *Kampfgruppe Wisliceny*, the following day against the Saint-Fromond bridgehead). Although his objectives were only partly achieved, Bradley could be satisfied with his American First Army; its two western army corps had pinned down and worn down the Germans while the second corps had just crossed the Vire. General Corlett had scored a resounding success at Saint-Fromond and Bradley let him commit the 3rd Armored Division the next day. Facing the 30th Inf.Div. was no more than the skeleton of *Kampfgruppe Heintz* and a tiny part of the *"Götz"*. The attacks on all fronts seemed to go the American command's way: a punch to the right, a punch in the center and a left hook to open up the way for the breakout south-westwards. But the Germans had two surprises in store for the Americans: *Kampfgruppe Wisliceny* came to the rescue and, that evening, coming from the east General Bayerlein, commanding the renowned *Panzer-Lehr-Division* (armoured training division) has just arrived at Carantilly, west of Canisy. On 2 June his tanks left the Tilly-sur-Seulles sector where they had been pinning down British troops for a month, and prepared for a great offensive west of Saint-Lô.

8 July

As the American armor prepared to cross the Vire at Airel/Saint-Fromond, the German tanks were also preparing for a "decisive" battle. The **Kampfgruppe Wisliceny** was a battlegroup made up of various units of the *"Das Reich"* Division, it was commanded by Lieutenant-Colonel Günther Wisliceny, a Silesian. Wisliceny was in charge of the *"Deutschland"* Regiment, one of *"Das Reich"*'s two grenadier regiments. Thus *Kampfgruppe Wisliceny* included the staff of that regiment *(Stab "D")*, its 1st Battalion *(I./D)* and its infantry gun company *(13. ID)*; these elements were reinforced by the divisional engineer battalion *(Pz.Pi.Btl. "DR.")* Also available in the sector was a tank company of *"Das Reich"*, the 6th Company *(6./Pz.Rgt. 2 " DR.")* and about fifteen Panzer IVs.

On 6 June 1944, the **Panzer-Lehr-Division** was the best equipped German armored division along the entire western front but a month of hard fighting had substantially reduced this unit's forces. It had 189 tanks on 1 June (97 Panzer IVs, 92 "Panthers" and 6 "Tigers"), but by 1 July was down to 68 (36 Panzer IVs and 32 "Panthers"), a mere third of the tanks initially committed. This armored division nevertheless remained a formidable force, commanded by Fritz Bayerlein, Rommel's assistant in Africa, with some very experienced and highly motivated commanders.

General von Choltitz then dispatched **Kampfgruppe Wisliceny** on a minor counter-attack in the Saint-Fromond sector, its objective being Hill 40, the crossroads between Le Désert and Saint-Fromond. The 6th company's fifteen Panzer IVs of the *"Das Reich"*'s tank regiment supported this action. The *Kampfgruppe* was to take charge of the elements of **Kampfgruppe Heinz** and **Pionerschule Angers** fighting in the sector. But the situation was confused and no contact could be made with these units holding out against the 30th Inf.Div. Elements of the **"Götz von Berlichingen"** established a front to the north-east in front of Hommet Wood, then **the engineer battalion of the "Das Reich" Division** (under orders from Captain Brosow) secured the D.8 road to Le

at most and less still for the veterans of the 4th Inf.Div., who lost another 600 men. American infantry took just 17 prisoners that day. As Martin Blumenson reports, the German paratroopers and SS grenadiers put up a tough fight, refusing to surrender, even when heavily outnumbered, and yielding ground only with despair and loathing. The veterans also had other enemies to contend with: the swamps and mud, but especially those "damned hedges" that compartmentalized the land with high embankments topped with screens of thick foliage. The GIs were ready to believe that this "damn war might last ten years" but as events later proved, **7 July was a great turning point in the fate of the American armies,** the calm before the storm leading up to the decisive blow. The terrible sacrifices that Maj.Gen. Middleton's VIII Corps and Maj.Gen. Collins' VII Corps had made in the period 3-7 July now made it possible for the entire right flank of the American front line to slowly slide, taking the Bauptois hills in the west (in the La Haye-du-Puits area), a hard nut to crack, and in the center, to weaken the defensive position established in front of Sainteny as far as Saint-André-de-Bohon. The action of these two corps now marked a pause but, in addition to gaining ground, made it possible to fix and wear down the entire German front throughout its length, from Vire to the sea, depriving

Désert, and from there to the Saint-Lô/Périers road, while the **1st Battalion of the "Deutschland" Regiment** covered the front line to the south-east. This last unit sustained losses, particularly from the fighter-bombers; its commanding officer, Commander Schuster, was killed. Although slowed down by this fresh opposition, the American forces committed by Corlett in the Saint-Fromond bridgehead did make some progress. **Saint-Jean-de-Daye** was taken the previous evening. The 113th Cavalry Group advanced towards Graignes and the 119th IR headed towards Pont-Hébert, while in the afternoon, CCA (Brig.Gen. Doyle O Hickey) of the 3rd Armored Division (Maj.Gen. Hobbs) was already racing into Airel to cross the Vire. This produced huge congestion, with armored columns mixing with infantry columns and the vehicles of the 30th Inf.Div. During the battle with the units of Kampfgruppe Wisliceny, the American units under General Corlett destroyed five of the *"Das Reich"* Division's Panzer IVs (there are photographs of these destroyed tanks that we will be seeing on the following pages).

The **"Das Reich"** Division also committed other elements that same day; in the center, in the Sainteny sector, to support the *"Götz von Berlichingen"* desperately clinging on to the terrain. The tank regiment's first battalion, Commander Kesten's "Panther" Battalion, was committed on the Périers/Sainteny line. Sergeant Barkmann of the 4th Company destroyed his first Sherman straightaway on 8 July.

The **"Götz"** suffered heavy losses that day. Commander Opificius, commanding officer of *II./37*, the keystone of resistance, received a direct hit to the head, and an officer and two men who came to his help were cut to pieces by shrapnel. The reconnaissance battalion dropped to a third of its strength but still held out in front of Sainteny. Reinforcements arrived however from Saumur, in the form of Commander Kurt Fleischer's engineer battalion.

9 July

Kampfgruppe Wisliceny ("Das Reich") attacked again, causing substantial losses to the 120th IR. Three tanks of the 743rd TD Battalion veered north instead of south.

This created disorder then panic while coming under attack by the men of the *"Das Reich"*. A terrific artillery barrage descended on the German lines to save the day, and the GIs regained what ground they had lost. The infantrymen of the 30th Inf.Div. were deadly. The Germans called them Roosevelt's SS, a nickname from which the men of the 30th drew no little pride, as it treated them as a crack unit. The oncoming panic was stopped by energetic leadership from Lieutenant-Colonels McDowell (3rd/117th Inf.) and Hugh T. Mainord (3rd/102nd Inf.). The 3rd Arm.Div.'s CCB arrived at Les Hauts-Vents. The 30th made swifter progress along the Vire, to Pont-Hébert. The tanks of the *"Das Reich"* were mysteriously pulled out, but in fact it was to make way for those of the *Panzer-Lehr*.

Given the narrowness of the front at Sainteny, the 9th Inf.Div. could not be lined up alongside the VII Corps, and so was placed in the Saint-Jean-de-Daye sector, to the north of the 30th Inf.Div., on its right flank. The 9th remained attached to the VII Corps, which now extended as far as the Saint-Fromond bridgehead.

On this 9 July, the *Panzer-Lehr-Division* set itself up on an attacking basis facing the Saint-Fromond bridgehead.

General Bayerlein was present to watch the 13th Parachute Regiment commanded by Count von der Schulenburg move up to the front line near Les Champs-de-Losques. Most of the soldiers were youngsters who had only just completed their training. They came under bombardment; of the 1,500 young paratroopers, 200 were killed or wounded. This terrible baptism of fire severely dented the regiment's confidence in its own ability.

10 July

This new day was a nightmare for the **"Götz von Berlichingen"** Division. A hurricane of fire came down on the German lines. Only a few Panzers were able to resist; the men fell one after the other. Companies were reduced to around fifteen men, battalions numbering 950 were reduced to 120. The 3rd Battalion of *SS-Pz.Gren.Rgt. 37*, which had numbered 945 men, was down to just 345. The division, which had two grenadier regiments now had just a core of a thousand infantry. The keystone of the German defense against Collins was almost wiped out. The Americans gained a foothold in **Sainteny**. The **"Das Reich"** Division reorganized around Raids, and its tanks, commanded by Lieutenant-Colonel Tychsen, retook Saint-André-de-Bohon, where they destroyed a battalion of the **83rd Inf.Div.**

That evening, a strange atmosphere came over the Saint-Fromond area. The infantrymen of the **30th Inf.Div.** and of the freshly arrived **9th Inf. Div.**, heard the noise of the engines of German tanks in the distance. Near their positions, they could hear the Germans digging in. All these rumblings and noises were interpreted as indicating "a general withdrawal of the German forces". But the *"Panzer-Lehr"* was located and was not even observing radio silence. In actual fact, this was the **Panzer-Lehr-Division** preparing for its great offensive due to start in the early hours

The young paratroopers of Count von der Schulenburg's Fallschirmjäger-Regiment 13 (5. Fallschirmjäger-Division) moved up to the front line near Champs-de-Losques on 9 July. They came under a terrific bombardment that cost them 200 casualties, killed or wounded. (Pipet/Heimdal Coll.)

of the following morning. Its major objective was to destroy and push back the Americans beyond the Vire-Taute Canal and remove the threat to the front west of Saint-Lô.

11 July

The **Panzer-Lehr-Division** launched its attack along two lines: - the 901st Grenadier Regiment (commander Colonel Scholze) reinforced by 12 Panzer IVs of the 2nd Tank Battalion and a tank destroyer company (Captain Oventrop) attacked north of the bridgehead against the 9th Inf.Div.; - the 902nd Grenadier Regiment (commander *Major* Welsch) reinforced by 20 "Panther" tanks of *I./Pz.Lehr.Rgt. 130* attacked south of the bridgehead against the 30th Inf.Div. and the 3rd Arm.Div.'s CCB. The attack fell behind schedule and did not start until 05.30. *"Panzer marsch!"* The armored columns got moving, and for the first time in nearly two weeks the German tanks went onto the offensive. The crack *"Panzer-Lehr"* troops were raring to go. At 06.30, the right flank of the Scholze group, its 1st Battalion (*I./901*) commanded by Captain Philipps had already penetrated 3 kilometers behind the American lines and passed Le Désert. Whenever the grenadiers came up against resistance, they called in the Panzers and crushed the American pockets of resistance. One battalion *headquarters* was overrun, then another. Prisoners were dispatched unescorted to the rear. The attack made rapid progress and Captain Philipps kept heading north until he came to the Vire-Taute Canal. By that time, Maj.Gen. Eddy's 9th Inf.Div. was completely encircled. But the *"Panzer-Lehr"* was not strong enough to put its plan into action. It was down to a third of its tanks and at barely half-strength had to face two American infantry divisions and an armored division, reinforced by various battalions.

It was attacking in fact against impossible odds of one to six. The weather cleared towards noon after a cloudy start to the day, and the "Jabos", or fighter-bombers, joined the fray. Of the 32 Panzers committed, 20 were hit and 12 carried on towards the canal. The planes *machine-gun*ned the columns, the grenadiers fell flat on the ground, leaving the tanks unprotected. By around noon, 500 grenadiers had fallen, either killed or wounded. The men of the 30th Inf.Div. tell the story: That morning, some of them saw four tanks and a command vehicle arriving along with twenty grenadiers. An American lieutenant jumped into a jeep equipped with a machine-gun and opened fire. Somebody fired a bazooka, one shot then another. Two officers tossed grenades through the open hatches and against the accompanying infantry on the road. The first tank exploded in a column of flames to terrified screams from the German crew. A German was caught in the explosion as he tried to warn the second tank. An American officer fired an FM BAR at the tank which brewed up as the third tank fell back. Altogether five tanks and four armored vehicles were destroyed, with sixty killed and countless men wounded or captured. Further on, confronting the 119th Regiment in the Pont-Hébert sector, four more tanks were destroyed and another thirteen were put out of action by P-47 fighter planes.

Captain Philipps did not escape, but ended up in captivity. Chief Warrant Officer Sohlbach returned to his lines with his twelve men and forty prisoners! For it he received the German Gold Cross. If this attack had succeeded, it would have blown away the Saint-Fromond bridgehead and earned several weeks respite for the German front. But General Fritz Bayerlein had failed. He had just lost 500 grenadiers and 23 of his tanks, and only had about forty left… The proud *"Panzer-Lehr"* was reduced to a *Kampfgruppe*. The 9th Inf.Div. had lost a little ground before the counter-attack was stopped, some 900 yards (820 meters).

In the sector of the **"Götz"**, the front folded up and **Sainteny** finally fell into the Americans' hands after eight days of fighting.

12 July

But, after the optimism of 7 and 8 July, the American offensive had become the battle of the hedgerows against reorganized German forces. From 7 to 13 July, the **30th Inf.Div.** lost 3,200 men, the battalion on US 119th IR's left flank, exposed to shellfire from right bank of the Vire still in German hands, registered 50% losses. "Old Hickory" was placed under the VII Corps' control on the 15th and on 20 July stopped all action to prepare for the final offensive.

South of Sainteny, **"Kampfgruppe Weidinger"** came to support the sorely tested **"Götz"**.

The **4th Inf. Div.** made its thrust towards Périers while the **83rd Inf.Div.** attempted to advance along the Taute valley. The 4th Inf. Div. was pinned down on 15 July and was committed in the reserve for the coming great offensive. In ten days, it registered 2,300

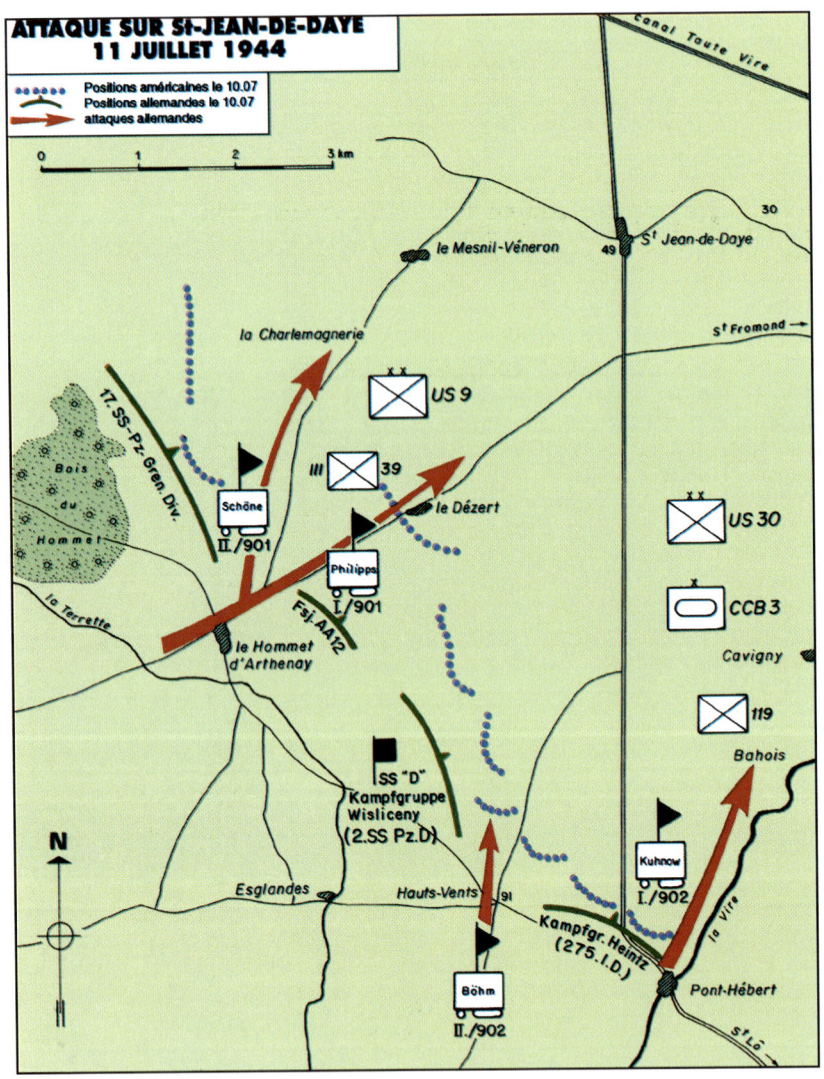

The Panzer-Lehr-Division's attack on 11 July towards the Taute-Vire Canal. (Heimdal.)

losses including 3 battalion commanders and 9 company commanders; losses too great to keep it in the front line.

The La Haye-du-Puits sector from 10 to 15 July

As we have seen, the **8th Inf.Div.** was brought in to reinforce Maj.Gen. Middleton's VIII Corps in place of the 82d Airborne Division. Its commander was Maj.Gen. William C. McMahon, assisted by Brig.Gen. Nelson M. Walker. It comprised the 13th, 28th and 121st IR. It was regarded as one of the best trained units. Even so, "hesitancy, inertia and disorganization" marked its beginnings in the front line in Normandy and its commitment coincided with some vigorous German local counter-attacks. Brig.Gen. Nelson M. Walker was killed while preparing an infantry battalion for an attack. Maj.Gen. McMahon made mistakes that led to his dismissal and replacement by 9th Inf.Div. executive officer Brig.Gen. Donald A. Stroh, who set about improving his unit's combat techniques. It occupied the north bank of the Ay on **14 July.**

On **14 July 1944**, the **8th Inf. Div.** at last occupied the north bank of the Ay after the Germans withdrew to the new line of defense, the *Wasserstellung*. This retreat was carried out on 13 July along the entire front from the Vire River to the sea, by order of General von Choltitz.

The **79th Inf. Div.** suffered heavy losses at the start of the month and it made no further progress after the capture of La Haye-du-Puits on 8 and 9 July. One of its infantry companies, which numbered only 94 men on the 7th, was down to just 47 another two days later. The 79th took Angoville-sur-Ay on **11 July** and it too reached the north bank of the Ay on **14 July.** Mopping up the coastal area from Montgardon to the Ay cost a further 2,000 men and Lessay remained in German hands. The **90th Inf. Div.** gained a foothold on the southern flank of Mont Castre on **10 July**, taking complete control the next day. The much depleted division did not reach the River Sèves until **14 July**, after the German withdrawal, linking up with VII Corps' right flank. Maj.Gen. Landrum finally achieved his *objective* but at the cost of a further 2,000 casualties.

Maj.Gen. Middleton's VIII Corps had completed the mission assigned to it on 2 July. But these twelve days of battle had left 10,000 casualties. It was now lined up along the Ay and Sèves rivers, but with no hope of a rapid German collapse; the Germans were only yielding ground step by step. The order to pull back was issued directly by von Kluge (Army Group B) to von Choltitz on the 13th owing to the lack of reinforcements to plug the gaps in the German front line. On this 14 July, Coutances, the planned objective at the time of the American offensive of 2 July, "seemed about as far away as Berlin".

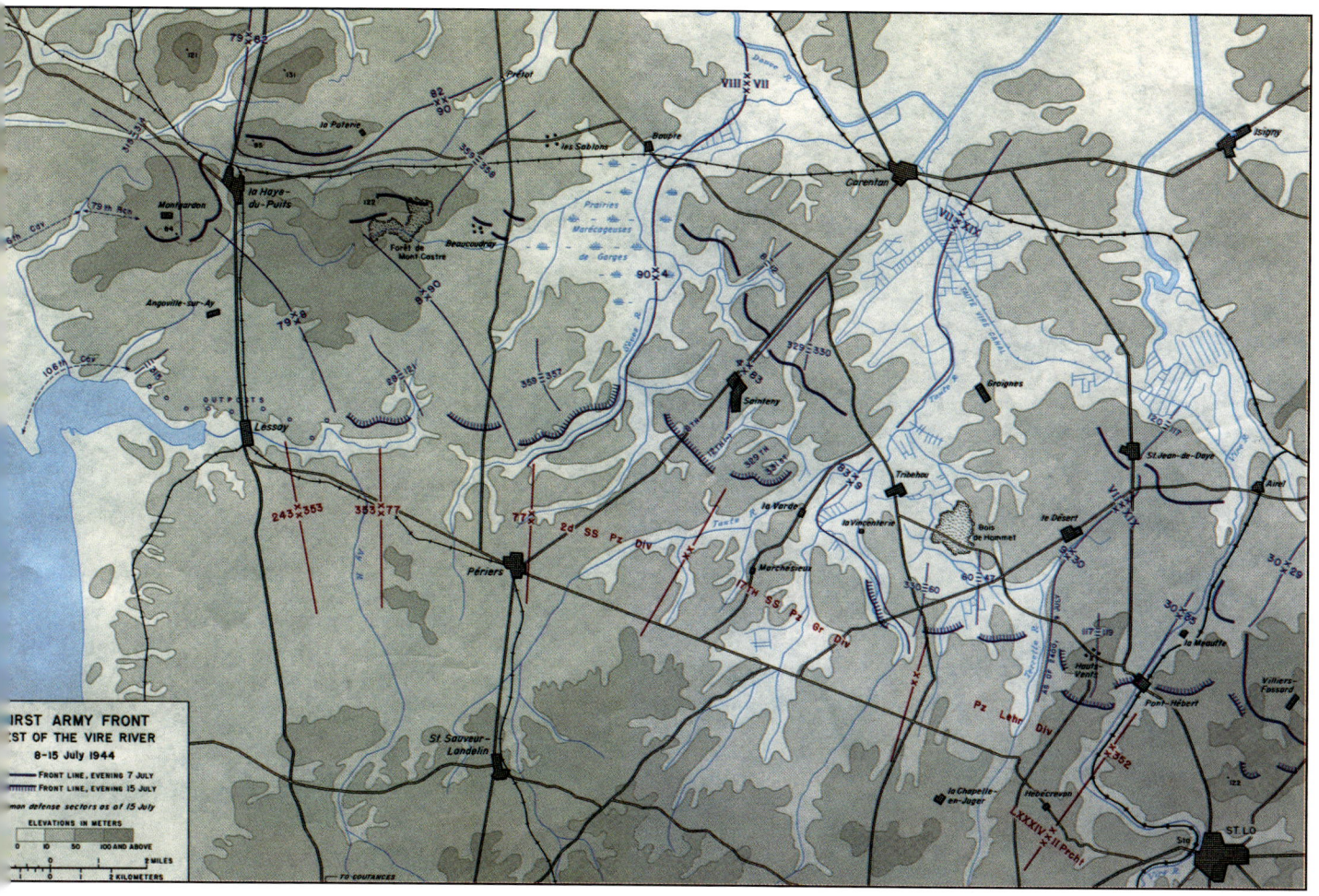

Map showing the advance of the American front from 7-15 July 1944. During this period, the VIII Corps profited from the German withdrawal to come up before Lessay. The VII Corps finally took Sainteny but remained 7 kilometers short of Périers. That same corps and the XIX Corps extended the Saint-Fromond bridgehead as they came close to the main highway. At this point in time, the XIX Corps had not yet taken Saint-Lô, but did so three days later. (US Army History Department.)

Cherbourg, 3 and 4 July.

As of 3 July 1944, La Presse Cherbourgeoise came off the press of the printing works of Cherbourg Eclair, a daily newspaper published in Cherbourg until June 1944. The new daily carries under the headline: "First daily newspaper in liberated France". It was headed by Daniel Yon (seen in the center of the photograph opposite) who was appointed by the Liberation and the Provisional Government committees. On this photograph, Daniel Yon hands over the first copy to Captain Patrick Dolan of New York, head of the PWD at Cherbourg. On a line with Daniel Yon, another PWD officer, Captain Fernand Auberjendois. Behind Daniel Yon, chief printer Caille. The following day 4 July, Charles Kiley also came to this printing works to print a GI newspaper: Stars and Stripes. Two contributors to that paper are pictured above: Sgt. Victor Harris (center) and Morrow Davis (right).

Below: Pfc John Allan piles up copies hot off the press, which reeled off eighteen thousand copies per hour under M. Caille's watchful eye. (Photographs courtesy NA and DAVA, Heimdal coll.)

As civilians and American soldiers examine photographs of the various theaters of operations that the PWD (the US psychological warfare division) submits to the public gaze, as an old local man peruses a copy of the La Presse Cherbourgeoise, Daniel Yon, surrounded by his colleagues along with Captain Auberjendois and Captain Patrick Dolan (right), examines the first copy of the new daily newspaper.
(Photographs courtesy NA, Heimdal collection.)

Cherbourg, early July.
Opposite, from top to bottom: the Germans had sabotaged the swing bridge in front of the commercial harbor. The Americans are at work repairing it. This view was taken facing towards the Val de Saire. – Supervised by the Americans, civilians make repairs to the roadway in the Quai Alexandre III.

Below: a house in Cherbourg smashed by bombs. Civilians clear up the debris. A bed sticks out hanging in an odd position.

Bottom of the page: American soldiers cross the railroad leading to the Harbor station; the Fort du Roule can be seen in the background.

Opposite, from top to bottom: even before the port was liberated and able to function normally, and although supplies were mostly conveyed by road, we see here the railroads in the station area being repaired by the Americans. In the background lies the flat area leading to the Montagne du Roule.

The Germans sabotaged the railroad to great effect, blowing up the Tunnel de la Roche which hangs in the Quincampoix valley. It was a spectacular operation. Three wagons of melinite are thought to have been used, and the mountainside was blown open… Blocks of stone piled up in the breach. Bulldozers are at work here to clear the tunnel.

On this other photograph, the work has advanced. The tunnel has been cleared, and is now a sunken road…

(Photographs courtesy NA, Heimdal collection.)

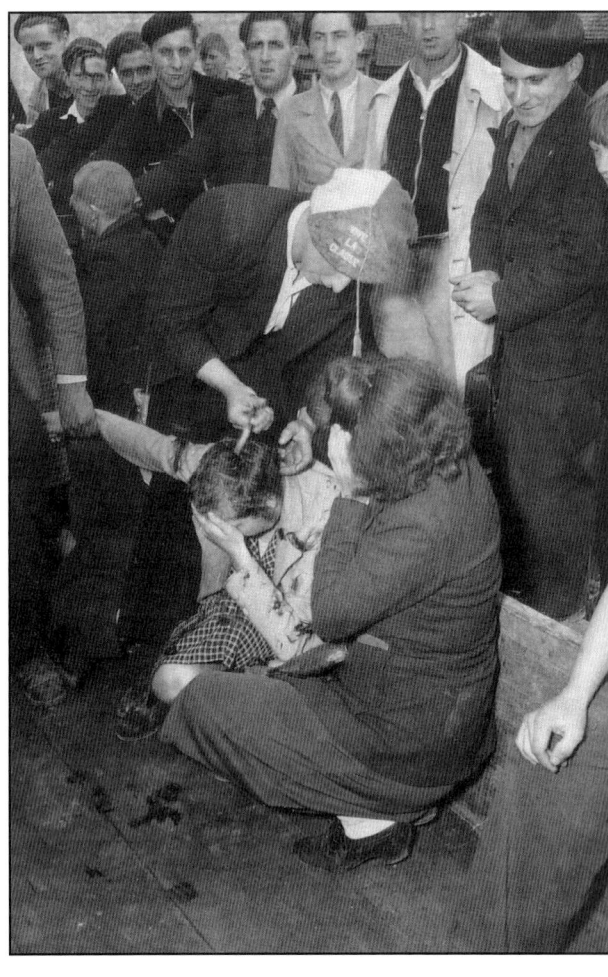

Cherbourg from 9 to 14 July, "purification".

Above and opposite: women were the first to come in for reprisals inflicted on collaborationists. On the morning of 14 July 1944, twelve Cherbourg women had their heads shaved under the mocking eye of onlookers and were paraded through the city in a truck, under a sign marked: "Collaborationist women's parade float". According to contemporary indications, these twelve women were waitresses or cleaning ladies in buildings occupied by the Germans and were suspected of sleeping with them, hence their punishment.

(Photographs courtesy National Archives, Heimdal collection.)

Two teenagers also paid. Roger L (an accountant), then 19 years old, and Jean T (a student), aged 22, were accused of helping the Germans by spying on their behalf behind the American lines. After a hearing lasting three and a half hours at the Court of Cherbourg, on 9 July 1944, they were convicted of espionage on behalf of the enemy and condemned to penal servitude for life. (Heimdal coll.)

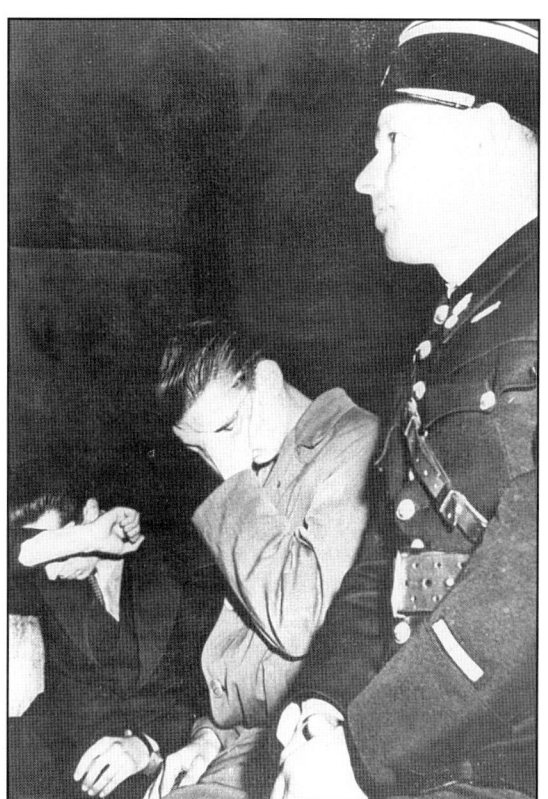

14 July 1944 In Cherbourg.

Two weeks after all German resistance ceased in the Cotentin, the people of Cherbourg celebrate Bastille Day on 14 July along with the American troops. On the photograph above, the municipal brass band arrives in the Place de la République from the Rue de la Paix. Below: the Hôtel d'Europe overlooks the Place de la République and made an ideal lookout post for these American soldiers. (Photographs courtesy National Archives, Heimdal coll.)

Opposite page, top: the City Hall is decked with British, French and American flags. A crowd gathers to listen to the speeches. Opposite page, bottom: the bandstand is now used as a speaker's platform, a French officer addresses a crowd of local people. The name of General de Gaulle was acclaimed on this occasion. The Hôtel d'Europe is on the left and the City Hall on the right. (Photographs courtesy National Archives.)

Cherbourg, 14 July 1944.

To mark Bastille Day on 14 July 1944, the American war correspondents photographed the people of Cherbourg present at the ceremony. Notice a priest on the left, and below, a young Norman who has sewn onto his jacket the cloth patch then worn by the American soldiers of the 79th Infantry Division. This was the division that captured the Fort du Roule. But this was the most popular badge among the local people because woven into it was a Lorraine Cross. This was because the division fought in Lorraine during World War I and later adopted the Lorraine Cross for its divisional insignia.

Opposite page, top: notice here a picture of the crowd looking north towards the bandstand, towards the sea (the City Hall is on the right). The young boy in the preceding photo is again pictured here. On the left, as their badges indicate, the two American soldiers belong to the 4th Infantry Division. The photograph in the middle pictures local fishermen listening to the speech. Notice also the World War I veterans proudly wearing their decorations. (Photographs courtesy National Archives and D.F./Heimdal.)

14 July victory parade at Cherbourg.

1, 2 and **3.** A ceremony was held in the theater square, formerly Place Maréchal Pétain and renamed Place du Général de Gaulle. In front of the theater, a wreath of flowers was placed in memory of local inhabitants who died during the German occupation. This wreath was surrounded by a guard of honor made up of French officials, American and even British soldiers.

4. Here is another picture of the 14 July celebration in the Place de la République, opposite the City Hall.

5. American troops in turn parade in the Place de la République.

6 and **7.** They then moved up the Rue François Lavieille. Notice on the right the Chamber of Commerce building which was requisitioned by the German authorities. The concrete sentry bunker seen in the 1944 photo has been demolished. In the 1944 picture, the bandstand in the background serves as a landmark.

8 and **9.** Finally, the American soldiers continue their parade "in honor of patriots killed during the German occupation" in the Rue Albert Mahieu, with the Place de la Fontaine in the background.

(NA, D.F. and E.G./Heimdal.)

Saint-Jores, Pont-l'Abbé, 6, 7 and 8 July.

1. Soldiers of the 90th Infantry Division pass through Gorges coming from the south from the front line on 6 July.

2. The next day, 7 July, near Saint-Jores, GIs of that same division (notice the standing soldier's divisional shoulder flash) advance along a hedge with cover from a Sherman of a tank battalion's Company C. The road has been cleared of mines.

3. But supplies had to be brought up to the offensive in progress and cases of ammunition are taken to the front following the mass methods developed by the US army. Photo taken on 8 July.

4. Three kilometers south of Saint-Jores, these men of the 90th Infantry Division are preparing heavy mortar shells brought up to them, photo taken on 7 July.

5. To cross the Sensurière marshes, 164th Engineer Combat Bn, Co B threw a Bailey bridge and a bridge of boats across from Pont-l'Abbé as a contribution to the offensive moving on Mont Castre.

6. Another view of this double bridge set up by US engineers.
7. At Prétot, these soldiers aboard a truck seem to be leaving the front line with no regrets…
8. At Lithaire, there were powerlines to be restored.
(Photographs courtesy D.F./Heimdal and Heimdal coll.)

79th ID

La Haye-du-Puits sector.

1. At the entrance to La Haye-du-Puits, on a level with the railroad, two German prisoners supervise one of their wounded comrades. This is east of La Haye-du-Puits.

2. On 7 July, near La Haye-du-Puits, an engineer unit waits to see action in a further operation near a house in ruins.

3. On 8 July, the attack against La Haye-du-Puits was launched by the 314th Infantry Regiment of the 79th Division. These GIs are now very close to the town, on the Barneville-Bolleville road to the north. However, for all the apparent tension, this is a staged photo taken on 9 July.

4. In front of La Haye-du-Puits Town Hall devastated in the blaze. An infantryman of the 79th Infantry Division supervises a young German soldier. A Signal Corps censor has camouflaged the soldier's shoulder flash on the negative. The US Army has since cleaned up some of its negatives so that now we find old prints with the insignia camouflaged and more recent ones with them visible again.

5. On 8 July, in the Rue du Château, in front of the café du Grand Marché, these German soldiers have just surrendered after being besieged for several hours in the medieval keep of the old castle, from where they come.

6. On 9 July, at the northern entrance to the marketplace, the Place Ducloux (a buttress of the church can be seen on the left), an engineer unit comes to inspect the damage and assess the equipment needed to clear the debris and reopen the road to traffic.

(Photographs courtesy US Army, NA and D.F./Heimdal.)

La Haye-du-Puits, 9 July 1944.

1 and **2.** The Norman town has just fallen and is invested by GIs of the 79th Infantry Division; here a crew transports an 80 mm mortar in several pieces. They are on their way back from the front line and heading off for Barneville.

3 and **4.** American infantry now patrol the town and pass in front of the post office.

5, 6 and **7.** More GIs continue to excavate the ruins of burned down houses in search of possible snipers of the 353. Infanterie-Division, survivors of Captain Pillmann's engineer battalion. Photograph n° 5 was taken on the Monbecq road. Photograph n° 6 was taken in the Rue de la Cavée, partly rebuilt; it was in the destroyed area on the eastern side of the big square.

8 and **9.** Near the old castle, a bomb has cut off the road, forming a huge crater.
(Photographs courtesy Heimdal collection and E.G./Heimdal.)

172

La Haye-du-Puits. 10 and 11 July 1944.

1. After the battle, civilians returned to the devastated little town; two old Normans are brought back home in a jeep.

2 and **3.** Two views of the marketplace lined with houses, some still intact, others damaged by fire or completely destroyed. The church has lost one of its steeples, which was never rebuilt. These vehicles are heading off south to supply the front now facing towards Lessay.

4 and **5.** The front of the church on 10 July with its destroyed steeple never rebuilt.

6 and **7.** The Rue du Château, the Saint-Sauveur road, a couple of old "Haytillons" (inhabitants of La Haye-du-Puits) returns hoping to find their home still standing.

8. Further on, many civilians, having loaded their most precious possessions in wheelbarrows, pass by the church front damaged by shrapnel, on their way to whatever is left of their homes.

(Photographs courtesy Heimdal collection and E.G./Heimdal.)

La Haye-du-Puits, 11-19 July.

1. From 9 July, the 8th Infantry Division came to relieve the 79th Division in the La Haye-du-Puits sector; pictured here is the 8th Division command post.

2. On 11 July, an excavator is at work to clear the debris, two days after the town was taken. A soldier of the 79th Division, Thomas Holland from Texas, listens to the commentary by the priest at Besneville, Henri Ryst.

3 and **4.** Again on 11 July, two old Haytillons already seen on the previous page (photo n° 6), have just returned from Doville. They are Eugene Sérée, a former barber, and his wife Honorine. But in view of the destruction, they applied to the Americans for rehousing. They were able to spend a few nights at the stud farm, which had not been damaged. The Town Hall then found them a room to live in in the Rue E Poirier. In the first photograph, Pvt. Bill W Lemak from San Francisco gives them a piece of chocolate. They also receive tins of American rations. In the second photograph, Eugene Sérée talks with a US Army officer and interpreter.

8th ID

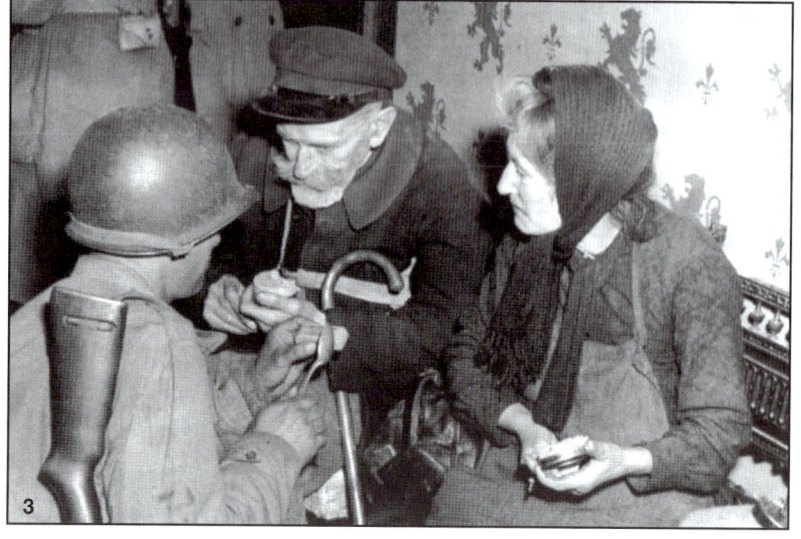

5. 14 July, a Sherman tank enters La Haye-du-Puits from the north, here on a level with the old castle.

6. On 14 July, ceremonies were held throughout the liberated areas of Normandy. Pictured here are some of those who gathered in front of the war memorial at La Haye-du-Puits. From left to right: Roger Abraham, Fernand Gosselin, Auguste Ambroise (grocer at Bolleville), an unidentified person, Jean-Baptiste Tardif (with the beard, he was notary Guilbert's clerk), Maurice Auvray (behind him - he owned a café in the square), an unidentified lady, the Abbé Pasturel (parish priest at Angoville-sur-Ay), Captain Letourneur (from Bolleville), an unidentified lady. The children in the front are Bernard Ambroise and Marie-Joseph Gosselin.

7. Ten days after the town was taken, on 19 July, the central square has now been liberated. In the foreground are the urinals sited near the church.

(Photographs courtesy US Army and NA.)

La Haye-du-Puits, 13 July 1944.

1. This aerial view of the town taken from the north-east shows the road from Saint-Sauveur-le-Vicomte leading to the church where the road from Portbail and Carteret arrives. Further on is the central square and the dead straight road to Lessay, the next objective.

2 and **3.** Here are two views of the marketplace.

4. This monument was erected at La Haye-du-Puits in memory of the 79th Infantry Division.

5. On the La Haye-du-Puits road, a soldier indicates that the graves of these two GIs (buried by French civilians) have been mined by the Germans.

6. On 13 July, in the La Haye-du-Puits sector, American wounded are evacuated. The front was held up for a fortnight in front of Lessay until 27 July, when the 79th Infantry Division managed to take the town during Operation "Cobra". For now though, it was more hard fighting in the hedgerows.

(NA and D.F./Heimdal.)

INFANTRY
DIVISION
UNITED STATES
OF
AMERICA
IN THE CAUSE
OF FREEDOM

4

5

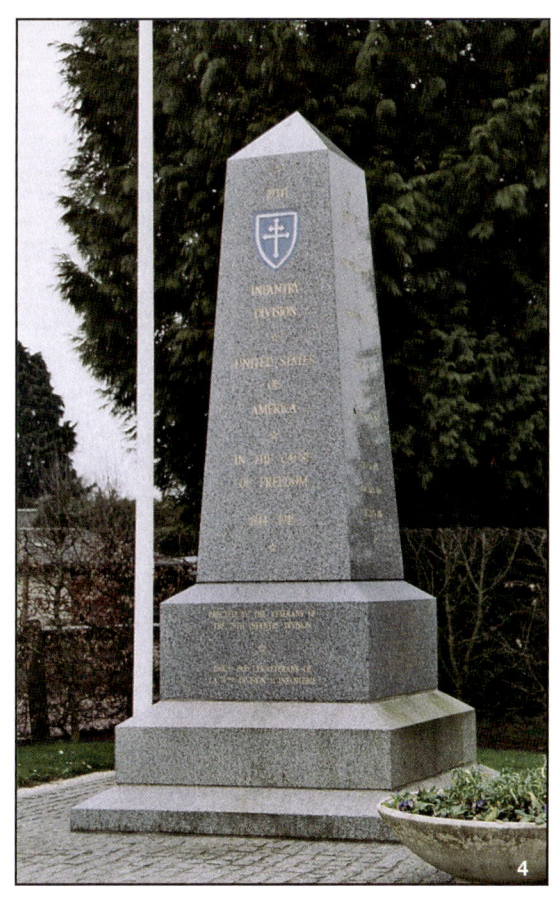

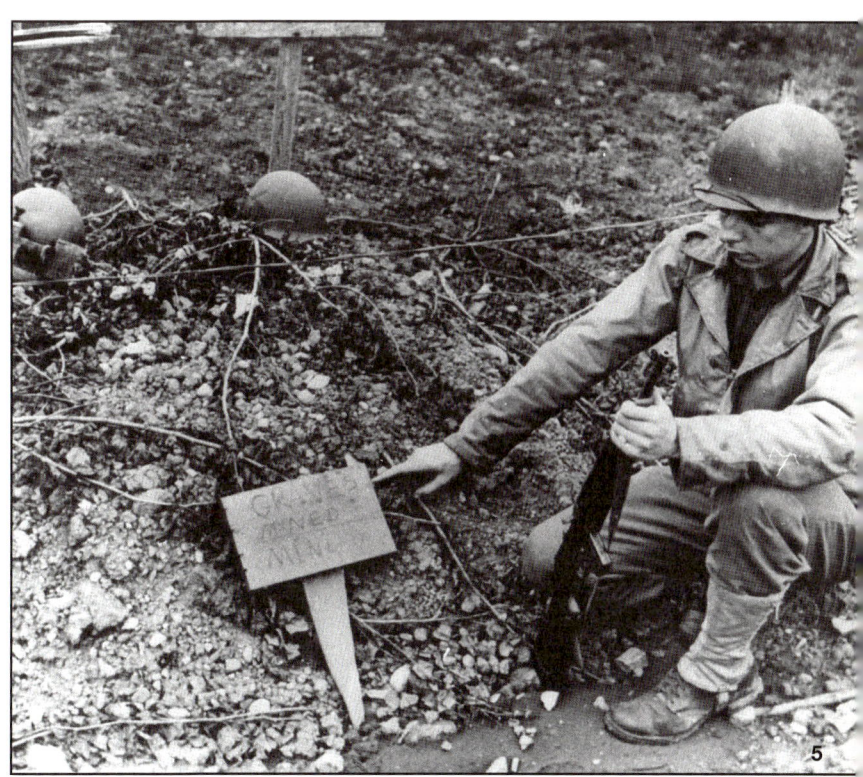

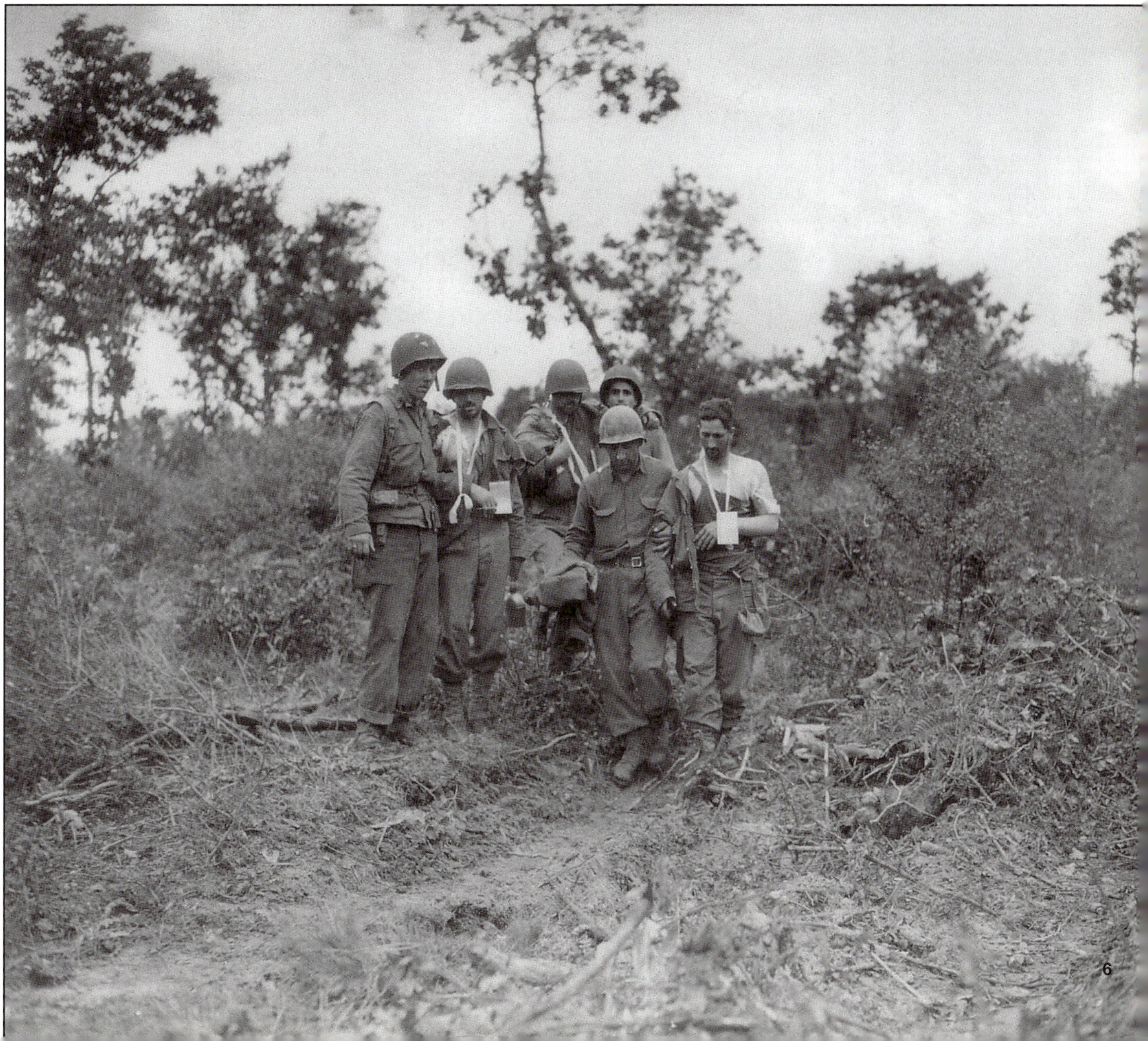

6

30th ID

On the front with the VII and XIX Corps, 7 and 8 July.

1. On 7 July, a Tank Destroyer M 10 advances before crossing the Vire River and taking part in the battle for the Saint-Fromond bridgehead.

2. 11 July, in the VII Corps' front line, a howitzer in action against the lines of the "Götz von Berlichingen".

3. On 8 July, these three soldiers of Kampfgruppe Heintz were shot by GIs of the 30th Infantry Division during the battle for the Saint-Fromond bridgehead.

4, 5, 6, 7 and **8.** On 8 July, coming from Airel (photographs 5 and 6), troops of the 30th Infantry Division cross the bridge over the Vire River leading to Saint-Fromond, set ablaze in the fighting (photo 4), with the tanks of the 3rd Armored Division already passing through. The Airel/Saint-Fromond bridge was reinforced by sappers of the 105th Engineer Combat Battalion, 30th Infantry Division. (Photographs courtesy US Army, Heimdal collection.)

**Saint-Fromond,
9 July 1944.**

1. A light tank of the 30th Infantry Division on its way from Saint-Fromond towards the crossroads leading to Le Désert passes by a 90 mm anti-tank gun set up in a defensive position.

2. A three-inch gun towed by a half-track of the 30th Infantry Division moves up into position to support the infantry advance.

30th ID

3rd AD

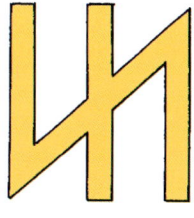
Das Reich

3, 4 and **5.** Two or three Panzer IVs of the 6th Company of the tank regiment of the "Das Reich" Division (6./SS-Panzer-Regiment 2 "DR.") were destroyed lending support to Kampfgruppe Wisliceny in its counter-attack on the American bridgehead. Fifteen tanks of this type were committed. Notice the "Das Reich" Division's tactical marking stencilled on the rear of the tanks pictured in photograph 3. Columns of Sherman tanks of Company D, the 33rd Armored Regiment (CCA, 3rd Armored Division) move up to the front line passing close by destroyed Panzer IVs lined up by the cemetery. All the photographs on these two pages were taken by American war correspondent Lovell. (Ets HQ. 44 - 7073, 7076, 7079, 7072, 7078) - photographs courtesy Nat. Archives and US Army - Heimdal collection.)

Saint-Fromond, 10 and 11 July 1944.

1. On 10 July, in a hamlet near Saint-Fromond, signallers stretch telephone lines while a light Stuart tank and infantrymen take a break.

2. Showing a certain sense of humor, this tank crew observing from their Stuart tank have placed a doll on a milepost looking in the direction from which the Germans are firing, 11 July.

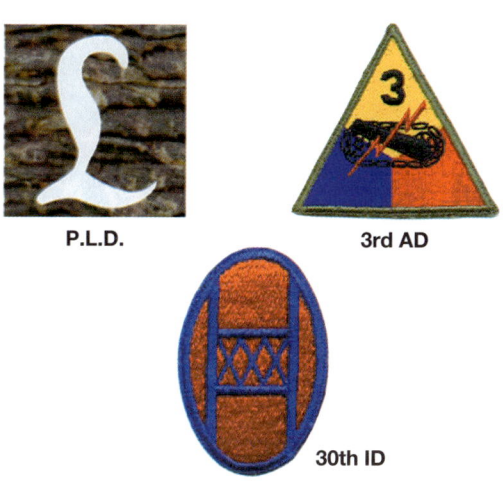

P.L.D.

3rd AD

30th ID

3. On this 11 July, near Saint-Fromond, these tanks and vehicles of the 33rd Armored Regiment (CCB, 3rd Armored Division) line up on a muddy road. A few hundred meters ahead, their comrades are resisting a counter-attack by the Panzer-Lehr-Division coming from Les Hauts-Vents. The light Stuart tank in the foreground christened "Carol" belongs to Company C of the 3rd Tank Regiment (33rd Arm. Rgt).

4. Near Saint-Jean-de-Daye, 11 July, as the Panzer-Lehr-Division attacks, this Tank Destroyer M-10 comes in support of the 30th Infantry Division.

(Photographs courtesy US Army, Heimdal collection.)

Sainteny, 11 and 12 July 1944.

1 and **2.** On the Carentan/Périers road, the village of Sainteny had been the objective of Maj.Gen. Collins' VII Corps since 3 July. It only fell into American hands on 11 July, after over a week of fierce fighting. The village of Sainteny is shifted slightly to the east of the straight highway, along which stretches the hamlet of Les Forges where this photograph was taken. On the corner of a house on the east side of the road (the village side), facing north-east, GIs of the 329th Infantry Regiment, the 83rd Infantry Division pose for the photographer – a picture taken after the 12 July.

3 and **4.** The GIs already seen in the previous photo fire a bazooka at a Panther tank of SS-Pz.-Rgt.2 of the "Das Reich" Division immobilized along the road, in the hamlet, during the battle this unit of German tanks fought here from 8-10 July. The "destruction" of this Panther is thus a reconstitution performed for the photographer on 11 or 12 July, to give an idea of the real battle fought here during the last few days.

5 and **6.** Continuing on the west side of the road, where the Panther was destroyed, after the crossroads to the south, a shell has just hit a house in Les Forges.

7 and **8.** In the center of the village of Sainteny, the church was badly damaged in the fighting: the choir was destroyed, the bell-tower was brought down by shellfire, and the nave was also hit. In the foreground, the war memorial has fallen off its base - the church has since been restored.

9. At the entrance to Les Forges.

10. In the village.
(NA and E.G./Heimdal.)

185

The artillery of the 9th Infantry Division in action near Saint-Jean-de-Daye on 13 July.

1. At Saint-Jean-de-Daye, 2,000 yards (1,800 meters) behind the front line, the 105 mm HM2 howitzers of the 84th Field Artillery Battalion (one of the of the 9th Inf. Div.'s four artillery battalions), concealed along a hedge under camouflage nets, open fire on the German positions. The artillerymen are wearing the divisional patch, easier to see in the next photograph.

2. We are now behind one of these 105 mm howitzers as the brass cartridge is ejected. Notice the gunner's patch. (7414)

3. The battery artillerymen remove the shells and brass cartridges from the packing in order to have complete rounds ready for firing.

4. The gun captain shouts down the telephone "Ready one the firing line". (7486)

5. Before assembling the round, the bomb disposal expert, a Pfc, screws a fuse onto the shell.

(DAVA - Heimdal collection.)

9th ID

186

12, 13 and 14 July.

1. On 11 July, the Panzer-Lehr-Division launched an attack against the American Saint-Fromond bridgehead. Pictured here are two of the division's Panther tanks; they belong to the 1st Company, the 1st Battalion (attached to the 902nd Grenadier Regiment under Major Welsch) which attacked from Les Hauts-Vents, opposite the 3rd Armored Division's CCB. This photo was taken on 13 July.

2. Another Panzer-Lehr tank belonging to the 1st Company and destroyed by a TD tank of the 3rd Armored Division. One of the tank crew got burnt trying to get out of his burning tank. Photo taken on 13 July.

3. Men of the 377th Antiaircraft Bn man an AA gun (12.7 quadruple machine-gun) pulling it clear of its camouflage net. This AA battalion was assigned to the 4th Infantry Division and so operated as a supporting unit in the Sainteny sector on this 12 July 1944. The gun is mounted on a half-track.

4. The gun now opens fire in support of the infantry with the devastating firepower of its four machine-guns.

5. On 14 July, a Sherman tank of the 3rd Armored Division (CCB) brewed up after being hit three days previously during the fighting against the Panzer-Lehr. Here it is towed off to a repair yard by two prime movers.

(Photos courtesy US Army and D.F./Heimdal Collection.)

4th ID

3rd AD

P.L.D.

189

13-18 July, "the calm before the storm".

1. While the Germans were getting very few supplies, the Allied reinforcements made up for losses and injected fresh units. Pictured here are dozens of (British) trucks in a port in southern England (the background in this photo has been censored).

2. On 13 July, a vehicle of the 21st Field Artillery Battalion, 5th Infantry Division is embarked at a British port on its way to the front east of Saint-Lô.

3. On 14 July, this puppy born a few hours before the landing was christened "Invasion" by Pfc. Jo-seph E. Day (from Belloire, Ohio) holding it here in a German helmet.

4. Another photo taken on 14 July - Pfc. Troy H. Risener, from Bradford (Arkansas) and Pvt. Berphe H. Sargent, from Mexico (Maine), use a flag of the Reich to clean the breech of an antitank gun. (7380)

190

5. These two Georgian volunteers from Tiflis, enlisted in the German army, were demoralized by a fight they did not choose (the Americans). They prefer to surrender to these soldiers of the 4th Armored Division, on 15 July. Here they inform their interrogators that they were in a group of 29 men commanded by two German officers; when the Americans advanced, they killed their officers and deserted. What they don't know is that the western Allies would hand them over to Stalin, who had an unenviable fate in store for them. Notice on the first Georgian's right sleeve the "Georgien" patch indicating his nationality and the 4th Armored Division's crest on one of the Americans' sleeve.

6. Near Le Désert, on 16 July, these men serving a 155 mm gun of Battery "A", 34th Field Artillery Battalion (9th Division) look proudly at the list of theaters of operations where their gun has seen action, from North Africa to the Cotentin. Their gun leader, on the left, is Staff-Sergeant Lyle Yoho from Taylorville (Illinois). (7661)

7. Mail was crucial to sustain morale among the troops. This photo of a US Post Office in Normandy was taken on 17 July.

8. With his colt at the ready, this Sergeant belonging to an artillery unit came on 18 July to inspect a wrecked Marder III type M 75 mm antitank gun mounted on a Czech 38 tank chassis) which was literally blown to pieces by accurate shellfire from his battery.

(DAVA and D.F./Heimdal.)

191

7 The Battle for Saint-Lô (11 to 18 July)

XIX Corps

35th ID

29th ID

V Corps

2d ID

A month after D-day, Saint-Lô seemed inaccessible. But fruitless efforts to reach it further stimulated the American commanders in their desire to take the town. Although destroyed in a terrifying apocalypse on 6 June it remained of vital importance. A strategic site, this ancient Gallo-Roman town, standing guard over a bridge over the Vire (Saint-Lô was formerly called Briovère, meaning bridge over the Vire), and later medieval town with ramparts along the line of the long rocky plateau overlooking the valley, and more recently capital of La Manche department. It was a major crossroads and checkpoint at the main place for crossing the Vire River. For the upcoming Operation "Cobra", it just had to be taken as it would otherwise be a thorn in the eastern side of the offensive, while its capture would be of help in bringing up the necessary reinforcements.

On the other side, the Germans dug in to the hills overlooking the town nestling in a dip, chiefly Hill 122 (to the north) and Hill 192 (to the north-east). The front line had to be held at all costs to avoid losing this strategic site. Here the sector of the front, from the Vire in the west to the Drôme in the east, was held by *II./Fallschirmjäger-Korps*, a parachute corps commanded by *Gen.Lt.* Eugen Meindl. He was in command of three battlegroups made up from the remnants of three infantry divisions, *KG 353* (remnants of *353. Inf. Div.*), *KG 266* (elements of *266. ID*) and *KG 352* (elements of *352. Inf.-Div.* which had faced the D-day landing at Omaha Beach). These three battlegroups were placed on the west of the front. In the east, the front was in the firm hands of *3. Fallschirmjäger-Division*, a parachute division commanded by *Gen.Maj.* Richard Schimpf, this division having been raised in the Rheims area late in 1943. It had in support an assault gun brigade, *Sturmgeschütz-Brigade XII* made up from volunteers from the paratroop army late in March 1944 at Melun and Fontainebleau. Among the gun crews committed, 2d Lieutenant Deutsch, a Knight of the Iron Cross, put up a stout defense of the Carillon sector. However, despite these crack paratroops, Meindl did not have enough men to hold such a huge front.

On its rocky promontory, Saint-Lô lay in a circus overlooking the Vire. Towering above and shutting in the site was a ridge to the north and east, which needed to be taken. To the **north**, high above the Pont-Hébert road, stood **Hill 122**, in the sector of Maj.Gen. Corlett's XIX Corps, an objective of the 29th Infantry Division located in the Villiers-Fossard sector that had been won so dearly. On its right (western) flank, as far as the Vire, stood the 35th Division, opposite the Carillon sector. To the **east**, it was still the 29th Division's sector and then that of the 2d Infantry Division (assigned to Maj. Gen. Leonard T. Gerow's V Corps) detailed to capture **Hill 192** overlooking the Bérigny/Saint-Lô road. Capturing this high ground was a prerequisite for the final assault and the attack was to be launched simultaneously by both corps on 11 July.

Hill 192. While further east, the 2d Armored Division and 1st Infantry Division covered the rest of the corps' sector as far as Caumont, the 2d Infantry Division under Maj. Gen. Walter M. Robertson had already failed in an attempt to take this high ground in June, losing 1,200 casualties in the process! The top of the hill was flat. It was protected by a maze of hedgerows well irrigated by sunken lanes which facilitated communications. The German paratroops had filled the hedgerows with well-equipped positions and reinforced them with a few assault guns. The main assault was to be launched in the west by the 38th Infantry (Col. Ralph W. Zwicker) with support from three tank companies and two heavy mortar companies. In the center, the 23rd Infantry (Lt. Col. Jay B. Loveless) would send a battalion onto the eastern slope. In the east, near the Bérigny crossroads, the attack had supporting fire from the 9th Infantry (Col. Chester J. Hirschfelder).

Morning mist ruled out the planned air support and the artillery opened fire alone for twenty minutes before the attack, launched at 06.00 hours on **11 July**. The previous night, Colonel Zwicker had pulled back his 38th Regiment to avoid it being hit by preparatory artillery fire. The Germans spotted their withdrawal and occupied the positions vacated by the Americans, which afforded them shelter against the impacts of the preparatory barrage. Then the six tanks in the first assault wave were destroyed or repelled by German *Panzerfausts*. However, with a rolling artillery barrage the advance went ahead regardless, albeit very slowly. Fifteen paratroopers surrendered, and three who refused to give themselves up were buried alive by a tankdozer! At noon the 38th Infantry reached the top of Hill 192 and the Germans were forced back. Although Hausser (*7. Armee*) gave orders for the hill to be retaken at all costs, the Germans' counterattacks proved ineffectual and they had to form a new line further south, overlooking the main highway.

On **12 July** the 2d Infantry Division made little headway, consolidating its position south of the highway. A more energetic attack might have broken through the German front which was by now seriously weakened in this sector. And yet the 2d Division took just 147 prisoners and sustained heavy losses : 69 killed, 328 wounded and 8 missing.

Towards Martinville ridge. In the north, Lt. Gen. Bradley dispatched a second division in reinforcement, the 35th Infantry Division, which arrived starting on 9 July, ready for the attack on the 11th, to support the 29th Division as Bradley felt that it would take more than one division to capture Saint-Lô. The 35th Division was to advance along the Vire River. The 29th Division had been reorganized by its commander, Maj. Gen. Charles H. Gerhardt, by reinforcing each infantry squad with a tank to take each hedged field. An engineer squad would reinforce each infantry platoon or every three fields (there were three squads to a platoon and so each platoon covered a front three fields long). Also, tanks were fitted with steel bars on the front carrying demolition charges.

Hill 122 was a German stronghold linked to the north of the Carillon position. Maj.Gen. Gerhardt decided to make his effort in the east with the 115th Infantry (Col. Godwin Ordway Jr.) along a broad front to the north and north-east of Hill 122. However Maj.Gen. Gerhardt's plan of attack was spoiled by a diversionary attack launched by the 2nd Parachute Corps in support of the *Panzer-Lehr-Division* attacking west of the Vire (see page 150); a German patrol cut down the 115th Infantry's telephone wires. German artillery and mortars and later two parachute companies overran the 115th's lines, encircling a battalion. At 07.30, having completed their diversionary attack, the German paratroops withdrew but the 115th suffered about a hundred casualties. After reorganizing, the American attack was postponed till that afternoon and was halted by gunfire coming from Hill 122.

In the east however, the 116th Regiment managed to progress slowly behind a powerful artillery barrage towards the Martinville ridge and the tanks knocked out an assault gun by the roadside cross. Six hedgerows were taken in five hours, then the 116th moved forward quickly in the south towards **Martinville ridge** and began to move down on Saint-Lô. So it was here that the main thrust was going to be made, especially after the success on Hill 192. On the evening of 11 July, Maj.Gen. Gerhardt gave Colonel Canham orders "to push on, if possible take St.Lô".

On **12 July**, the 29th Division's attack made little progress; nearly 1,000 men had been lost in two days! Generals Corlett and Gerhardt were by now convinced that Hill 122 had to be captured first; the front was realigned on the 13th and it would be the 35th Division's *objective* while two regiments of the 29th Division (the 115th and the 116th) would carry on their effort on Martinville ridge. On **13 July**, the 35th Division under Maj.Gen. Paul W. Baade resumed their effort on **Hill 122**, now in its third day. The division was inexperienced and fighting in very difficult terrain dotted with hedgerows, and Le Carillon was firmly held. Help finally came in the form of an advance by the 30th Division on the other bank in the Pont-Hébert sector, and on **14 July**, its 137th Infantry lost 125 men and 11 medium tanks, but rounded up 53 prisoners as it gained ground. The joint attacks by all US divisions in the sector finally caused the entire German front to fold up. And the American artillery proved highly effective against dogged and effective German infantry. *KG 352* lost 840 wounded to the artillery in just two days, not counting those killed!

General Meindl was by now extremely concerned over *KG 352*'s plight, as it held the front north of Saint-Lô and might completely collapse at a moment's notice. On **15 July**, the 35th Division pursued its attack and overran the Germans east of Le Mesnil-Rouxelin, now threatening Saint-Georges-Montcoq just two kilometers north of Saint-Lô. Following a deluge of artillery fire with fighter-bombers in support, Hill 122 was finally captured. With their backs to the Vire, the Germans were forced to withdraw in this sector. In the center, the 29th Division made little progress, apart from Major Bingham's 2/116 which reached the Madeleine crossroads east of Saint-Lô (where the Crédit Agricole bank now stands) but the Germans still held Martinville ridge overlooking the sector. Major Bingham's battalion was surrounded.

On **16 July**, 2/116 was still encircled but the German front was exhausted to breaking point. On **17 July**, the left flank of *II. Fallschirmjäger-Korps* collapsed before the 35th Division, possibly the first to enter Saint-Lô, although that honor was reserved for the 29th Division. As early as the morning of **18 July**, Maj.Gen. Corlett ordered Maj.Gen. Gerhardt to dispatch a task force into the town to take control. This task force's commander was Brig. Gen. Cota, who fought well at Omaha Beach, and had been ready for two days. While the German front was withdrawing everywhere to avoid collapse, the Cota Task Force set off north of La Luzerne at 15.10 on **18 July,** arriving in Saint-Lô from the north-east along the Isigny/Saint-Lô road (now the D6 road). 1/115 (Major Johns) joined this task force. At 19.00 hours, the ruined town was in American hands. 2/116 was pulled free. Major Howie, who had attacked on the Martinville ridge with his 3/116, was killed; his men carried his body all the way to Sainte-Croix church in Saint-Lô, and he became known as the "Saint-Lô Major". The 35th Division in turn entered the "capital of the ruins" on **19 July**, relieving the exhausted GIs of the Blue and Grey division. This hardfought victory released the left flank of the First Army, enabling Lt.Gen. Bradley to launch Operation "Cobra".

Sidney V. Bingham. Jr.

The final battle for Saint-Lô, from 11 to 18 July. Areas in blue show advances up to 11 July: in the north facing Le Carillon towards Hill 122 by the 35th Division, in the center, towards Martinville ridge by the 29th Division and in the east, with the capture of Hill 192 by the 2d Division. Notice the position of 2/116 encircled near La Madeleine and the line of penetration of the Cota TF. (US Army. Hist. Dept.)

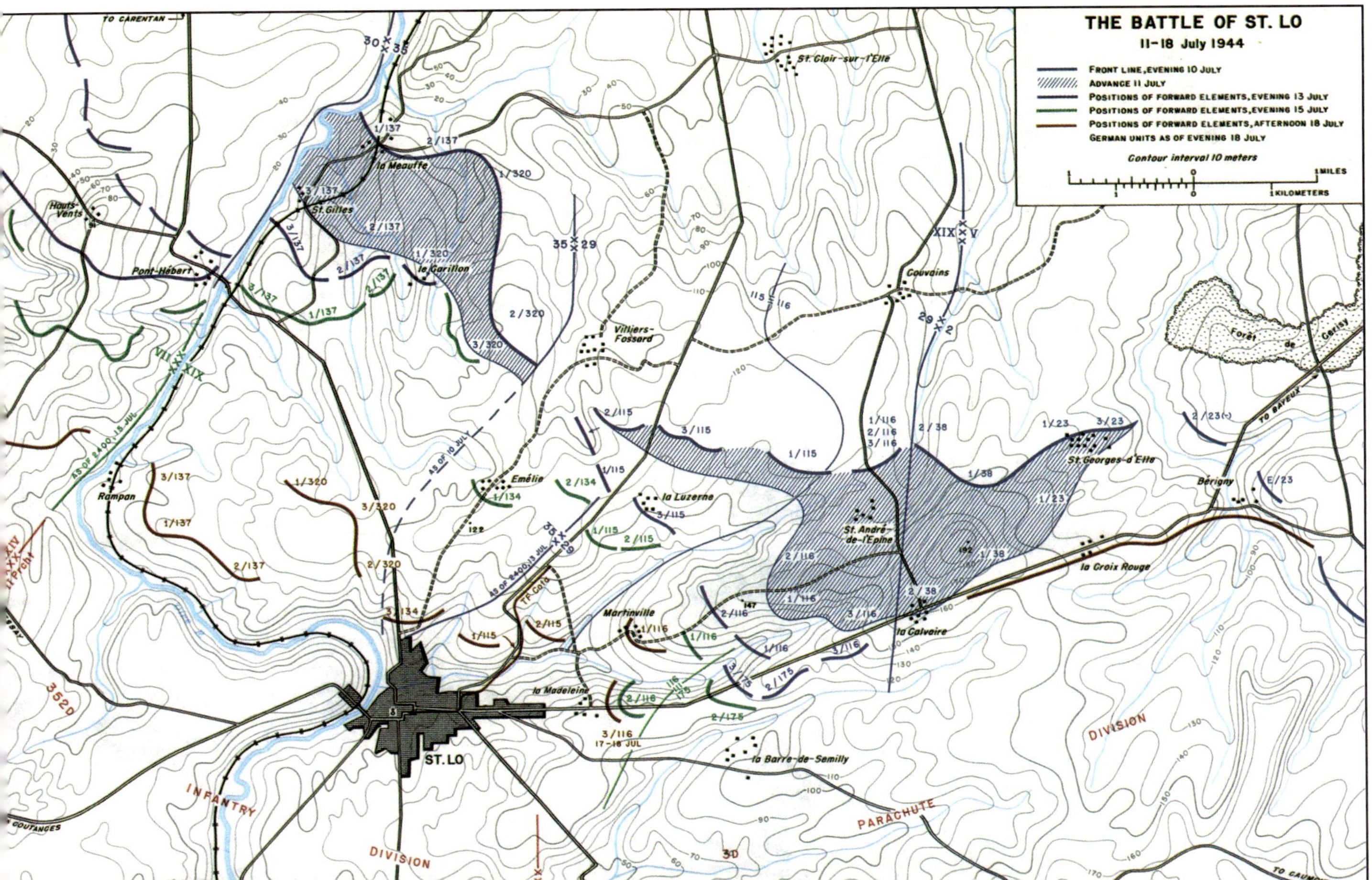

29th Infantry-Division

Hedgerow hell, 6 July.

1. The battle the American troops had to fight in the hedgerows took place at infantry platoon or battalion level. A testing, confused, seemingly never-ending form of combat. An American patrol has surprised a German battalion which has had to leave behind its collective weapon, an MG 42. The GIs now had to neutralize grenadiers concealed among all the vegetation. One of them is dangling his helmet on the end of his rifle to coax the enemy into firing and betraying his whereabouts. An old trick…

2. July 1944, a group of American infantry has been surprised by a German sniper firing on them. They take cover and then prepare to take him out with rifle grenades.

3. Two men of the 29th Infantry Division, notice the divisional badge stencilled on their helmets, race forward along a hedge, with their bayonets at the ready. Two American soldiers have been killed, their bodies can be seen along the hedge on the right side of the road.

4. An American sten gunner armed with an Browning automatic rifle in a position overlooking the Saint-Lô sector. (7161)
(Photographs courtesy Heimdal coll.)

Saint-Lô sector.

1. A front line observation post in the Saint-Lô sector. (7163)

2. Captain William Bouton pokes his gun through one of the German positions admirably camouflaged among the hedges. It has just been captured. Such positions were below ground level and could only be taken by hand-to-hand fighting, using grenades.

3. American infantrymen have just taken another hedge and jump into the shelter of shell craters and positions dug by the Germans.

4. A platoon of American infantry advances along a road, mopping up the entire sector, flushing out German snipers, often a costly operation in terms of men. In the foreground, an American sergeant looks through a gap in the hedge. At his feet lies the body of a German soldier who must have been an MG ammunition server. The box of MG belts he was carrying can be seen. (8116)

5. These soldiers have come under German mortar and machine-gun fire. They have left their jeep and taken cover in the ditch. They then advanced on Saint-Lô which they soon captured.

6. Just north of Saint-Lô, men of the American medical service administer first aid to the wounded. They sometimes operated for 24 hours under artillery fire. Their main problem was bringing in plasma of which large quantities arrived daily from England.

(Photographs courtesy Heimdal coll.)

Saint-Lô sector around 10 July.

1 and **2.** In the midst of the ruins of Saint-Lô, the church of Notre-Dame stands with its two steeples still intact. But the vault of the nave has collapsed under the Anglo-American bombs. These photographs were taken by a German war correspondent barely a week before American troops entered the town.

3. General-Major Richard Schimpf commander of the 3. Fallschirmjäger-Division, a parachute division committed in the Saint-Lô sector, receives a report from a captain under him (left). The general officer is carrying a Fallschirmgewehr 42, a weapon reserved for German paratroopers but issued in very small numbers.

4. Under cover in a trench, a Gefreiter (corporal) with a parachute unit writes a quick letter home. The atmosphere is euphoric during this lull in the fighting for the Marketen have just been distributed, witness the cigars and cigarettes.

5. The German PK has caught the expression of a Fallschirmjäger, a German paratrooper, marked by the tense atmosphere of the battle. With a few ferns around his helmet, his face covered in mud, and rainsoaked jump smock, the man gazes intently at the ground he has been detailed to hold. He is probably an NCO and platoon leader as suggested by the MP 40 clip-holder, holster, and strap of the binocular case appearing under that of the gas mask case.

(Photographs courtesy Bundesarchiv.)

This 3. Fallschirmjäger-Division badge is here worn on Gen. Maj. Schimpf's cap.

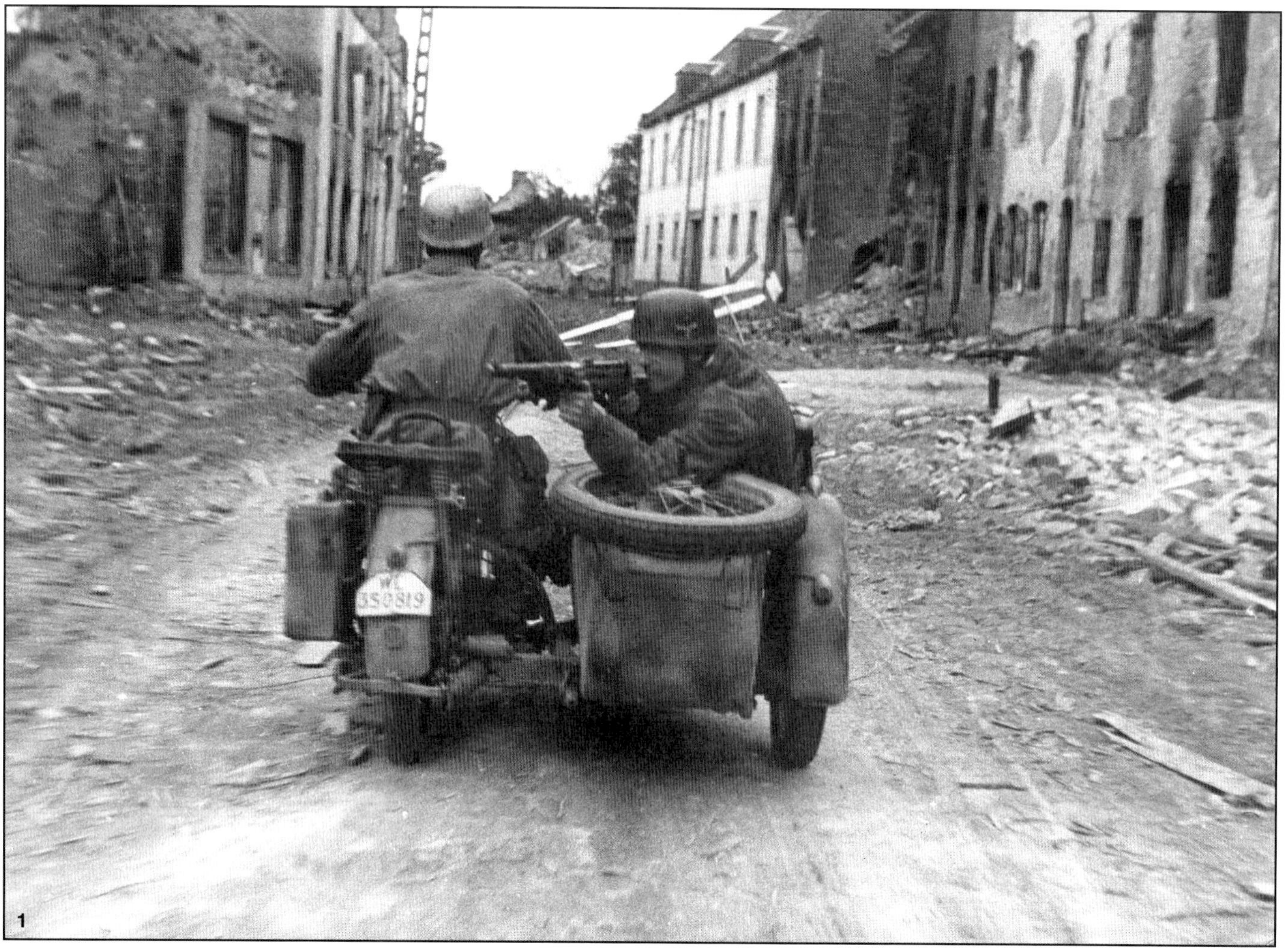

1

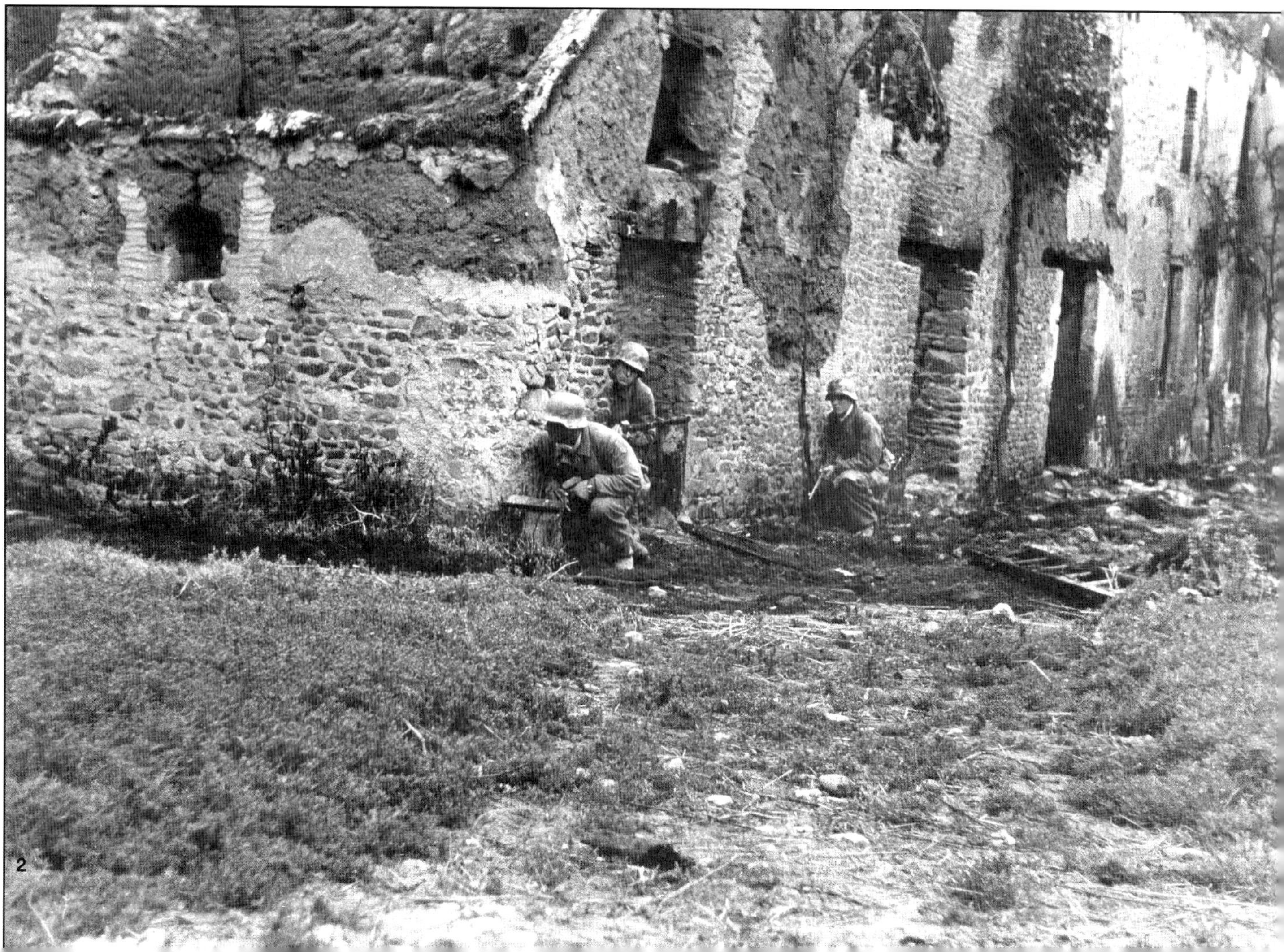
2

German paratroopers in the Saint-Lô sector.

1. A parachute unit's recce or liaison sidecar (the troopers are wearing their characteristic headgear) races through a locality in ruins. The passenger aims his Beretta machine-gun – a souvenir from Italy - towards a hypothetical infiltrated enemy forward element.

2. A patrol dispatched to a burned-down farm stops to take a look. At the corner of the farm wall, the platoon leader, with his P-38 gun at the ready, gives the area to be reconnoitered a careful once-over, in a scene obviously staged for the photographer.

3. A severely wounded man is carried to the dressing station on a makeshift stretcher, just a wooden door. Most of the paratroopers in the battalion wore the all-arms helmet and hiking boots. Only the camouflaged jump smock distinguishes them from other soldiers of the Luftwaffe.

4. For their daytime movements, the military police of the 3. Fallschirmjäger-Division in their Stöwer covered with branches for camouflage, had to scan the sky to watch for Jabos (fighter-bombers) appearing out of the sky spitting death.

(Photographs courtesy Bundesarchiv.)

11-13 July 1944.

1. On 11 July, a Technician 5th Grad brings in his jeep Pvt Vincent Lucas of Braddock, Pennsylvania; he was wounded by a mine and so was taken to the dressing station. Notice the badge of the 29th Division stencilled on the driver's helmet. (7223)

2. Medics bandage another GI who sustained a wrist wound.

3. Pvt Louis A. Mayerski, from Cleveland Ohio, is engrossed in reading his prayer book while sheltering in his foxhole, on 12 July, north-east of Saint-Lô.

4. On 13 July 1944, GIs Allen R. Mitchell (left), of Watertown South Dakota, and Bryant W Gillepsie from Indiana, members of Counter Intelligence Corps (CIC, responsible for interrogating prisoners and all intelligence relating to the enemy) of the 29th Inf.-Div. taking cover in a storeroom at Villiers-Fossard, all the more pleasant a shelter for being lined with barrels filled with cider served up here by Miss Renée Marie.

5. Our two CIC men are now comfortably installed in their storeroom; in the background is one of the GIs' jacket bearing the 29th's patch. (7763)

6, 7, 8. Villiers-Fossard today. All that remains is the bell-tower of the rebuilt church. The small cupboard was probably left by some Germans.

35th ID

13 and 14 July 1944.

1. The 35th Inf.-Div. is now in the line on the 29th's right flank, north of Saint-Lô. Men of this division, belonging to Company A of the 137th Infantry Rgt., take cover from German fire along a column of vehicles of an artillery unit. 14 July 1944.

2. That same day a mortar platoon crew of the 35th US Inf. Div. in action north-west of Saint-Lô. From left to right:
- the loader, Pfc Wilford Clemens, of Wilson, Michigan,
- the gun-layer, Cpl. Denzel Strictling - and the gun captain, S/Sgt. Harold Purdy of Mont Vernon, Ohio. Notice the care taken to protect the position. (7377)

3. The previous day, 13 July 1944, engineers and signallers lay telephone wires along a sunken lane.

4. Near Saint-Lô, 14 July, medics of the 35th US Inf. Div. bring a casualty to a dressing station.

(Photographs courtesy Heimdal collection.)

Hedgerow hell, 11-16 July.

1. This photo shows a detail of the German positions at Le Carillon taken by the GIs. Pictured here is an entrenchment with firing-step in the hedges at this German strongpoint: lookout and gunner emplacement, on the left, and on the right, a tunnel to communicate with the shelter and the nearby field. (Heimdal Coll.)

2. Pvt. Joseph Battaglia resting on 16 July, in a carefully prepared shelter cut in a hedge, well protected and… decorated with the inevitable pinups.

3. In another shelter, obviously captured from the Germans, a GI examines the small library built up by the German soldier who preceded him here. He is browsing a copy of the Das Reich magazine.

4. Each hedge had to be taken one after the other, and the Germans left few prisoners. So this captured corporal made a good subject for the war correspondent.

5. Still more interesting, this German lieutenant gets all the attention of the war correspondents, the one taking the photograph and the other getting out his camera, opposite.

6. In the Saint-Lô sector, the roads are lined with wrecked German vehicles.

7. Advancing also meant clearing the roads of all the debris getting in the way. Between Saint-Lô and Saint-Fromond, on 11 July, to the west of the town, these soldiers are clearing a smashed wall and salvaging material that will be useful for marking out a new road. (7171).

(Heimdal coll and D.F./Heimdal.)

The artillery in action. 16 July 1944.

1. 16 July 1944, Pvt. Nathan Melton of the 35th Inf.-Div. (notice the divisional patch on his sleeve) unpacks a cartridge (powder charge) to prepare a 155 mm shot. This artilleryman belongs to the 4th Gun Sector, Battery B, 127th Field Artillery. During the battle for Saint-Lô this artillery regiment of the 35th Inf.-Div. was committed alongside the 29th Inf.-Div., to its right. (7612)

2. Artilleryman Melton now places the primer in the nose. (7611)

3. The nose is then screwed onto the 155 mm shell (7615)

4. This field artillery position fires on the German lines to cover a night attack by the infantry; the gun pictured here is an M5 76.2 mm (3 inch) anti-tank gun, with the same barrel as on the Tank Destroyer M 10. (7879)

35th Infantry Division

5. The American field artillery pounds the German lines to open up the way to Saint-Lô; this is a 105 mm Howitzer HM2.

(Photographs courtesy Heimdal coll.)

15-18 July 1944.

1. Maj. Gen. Charles H. Gerhardt, commander of the 29th Infantry-Division.

2. Near Saint-Lô on 18 July, Major General Charles H. Gerhardt discusses new assault tactics with staff officer Major William W Bratton.

3. Men of the 175th Infantry Regiment of the 29th dig emplacements behind a hedge on 15 July 1944, shortly before the great offensive on Saint-Lô.

4. A German soldier was killed on 16 July in a well camouflaged trench.

5. A GI, probably of the 35th Inf.-Div., advances near the church at Saint-Georges-Montcocq (north of Saint-Lô), probably on 18 July.

6. The same spot in 1984.

7. On 18 July 1944, medical officer John R. Hines examines a German hand grenade; notice the two German anti-tank mines in front of him. The photograph was taken near Saint-Lô.

(NA and D.F./Heimdal.)

211

In front of Saint-Lô.

1. These soldiers of the 29th Infantry Division advance cautiously into a field in which lies the body of a German soldier.

2. Further on, a medic examines a German with a serious facial wound.

5. These Americans have made a sign to try and get the encircled Germans to surrender.

6. These GIs come under mortar fire at the entrance to Saint-Lô.
(D.F./Heimdal.)

3. Damage caused by a mine on a small road east of Saint-Lô on 20 July. Two four-wheel drives tried to bring ammunition up to a battery. The first vehicle was destroyed by a mine and the engineers were called in at once. The second vehicle, unable to move, waits for a sapper, with his detector, to clear the road, while the other soldiers excavate the ground around the destroyed truck with their knives.

4. Hedges and sunken lanes turned the GIs' advance into sheer hell, with destruction everywhere. This photo was taken on 17 July on Hill 122 overlooking Saint-Lô, on the north side of the town, a vital objective for the 29th Infantry Division.

**18 July 1944.
On the GC 6 road.**

1. Coming from the Couvains crossroads, on the GC 6 (the road from Lison to Saint-Lô), the Cota Task Force attacked with infantry and tanks. In a small lane, the American infantry take cover from artillery fire by German guns in position to the south of the town.

2, 3 and **5.** An American patrol cautiously approaches Saint-Lô guided by a French gendarme, these three photographs are taken from a report by Richard Boyer.

214

4. The Cota Task Force is 700 meters from the first houses of Saint-Lô, a German soldier surrenders.

6 and **7.** A member of the Military Police, Pvt. Arthur Landbish of New York, poses in front of the signpost at the entrance to the much coveted town.

(Photographs courtesy Heimdal coll.)

Saint-Lô sector, 19 July.

1. With an officer looking out, his men leave the shelter of a hedge before advancing.

2. Pictured here is a Weasel Bren carrier used for transporting ammunition or supplies for the 121st Engineer Battalion (Company C, the "C" is painted on the right) 29th Infantry Division. This unit's rallying cry - Let's go! - is marked in chalk in front of this machine known more officially as the "St-Lo Special". More inscriptions can be read, Essayons (in French! – meaning "let's give it a try") or Nihil Timemus (in Latin) immediately translated into English ("we fear nothing"). Young Jim seems to be the name of the driver of this Weasel.

29th ID

3. After final victory on this 19 July, some GIs of the 29th (their badges have been censored) opened the first cafe in Saint-Lô (open the first cafey in St Lô by Cpl Martin owner, operater, No dish warm, waitress wanted).

216

4. Then mail is distributed to the soldiers.

5. East of the positions held by the 29th Infantry Division were those of the 2d Infantry Division. Pictured here are two soldiers of this division at Cerisy-la-Forêt helping a Norman woman to collect water. The man in the center is Staff-Sergeant Bernard Dargols. He was actually a Frenchman living in the USA, where his father had settled for business reasons. At the age of 22, this Parisian joined the US Army and, thanks to his knowledge of France, was assigned to Military Intelligence. This photograph was used on the cover of Yank.

6. Bernard Dargols at a ceremony at Omaha Beach on 6 June 2003.

(D.F./Heimdal and G.B./Heimdal.)

2d ID

19 and 20 July 1944.

1. Armed with an M1 rifle, this American infantryman observes the center of Saint-Lô (notice the imposing ruins of the Post Office), while taking cover from possible German sniper fire.

29th Infantry-Division

2 and **3.** As the Cota Task Force advances towards the center of Saint-Lô, some American infantrymen take a break in front of a German signpost indicating a diversion to bypass the town center. This road from Lison came under German artillery fire, so the Americans called it "88" Alley for the famous German 88 mm gun. A half-track armed with an AA gun (12.7 quadruple machine-gun) covers the roadside. In actual fact, this photo was taken on a small lane running perpendicular. Then, in the second photograph, the advance resumes.

4. A Dodge Command car has just been hit by a German shell and is still burning as American troops enter Saint-Lô.

5. The 29th Inf.-Div.'s reconnaissance vehicles, M8 armored cars, cause congestion in the ruined center of Saint-Lô.

6. The center of Saint-Lô is still under German artillery fire and the men of the 29th race for cover.

(Photographs courtesy Heimdal coll.)

19 July 1944. La Bascule crossroads.

1. Task Force Charlie arrives in Saint-Lô and comes to the La Bascule crossroads where the roads to Bayeux, Isigny and Torigni-sur-Vire and streets from the town center all converge. The troops arrive along with tanks and bear right towards the town center.

2. Major Johns (1st Battalion, the 115th Infantry Regiment) set up his command post in the restaurant on the corner, now flying the gray and blue flag of the 29th. But this CP came under German 88 mm gunfire, opening holes in the wall and destroying Captain Sidney A. Vincent's Tank-Destroyer.

3. We approach the crossroads. The flag raised by Sergeant Davis of Bellefontaine, Ohio, unfurls to reveal the figure "29" embroidered in the middle.

6. A Sherman tank advances through streets piled up with rubble.

4 and **5.** We continue advancing and come to the sign indicating the direction to Isigny; the road on the right which passes in front of the burned down house leads to the Place Sainte-Croix and the town center. (Photographs courtesy Heimdal coll.)

19 and 20 July 1944. Center of Saint-Lô.

1. An American patrol cautiously makes it way down the Rue Saint-Georges searching any houses where German snipers might be concealed.

2. American infantry of the 29th have thrown themselves onto the ground and are crawling to avoid German sniper bullets.

3. Mopping up a house.

29th Infantry-Division

4. The infantry and armor advance along streets strewn with rubble, between the Place Sainte-Croix and the town center.

5. The infantrymen of the 29th have passed the Place Sainte-Croix and are advancing along the Rue du Neufbourg towards the town center.

(Photographs courtesy Heimdal coll.)

1. US infantry of the 29th advance through Saint-Lô, probably in the Rue du Neufbourg, passing in front of an American anti-tank gun destroyed by German fire.

2. Amid the ruins of the devastated town, a GI of the 29th has just rounded up three German prisoners; two of them have lost their jackets and boots.

3. A German sergeant has been wounded in the leg and captured.

4. He is now loaded aboard a half-track on his way to an American field hospital. The vehicle probably belongs to the 13th Cavalry Group temporarily assigned to the 29th from 18-20 July 1944.

5. On being placed on board the half-track, this German sergeant grimaces with pain from his wound. With these three photographs (their 1944 code numbers are respectively as follows: Eto-hq-44 8226, 8230, 8231) came a full report. (Photographs courtesy Heimdal coll.)

1 and **2.** On 17 July Major Howie, commander of the 3rd Battalion, the 116th Infantry Regiment, told his men: "See you in Saint-Lô!". He was killed shortly afterwards by a mortar shell exploding near him when he was at La Madeleine crossroads east of Saint-Lô (where a Crédit Agricole branch bank now stands). His men brought his body right into town and placed it on the ruins of a side aisle at Sainte-Croix church. In the foreground, two soldiers of the 29th are in position in a bomb crater to man a Browning machine-gun.

3 and **4.** The body of Major Thomas D. Howie has been placed on blocks of stone dislodged during the bombardment of Sainte-Croix church. The Major's body has been draped in a US flag with flowers around it. Major Howie passed into posterity as the legendary "Major of Saint-Lô".

5, 6, 7, 8, 9, 10, 11. It was in the cemetery, and more specifically in the Blanchet family burial vault, north-east of the Carrefour de la Bascule crossroads, that Major Johns had his command post after 19 July. (8348)

12, 13, 14. The impacts are still visible.

15. This GI has inscribed the butt of his Garand rifle with the words "Cry baby!" with the dry humor then appreciated by many American soldiers. The scene is in the town center in a cellar where a telephone exchange has been set up.

(DAVA and E.G./Heimdal.)

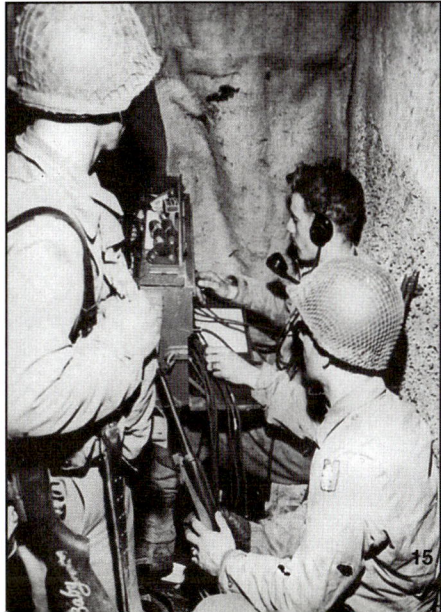

The Americans at Saint-Lô, 19 July.

1. This light Stuart tank, reinforced with sand bags on the front, passes through the center of Saint-Lô between two broken gas pumps. It is coming from the Carrefour de la Bascule crossroads into a less badly hit neighborhood.

2. A little further on, towards the upper town, this German armored reconnaissance vehicle was knocked out, obviously during the terrific bombardment. It is a Schwerer Panzerspähwagen (8 Rad) (Sd.Kfz 231). This was an eight-wheeled armored reconnaissance vehicle carrying a crew of four and armed with a 2 cm KwK 30 and a MG 34 gun. It had a consumption of 45 to 50 liters per 100 kilometers (c.5 miles to the gallon).

3. This photograph is something of a symbol of the 29th Infantry Division's battle for Saint-Lô, which took a month and twelve days of fierce fighting to reach. Pictured in the background is the church of Notre-Dame which still has one of its two steeples intact (the spire was destroyed by German artillery a few days later). On the left, behind the Sherman, notice the upper section of the ruins of the law courts and the prison. The tank bears the name of "Hun chaser" (the Germans earned this nickname from Attila's tribe of invaders a thousand years ago).

4. The upper town emerges from the ruins; the rubble had to be cleared to let traffic through.

5. Between the upper town and the Vire river, a German soldier lies amid the rubble.

(D.F./Heimdal.)

229

Saint-Lô after the battle, late July.

1. On 29 July, vehicles pass at the foot of the upper town on the left, on their way to the front, west of the Vire (to the right of the building in ruins). (9001)

2. Columns of ambulances and transport vehicles move up to the front, passing through the ruins of Saint-Lô. (9837)

3. But US engineers are already at work with their machinery clearing the streets blocked by debris; reinforcements and supplies had to pass through Saint-Lô on their way to the front. (8991)

4. At the foot of the rocky plateau of the upper section of Saint-Lô, this photo was taken at the same time as photo n° 1. (9000)

5. To the west of central Saint-Lô, between the upper town and the Vire river, US army vehicles ply up and down the devastated streets. (9003)

6. In the same sector as the previous photo, pictured again in this contemporary color photograph is the corner tower dominating the valley from the rock on which stands the upper town. Master Rear on the sign was the First Army's codename. This code was used to designate the formation's HQ. All units in a corps had a codename, down to battalion level.

(Photographs courtesy US Army and NA/Heimdal.)

1. Bypassing the upper town of Saint-Lô on the north side, this American column overlooks the Dollée valley which has been crushed by bombs and turned into an apocalyptic landscape. The debris has blocked the course of the Dollée, forming a small lake. This lunar landscape made such an impression that it was photographed many times over and came to symbolize the destruction of Saint-Lô. The jeeps are coming from the east on their way down to the Dollée valley passing at the foot of the upper town.

2. This color photograph taken in the summer of 1944 helps to realize the scale of the destruction and the size of the lake created by the overflowing Dollée, dammed up by the pile-up of debris. The road at the foot of the upper town has been cleared and is being used by columns of vehicles bypassing the city via the north on their way south.

3. This other color photograph was taken looking north towards the Dollée valley. The jeep here is heading eastwards up the road, in the opposite direction from the jeep pictured in photo n° 1.

4. This other color photograph was taken looking north shows the "lake" overlooked by seriously damaged old houses of the Dollée nieghborhood.

(Photograph courtesy NA/Heimdal and DR.)

The Dollée nieghborhood.

1. Since the remaining bell-tower of the church of Notre-Dame, the Dollée valley presents a spectacle of desolation; the blocked river form a small lake in the medium of ruins.

2. We see here the ruins of the building already seen in the previous photo, the Prefecture, then located above the Dollée.

3. The small lake formed by the Dollée river with the Pont-Hébert/Carentan road in the background.

4. Another view of the Dollée valley looking to the right from the upper town.

5. Looking leftwards towards the lane leading to the Pont-Hébert road. Photos n°s 3 and 4 were taken in 1945, a year later; with the area still in total desolation, civilians had to pass through these fields of ruins.

(Photo n° 1 : La Manche Libre coll.; photo n° 2: DR.; photos n°s 3, 4, 5: Heimdal coll.)

The Dollée valley.

1. At the foot of the upper town, from the Dollée valley, this color photograph taken in the summer of 1944 pictures the upper town, its ramparts, the church of Notre-Dame with its truncated tower, and the ruined Prefecture building on the right.

2. At the same spot, American convoys raise clouds of dust as they take the road across the Dollée.

3 and **4.** From the same spot, towards the right, more views of the ruins including the Prefecture. Photo n° 4 was taken by photographer Heinrich Hoffmann on 16 June when the Germans still held the town, which was already completely destroyed by the terrific bombardment of 6 June. The Germans used this photograph as a propaganda picture, with the caption "hundreds of French people are buried under the ruins of their houses".

(NA and Heimdal.)

1. An aerial shot of Saint-Lô taken taken at 400 feet on 28 July 1944. The photograph was taken from the south-west and pictures the Vire river and, east of it, the ruins of the town center.

2. On this other, very clear aerial photograph, taken from the south, we can see the Vire with that all-important bridge, and the station on the left, on the west bank. Above the major crossroads of the Place des Alluvions, the upper town rises up out of the ruins to overlook a field of rubble. The mutilated church of Notre-Dame remains a key landmark.

3. Again from the south, looking north, the upper town emerges with the Dollée valley in the background, and the road to Pont-Hébert.

4. At the foot of the rock on which stands the upper town, American vehicles come onto the Place des Alluvions to turn right to take the bridge over the Vire.

(NA, Heimdal and DR.)

Saint-Lô, "Capital of the ruins".

1. An aerial shot of the upper town of Saint-Lô, on the right is Notre-Dame church which has just lost its second steeple. All the upper town around the church has been reduced to a vast expanse of rubble. Pictured in the top left are the Vire and the station.

2. An American patrol advances, on 26 July, inside the ruined church of Notre-Dame.

3. Ruins of the façade of Saint-Lô's Notre-Dame church when the 355th Engineers arrived.

4. The ruined façade with its collapsed tower.

5 and **6.** The ruins of Notre-Dame church, seen looking west from the choir towards the collapsed façade, this photograph was taken in the opposite direction from photo n° 2.

7. Another view of the interior of the ravaged nave.

8. Color photo taken in 1944, showing the church amid the ruins, facing west.

(NA and Heimdal coll.)

Saint-Lô. Ruins of the upper town.

1 and **2.** The Saint-Lô law courts were smashed in the bombardments, the then adjoining prison collapsing and killing its inmates.

3. A year on, the ruins of the law courts were still as they had been, there were plans to preserve them as a "monument to the ruins", but in the end only a small section was preserved.

4. Pictured here is the post office, devastated in the initial D-day bombardment, which caused many civilian victims.

5. Looking eastwards from the bell-tower of Notre-Dame church, the ruins of the upper town. The law courts are in the middle, on the left the ruins of the Prefecture and the post office. In the background is the stud farm.

6. Unusual color photograph taken at the same spot in 1944.

7 and **8.** The ruins of the prison preserved as a memorial, today, with the list of victims.

(NA and E.G./Heimdal.)

244

Saint-Lô, the "devastated upper town".

1. This photo was taken from the still standing tower of Notre-Dame church, and pictures, on the left, the Rue Torteron, the Hospital (or Alluvions) crossroads, la Vaucelle.

2. Color photo taken at the same spot in 1944.

3 and **4.** This other photograph, taken from the tower of Notre-Dame, looks further to the right and pictures the Place des Beaux-Regards, the Rue Thiers and the Rue Dame Denise. The whole neighborhood has since been entirely rebuilt, and the new Prefecture was built there. Further down is the station, with the Institution Saint-Lô d'Agneaux in the background. The second photo is a close-up view with a German signpost.

5. Pictured from the plateau south of the Rue Torteron are the ruins of the upper town dominated by the mutilated church of Notre-Dame.

6. The upper town is awash with an ocean of rubble with, standing in the middle, the single tower of Notre-Dame church which survived the storm.

(Photographs courtesy La Manche Libre Coll. and NARA/Heimdal.)

The ruined upper town of Saint-Lô.

1. This photograph was taken facing north-west from halfway up the tower of Notre-Dame church, and pictures the ruins of the houses lining the north side of the church square. A huge bomb crater has been marked off in the middle of the square.

2. This second photograph was taken facing in the opposite direction. The large section of wall on the right is the western side of the one in the middle of the previous picture.

3. The Rue des Prés is nothing but burned-out ruins. What had taken generations to build was destroyed in a few hours.

4. This photo was taken facing westwards from a good way further back than photo n° 1. Pictured on the left is the east end and north side of Notre-Dame church (along which the outside pulpit can be made out). The ruined gable, way in the background, is the same as the one pictured on the right in photo n° 1.

5. The chaos of ruins near the church of Notre-Dame. One can guess what a tragedy it was for civilians caught in this nightmare.

6. Through the ruins of a movie theater.

7. This building was occupied by the Wehrmacht as marked by the sign swung over the door.

8. In this gutted house, smashed beds and the cooker can still be seen hanging in midair next to the fireplace.

9. At the end of the upper town, overlooking the station, this is the only house where there was any furniture still unbroken.

(NA - La Manche Libre and DR and Heimdal coll., photo n[os] 4 to 9 were vetted by the SHAEF censor on 1 August 1944.)

The Rue Torteron and the Dollée.

1. This other color photograph from 1944 pictures the Rue Torteron, which passes along the foot of the upper town, on its southern slope, turning our backs to the Vire river to face east. Standing out from the flat upper town is what remains of one of the two towers of Notre-Dame church. In the background is a cedar also pictured in the next photograph.

2. Still in the Rue Torteron, a little further on, is the cedar which served as a landmark amid this scene of desolation.

3. The same spot, facing the other way. Notice the intact upper town house already pictured in photo 1.

4. View from above onto the Rue Torteron from the upper town.

5. And now on the other side, on the northern slope, the road located between the upper town on the left and the Dollée. Agneaux college can be seen in the background.
(US Army/NA Heimdal and DR.)

Saint-Lô. The station. A bunker, 29 July.

1. Like all rail junctions, Saint-Lô station came under Allied aircraft attack. This photograph taken on 29 July 1944 shows the railroad churned up by the bombs. (9007)

2. The station depot has been devastated, and the platforms and lines are strewn with debris. (9008)

3. Pan shot showing the station, the rail lines and platforms devastated by bombs. The station was completely rebuilt.

4. The station seen from the upper town.

5. Outside view of a German control bunker we shall be seeing again in photo n° 7. (25854)

6. Interior of a German bunker at Saint-Lô showing quartering and telephone installations which were sabotaged before the Germans left. (8994)

7. Another view of an abandoned German bunker.

(DAVA and D.F./Heimdal.)

Civilian victims at Saint-Lô.

Saint-Lô came under bombardment as of D-day. At around 16.30 on Tuesday 6 June, the first bombs fell on the station. A few hours later, at 20.00 hours, fourteen Flying Fortresses flew over the town and dropped their bombs haphazardly, hitting various neighborhoods. More and more people began to move out but already there were many dead and injured lying under the rubble. During the night of 6-7 June, the destruction continued at midnight, at 3 and again at 5 am. Planes in their hundreds continued to wreak death and destruction. At dawn, Saint-Lô was reduced to one huge blazing inferno. Over five hundred bodies of local people were pulled out of the debris, with a similar number reported missing. It is estimated that out of a then population of some 10,000 inhabitants over eight hundred were killed in these bombing raids.

1. This photograph, showing the last mutilated bell-tower of the church of Notre-Dame at Saint-Lô surrounded by crows as night falls symbolizes the terrible tragedy suffered by the town.

2. This photograph taken by the Germans before the final battle pictures the devastated Rue Torteron looking towards Agneaux and its college visible in the background.

3, 4, 5, 6, 7 and **8.** Close to the church of Sainte-Croix, graves of civilian casualties during the bombardments testify to the horror the town went through. Successively, in these few examples:
- bones in the Rue de la Poterne; - bones in the Rue de la Marne; - bones at the hospital; - girl, gendarmerie; - Madame Marie Marguerite, presumedly; - human remains in the Rue Dame Denise…

9. These civilian victims, women and children of Saint-Lô, were more fortunate. They are leaving the shelter where they had sought refuge during the bombardments - photo taken on 26 July. (8662)

(Photographs courtesy DR, Heimdal coll. and E.G./Heimdal.)

253

8

Preparation of Cobra (15 to 23 July)

For Operation "Cobra", four armored divisions were thrown into the battle. Pictured here is a Sherman of the 69th Tank Battalion, 6th Armored Division advancing along a lane in Normandy among the hedgerows. This photo was taken on 1 July when its leading elements had just come ashore; it was at full strength in Normandy by mid-July, shortly before "Cobra". For the breakout it was the armored division farthest to the west, in the Lessay sector, racing along the coast. This countryside was representative of this area – narrow lanes lined with a very dense network of hedgerows. It prevented units from being deployed but it was very useful for bringing up reinforcements to the front and for attacking in several different directions at once. (DAVA/ Heimdal.)

For the American infantryman, these two weeks of combat in the bocage of the Cotentin, in the first half of July, were pretty demoralizing. The capture of Saint-Lô on 19 July added the finishing touch to the *1st Army* offensive launched on 2 July enabling it to establish a starting base on the Lessay/Caumont-l'Eventé line, before launching a further, even more decisive offensive.

But the offensive of General Bradley's *1st Army*, lining up a dozen divisions, made inroads of only about 7 miles (11 kilometers) west of the Vire River and only led to the Germans falling back onto a new line. This retreat was carried out in orderly fashion on the 13th with no indication of the German front facing imminent collapse. In gaining this 11 kilometer-wide zone, the *1st Army* lost 40,000 men (killed, wounded and missing) the vast majority of whom were infantry (90% of these losses). By the end of the offensive, certain infantry companies were down to the strength of an overstrength platoon. In his history of the 329th IR, 83rd, one of the "surviving" veterans, Raymond J. Goguen, wrote, "We won the battle of Normandy (but) considering the high price in American lives, we lost." This war of the hedgerows being a partitioned war carried out by small groups of infantry directed by subalterns who had to stay offensive-minded all the time, there were huge numbers of casualties among the officers, which posed a serious leadership problem. This leadership problem was, paradoxically, only made worse by the problem of infantrymen coming up in reinforcement to fill the gaps. After some "initial wavering", the American infantry divisions that had fought amid the hedgerows for two weeks (8th, 90th, 83rd ID), were now battle-hardened with plenty of experience. But the arrival of the rookies to bring them back up to strength, meant that there were again a large number of inexperienced troops. It must be remembered that a motorized division involves considerable logistics and many technicians such as drivers, suppliers, telephone operators and cooks. An American infantry division of 15,000 men that had lost 4,700 men in twelve days (83rd Inf.Div.) or 2,300 men in ten days (4th Inf.Div.) would be down to one third or two thirds (respectively) of its fighting forces bearing in mind that these represent only about half of total numbers, i.e. around 7,500 men. The same went for the German army; when an armored division like the *"Panzer-Lehr-Division"* was already reduced to half strength as of 10 July, this meant that there was not much left of its infantry and so to keep it in the front line was only possible by "transforming" into infantrymen drivers, telephone operators, secretaries, cooks and other members in the service units, or even tank crews who had run out of tanks to use. Paradoxically, this terrible loss of fighting men on both sides led to very different results:

- the Americans very often replaced 100% of casualties sustained by their divisions and had full strength divisions ready in the front line when the next offensive came; a ten-day break (15 - 25 July) was used to bring up these reinforcements. But this massive influx of young recruits brought down the military worth dearly acquired by the units in the front line. These young recruits were quickly dispatched to a sector of the front where they had no opportunity to get to know their commanders and where they saw very little of their comrades (given the highly partitioned battlefield); they proved an obstacle to blending units into coherent formations, with the "team spirit" that was so crucial to building up their offensive-mindedness.

- the Germans saw their front line units bled white, with most of their divisions reduced to the fighting strength of a regiment or even a battalion (by 17 July only 12% of their losses had been made up - see our paragraph on German casualties). But paradoxically, although these were already very good quality divisions on going up to the front line, the stout resistance put up by the "survivors" - in spite of the appalling losses - is explainable by the close friendship and spirit of camaraderie of the German fighting troops, who had known each other since the hard months of training and who had suffered long weeks together in the firing line. A German grenadier or tank crew member died for his comrades rather than "for the Führer". Phrases keep cropping up in these men's recollections like: "if I give myself up, my comrades in the troop or platoon next to us will get killed". One should also note that a crack division like the *"Götz von Berlichingen"* was partly formed from Germans from Romania who had thus never lived in the Reich and so had not received the usual brainwashing. The recruits, very often of average quality, by no means hand-picked, were transformed by their team spirit or loyalty to their unit. This attitude characterized all the crack units (paratroopers, Rangers, tank units, commandos, etc.) and frequently transformed a very ordinary person into a top class soldier. In addition to this "total solidarity with one's comrades", another factor explains why the German troops fought so fiercely in the front line.

The fighting efficiency of the German arms was due first and foremost to the quality of its leadership. Germany had the best body of officers (this was nothing new and was already the case in 1914) and an excellent body of NCOs. Its equipment was excellent (especially the tanks), superior in quality although inferior in quantity. It was operated by tough and skilful fighting troops with vast experience. Martin Blumenson (op. cit. p. 177) notes how good the German troops were, except for the *"Osttruppen"*. The regular Wehrmacht units were not invincible but resisted well while the *Waffen-SS* and the paratroops were crack troops with unshakable morale who asked for no quarter and certain gave none (according to a conversation between Corlett and Gerhardt). The Germans made skilful use of the terrain, mounting local counter-attacks with local reserves supported by a few tanks, and similarly skilful use of their machine-guns and mortars to support their strongpoints.

So the GIs were up against a formidable enemy and no less formidable terrain. Being surrounded by the hedgerows of the Bocage created a feeling of oppression. You felt cut off from the rest of the world, cut off from America, from England, from everything familiar, in a country devastated by war, backward almost, with tarmacked roads, electricity and running water still something of a rarity. Most of the roads turned into muddy quagmires whenever it rained - and it rained a lot during that summer of 1944 - or raised clouds of dust in the hot sun. In such conditions, there were numerous cases of "combat fatigue" (exhaustion, nervous breakdown due to fighting conditions). Most of the men suffering from combat fatigue spent 24 to 72 hours resting in a field hospital and were then sent back to their units; the most serious cases were evacuated. In addition to casualties, 25 to 30% of the men treated in the field hospitals were combat fatigue cases. But there were many more casualties with shrapnel wounds. Although the German artillery could fire a lot fewer rounds than the Allies (on 10 July, on the British front, the British fired 80,000 shells when the Germans could only manage 4,500), in the American sector it aimed them with terrifying accuracy. Otto Weidinger (in his history of the "Das Reich" Division, T 5, p. 232) notes that it had 132 pieces of ordnance to support his *"Kampfgruppe"* at the time of its counter-attack against La Haye-du-Puits on 8 July; there was the artillery of the *"Das Reich"* (32 guns), a troop of the *"Götz"* (12 guns) and various troops of the infantry units in the sector (7 troops). It also had a battalion of 150 mm rocket launchers *(SS-Werfer-Abt. 2)*; each one had 6 guns, the unit represented 108 extra guns, i.e. a total of 240 guns committed against Maj.Gen. Middleton's VIII Corps. The sky also seems to have leagued against the Allied offensive. It was the most appalling weather seen since the start of the century. While the rain and low cloud meant 50% less action than planned – the German forces nevertheless came in for a terrific amount of devastation. The mud and rain meant the men could not dry out or warm themselves, caught in the thick hedgerows. The disillusioned GIs likewise could see no end to the adventure, saying: "We could see the war lasting for twenty years".

But the American army was undoubtedly the best component of the Allied front line in Normandy. It suffered from two weak points to start with: - initial lack of experience of most units (the British fighting man was generally more experienced), - the lack of ideological motivation of the fighting troops. On this last point, we gathered the testimony of the Rangers historian, Lieutenant-Colonel Lane, and of a veteran, Lieutenant Allsup. The naturally isolationist mindset of the American citizen, and being so far from home made it hard to motivate the GI in this campaign for freedom, even for the Jewish soldier, although more closely concerned. Some forceful propaganda sought to motivate the American fighting forces. As it turned out, motivation was not long in coming once in Normandy, with the first bloodshed and the first comrade killed. The GI had much to learn but he learned it fast. The 83rd I.D., which fought poorly when first committed, became battle-hardened within days. After two days of engagements, the men had become veterans. Without having the experience of the German soldier, the American fighter was almost his equal in courage, a reckless courage seen in the scale of casualties, at this stage 50% higher than British losses.

The GI had a very a limited view of the battlefield from behind his hedge. He faced a still formidable and offensive-minded enemy who had just fallen back onto a new line of defense and felt it was going to take him another fortnight of fighting to push the Germans back to a new line, a dozen kilometers further on, and that many more of his comrades were going to fall all around him, and so on. Readers will readily recall the picture of the victorious American armored columns advancing in August 1944, and imagine the GI with rifle slung, advancing unopposed. The fact of the matter lies in the huge sacrifices made by the US infantry. As we have seen, the American divisions were kept up to full strength by the continual injection of reinforcements, thus hiding the terrible reality. By the end of 1944, on reaching the border with the Reich, after a seven-month campaign in Europe, statistically the American infantryman had a much better chance of being killed or wounded than of finishing the war on his feet. It was not unusual to find infantry regiments in which all the men had been replaced one and a half times over… the terrible reality was rain, mud and death in the hedgerows.

However, there was a reality unknown to the ordinary GI but known to the top commanders. Although objectives had only been partly achieved and Saint-Lô was still under German artillery fire on 20 July, Lt.Gen. Bradley knew that the Germans were exhausted and making one last desperate stand. So tactically he made the right move. He attacked on all sides with the whole corps to escape the trap of the hills around La Haye-du-Puits and the endless swamps that cut the terrain into narrow strips. He finally left the trap behind him, the worst terrain of the entire Normandy battlefield. And especially, by launching an all-out offensive, he literally wore out the German front along its entire length, bringing up to the front line all the reserves that the Germans wanted to hold back to counter a breakthrough. The *"Das Reich"* Division, called up from the south-west to be used as operational reserve, was finally committed in various *"Kampfgruppen"* from 7 to 13 July (*"KG Weidinger"* in the west and *"KG Wisliceny"* in the east) before being put en bloc in the front line. The 5th Parachute Division (Wilke) was disbanded; its 15th Regiment was committed on Mont Castre on 5 July while the 13th Regiment (commanded by Count von der Schulenburg) was thrown into the battle on 10 July in the Champs-de-Losque sector against the Saint-Fromond bridgehead. This division was down to one parachute regiment (the 14th) and its artillery regiment. It was the same for *275. Infanterie-Division* (General Schmidt) which arrived from Saint-Nazaire; it had already lost one unit early in June (*"Kampfgruppe Heintz"*), one of its regiments was committed in the Lessay sector in mid-July (along with the 91st). Thus, three powerful divisions (including two elite divisions) were split up to plug the immediate gaps. And while the Americans suffered very heavy losses, German losses were dramatic insofar as there was no-one to step in the breach. From 6 June to 9 July, losses for the entire German front in Normandy were: - 150 Panzer IVs, 85 "Panther" tanks, 15 "Tiger" tanks (making a total of 250 tanks), 167 75 mm guns (assault and anti-tank guns), 30 88 mm guns; this represents more equipment than needed to fit out an armored division (according to OB West KTB on 10/7). But the losses in men were even more worrying: from 6 June to 11 July, the German army lost 87,000 men in Normandy (including 2,000 officers). The division by division casualty figures speak volumes:

- over 8,000 men for *243. ID*, around 8,000 men for *352. ID*, over 6,000 men for *716. ID*, 4,485 men for *12. SS-Pz.-Div.* , 3,411 men for *21. Panzer-Division* (according to OB West KTB on 12/7). Allied losses were about the same, **61,549 men** (39,341 Americans and 22,208 British) up to **10 July** and **96,728 men** up to **19 July** (62,028 Americans and 34,700 British). The sharp increase in American losses between 10 and 19 July is explained by the sacrifices made during the capture of Saint-Lô. The significant difference between American and British casualties shows the greater effort made by the Americans and the heavy price paid for lack of experience. In particular, the losses incurred by the tactics of Lt.Gen. Bradley in attacking along the entire front (contrary to the method use by Generals Montgomery and Dempsey in the British sector, involving the mounting of limited operations easily countered by the German defenses). Bradley's tactics paid better dividends.

Indeed, with American losses on one side, the German casualties on the other had General von Choltitz saying that the "battle of the hedgerows is a monstrous bloodbath" (Telecom. to General Max Pemsel of 7th Army, 15 July 23.50). By **17 July** German losses had risen to **100,000 men** (including 2,360 officers). Losses were about even on either side as the Allies caught up two days later; so, theoretically, the GI was right; this was a return to the war of attrition that characterized the First World War. The great difference lay in the reconstitution of these forces. While the Allies were able to maintain 100% strength, owing to difficulties bringing recruits up to the front or of not having them in the first place, by **12 July**, the Germans had only brought up 5,210 men, a 6% loss replacement rate, with another 7,500 others promised or on the way, i.e. a further 9 %, making a total of **just 15%.**

Lt.Gen. Bradley knew this. He knew that the German front might crumble. On 10 July, his army emerged from the trap of the marshes: Montgardon and La Haye-du-Puits had fallen, Sainteny would fall the next day, the Saint-Fromond bridgehead was secure. Within a few days, he would have his start line from Lessay to Saint-Lo, from which to launch his great offensive. The plan was hatched on 11 July. It became the 1st Army plan on **13 July** (the day of the German withdrawal!). It took the name of a snake which uncoils the better to strike its prey: **"Cobra"**.

This was the scheme to escape the trap of the war becoming bogged down in Normandy, the idea of a "Breakthrough". To move on from the "static period" several possibilities had been aired: - that of a secondary amphibious operation in Brittany to take Brest and Quiberon, but there were only four divisions available for what would have been a risky operation; - an airborne operation, but there were not enough aircraft, as a good number were mobilized for the upcoming landing in Provence. In late June, Monty decided that the entire front should swing round with Caumont the hinge. The *objective* of the offensive was Brittany and its ports. But it was Lt.Gen. Bradley who had the idea of a "massive blow" in front of VII Corps to rip through the German front and break out so as to envelop part of the front and the forces in it.

The "Cobra" plan

Inside twelve days, the "Cobra" plan was worked out by General Bradley and carried out by General Collins, whose corps spearheaded the operation. At this stage, it was merely a matter of making a breakthrough, of gaining much more ground at a single stroke ensuring a still better starting base for a second thrust towards Brittany. This operation might also make it possible to encircle and destroy the German forces facing the VIII Corps, as well as those facing the VII Corps. US Officers Intelligence reported to Bradley and Collins that the enemy forces numbered no more than 17,000 (barely the strength of a German division although in theory eight or nine were represented on the front line, which gives an idea of the strength of each...) and less than 100 tanks. Odds of at least five to one in favor of the Americans! However, it was possible that the Germans, who were very quick to reform the front lines in times of crisis, might contrive to withdraw some of their forces. They had a string of three opportunities to do so: - along the line Coutances/Canisy (highly unlikely, considering the plan), - in the Gavray sector (this was actually attempted), - near Avranches (the Mortain offensive tried to re-establish this line). But intelligence reports showed the weakness of the German front and the lack of reserves. All this was true enough but, as usual, it underestimated the Germans' energy and moral fibre capable of holding a front in the worst conditions. Despite the plan's relatively limited goal (Coutances, Gavray or Avranches), some had dreams of a broad penetration into the rest of France, the **"Breakout"**; for now, it was just a **"Breakthrough"** with Lt.Gen. Collins hoping to be in Avranches within the week.

To launch this offensive, the 1st Army now had a number of advantages. The infantry had gained experience of fighting against tanks. The bazooka taught the GI that he was not entirely helpless against these steel monsters. The partitioned terrain meant short range combat and the German tanks lost the edge they would otherwise have had with longer range guns than the Sherman. Lastly, as of 5 July, the 79th Inf.Div. designed a "hedgecutter", improved by Sergeant Curtis G. Culin Jr. of the 102d Cavalry Reconnaissance Squadron. This was a set of teeth fitted onto the front of the tanks to cut through the hedges. They were made from German beach obstacles, in plentiful supply along the coast. These tanks were called "Rhinoceroses", then just "Rhinos". The 23rd Armored Engineer Bn. (3rd Armored Division, commanded by Lieutenant-Colonel Lawrence G. Foster) also claimed to have invented the hedgecutter. At the start of "Cobra", three out of five tanks were fitted with the device, but for tactical surprise, Lt.Gen. Bradley forbade their use in advance of the operation.

The landscape, where the offensive started out, was firm terrain, quite different from the marshy areas the 1st Army had just extricated itself from. But it was undulating country still with plenty of hedgerows. However, the sector had a good road network to facilitate operations. The major roads took two way traffic and were tarmacked (fairly unusual for the time). There were two straight highways running parallel to the front line: - the Saint-Lô/Périers/Lessay road which was to be used as the start line although still mostly in German hands, - the Saint-Lô/Coutances road. And there were highways running north-south along which the units of the VII Corps could make deep inroads: - the Saint-Gilles/Canisy road (in the east), - the Marigny/Carantilly road (further west). And there were major crossroads at Coutances, Marigny, Saint-Gilles, Le Mesnil-Herman and Notre-Dame-de-Cenilly.

There were by now plenty available American **troops**. Before "Cobra", four armored divisions and four infantry divisions were brought in in reinforcement. General Bradley's 1st Army now had four corps and fifteen divisions. One corps, General Collins' VII Corps, was substantially reinforced because it was to spearhead the attack. So we have, from west to east: - **VIII Corps** under Maj.Gen. Middleton, freshly reinforced by three divisions (two armored and one infantry), it had, from west to east **79th ID** (Wyche), **8th ID** (Stroh), **90th ID** (Landrum), **4th AD** (Wood), **83rd ID** (Macon) and one armored division in reserve, the **6th AD** - Maj.Gen. Collins's **VII Corps** aligned from west to east **9th ID** (Eddy), **4th ID** (Barton - his division came in support of the 9th and 30th, sorely tested in the fighting of the previous days), and **30th ID** (Hobbs); **1st ID** was detached from V Corps to lend support, and its presence was to remain a secret until the offensive was launched; two armored divisions, **3rd AD** ("Spearhead") and **2d AD** ("Hell on wheels") were to rush into the breach. - **XIX Corps** (Corlett) was down to just one division, **35th ID**, 29th ID having been withdrawn exhausted from the front at Saint-Lô. - **V Corps** (Gerow) since the transfer of 1st ID was reduced to two divisions, **2d** and **5th ID**. XIX and V Corps only played a secondary role. Notice how the two corps in the west each had two armored divisions. They were responsible for crushing the German front. But the gap was to be opened up in front of Collins' VII Corps, which is where the air force dealt the "massive blow" envisaged by Lt.Gen. Bradley.

The **bombardment** was intended to crush the German front along a sector 7,000 yards (6.4 kilometers) wide by 2,500 yards (2.3 kilometers) deep. This carpet bombing zone covered the sector south of the Saint-Lô/Lessay road where lay the villages of Montreuil-sur-Lozon, La Chapelle-en-Juger and Hébécrevon. The bombs were to **crush the German lines** along the entire sector of the front (where stood the remnants of the *Panzer-Lehr-Division* with 5,000 men including 2,200 fighting troops and 40 tanks, the remnants of the 13th Parachute Regiment of the 5th Parachute Division and those of *Kampfgruppe Heintz*) to break through the German **lines of communications, neutralize the German reserves** and **reduce their will to fight** using terror tactics. General Bradley went to England on **19 July** to settle all these matters with the air force commanders: Air Chief Marshal Leigh-Mallory, "Commander AEAF", General Brereton (9th US Air Force) and General Quesada (IX Tactical Air Command). To crush the German front, the bombardment was to take place right in front of the American lines. And, to avoid the risk of bombs falling short on the American units, Lt.Gen. Bradley suggested moving his men 800 yards (730 meters) back one hour before the bombardment. The air command got them to withdraw 1,200 yards (1,100 meters). Bradley also request a flight path bringing the planes in from the west, parallel to the front so as to avoid the risk of bombing the American lines. But this request was turned down as the air force would be exposed to German flak on the west coast of the Cotentin and the arrival through this narrow sector would cause congestion. So the bombers were sent in from the north.

All the 8th US Air Force's heavy bombers and the 9th US Air Force's medium bombers and fighter-bombers took part in the operation. General Quesada of IX Tactical Air Command coordinated the air attack with the ground troops. The operation was planned as follows:

- 80 minutes before the attack, 1,800 heavy bombers would crush the saturation zone for an hour under a carpet of bombs;

- at the moment of the attack 350 fighter-bombers would *machine-gun* and bomb a narrower strip for twenty minutes; - 10 minutes later, 396 medium bombers would bomb the southern half of the zone for forty-five minutes; - throughout the operation, 500 fighters would cover this aerial armada. Altogether **over 3,000 aircraft** were committed! An hour later, IX TAC fighter-bombers and RAF Typhoons were to join in the offensive, "Cobra" to be launched on or after 23 July as soon as the weather was right.

The **ground attack** was to begin with the VII Corps infantry advancing. From west to east, **9th Inf. Div.** was to descend on Montreuil-sur-Lozon then Marigny before handing over to **1st Inf. Div.** in that direction. **4th Inf. Div.** would pass through La Chapelle-en-Juger towards Carantilly, **30th Inf. Div.** passed through Hébécrevon, Saint-Gilles, Canisy and Le Mesnil-Herman to cover the left flank of the offensive and see off a possible German counter-attack from the east bank of the Vire. In fact: 4th Inf. Div. was in the center with the right flank covered by 9th Inf. Div. and the left flank covered by 30th Inf. Div. 1st Inf. Div. (motorized) would race towards Coutances in conjunction with CCB, 3rd Arm. Div. Light bombs were to be used so as to avoid heavy bomb craters such as would hinder the advancing vehicles (as had happened during the bombardment preceding the capture of Caen on 8 and 9 July). The infantry were to open the breach after the bombardment, and clear the way for the tanks of **3rd Arm. Div.** and **2d Arm. Div.** to burst through the gaping breach.

The two armored divisions would sweep forward to the south-west (Tessy-sur-Vire), south (Villebaudon), south-west (Hambye on the one hand and Lengronne/Cérences on the other). **Further west**, **3rd Arm. Div.** would advance westward along two parallel lines, the southern one to Hyenville (CCA), the northern one to Coutances (CCB). **VIII Corps** was to march at dawn on day three and descend on Coutances with two armored divisions, **6th Arm. Div.** along the coast and **4th Arm. Div.** directly on Coutances.

Further bombing was designed to destroy the bridges over the Vire, in the east, and below the Cérences/Villebaudon line, in the south, to cut off the battlefield so as to prevent the arrival of German reinforcements. In VII Corps' sector, the corps had considerable artillery oiwer in addition to the divisional artillery: 9 heavy, 5 medium and 7 light batteries, altogether 258 guns with 140,000 rounds.

Given the prospect for a possible exploitation of this breakthrough, the staff of Lt. Gen. Patton's **3rd Army** gathered in the northern Cotentin. On **22 July**, its forward echelon was already around Valognes. The presence of Patton a few days before the launch of "Cobra" led to certain adjustments being made to the plan. Patton and Bradley had known each other well since North Africa. The boldness of "Cobra" is a sign that Patton had a hand in Lt.Gen. Bradley's plan. In this brilliant plan, the Americans made German "Blitzkrieg" principles their own: - to bring in the air force to crush the attack zone along a narrow front, - to use infantry to mop up and hold the gap open, - then to launch the armored forces, - to make deep inroads into enemy territory, - to carry out a broad sweeping movement in order to enve-

The American order of battle on the eve of "Cobra". From left to right: VIII Corps with 79th ID (Lorraine), 8th ID (Golden Arrow), 90th ID (Tough Ombres or Texas Oklahoma), 4th AD and 6th AD (in reserve), 83rd ID (Ohio), VII Corps with 9th ID, 30th ID (Old Hickory), 1st ID (Big Red One), 4th ID (Ivy), 2d AD (Hell on wheels), 3rd AD (Spear-head), XIX Corps with just 35th ID (Santa Fe), V Corps with 2d ID (Indian Head) and 5th ID (Red Diamond). (Heimdal.)

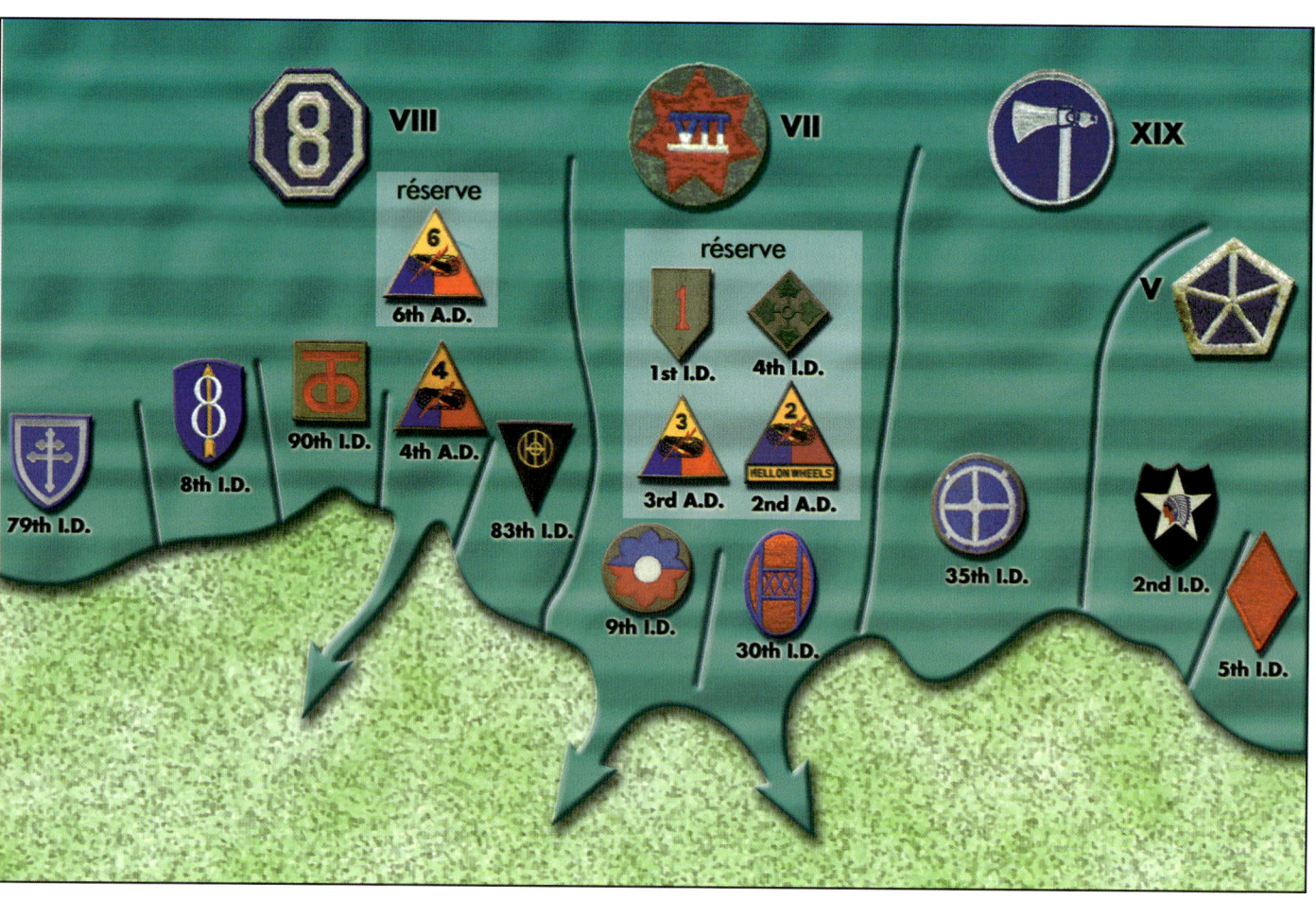

lop and capture enemy forces overtaken before they had time to withdraw to new lines of defense, - to continue to exploit the in-depth advantage before the enemy could recover. And of course the watchword of the *blitzkrieg* was *speed.* It was on this point that the main instigator of this type of modern warfare, General Fritz Guderian, always insisted. This was a lesson that was not lost on go-ahead Patton. Also, the American air force offered huge possibilities. General Fritz Bayerlein, commander of the *Panzer-Lehr-Division*, a witness and victim of this massive bombardment, rued at what the Germans might have done if just once they had had such resources available to them.

Saint-Germain-sur-Sèves and La Varde

However, there was one small downside to this picture before the operation was launched. While Lt.Gen. Bradley had managed to line up the eastern half of his front near Highway 800, the VIII Corps was behind schedule in fulfilling its objectives: Lessay and Périers were still not taken and Saint-Germain-sur-Sèves and La Varde were two German salients in the American front. So he issued orders for them to be reduced.

La Varde was a small hamlet a kilometer north of Marchésieux. This hamlet was on a spit of land which advances like a ship's hull between the swampy Taute and Lozon valleys. The sector was held by the remnants of SS grenadier regiments (under their commander Lieutenant-Colonel Fick) belonging to the *"Götz von Berlichingen"* Division. They were *Kampfgruppen* **Ertl**, **Lorenz**, **Ullrich** and **Hoffman** then the engineers of commander Kurt Fleischer's engineer battalion. These exhausted units in the La Varde sector had the strength of a large company reinforced by assault guns. Late in the afternoon of **18 July**, Maj.Gen. Macon, commander of the **83rd Inf. Div.**, ordered an offensive against La Varde. At around 18.00 hours (British time), Colonel Crabill's 329th IR launched a diversionary attack. The maint thrust was to come from the **331st** under Colonel York and the engineers worked under cover of dark to restore the destroyed bridge over the Taute. After crossing the flooded valley, the assault battalion (3rd) led by Colonel York secured a bridgehead at La Varde at nightfall but his muddy and soaked men's weapons were no longer in working order. The next morning, the 19th, under cover of fog, reinforcements managed to pass through German machine-gun fire that was too light to halt the men of the 331st Inf. Rgt. The engineers set up a Bailey bridge during the night and the tanks could then come to support this bridgehead. Unfortunately, destructive charges had been placed on this bridge set up by the engineers and, by a stroke of bad luck, they were hit by a German shell and the metal bridge was blown up. On the German side, *KG Lorenz* was too weak to attempt a counter-attack. This was launched by *KG Ullrich* supported by two assault guns. The GIs managed to bring up two anti-tank guns which destroyed the first German assault gun; the damaged gun was pushed to the right side of the road to let through the second gun. It reached the northern part of the road and opened fire on the roadway running through the middle of the valley. Colonel York's GIs had already 50% losses, and a battalion commander was reported missing. The survivors of the 331st Inf. Rgt. fell back that the afternoon through the flooded Taute valley suffering heavy casualties as they went. As Martin Blumenson notes (op. cit., p. 201), the failure at La Varde was due to bad luck and also to problems arising with new recruits; the 83rd Inf. Div. "had incurred more casualties and received more replacements" than other units. Colonel York said: "We have quite a few new men and they are really new, they don't know their officers and the officers don't know their men."

The defensive point at **Saint-Germain-sur-Sèves** posed the same problems. This was a small mound of earth cut off amid some flat marshy land and defended by the remnants of a German battalion with support from assault guns and tracked vehicles of the *"Das Reich"* Division. The attack was to be carried out by the **358th Inf. Rgt.** (Lt.Col. Christian E. Clarke, Jr), the **90th Inf. Div.** (Maj.Gen. Landrum), which was to launch two battalions advancing along each of two roads leading to "the island". Here again the engineers were to build a metal bridge as soon as a bridgehead was secured. The attack initially planned for the 18th was postponed until **dawn on 22 July**. Poor visibility meant no fighter-bombers could be used. The men of the 358th started out with little support, on flat ground in full view of German lookouts (the sector was held by the paratroopers of the 6th Regiment and men of the *"Das Reich"* Division) with an ideal shooting range in front of them. One of the assault battalions lost 50% of its men crossing the marshes, fording the river and reaching "the island" where it secured a bridgehead. The other battalion came under artillery and mortar fire, machine-gun crossfire from the German positions, and could not keep up. At nightfall, the first battalion was down to 400 men (i.e. half-strength) with no supporting mortars or tanks, these being held up in another part of "the island" in the Le Closet sector. Some of the men were demoralized by a combination of fear and fatigue in the dark night on this strip of land on the edge of the marshes, and facing the enemy. Some fell back without permission to join the lines.The battalion commander back in the rear lost his way in the pitch-black swamp trying to move up to his battalion's forward positions. But the American bridgehead was two kilometers wide and a kilometer deep. The situation worried Otto Weidinger commander of *"Der Führer"*, *"Das Reich"* Division (holding the sector to the left of the paratroops of the 6th Regiment), the 3rd Battalion *(III./DF)*, commanded by Captain Werner, was dispatched to counter-attack at 21.30 with support from the tanks of *SS-Pz.-Rgt. 2 "DR."* Facing this fierce armored attack with no commander, few GIs stood their ground, but the panic-stricken majority retreated in disorder under enemy fire. By 22.30, it was all over, the Germans had regained their positions and reported the capture of 308 surrendering GIs. At daybreak on 23 July, the 90th Inf.Div. commanders took stock of this setback: 100 killed, 500 wounded, 200 prisoners (the German figure is more precise and must be correct, the number of wounded was probably only 400). The reasons for the failure: the overcast weather, the terrain, a skilful enemy and a gap in the chain of command, and most of all young recruits with as yet inadequate training. These two failures meant that it was not possible to line up VIII Corps' left flank on the start line planned for "Cobra". This forced a slight change of plan on Lt.Gen. Bradley. While he had been planning to commit the VII Corps within hours of launching the attack of Maj.Gen. Collins's VII Corps on 24 July, as we saw in our study of the "Cobra" plan, Maj.Gen. Middleton's VIII Corps

On 17 July, around the Château d'Esglandes, numerous American attacks were repelled. The engineer company of the Deutschland Regiment (16./D) repulsed nineteen. The company commander was Ostuf. (lieutenant) Heinz Macher. Three of his men, sappers Heinska, Jerserik and Kloeppel, aged nineteen, destroyed two American tanks with grenades. This salient, like the La Varde salient (see overall map), gives a good idea of the fierceness of the fighting in the sector. Crack German troops hung onto their ground as the GIs launched attack after attack, with heavy losses on this difficult terrain. (Map courtesy Munin.)

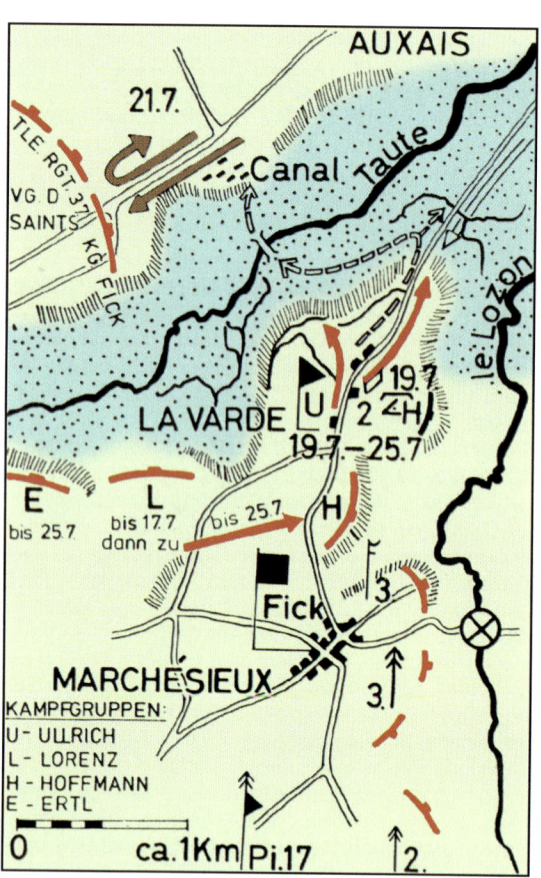

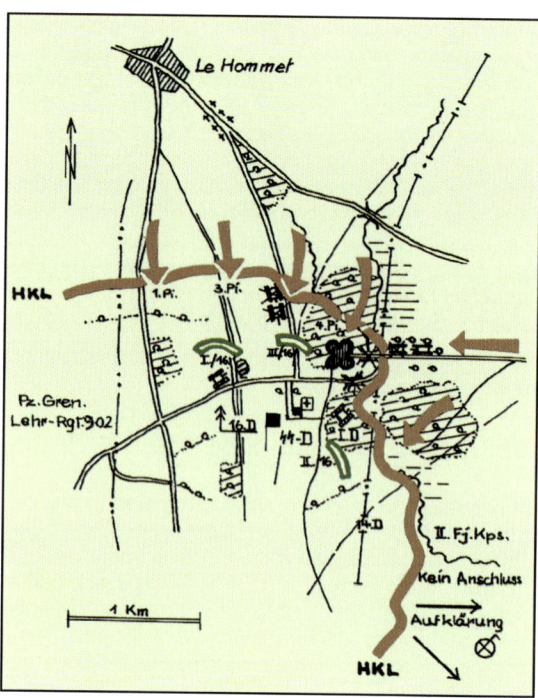

The La Varde strongpoint and the German attack of 19 July (brown arrows). Battlegroups (Kampfgruppen) Ullrich, Lorenz, Hoffmann and Ertl leaning on this salient overlooking the marshes.

The successive front lines from 7 to 25 July showing clearly how the VII Corps troops advanced slowly but surely between Ca-rentan and Sainteny against the grenadiers of the Götz von Berlichingen and the role, destabilizing the German front, of the Saint-Fromond bridgehead. Notice too how Lt. Gen. Bradley gradually contrived to align his front in this sector near the Saint-Lô/Périers road. (Heimdal.)

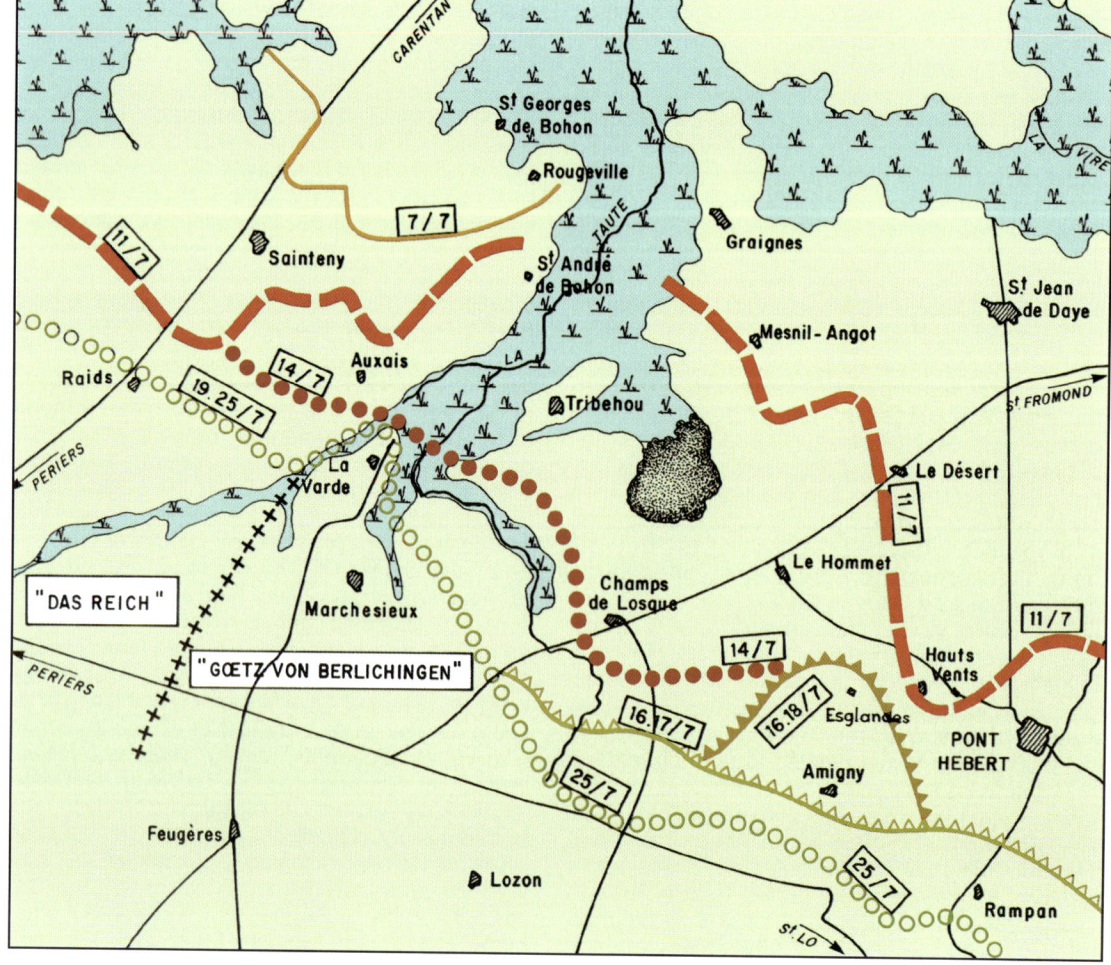

finally did not attack until dawn on the third day of the offensive. In the VII Corps' sector, *Kampfgruppe Wisliceny* also held a salient in the American front around the Château d'Esglandes; it was finally reduced on 18 July.

The failure of "Goodwood"

Shortly before "Cobra" was launched, a great British offensive began on the eastern front in Normandy to divert the Germans' attention and prevent them from sending reinforcements to the American sector, to make Lt.Gen. Bradley's offensive easier. However, General Montgomery finally thought that "Goodwood" should not be just a diversionary attack but a real breakthrough against the German front. Montgomery also requested the full weight of air power and General Eisenhower was really taken with the idea (cf. M. Blumenson, *Op. cit.*, p. 190). It is certain that had the German front in Normandy been broken through in two places - east of Caen and west of Saint-Lô - the Allied victory could only have been quicker and more decisive. "Goodwood", the Second British Army's attack, was launched on 18 July. The British tank divisions ("Guards", 7th Arm. Div., 11th Arm. Div.) raced towards the German defense in depth, offering sitting targets for the 88 mm guns of *III. Flak-Korps.* The first day, 270 tanks and 1,500 men were left behind in the field. By the time this bloody offensive was finally stopped on 21 July, Lt.Gen. Dempsey's British Army had lost 3,600 men and 469 tanks! These huge losses of tanks accounted for 36% of all British tanks available on the mainland of Europe, for very little ground gained. Another two costly offensives like this and the British army would be out of tanks altogether. On hearing of this disaster, Eisenhower was furious and submitted to Winston Churchill an order to have General Montgomery dismissed; but Monty somehow survived. Certainly Montgomery, generally "overcautious" (which caused dissatisfaction among American opinion and commanders alike), launched some overbold offensives as well - "Goodwood" was one, "Market-Garden" later on another. Lt.Gen. Bradley did not make the same mistake for "Cobra"; before launching his precious tanks into a possible trap, he first had the area mopped up by his infantry. More than ever after this setback on the eastern front in Normandy, the outcome of the battle depended on the success of "Cobra" and the 1st Army.

On this **23 July**, von Kluge suggested to Hitler a general withdrawal of German forces in the West, which was finally accepted. But it was too late. The very next day, a real firestorm came down on the German front west of Saint-Lô. The aircraft used to support "Goodwood" were now available for "Cobra".

This photo, taken by George Greb at the start of Operation "Cobra", is very symbolic of what the offensive was going to be like. (Heimdal.)

Tanks against the hedgerows

1. Lieutenant-Colonel Lawrence G Foster, commander of the 23rd Armored Battalion which developed the "hedgecutter".

2, 3 and **4.** The hedges were a major headache for the American tank units. To allow them to move off the narrow lanes, the engineers needed to blow out a section of hedge. Certain tanks, the Tank-dozers, had a bulldozer blade fitted onto the front end. Although effective, these machines were few and far between and not so maneuverable as an ordinary tank. Pictured here **(2** and **3)** is one of them belonging to the 3rd Armored Division performing two maneuvers (D.F. and DAVA/ Heimdal Coll.)

5, 6 and **7.** After the experience of battle at Villiers-Fossard and Les Hauts-Vents, the 23rd Armored Engineer Battalion, 3rd Armored Division, devised teeth to be mounted on the front of their tanks; this is how the hedgecutter tank was born. This accessory was manufactured by cutting up and welding German beach obstacles, of which there was an abundant supply all along the coast. The idea was so childishly brilliant. Pictured here is a Sherman tank of the 3rd Armored Division **(photo 5)** just coming through a hedge, and a Stuart tank of the 705th Ord. Company, 5th Infantry Division **(6** and **7)** fitted with these "teeth". (DAVA and D.F./Heimdal.)

15 and 16 July 1944.

1. The tank regiment of the "Das Reich" Division commanded by Lieutenant-Colonel Tychsen comes up to support the "Götz von Berlichingen" Division. One of the 1st Battalion's Panthers was destroyed here by a bazooka rocket fired by the Texan Pvt. Ward Watley. On 16 July, Ward Watley, who belonged to the 22d Inf. Rgt., the 4th Infantry Division, came back to survey his "kill".

2. Near Sainteny, on 16 July, a 155 mm howitzer of Battery "B", the 20th Field Artillery Battalion (one of the 4th Division's four artillery battalions) opens fire on positions held by the "Das Reich" Division. (Photo courtesy Heimdal collection.)

3. South-west of Sainteny, these three German paratroopers of the 6th Regiment were killed while on a reconnaissance patrol. Their vehicle, a Schwimmwagen, is examined (in the background) by two men of the 4th Infantry Division. Photo taken on 16 July.

4. Meanwhie, the bridge at Saint-Fromond enabled the vehicles of the XIX Corps to come up to reinforce the broad bridgehead west of the Vire river. The sector was by now fairly quiet, and the crossing of the Vire of a few days ago in assault vessels under mortar fire is just a distant memory; the GIs (in the foreground) take time to relax on a river bank that has become pretty peaceful here. (Photographs courtesy Heimdal collection.)

5. In this photograph taken a few days earlier, pictured on the left is the hotel next to the bridge entrance before it again came under fire, probably from German artillery. (D.F./Heimdal.)

18, 19 July 1944.

1. Pont-Hébert, 19 July, three knocked-out Sherman tanks are there to remind us that the *"Panzer-Lehr"* launched an attack from this locality on 11 July.

2. Pending the construction of a bridge of boats, ambulances ford the river here at Pont-Hébert. The locality located on the right bank of the Vire (here facing north) is now in the hands of the Americans.

3. Pont-Hébert, the two banks are now linked by a bridge of boats.

4. The American tank units also had heavy losses but a good number of damaged Shermans were towed off back to the repair shops. Those undergoing repairs on 18 July were soon back in the front line.

5 and **6.** On 19 July, American P-47 Thunderbolt pilots come to examine their "kills" to see the damage their planes did to the steel monsters and find their most vulnerable spots. On tank "215" (photo n° 5), the "Zimmerit" (antimagnetic plaster) all over this "Panther" is almost intact. As the location is unspecified, we cannot tell whether this 2nd Company tank belongs to the "Das Reich" or the "Panzer-Lehr" Division destroyed by P-47s on 11 July. The "Panther" pictured in photo n° 6 was worse hit. A rocket has dislocated the left bogie, another the right bogie, and a third the engine compartment and the fuel tanks in the rear. In this last photograph, pictured around the tank are, from left to right, 1st Lieutenant Henry W Collins (from Atlanta), 1st Lieutenant Bayard B Taylor (from Lincoln) and 1st Lieutenant Joe F Richmond (from West Union, Ohio). They belong to the 366th Fighter Group.

(Photographs courtesy DAVA, Heimdal collection.)

18 July 1944, the 79th Infantry Division in the Lessay sector

1 and **2.** After the Germans withdrew onto their third line of defense, the "Wasserstellung" (the "water position", being backed by several rivers: the Ay, Sèves, Taute and Terrette), General Wyche's 79th Infantry Division set up outposts north of the Ay river, in front of Lessay. Pictured here, a few hundred meters east of Lessay (the milepost gives us a precise indication), along the Lessay/Périers/Saint-Lô road that was to prove so crucial in the upcoming American offensive, is a 243. Infanterie-Division first-aid post. The remnants of that division under its commander Colonel Kloster-Kemperer held the entire sector between Lessay and the coast. (BA.)

3. On 18 July, some men of the 79th Infantry Division prepare to leave on night patrol; they paint their faces with lampblack. From right to left: 1st Lieutenant Wendell Shreve (patrol leader), Pfc George Peterson (interpreter) and a Norman, Aubert Ton, acting as their guide. Notice the very large mesh camouflage net worn on the helmet, the model usually worn by the men of the 79th. (D.F./Heimdal.)

4. A machine-gun battalion of the 79th Infantry Division crosses a field in the Lessay sector. (DAVA/Heimdal.)

3

79th Infantry Division.

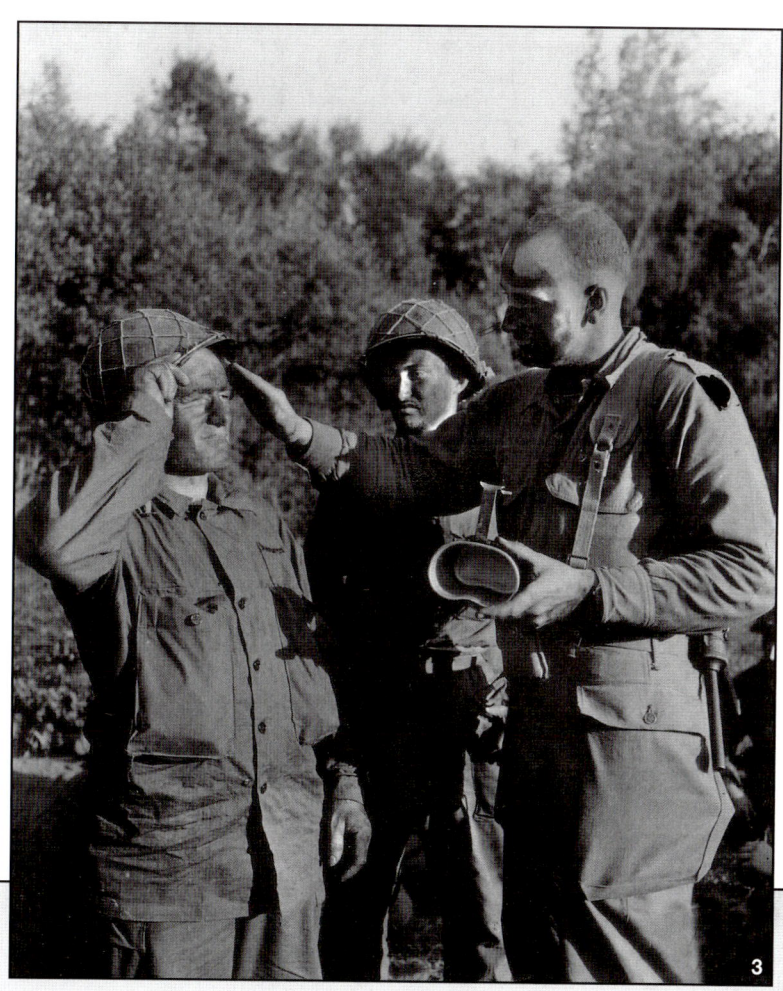

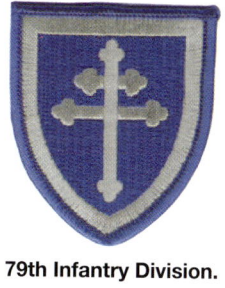

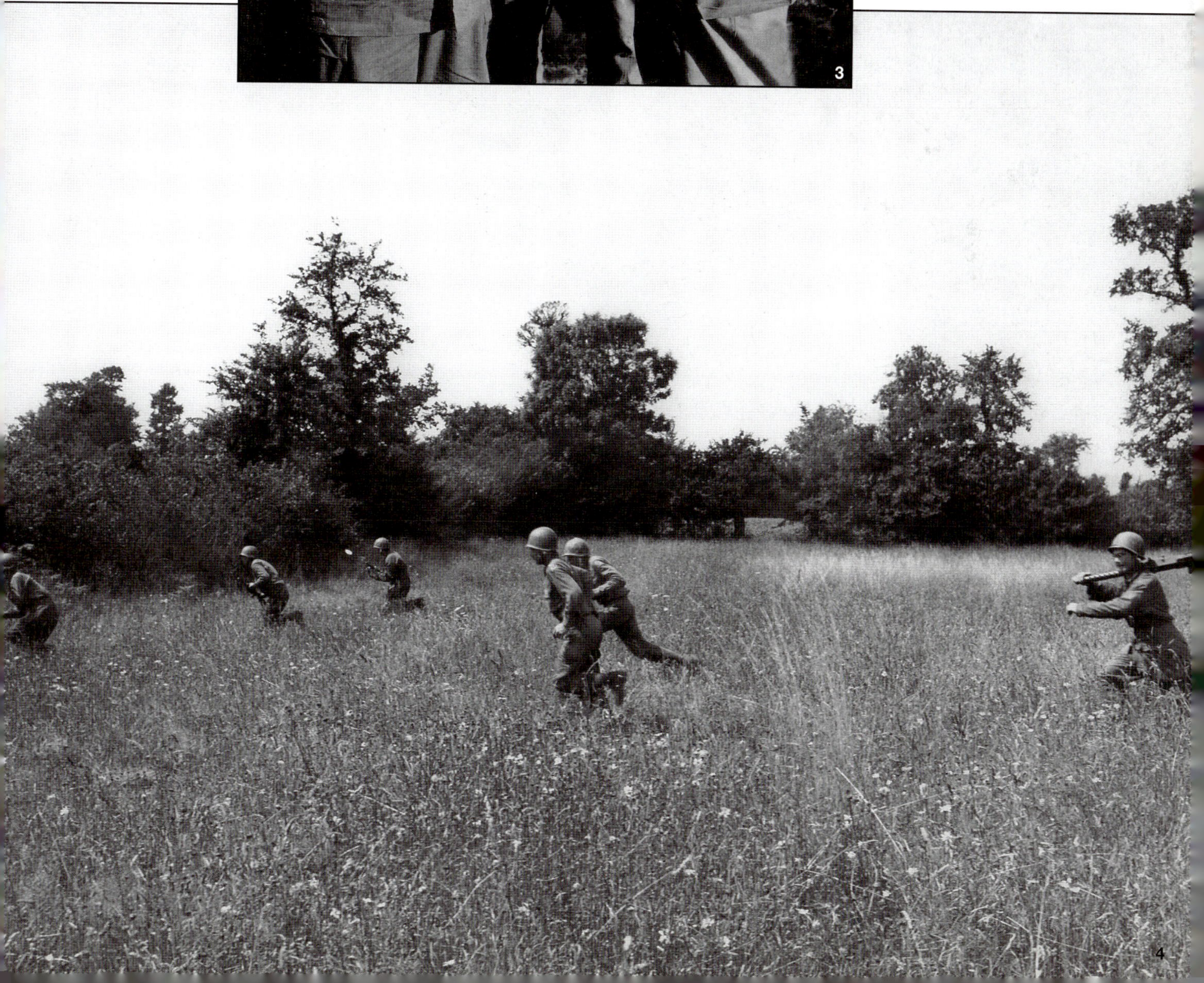

4

18 July 1944, the 79th Infantry Division in the Lessay sector.

1. War correspondent Collier made an interesting reportage showing combat techniques used by the 79th Infantry Division in the bocage; it includes the two American photographs on the previous page. With these seven photographs, we have reconstituted this reportage. The five photographs in these two pages were taken at the same spot along a hedge, the same oak is pictured in two photographs. In view of the limited view, weapons firing in curved trajectories were particularly useful, and especially, for the infantry, the defensive rifle grenades fired with the Garand rifle.

2. As the infantry fire with their rifles, their comrades set up a heavy 30 cal. machine gun.

3. The GI pictured in photo n° 1 has just fired his "fragmentation grenade". Notice, sewn onto the man's left sleeve, the badge of the 79th Infantry Division (a white cross of Lorraine on a blue background recalling how the division saw action in that region in 1916).

4. An infantryman, nestling among some luxuriant vegetation, fires at the hedge opposite to cover his comrades who prepare to cross the field.

5. Against the German strongpoints, the M1 bazooka, in theory an anti-tank weapon, could nevertheless render invaluable services, its rocket being capable of blowing up a hedge embankment.

(Photographs courtesy US Army - Heimdal collection.). The seven photographs by war correspondent Collier in 1944 (they are no longer in use) carried the n[os] Eto-hq-44-8036, 8037, 8038, 8039, 8040, 8041, 8042.

Behind the front, 23 and 24 July.

1. A reception center for refugees fleeing the front line was set up at Sainte-Marguerite-d'Elle. Here Stuart Scheftel, of New York City (N.Y.), of the Psychological Warfare Division (PWD) questions Pierre Lethouayes and his family, the last family to leave the ruins of Saint-Lô. By way of shelter, they lived for twenty days in a dry well. This photo was taken on 23 July by war correspondent Gedicke. (8378)

2. This other photo taken on 24 July at the Sainte-Marguerite-d'Elle reception center by war correspondent Moore and features some of the refugees who were resettled there. (8525)

3. This German travelling kitchen was salvaged to prepare meals for refugees at the center managed by the Allied Civil Affairs Bureau. This photo was also taken on 24 July.

4. A Norman woman proudly shows off to a GI the decorations won by her husband during the Great War and which she has had framed.

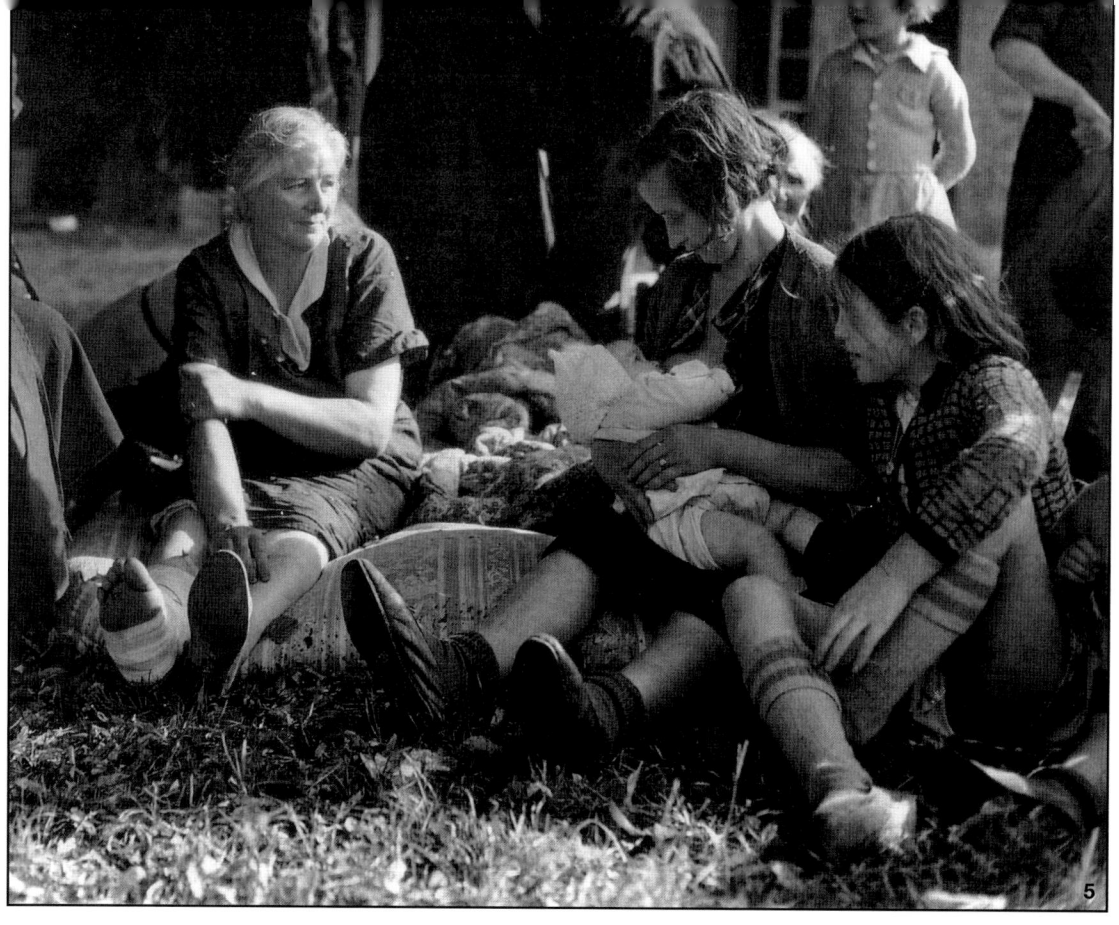

5. As the fighting progressed, civilians were thrown out onto the streets, often losing everything they had. Some women and children have taken up a place on no more than a mattress laid out directly on a lawn. A mother is breast-feeding her child.

6. This photograph of German origin recovered by American troops gives an idea of the apocalyptic conditions faced by the civilian population of Saint-Lô. This photo was taken in the square in front of the church of Notre-Dame, facing north-east.

7. These American soldiers have come to examine a Russian 152 mm Pushka obr. gun re-used by the Germans and photographed here on 23 July. (8375)

(Heimdal Coll.)

in the upcoming offensive **(3)**. The men of the infantry units stack their light kit. (Photographs courtesy D.F./Heimdal.)

24 July, the artillery and mortars prepare to help crush the German lines. The 87th CML Battalion has sited its 4.2 inch mortars 600 yards (550 meters) from the German front **(4)**. Transported by Weasel M29 Bren carriers, the 1st Platoon of the battalion's Company "C" takes up position again **(5)**. A mortar crew unloads cases of 4.2 inch (just over 100 mm) shells from a Bren carrier. (Photographs courtesy D.F./Heimdal.)

23 and 24 July. Preparations for the offensive

23 July, before moving up to the front line and taking part in Operation Cobra, the GIs often completely refitted. The US army was a rich army. Meanwhile, the Germans were short of everything and their uniforms were worn to a shred **(1)**. Helmets are checked and changed **(2)**. GIs get rid of any equipment that no longer served so as to have less weight to carry

23 July 1944. The troops move up to the front line for "Cobra".

1. Trucks come to the rear to fetch men to reinforce the front lines prior to the offensive.

2. One way traffic: "Ahead!". These men of the 4th Infantry Division prepare to go onto the attack between La Chapelle-en-Juger and Hébécrevon. (8621)

3 and **4.** Another unit of the 4th Infantry Division moves up to the lines on foot; a Norman farmer's wife watches them pass, at the farm at a place called La Maison Basset at Le Hommet d'Arthenay. Here again, the men take roads following the "One way" signs. (8629 and photo taken in 1987).

5. T/S Charles J Jozefik and Pfc Frank J Zielinski of the 142nd Armd. Sig. Company reconnoiter by Jeep along a dirt track turned into a mud bath by the heavy rain of the last few days.

6. A mine clearance squad of the 3rd Battalion, the 8th Infantry Regiment (4th Infantry Division) moves up towards the lines, near Amigny, north of the Saint-Lô/Lessay road, as tanks of the 2nd Armored Division wait on the right side of the road to let the infantry through. (8623)

All these photographs were taken on 23 July by war correspondents Collier, Barth and Parker. (Nat. Archives and US Army, Heimdal collection.)

Preparations and launch of the offensive – 21-24 July.

1. North of Marigny, in the sector where the offensive would place in a few days time, infantrymen clean the barrel of a bazooka.

2. A heavy artillery gun is moved by a tracked prime mover along a narrow lane before being set up to bombard the German front. While the roads were narrow, there were plenty of them, enabling reserves to be brought up close to the front line.

3. At Le Désert, this GI examines a pile of horseshoes. Normandy is a large stock-breeding area and there were also horse-lovers among the Americans.

4. On 21 July, Major General Barton, commander of the 4th Infantry Division, explains their mission in three days time to the men of his 22d Infantry Regiment. Photograph by Massenge. (8110)

5. On 24 July, west of Saint-Lô, this tank-destroyer is also being set up near the front. Its front end is reinforced with sand bags.

6. Aircraft came over on this day and here a 155 mm howitzer is in action as the VII Corps artillery lends support to the air force.

9

"Cobra" 24 to 30 July

24 July

The bombardment was scheduled for 13.00 hours. Six groups of *IX TAC* fighter-bombers and three bombardment divisions of the *8th US Air Force* (some 1,600 heavy bombers) took off from England. The great day had arrived. In Normandy, Maj.Gen. Collins had the front lines of his *9th* and *30th Inf.Div.* fall back 1,200 yards (1,100 meters) as planned to keep them clear of the bombed area.

However, there was poor visibility in England. Accordingly, *Air Chief Marshal* Leigh-Mallory decided to postpone the bombardment. His message came through just minutes after the squadrons were dispatched, so most of the medium bombers remained on the ground; three of the six fighter-bomber groups were informed but the three others dropped their bombs. As for the heavy bombers, given the poor visibility, 500 of them decided to turn back, 35 bombers in the second wave dropped a few bombs rather haphazardly, killing 25 men and wounding 131 of the **30th Infantry Division**. Despite this botched bombing raid, *Maj.Gen.* Collins tried to make the best of the situation and most of all to prevent the *"Panzer-Lehr"* from seizing the positions evacuated overnight. The **9th Infantry Division** launched its *60th Infantry Regiment* to repulse any infiltrated Germans. A battalion of the 47th IR fought for a single hedge and the *39th IR* lost 77 men after an eight-hour battle to recover a position.

This false start to Operation Cobra raised a few eyebrows. *Lt.Gen.* Bradley protested to the air commanders because the approach of the heavy bombers had not proceeded exactly as planned, although the operation had been carefully worked out over the previous two weeks. But there was no time to lose, the surprise effect had been squandered and the Germans must not be allowed time to take preventive measures. The weather forecast for the following day was good. Bradley decided to launch "Cobra" at 11.00 hours on 25 July.

Modifications were made to the flight plan to avoid repeating the various casualties of the day before among the US infantry.

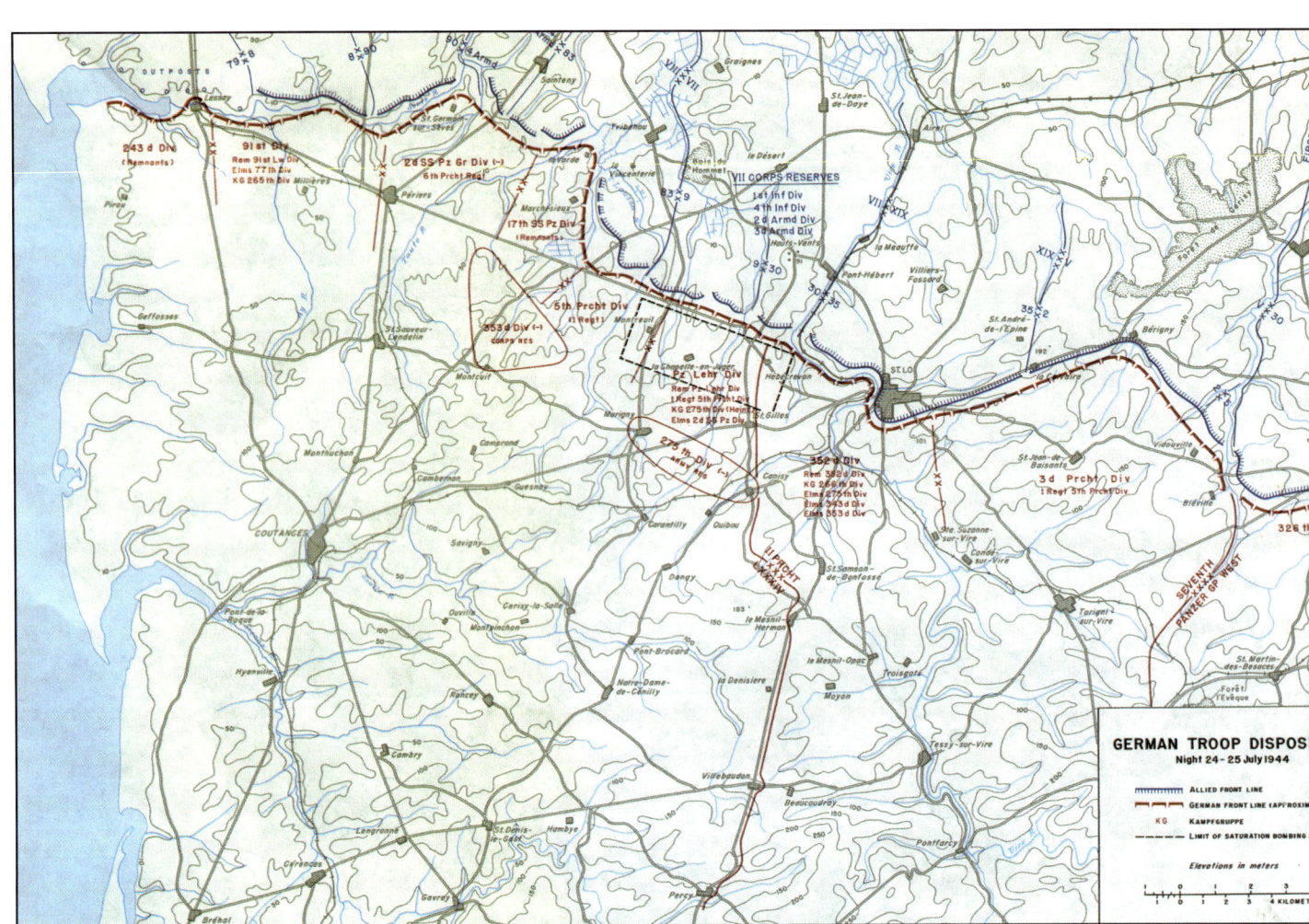

American and German positions on the eve of Operation Cobra. The rectangle between Montreuil-sur-Lozon and Hébécrevon marks the objective of the carpety bombing, chiefly the remnants of the Panzer-Lehr-Division, the FJR 13 (1 Regt 5th Prdt Div.), KG Heintz (275. ID), and elements of the "Das Reich" Division. (US Army History Department)

280

Oddly enough, the German command failed to notice this abortive bombardment. Late in the morning of this 24 July, the **"Panzer-Lehr"** was not really holding a front line as such, more a string of fairly well spaced strongpoints (each comprising a small group of grenadiers supported by a few machine-guns and one or two tanks), most of them just south of the road. The young paratroopers of the 13th Regiment formed an anchor point north of Marigny (towards Montreuil-sur-Lozon). The rest of the sector as far as Hébécrevon was held by the men of the *"Panzer-Lehr"*. Given the heavy cloud cover, they did not expect to be attacked by fighter-bombers but rather hoped to have a quiet day patrolling the American lines. Suddenly, the sky was filled with the tremendous drone of an air fleet flying above the clouds, but how could this be in such overcast weather conditions? A whistling noise followed by explosions, 800 tons of bombs, including 550 tons of high explosive bombs and 135 tons of fragmentation bombs were dropped. Losses among the *"Panzer-Lehr"* were estimated at 350 men and 10 tanks and assault guns. However, as the ground attack did not make much headway (*Maj.Gen.* Collins seeking mostly to regain the ground lost as his troops fell back), General Bayerlein thought he had repelled a large-scale offensive. This failed attack gave him confidence in his ability to hold out. He expected that the attack would be renewed on the 25th and requested 200 men from *275.Infanterie-Division* (kept in reserve in the rear). However, he thought the main bombardment was over and that there would only be a ground attack the next day. That is why in what proved a fatal move he did not pull back his troops. So what actually happened was that paradoxically the failed bombardment worked like a ploy that further contributed to the final success of the operation.

25 July

At **09.00 hours**, 1,500 B-17s and B-27s came over their objectives and laid a carpet of 3,300 tons of bombs on the area from Montreuil to Hébécrevon. All hell was let loose. There were further heavy losses in the American sector. The leading bomber of the third formation made an aiming error. This bombardment on the American lines north of the highway killed 111 GIs and wounded another 490. Among the casualties was *Lieutenant-General* Lesley J McNair, commander of *1st US Army Group* (a dummy formation, part of the *"Fortitude"* plan for which so many divisions were held back in the Pas-de-Calais); his death was kept secret. Every American division in the front line was hit:

- 14 killed and 33 wounded for the *47th IR, 9th ID* ;
- 15 killed and 23 wounded for the 15th Engineer Battalion *(9th ID)* ; - 4 wounded for the 60th Field Artillery Battalion *(9th ID)* ; - 1 killed and 2 wounded for the *84th Field Artillery Battalion (9th ID)* ; - 10 killed and 27 wounded for the 4th ID ; - 61 killed and 374 wounded for the *30th IR*. The heaviest losses were thus registered by this division which was to advance on the left flank of the attack (figures taken from M. Blumenson, op. cit., p. 236). The additional figures taken from the history of that division (by Robert L Hewitt, p. 37) speak volumes: *the bombardment of the 25th caused the division as many casualties as a very hard day's fighting. In this brief bombardment the 30th suffered 662 losses, i.e. 64 killed, 374 wounded, 60 missing and 164 cases of combat fatigue, taking total losses for the two days to 814.*

On 25 July, the Allied bombardment also fell on the US positions. American medical officers pull out GIs buried under masses of earth blown up by the bombs. (8614). (DAVA/Heimdal.)

Many men suffered from combat fatigue, in a state of shock with bombs falling all around them, and incapable of fighting. The Command Group of the 3rd Battalion, the *47th IR (9th Inf.Div.)* was wiped out. But what was the effect of the bombing on the German lines?

While the bombardment caused heavy losses in the American lines, the carpet of bombs had a devastating effect on the German lines. Of the 40 Panzers committed in the front line, there was just one tank still in working order. Some were hit and exploded, others were flipped over on their backs or thrown into bomb craters. Colonel Gerhardt, who commanded what was left of *Pz.-Lehr.Rgt. 130*, was down to the 7 tanks he held in reserve – to fend off four infantry divisions and two armored divisions! General Bayerlein took the view that his already very weakened division had now been wiped out of existence. On going to the Amigny sector at around noon, he saw "nothing but smoke, dust and flames". Of the 5,000 men which the division still numbered (including 2,200 grenadiers), there were just 2,500 survivors! And those who survived the bombs were very often in a state of shock as well.

The American field forces attacked: the **4th Inf.Div.** in the center flanked, on the right by the **9th Inf.Div.** and the **30th**, on the left. The **2d Arm.Div.**, arriving from Les Hauts Vents, raced to the crossroads on the main highway. The **1st Inf.Div.** and **3rd Arm.Div.** followed the 9th ID. Outnumbered one to thirty, the last survivors of the *"Panzer-Lehr"*, a few paratroopers of the 13th Regiment and a handful of survivors of **"Kampfgruppe Heintz"** tried to stem the surge before being completely overrun! On the American side, a battalion of the **30th Inf.Div.** and a regiment of the **9th Inf.Div.** could take no part in the attack. Some German nests of resistance slowed down the American advance. Two tanks and a line of grenadiers blocked a battalion of the **8th IR, 4th Inf.Div.**; the line of resistance butted up against a sunken lane running parallel to the main road on the south side. The battalion outflanked this pocket of resistance, destroyed the two tanks with a bazooka but failed to take the position. The thrust made no further headway and by nightfall the **4th Inf.Div.** was still some way short of **La Chapelle-en-Juger**.

The **47th IR, 9th Inf.Div.** took Montreuil-sur-Lozon but *Maj.Gen.* Eddy, surprised by unexpected resistance from isolated groups defending fiercely, hesitated to fully commit his division. The Saint-Lô/Périers road was by now in the hands of the American troops but the conquered area was less than two kilometers deep. The main objective — the Saint-Lô/Coutances road and the localities of Marigny and Canisy — was far from having been achieved. *Lt.Gen.* Bradley was anxious. Was the great offensive going to fail? He noted how weeks of war in the Bocage had made people cautious, and being so conditioned it was difficult to expect his infantrymen to throw caution to the wind overnight, especially after the shock of the bombs falling short on them. His watchword of racing ahead was not followed. And the determination of the German nests of resistance does not explain everything. This night of 25-26 July was a night of agony for both sides. However, *Lt.Gen.* Bradley had just been informed that *Maj.Gen.* Hobbs's **30th Inf.Div.** had finally seized the ruins of **Hébécrevon** and Intelligence Officers's reports told of the first prisoners being still dazed at the violence of the bombardment. And next morning, there would be another air strike.

26 July

To reconstitute the pulverized front, the German command had few resources and weak reserves. General von Choltitz decided to dispatch forthwith a reinforced regiment of *353. Inf. Div.* to the threatened sector. Also, the 7th Army commander (Hausser) was still unaware (the telephone lines had been cut, crushed under the bombs) of the real state of *the* "*Panzer-Lehr*". Confronting the **3rd Inf.Div.**, elements of the German **5th Parachute Division** determinedly held out the day before (their defense favored by some rough terrain and the deep Lozon valley). The 353. Inf. Div. prepared to counter-attack against *La Chapelle-en-Juger*. What was left of the **"Panzer-Lehr"** also attempted to hold out. Colonel Gerhardt managed to have some damaged tanks repaired and was able to align 14 at Canisy and another 14 joined **Pz.-Lehr-Rgt. 130** the following day.

In the first hours of the day, the situation appeared none too rosy to the American command, with very little ground gained in view of the resources expended. However, this was the day the offensive really broke through. The last pockets of resistance yielded, the assault troops reasserted themselves and forged ahead irresistibly. At dawn, the **8th IR, 4th Inf.Div.**, took **La Chapelle-en-Juger**, secured the crossroads passing through the ruined locality and carried on southwards, eliminating a few pockets of resistance as it went. That afternoon, the regiment overran elements of the 353rd and put to flight the *"Panzer-Lehr"*'s artillery units. To the right, the **9th ID** gained a little ground but no more than the previous day. *The 30th Inf.Div.,* on the other hand, raced ahead on the left flank. The **117th IR** (Kelly) advanced due east towards Saint-Lô in the bend of the Vire. The **119th IR** moved quickly down south while cutting south-east to reach and cover the west bank of the Vire. In the afternoon, it cut off the Coutances/Saint-Lô road and set off to take its next objective: the Canisy/Saint-Lô road, a mission half

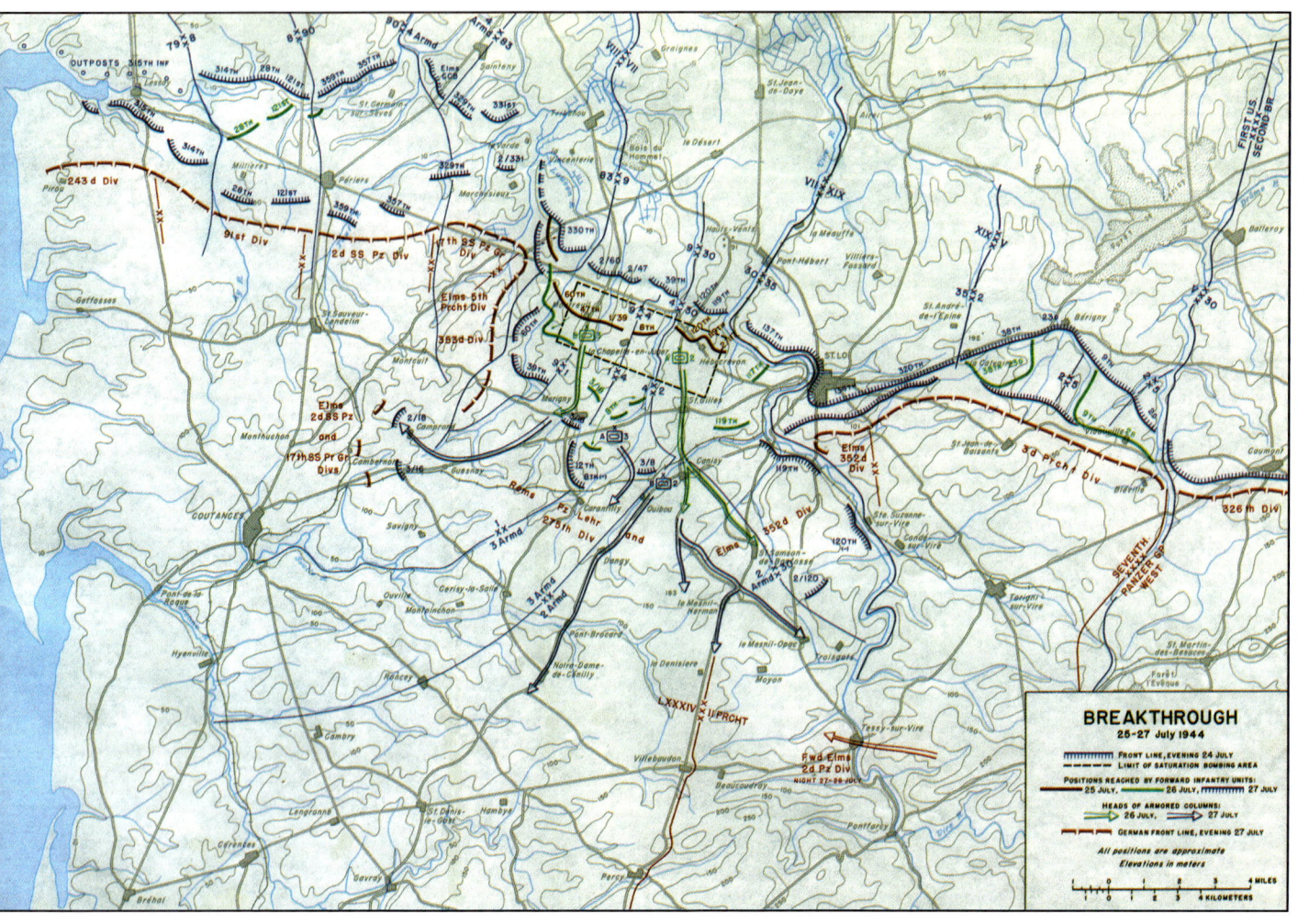

The initial phase of Cobra, the Breakthrough, 25-27 July. Already two armored divisions are pouring into the breach, the 3rd in the west and the 2d in the east. (US Army History Department)

completed by nightfall. Maj.Gen. Hobbs was exultant: "This thing has busted wide open". All he now had in front of him were a few soldiers who surrendered without a fight; there was no more German front facing his sector.

On hearing this good news, Maj.Gen. Collins had a decision to make as to whether to use his tanks. His fear was that committing the tanks might congest the battlefield (as had happened in the Saint-Fromond bridgehead) and the role assigned to his armored divisions involved deepening the breach after the infantry had broken out. In view of the rapidly changing situation and the Germans' disappearance from a whole section of the battlefield, he decided to commit his tanks. Major-General Clarence R. Hubner (**1st Inf.Div.**) was to clear the crossroads for **CCB** (Boudinot), **3rd Armd. Div.**, passing through the lines of the **9th Inf.Div.** and reach **Marigny**. Close to this locality, the Americans ran up against two companies of the **"Das Reich"** Division (supported by a few Panzer IV tanks and anti-tank 75 mm guns) and elements of **353. ID**. Further east, **CCA** of the **2d Arm. Div.** broke out from **Saint-Gilles**, profiting from the mopping up operations already performed in the sector by the infantry of the *30th Inf.Div.*, the tanks of the *2d Arm.Div.* made good progress towards Canisy, more hindered by bomb craters than by enemy resistance. At **Canisy**, **CCA** of the *2d Arm.Div.* was divided into two columns: one veered off towards Hill 122 in the direction of Le Mesnil-Herman and the other towards **Saint-Samson-de-Bonfossé**, reached without a fight by midnight.

Thus, this new day brought the much-awaited breakthrough, one that could even be exploited by committing the tanks. In the south-east, in the sector of the **30th Inf.Div.** and **2d Arm. Div.**, the American lines moved a dozen kilometers forward through a gaping hole where the German front no longer existed. "Cobra" had succeeded.

Further west, in the sector of Maj.Gen. Middleton's *VIII Corps*, the **79th** and **8th Inf.Div.** took **Lessay** from the German **243.Inf.-Div.** and a strip of ground from a *Kampfgruppe* of the **91st**. To avoid the encirclement that loomed ahead, General von Choltitz issued orders for the units of his corps' left flank to withdraw to Coutances, then Bréhal and Gavray where a second line of defense would be established.

27 July

The breakout went ahead at great speed. In the east, the **2d Arm. Div.** made the swiftest advance – with no opposition, fanning out deeply into the hedgerows, as planned. It reached Hill 183, passing **Le Mesnil-Herman** and reaching **Le Mesnil-Opac**, with its **CCA**. Further west, from Canisy, **CCB** of this division passed **Quibou** then **Dangy** before reaching *Pont-Brocard*. Fourteen tanks of the *"Das Reich"* Division were sent to Quibou to try and cut off CCB's breakthrough, to no avail, as it arrived at **Notre-Dame-de-Cenilly** at day's end. The German command had counted on *the* **"Panzer-Lehr"** to halt the southward rush of *"Hell on wheels"* – the **2d Arm.Div.**, whose motorized infantry advanced through the hedgerows in camouflage smocks), *the "Panzer-Lehr"* no longer existed as a motorized unit and so was not up to the job.

In the west, building on the breakthrough also took shape quickly. **CCA** of the **3rd Arm. Div.** advanced on **Carantilly** to cover while, further north, **CCB** (Boudinot) extended due west the northern pincer of the planned encirclement. The **3rd A.D.** had support from the **1st Inf. Div.** (Huebner) with the **18th IR** (Col. Smith) and **16th IR** (Col. Frederick W Giobbs). The **18th IR** was at **Camprond**. The American advance in this sector arrived 7 kilometers east of Coutances with Huebner's and Boudinot's men to cut off the line of retreat of the remnants of two crack divisions — **2.SS-Panzer-Division "Das Reich"** and **17.SS-Panzer-Grenadier-Division "Götz von Berlichingen"** — down to a few thousand men. The Germans then set up a north-south line of resistance east of Montcuit, and pass in groups south beyond the American positions or across the Saint-Lô/Coutances road already being taken by the American convoys. *SS-Oberscharführer* (WO) Ernst Barkmann was part of two that tried to break out. He belonged to the "Panther" tank battalion of the *"Das Reich"* Division *(I./SS-Pz.Rgt.2)* that was near Périers. He was in Le Lorey with his tank and about to counter-attack towards Marigny when he received orders to withdraw southwards through the American lines. He arrived from Le Lorey along a sunken lane and came to Highway 172 at a crossroads where his tank was protected between two tall hedges. The American tanks of CCB were arriving from the left, at 200 meters, *"Feuer!"*. One tank brewed up, followed by jeeps, half-track vehicles and tankers. Two more Shermans were destroyed. On being informed, fighter-bombers suddenly appeared in the sky and engaged Barkmann's Panther "424". He was hit but not seriously; he destroyed another two Shermans. Some German grenadiers who were there kept his tally: Barkmann and his Panther accounted for nine Sherman tanks. He pulled back to Neufbourg, the damage was repaired, and he made it to Coutances. This took his tally to 15 tanks in two days; in September Barkmann received the Knight's Cross of the Iron Cross for his action in Normandy. On this day of the great breakout, many Germans tried to withdraw to the new Bréhal/ Gavray/Percy line, and some managed to cross Highway 172.

28 July

On this fourth day of the American offensive, some unhoped-for successes enabled most of the objectives to be achieved and part of the retreating German forces to be encircled. To the east, **CCA** of the **2d Arm. Div.** carried on due south, reaching **Villebaudon**. During the night, elements of **2.Panzer-Division** crossed the Vire and mustered near Beaucoudray to counter-attack this armored spearhead, which they did the next day at La Denisière (between Villebaudon and Le Mesnil-Herman); one *Kampfgruppe* setting up a hedgehog formation by knocking out 25 American tanks before being destroyed on 30 July and 1st August. The division's other column, **CCB**, performed a particularly decisive assignment. Its tanks were at **Saint-Denis-le-Gast** where they were diverted to **Cambry** and **Lengronne** in an operation to encircle the German forces south of Coutances. From Lengronne, it was only about ten kilometers to the sea. The German's road to retreat had almost been cut off.

Now that **Lessay** and **Périers** were in the hands of the Americans (the *90th Inf.Div.* captured the latter locality the previous day), two new armored divisions were committed to the battle. The **6th Arm. Div.**, coming from Lessay, raced due south on the D2 road, arriving within four kilometers of Coutances by evening. The **4th Arm. Div.** (Major-General John S.

SS-Oscha (WO) Ernst Barkmann, with his Panther "424" of the "Das Reich" Division's tank regiment, contrived to destroy nine US tanks and numerous vehicles on the Saint-Lô/Coutances highway, on a level with Lorey. He was 24 years old, and a month later he was awarded the Knight's Cross of the Iron Cross.

Wood) moved down in the same direction, starting from Périers, crossing **Saint-Sauveur-Lendelin** and reaching **Coutances** by day's end. General Bradley committed these two armored divisions close on the heels of the German units which were retreating in good order (remnants of *243rd, 91st, 2nd SS-Pz.Div.* and *17th SS-Pz. Gr.Div.*); they advanced quickly in pursuit of the fast withdrawing Germans. Leading elements of *Maj.Gen.* Wood's 4th A.D. finally arrived in the northern outskirts of the episcopal city which was now covered just by rear-guard elements. The main streets were mined and booby-trapped. Coutances was not completely invested until the following day.

29 July

Since 26 July, the day "Cobra" really broke through, the race was on between the Americans and the Germans. The Germans hoped to hold out long enough against the American thrust in the east to enable all of their troops to withdraw to a new, rather favorable and shorter line and leaning up against some hilly ground. With an extra twenty-four hours, they might have succeeded.

The previous evening, while the armored columns had already reached Coutances in the north, the **3rd Arm.Div.** barred the way in the east from Coutances along the Savigny/Cerisy-la-Salle line, while the **2d Arm. Div.** cut off the exit route south.

Actually, the Germans had planned an intermediate line – the *"Weisse Linie"* ("white line") - before finally withdrawing to the Bréhal/Gavray/Percy line. The *"Das Reich"* Division had taken up a defensive position after withdrawing, around Courcy and **Roncey** with the *"Der Führer"* Regiment to the north (successively, from west to east: *I./DF, III./DF, II./DF*) and the *Deutschland* Regiment to the east (from north to south: *III./D, I./D, II./D*). Its positions formed the edge of a pocket, as the 2d Arm.Div. reached Cambry and Lengronne to the south: **"the Roncey Pocket"**. In addition to men of the *"Das Reich"* Division, the paratroopers and infantry of the *"Götz von Berlichingen"* Division were all together here. The crack troops of *LXXXIV.Armee-Korps* were "trapped" around Roncey. In front of this encirclement in progress, some of the men caught there managed to slip out of the sector via the west, to Gavray and Cérences while, further west, along the coast, the surviving infantrymen of German *243., 77.* and *91. ID* retreated southwards. SS-Obersturmbannführer (Lieutenant-Colonel) Christian Tychsen, temporary commander of the *"Das Reich"* Division since 26 July, was killed the previous day near Cambry. SS-Standartenführer (Colonel) Otto Baum then took over command of the division while staying on as commander of the *"Götz"*

The encirclement was completed on this day; the **4th A.D.** passed through liberated Coutances, reaching Cérences and Lengronne and the pocket was closed. Until eight that morning, various units continued to break out through the thin American lines without too much difficulty. At dawn, this all changed, with fighter-bombers flying in to machine-gun the long columns of vehicles trying to escape from what the Germans called *"der Kessel von Coutances"*. Long columns of smoke rose up over the whole sector,

The American breakthrough broadened out on 28-29 July, threatening the German units holding the coastal sector in rear and forcing them to withdraw. Two armored divisions were in hot pursuit to the west, the 6th and the 4th, which entered Coutances on 28 July. But the 2d Armored Division conducted a sweeping attack, trapping numerous German units in the Roncey pocket. The Germans fell back onto a Bréhal-Gavray-Percy line on the evening of the 29th. (US Army History Department)

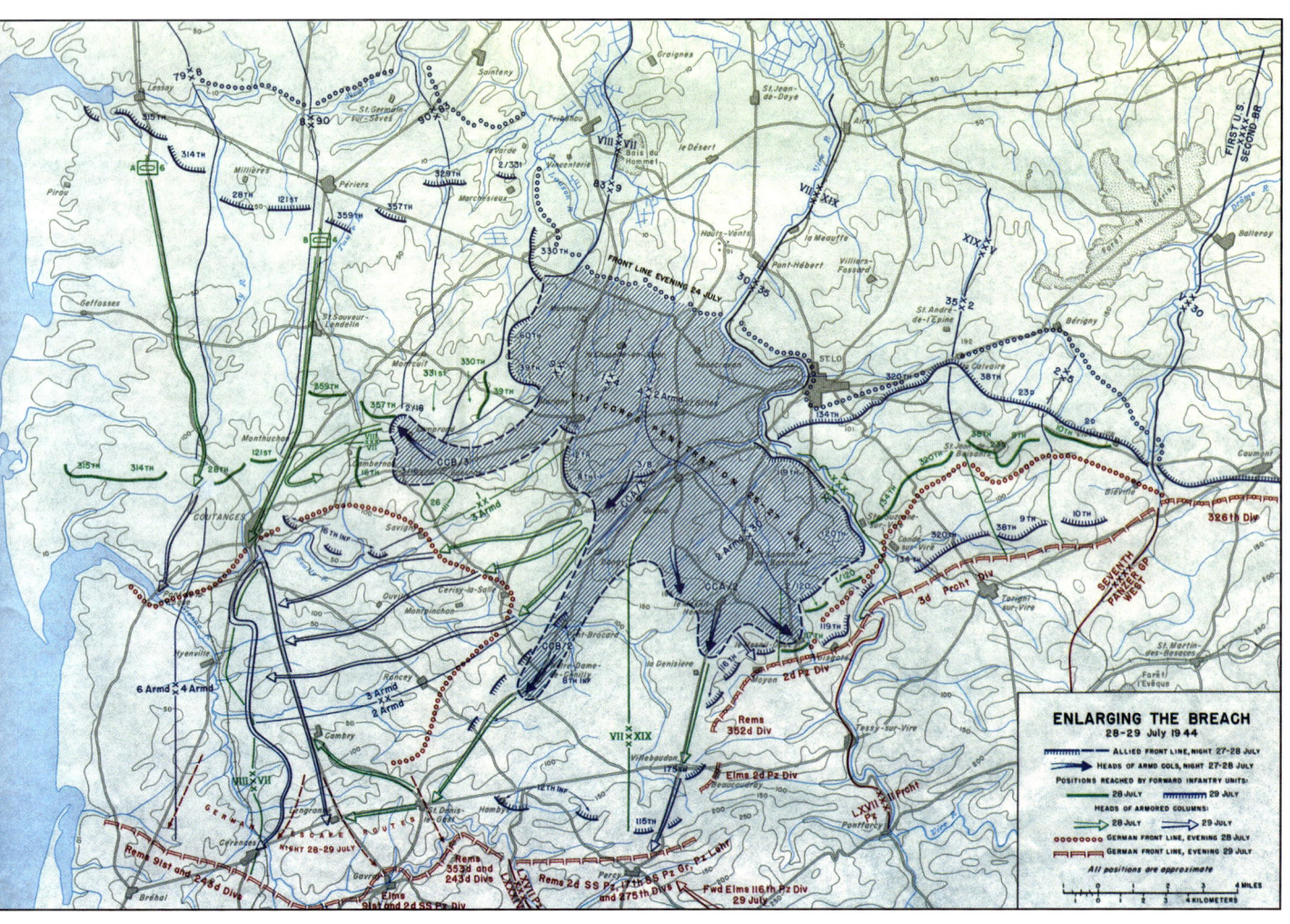

marking the cataclysm that had come down on all parts. Losses here were extremely high. But, once more, German organization and courage avoided this infernal pocket turning into a total rout. Units would go to ground by day awaiting nightfall and a last chance to break out in several sectors, notably at Saint-Denis-le-Gast, with further casualties. Three American divisions now crushed the pocket which was cleared the next day.

The *2d Arm.Div.* alone put 1,500 German soldiers out of action and captured another 4,000. This division closed the pocket from the south, with the *3rd Arm.Div.* mopping up from the east. **That evening**, the German elements able to withdraw were on the line of retreat passing through Bréhal, Gavray, Percy, Beaucoudray, Moyon, Troisgots and Torigni-sur-Vire After the successful breakthrough, the American troops thus completed the second phase of "Cobra": the pursuit of the German elements on the run, and as far as possible their destruction or capture. They now needed to set about the weak German line of retreat and carry on southwards, without worrying about the eastern flank of the offensive.

30 July

30 July. The German line of retreat was held all too briefly and lightly. From **Hambye**, the 3rd Arm.Div.'s CCB broke out southwards and approached Villedieu-les-Poêles that evening. Further west, that same division's CCA took **Gavray**, a bridge was thrown across the Sienne, the 26th IR, 1st Inf.Div. set foot on the other bank facing elements of the "*Das Reich*", on difficult terrain. Still further west, the 4th Arm.Div., coming from Coutances, took positions held by a few infantry and raced due south from *Cérences* to **La Haye-Pesnel** and even **Avranches,** which it reached that evening! Along the coast, the 6th Arm.Div. took **Bréhal** and approached **Granville**.

This operation had now turned out a masterly success. *Lt.Gen.* Patton and his 3rd Army then took over. With his armored divisions, he would charge ahead leaving the skilful Germans no breathing space to reorganize on a new line of defense within a day or two. On **31 July**, the town of Avranches was behind him. The 4th Arm.Div. was at **Ducey** and **Pontaubault**. The Americans had only to overrun a few survivors of the German *91.ID* and those of *"Kampfgruppe Bacherer"* (survivors of the 77th). The road to Brittany was open, "Cobra" was a famous victory, beyond people's wildest dreams.

Conclusions

As assessment of the Roncey Pocket

The first tangible result of the success of "Cobra" lies in the outcome of the "Roncey Pocket". The hoped-for breakthrough was to lead to the encirclement and destruction of a maximum of units in von Choltitz's corps. The assessment drawn up by the Americans of Germans losses is eloquent: 2,250 killed, 5,000 prisoners, more than 100 tanks, 150 tracked armored vehicles, pieces of ordnance, all kinds of vehicles, making a total of 539 vehicles. The Germans lost men in three pockets during the Battle of Normandy: the Cherbourg pocket in late June (40,000 men), the Roncey pocket at the end of July (7,200 men), and the Falaise pocket at the end of August (50,000 men). The Roncey pocket was the least costly for the German army in terms of numbers but probably the most expensive in terms of quality. In Cherbourg, infantrymen belonging to second rate infantry units were captured. The same may also be said for most of the men killed or captured in the Falaise pocket. In spite of the dramatic and spectacular side of this last pocket, it trapped mostly the rear-guard of second rate infantry units, Asian soldiers belonging to the "eastern troops" and very few men from armored divisions or the *Waffen-SS*. Conversely, most of the men killed or captured around Roncey belonged to crack units (paratroopers, *2.SS-Pz "Das Reich", 17.SS-Pz.Gren.Div. "Götz von Berlichingen"*). The German army also suffered very heavy losses in terms of equipment. Otto Weidinger (*op. cit.* p. 264) gives figures which tell us the percentage of equipment salvaged from the armored artillery regiment of the *"Das Reich"* Division (*SS-Pz.Art.Rgt.2 "DR"*), compared to the issues of 28-7-1944: -30% for the command battery, -0% for the 2nd Battalion, -40% for the 4th Battalion, -60% for the observation battery. The tank regiment of this same division (*SS-Pz.Rgt. 2 "DR"*) salvaged 70% of its machinery and the AA battalion (*SS-Flak-Abt. 2 "DR"*) evacuated only 10% of its guns. Otto Weidinger notes that almost all the losses in *matériel* were due to the action of Allied aircraft. But, in spite of the impressive figures for these losses, the energy of the Germans encircled at Roncey averted disaster. As Martin Blumenson observes (op. cit., p. 281), the *"Das Reich"*'s battalion of Panzer IVs slipped quite safely out of the Pocket (which accounts for Otto Weidinger's figure of 70% machines saved by the tank regiment of the *"Das Reich"*) and many soldiers of the 6th Parachute Regiment (almost all of whom broke out eastwards behind their commander, Major von der Heydte) and of the *"Götz von Berlichingen"* Division found a way out of the Pocket, over 7,000 men, which is more than half of the number encircled. This determination to avoid capture, as testified by many Germans who fought in Normandy, is explained by the motivation of the troops but more particularly by the presence of many who had previously fought on the Eastern front (particularly in the armored units). There, capture was almost always synonymous with a quick or a slow death: summary execution or the very high death rate in the prison camps of the Soviet Union. The chances of a German prisoner on the Eastern front ever seeing his homeland again were less than 10%; out of the 107,800 German prisoners taken by Soviet troops at Stalingrad, only 6,000 survivors made it back to Germany some fifteen years later (figures provided by Paul Carell). This explains the German soldier's kneejerk reaction and his savage determination to fight with no thoughts of surrendering and to break out at all costs in the event of encirclement.

As Martin Blumenson further notes, there were enough troops along the line from Percy to the sea, but the problem was that the men were exhausted. So, the Roncey Pocket was a major step towards success for the Allies in Normandy but, as later with the Falaise Pocket, it was less than a total success. The 2d Arm.Div. played a decisive role in cutting off the German line of retreat to the south, but it was not strong enough to close the gap altogether. The *"Das Reich"* and *"Götz von Berlichingen"* divisions lived to fight another day in the Battle of Mortain (albeit in considerably smaller numbers) when they might have been completely engulfed in the trap.

An assessment of "Cobra"

"Cobra" was without doubt the greatest Allied success of the Battle of Normandy (after the D-day Lan-

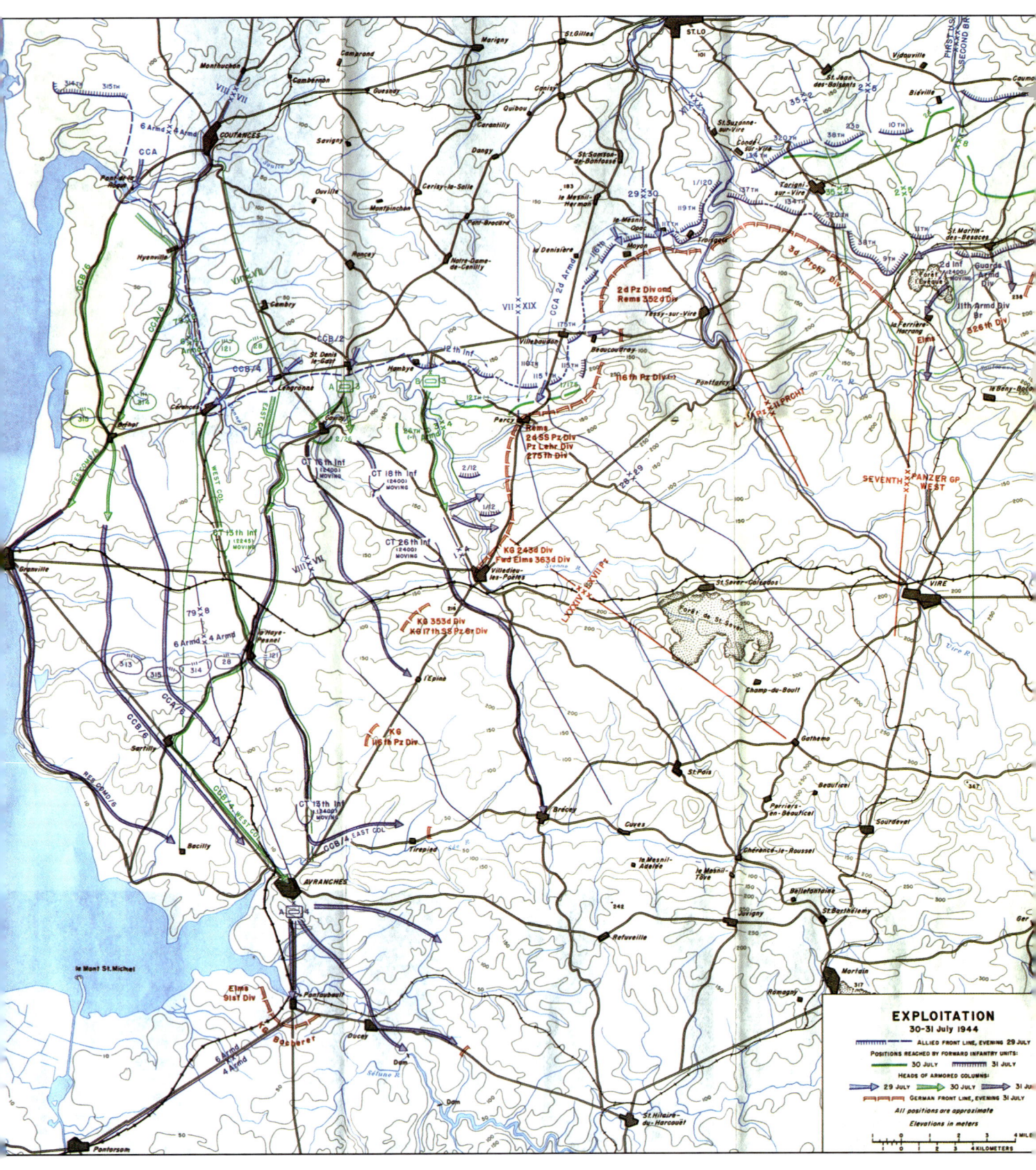

Cobra was a success, Pontaubault was reached on the evening of 31 July. This came to be known as the breakout at Avranches. (US Army History Department)

ding itself). Whereas the Germans had almost reduced the western Allies to a war of position and attrition (with losses even), "Cobra" finally got the Normandy front moving and succeeded beyond their wildest hopes by making up at a stroke for all the time lost in the execution of "Master Plan", taking apart the German front and advancing unopposed across the rest of France (this was not planned).

In the "Great controversy" which divided the American and British Allies – and still does – General Montgomery's supporters claim that he gave the British army a crucial role to play in pinning down the greater part of the German armor around Caen, leaving General Bradley a free hand in the west to launch his victorious offensive. American criticisms of Montgomery's "overcautiousness" do certainly seem fairly well grounded. The 1st Army had to tackle the most difficult terrain of the Normandy front, with swamps and high ground (Mont Castre among others) to be taken, they suffered much heavier losses than the British, partly owing to the lack of combat experience of many of the units but most of all on account of the 1st Army's more aggressive stance in launching an all-out offensive along the entire front from 3 to 15 July, a tactic that paid off since it bled to death von Choltitz's corps to the point of no longer being able to withstand "Cobra".

True, two thirds of the German armored divisions committed to the Normandy front were around Caen (which was only normal in view of the fact that the terrain in the Plain of Caen was much more suited to tank warfare). But the Americans were confronted with crack troops along two thirds of their front line, from east to west: II Parachute Corps, "*Panzer-Lehr*", "*Götz von Berlichingen*", 6th Parachute Regiment, "*Das Reich*". The great merit of the American command was to implement these tactics of all-out offensive to weaken the enemy, crush him at one specific point along the front with tremendous means (carpet bombing), then race through the open breach without worrying over their flanks, and to make a success of the breakout through sheer speed which brought ultimate success. British tank warfare followed rather more antiquated principles: the tanks progressed in successive leaps, waiting each time to be covered by the infantry; this tactic proved fatal in the failed Operation "Epsom". It was the speed of the offensive that made "Cobra" such a masterly victory. Even the German counter-attack at Mortain failed to slow down Patton's tanks advancing across the rest of France.

Role in the overall context of the world war and human losses

As we have just seen, "Cobra" marked the major turning point in the Battle of Normandy and therefore in the "War in the West" which led to the campaign in Germany and ultimate victory.

How did such a success come about? The scale of the Allied victory in Normandy can really only be seen in the light of the war on the Eastern front, which is where destiny was really played out. One only has to consider the figures for military losses. The USA lost 250,000 men (including in the Pacific) and Great Britain 350,000 soldiers (not that many, considering that the United Kingdom had been fighting in various theaters since the first day of the war). On the other hand, the two armies battling it out on the "Eastern front" suffered truly huge losses. The Soviet Union lost 13,600,000 fighting men (some historians put the figures a good deal higher than that: thirty million and more, there were no accurate statistics at the time and the exact figure will probably never be known) and the Reich registered 2,500,000 men who fell in the front line and a total of four million military losses (total German losses came to seven million – with three million civilians killed). The difference between these two figures (see Müller-Hillebrandt's official account) represents German prisoners-of-war who died in captivity, i.e. a million and a half (!) POWs who never returned home (the great majority of them died in Soviet captivity). The Soviet Union played a major role in human terms in the Second World War. It utterly committed its men in human waves, with no concern for losses. The German army was completely worn down there. Thus by the end of 1944 the *Wehrmacht* had been bled white, and was a poor army with very few reserves. The Allied landing in Normandy, backed by such tremendous material support (from 1941 to 1945 the USA built 300,000 aircraft!), was the last straw that broke the camel's back. But, more than a war of hardware, this conflict was a fantastic battle of men. Just before battle commenced in Normandy, the Soviets launched their summer offensive and committed against the German Center Front no less than a hundred divisions of the Guard! Confronted with such a tremendous force, the German front in Bielorussia just collapsed. A German tank army was encircled near Tarnapol. The Roncey and Falaise Pockets pale into insignificance compared with the great battles to destroy the Eastern front. The war was fought first in Russia and then in Normandy. But "Cobra" and the Battle of Normandy were nevertheless the major watershed in the war, marking the beginning of the end.

To close this evocation of "Cobra", let us not forget the civilian losses which came to 15,000 among the Norman population of the Manche department, out of a total of nearly 50,000 for the whole of Normandy, losses which are not so very far short of the military losses.

30th Infantry Division

1st Infantry Division

3. Private Victor Dowdle of Blackfoot, Idaho, a member of an anti-tank unit with the 1st Infantry Division (notice the divisional badge on his sleeve - "The Big Red One") paints the Allied white star and the name of his anti-tank company on a captured German half-track. This vehicle, an SPW, belonged to the Panzer-Lehr-Division's assault gun battalion, as can just be made out from the two tactical markings above and to the right of the star.

4. William M. Textee and Henry Zimmerman of the 2nd Battalion, the 47th Infantry Regiment (9th Infantry Division) examine German propaganda leaflets (they are near their comrades pictured in photo n° 2).

5. On this 24 July 1944, the infantry and armor get into position before the decisive assault.

(D.F./Heimdal.)

Preparations, 24 and 25 July.

1. On 24 July, an off-target bombing raid left 25 killed and 131 wounded among the ranks of the 30th Infantry Division. Pictured here are medical orderlies of this "Old Hickory" division picking up casualties. Notice the divisional badge on the sleeve of the medic in the foreground.

2. As bombers come over their objective on this 25 July, Corporal Anthony Pinto of the 47th Infantry Regiment, 9th Infantry Division takes a light meal before the attack. The 3rd Battalion of this regiment had its Command Group destroyed by the bombs. The divisional badge is visible on these two men's sleeve.

9th Infantry Division

Bombardment of 25 July.

1. The huge armada of Allied bombers fills the Cotentin sky. This extraordinary photograph pictures formations of great winged creatures of steel about to sow death and destruction in a few minutes.

2. These four infantrymen of the 3rd Battalion of the 8th Infantry Regiment (4th Division) gaze with satisfaction at this armada crossing the sky: it is 10.35 (we checked) on one of the GIs' watch: the time of the bombardment!

3. The day before, 24 July, a fighter-bomber hit a vehicle. This photo gives a good idea of the type of terrain on which the troops had to operate.

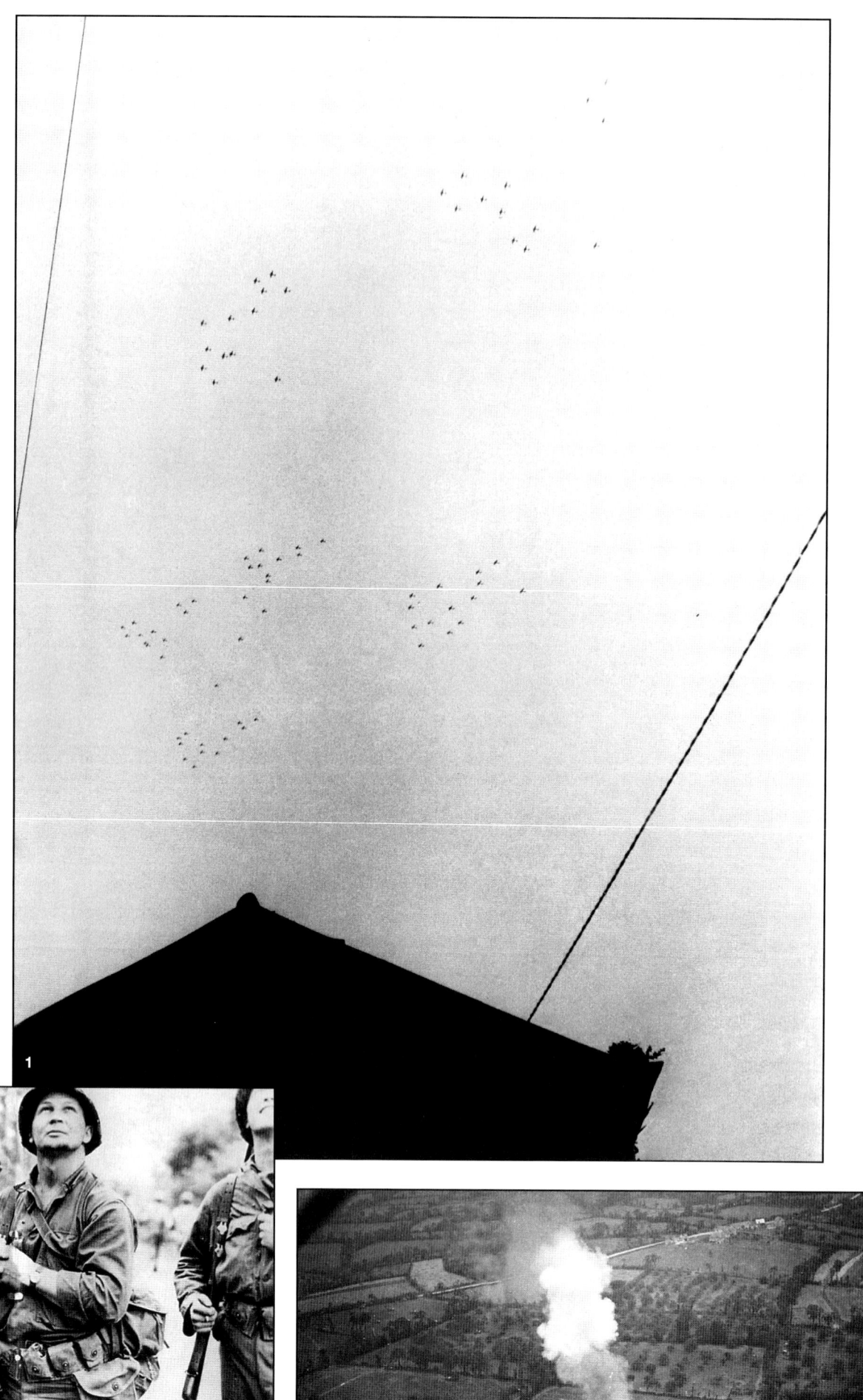

290

4 and **5.** These two aerial photos show the outcome of the bombardment in the Saint-Gilles sector. The bomb craters are huge. The photographed sector is the same (identifiable as such from the road and the track marks left by the tanks). (NA/Heimdal - Heimdal Coll.)

Bombardment of 25 July

1 and **2.** The time is 09.00 hours on 25 July 1944, 1,500 B-17 and B-27 bombers fly over their objectives about to drop a carpet of 3,300 tons of bombs on the area from Montreuil-sur-Lozon to Hébécrevon. All hell is let loose; the Americans also suffered heavy losses among their own ranks: 111 killed and 490 wounded, almost the strength of a battalion! In this photograph, medics dig out GIs buried under earth blasted into the air by the bombs.

3. One of the victims was Lieutenant General Lesley J McNair, commander-in-chief of the ground forces and commander of the First Army Group. Given his role in the "Fortitude" plan, his death was kept a secret. This photo was taken just hours before his death, on 25 July.

4. After the bombardment started at 05.00 hours, following the failed raid of the previous day, and despite the losses, GIs race through the hedges to overpower whatever remains of the German positions crushed under the bombs.

5. The bomb craters sometimes cut off roads and bulldozers set to work to enable troops to be brought quickly up to the front. Pictured here are men of the 30th Infantry Division (notice the unit's patch on the sleeve of the infantryman on the left). These troops covered the left flank of the breakthrough.

(Photographs courtesy D.F./Heimdal.)

The throes of the "Panzer-Lehr" (1)

War correspondent George Greb followed the American armor as it raced towards Marigny on 26 June 1944. He left an outstanding reportage on the catastrophe that hit the Panzer-Lehr-Division. He took pictures of the wreckage of at least three Panther tanks, a Panzer IV and two half-tracks.

1 and **2.** These two photographs are of a destroyed 45-ton Panther, cast into a bomb crater like a straw in the wind. (Heimdal Coll.)

3. Further on, another Panther had its track blown off and brewed up. According to the caption to this photograph, the two motorcyclists resting in the foreground were involved in the destruction of this Panther by bazooka with an anti-tank crew; possibly so, for there is no bomb crater to be seen. They are Pvt. Raymond Bennett (right) from Irwin, Tennessee and Sergeant Harvey Davis from San Diego, California. (Heimdal Coll.)

4. This photograph, taken from a different angle, also pictures the burnt-out Panther and the motorcyclists, in the background; in the foreground, a half-track belonging to the engineer battalion (Panzer-Pionier-Battalion 130) of the Panzer-Lehr-Division carries crossing ramps seen here on the vehicle. (Heimdal Coll.)

294

The throes of the "Panzer-Lehr".

After the bombardments of 25 July, the 40 tanks lined up by the Panzer-Lehr-Division were all destroyed. Some exploded on impact, others were flipped upside down and thrown into bomb craters... One had its turret completely ripped off **(3 and 4)**, while another brewed up **(1, 2 and 5)**.

(Reportage by George Greb, Nat. Archives, Heimdal collection.)

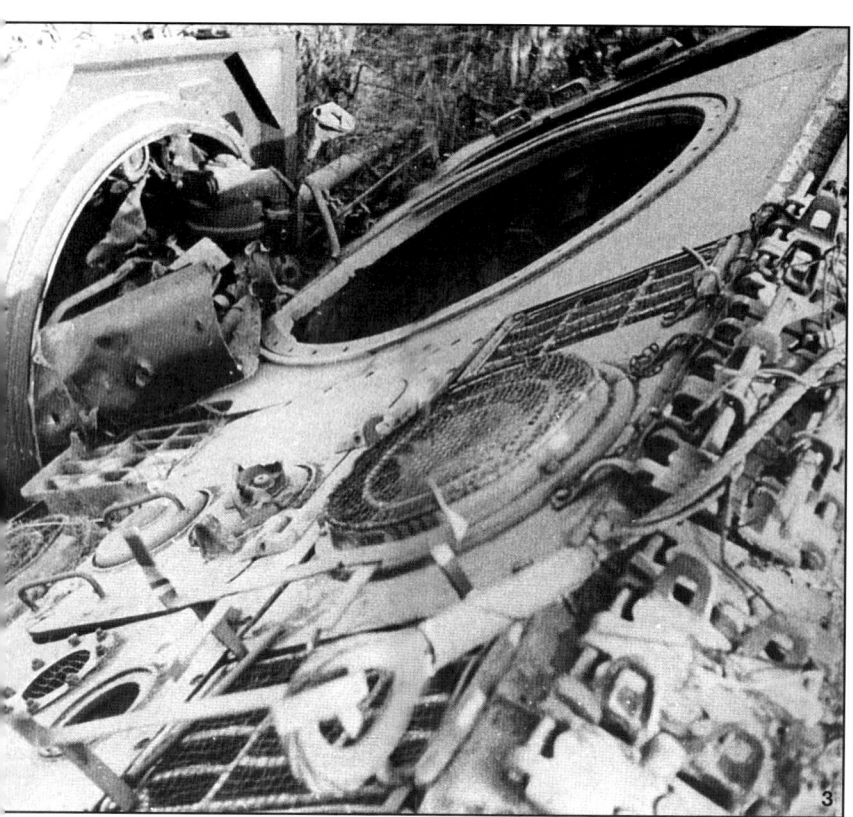

The throes of the "Panzer-Lehr".

Photographer George Greb made this reportage in the wake of the 2d Armored Division, near Saint-Gilles.

On the way, a Jeep belonging to a 2d Armored Division staff passes by a destroyed Panzer IV of the 8th Company **(3).** The same tank is pictured in photo 1. Further on a Panzer-Lehr (SPW) vehicle with its track blown off has been destroyed and pushed onto the roadside **(2).** Another shot of the Panther tank destroyed by Sergeant Harvey Davis, the tank that had its track blown off and brewed up **(4).**

5. Another destroyed Panther was thrown onto the verge. These men of the 2d Armored Division pose in front of the defeated monster.

6. A team of medics races towards Saint-Gilles.

(Reportage by George Greb, Nat. Archives, Heimdal collection.)

The throes of the "Panzer-Lehr".

1. There were Tatars and Mongols in the line alongside the Panzer-Lehr, they are now prisoners with their German comrades.

2, 4 and **5.** The 2d Armored Division military police round up some German prisoners and a few Tatars, including those already seen in photo **1.**

3, 6 and **7.** On this 26 July, on entering Saint-Gilles, the Americans found only one civilian, with a leg broken just above ankle. When these medics from a Tank Destroyer unit (see the badge of this type of unit in the three photographs and more particularly photo 6) tried to speak to him in French, he answered in Russian: "Tovarich, Tovarich!" He was a Russian who had been captured near Leningrad and enlisted as a forced laborer at Cherbourg whence he contrived to escape during the battle and take shelter here, where he was wounded. The American medics administer first aid before evacuating him in the jeep.

(Photographs courtesy George Greb/ Heimdal Greb Coll.)

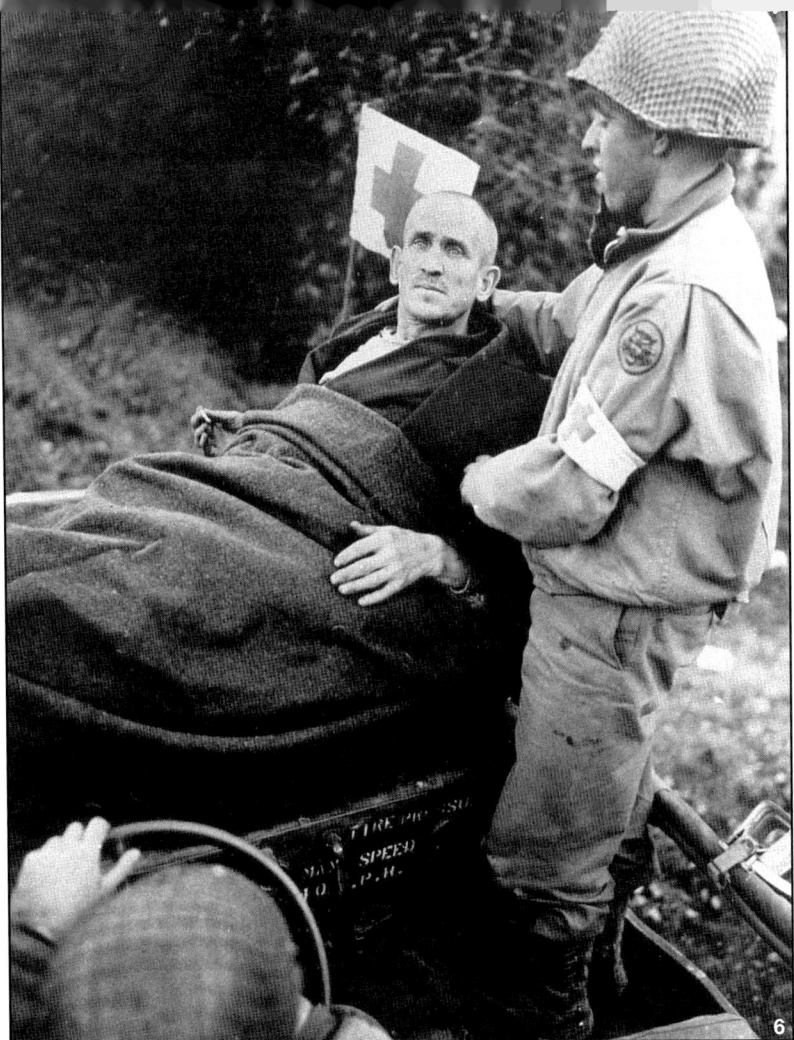

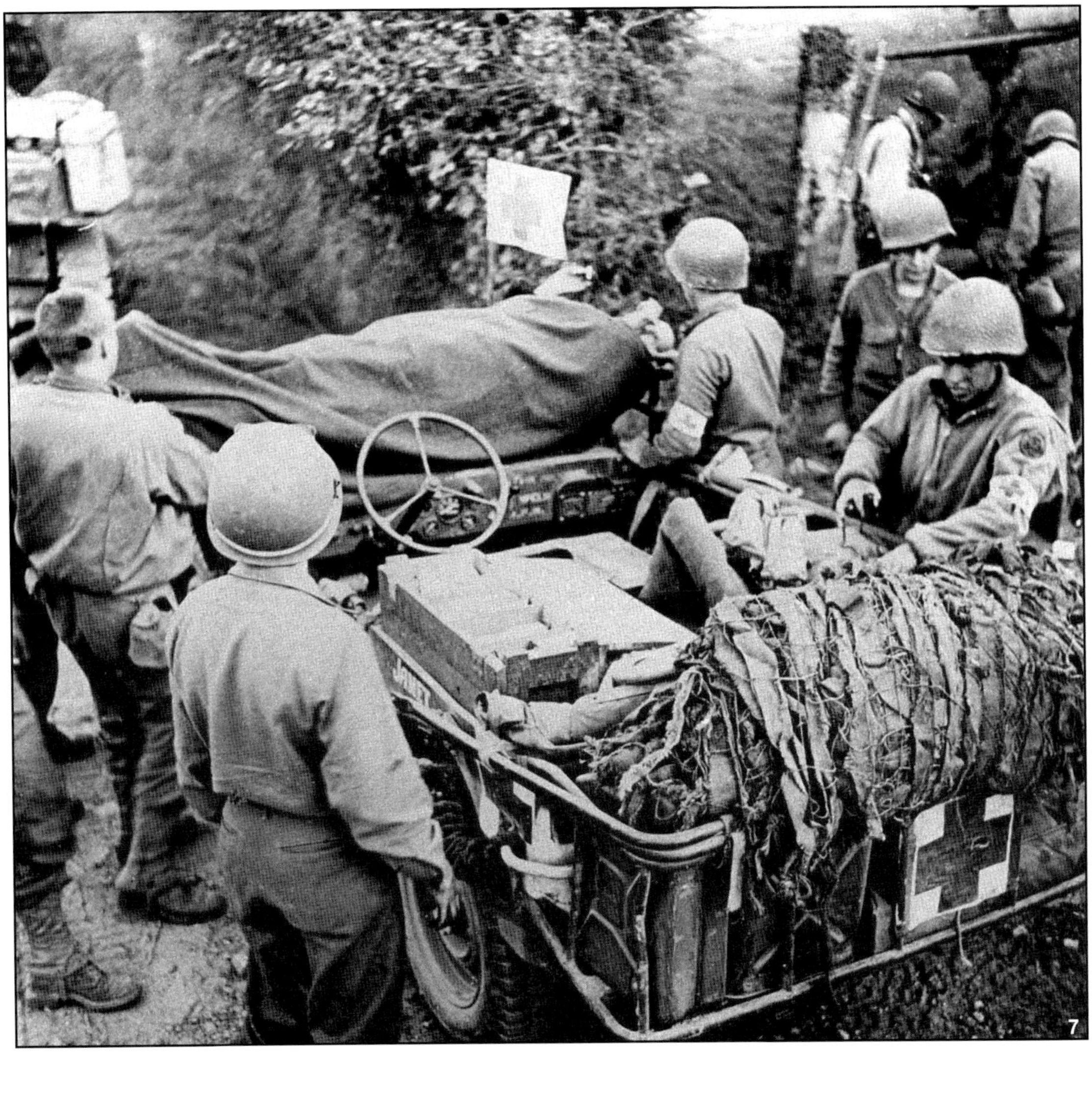

301

**The throes of the "Panzer-Lehr".
(Reportage by George Greb, Nat. Archives, Heimdal collection - photographs 1 to 5).**

1 and **2.** A mine clearance team west of Saint-Lô near Hébécrevon. From left to right (in photo n° 2): Pvt. Barnie Forrest from Chipewaw Missouri, Pvt. Wilson Smith from Graceville Florida and Pvt. Dalton Farmer from Big Sandy Tennessee.

3. A bulldozer clears the road for the 2d Armored Division's tanks. In the background, a Sherman tank has fallen into a bomb crater, beside a destroyed German SPW half-track.

4. American matériel abandoned on the battlefield near Saint-Gilles, probably the equipment of GIs killed or wounded in the bombardments; notice the photograph of a woman glued onto a rifle butt.

5. Lieutenant George Williams from Houtzdale in Pennsylvania defuses a German booby-trap near Saint-Gilles. A grenade had been connected to a compass; any GI picking up the compass would have set off the grenade.

6. North of Marigny, these engineers are trying to pull clear a bulldozer that has fallen into a muddy bomb crater (this photograph is not by George Greb, photograph by Collier - 8863).

(Nat. Archives/ Heimdal Collection.)

303

Marigny sector, 26 July.

1. As the 9th Infantry Division advances on Marigny, the tanks await the order to attack. Five tank crew members of the 3rd Armored Division, sheltering under their TD tanks, will soon be racing towards Marigny.

2. On the afternoon of 26 July, the tanks of CCB of the 3rd Armored Division finally race towards Marigny. Pictured here are two light Stuart tanks of Company "B" of the 33rd Armored Regiment advancing due south. The front tank is fitted with a hedge-cutter. (8791)

3 and **4.** Major General Manton S. Eddy (on the right in the jeep, with his hand on the windshield), commanding the 9th Infantry Division, is here at the farm at the place named La Courmiette, at Champs de Losques. He has come to monitor on the ground his men's advance on Marigny; he was surprised the previous day by unexpected resistance although the Germans had come under heavy bombardment. Like most of the buildings in the sector the farm pictured here (photographed in 1991) was made of earth.

5. Infantrymen advance through the ruins of Marigny.

6. A 75 mm MK 8 howitzer mounted on an armored chassis of the 33rd Armored Regiment, the 3rd Armored Division passes through Montreuil-sur-Lozon as a bulldozer is already hard at work clearing rubble. The howitzer is followed by more vehicles of the 33rd Armored Regiment (CCB): Dodge, MÁ1 half-track, M8 armored car, moving on Marigny on this 26 July.

(Photographs courtesy DAVA and D.F./Heimdal.)

The front explodes

1. This young German paratrooper, 17 year-old Georg Eidloth, was one of the first German prisoners. He was captured north of Marigny by First Army photographer Corporal Alex H. Kapitanski, pictured behind him. This photo was also taken at La Courmiette, Champs de Losques. The montage below was made with the photograph on the previous page, taken at the same location.

2. More paratroopers of the 5. Fallschirmjäger-Division, most still wearing their helmets, are taken to the rear and pass a heavy truck with cab and armor-plated engine belonging to their unit (it has a "WL" registration).

3. Further on, after an intial check, their guards have made them give up their helmets and belts.

4. A halt. The photographer has followed the same group. We recognize the leading paratrooper in the previous photo.

5. The check continues.

6. The men in the previous photo have received a label; they are now prisoners-of-war.

(US Army and D.F./Heimdal.)

Prisoners gathered on 26 July.

1 and **2.** A whole group of captive paratroopers, already labelled, is taken to a farm supervised by Cpl. Everett Paw, Mayfield Hgts., Ohio, an MP, prior to transfer to a prison camp. These paratroopers formed a highly motivated crack troop. They are the survivors of the 5. Fallschirmjäger-Division whose already sorely tried 13th Regiment was completely wiped out under the carpet of bombs. (8792-24 and 30)

3. Another view of this group.

4. Near Pont-Brocard, a small party is supervised by a soldier of the 2d Armored Division, recognizable by his camouflage smock.

5. An American photographer of the Army Signal Corps by the body of a German paratrooper killed in position with no time to use his Panzerschreck (German bazooka) or his MP 40 submachine-gun. He is wearing a paratrooper's jump boots but an Army helmet, which was common practice among German parachute units used almost exclusively in ground operations in 1944.

6. This GI is inspecting some German graves.

(US Army and D.F./Heimdal.)

The prisoners are rounded up, 27 July.

1. On 27 July, an officer of the 9th Infantry Division (notice the divisional badge on his sleeve) questions German prisoners captured during the battle fought in the Marigny sector. They include paratroopers of the 5. Fallschirmjäger-Division and infantrymen of the 353. Infanterie-Division. Photo taken by Spangle. (8830)

2. That same day, in the Carantilly sector, men of the 4th Infantry Division bring back a German prisoner assigned to the 275. Infanterie-Division.

3. Here now is a group of prisoners from an infantry division, probably the 275. ID.

4. Prisoners are rounded up, some are paratroopers, most are wounded.

5. Captive paratroopers collapse with exhaustion after the terrible ordeal they have been through.

6. Pictured here are the same paratroops behind barbed wire.

(US Army and D.F./Heimdal.)

German prisoners, 25 and 26 July 1944

1. A young parachutist (of the 13th Regiment) reads one of thousands of leaflets dropped over the German lines. This one refers to the 20 July attempt on Hitler's life and encourages the Germans to surrender.

4th Infantry Division

2. North of Saint-Gilles, on this 25 July, Donald Mackenzie, correspondent for the New York Daily News (left) with the assistance of S/Sgt Ralph A. Hirst (center) provided to translate for him, questions a German Panzer-Lehr prisoner who is wearing the Feldgrau jacket of the assault gun or motorized artillery units. He questions him about morale in the German Army following the 20 July attempt on Hitler's life.

3. A Feldwebel (sergeant) of the 13th Parachute Regiment, taken prisoner on 26 July, quietly smokes a Bavarian pipe. The American caption mentions his Hitler moustache. He is decorated with the Wounded Medal.

4. La Chapelle-en-Juger on 25 July, Lieutenant Walter V Bodlanger (center) and Lieutenant-Colonel Hanson (right) ask a German parachutist (left) for information about his regiment's positions. Notice the 4th Infantry Division's patch clearly visible on Lieutenant Boldanger's sleeve. The two American officers belonged to this division advancing in the center of the disposition.

5. On 26 July, this is the first party of German prisoners to be sorted and gathered after the first shock of "Cobra", and later sent to the rear on their way to a prison camp. The fourth prisoner in the right foreground is one of the Tatars photographed by George Greb (see our reportage on "the throes of the Panzer-Lehr").

(Photographs courtesy US Army and D.F./Heimdal Collection.)

313

3rd Armored Division

9th Infantry Division

Marigny 26 and 27 July, 9th Infantry Division, 3rd Armored Division

1. Hot on the heels of the tanks of the 3rd Armored Division, the infantry enter Marigny late on 26 July. German tactical signs on the signpost on the right: at the top that of the 2. SS-Panzer-Division "Das Reich" and, below, the way to Kampfgruppe Heintz. Notice in the background the square in front of the church with the grain store and the bakery which we will be seeing in the photographs on following pages. (D.F./Heimdal.)

2. In the church square, a GI passes by an abandoned German 105 mm gun, a 10.5 cm leichte Feldhaubitze 18, a howitzer used a great deal by German artillery regiments. The church dominates the square. Photo taken on 28 July. (D.F./Heimdal.)

3. The destroyed houses have been rebuilt. The road signs indicate north, the direction from which the Americans arrived: Saint-Sauveur-Lendelin and the German military cemetery now located on the north side of the locality. (E.G./Heimdal.)

4. Moving forward and turning round to face north, we see the gun again at the foot of the destroyed houses.

(D.F./Heimdal.)

5. In this photograph, taken from a little further back, American engineers have cleared the rubble that had spilled out onto the street, blocking the traffic. The 105 mm howitzer was pushed back into the debris piled up beside the church (the gun can be seen). The house which got in the way in the bend was dynamited on 29 July, raising a cloud of dust. (D.F./Heimdal.)

6. Today, the houses on the left survived the war. (E.G./Heimdal.)

7. A rare color photograph taken in 1944 showing the 105 mm howitzer amid the debris. (U.S. Army.)

Marigny 26-28 July, 9th Infantry Division, 3rd Armored Division, 1st Infantry Division

1. CCB of the 3rd Armored Division and the 1st Infantry Division now pass through Marigny before carrying on due west towards Coutances. From the church, the war correspondent has taken a photograph of the square. Pictured are Monsieur Deshayes' grocery store already seen on the previous page. On the left are the grain store, the bakery and Pacary's butcher's shop. (DAVA/Heimdal.)

2. A GI rests beside Benoist's bakery, photograph taken by war correspondent Spangle on 28 July. (D.F./Heimdal.)

3. Today, a bank has replaced the grain store. (E.G./Heimdal.)

4. On 26 July, A Company of the 296th Engineers, 111th Engineer Combat Group is at work clearing rubble (see also the photographs on the previous pages). (NA/Heimdal.)

5. The interior of the church shows the damage caused by American barrage fire that fell on the place. While the façade is almost intact, the south side (on the right in the photo) was laid low by shellfire. Photo taken on 28 July by war correspondent Petrony. (D.F./Heimdal.)

6. Today, the south aisle has been restored. (E.G./Heimdal.)

7. The American army passes through Marigny and a French flag has been hung from the front of Benoist's bakery. At the foot of the shop are German stakes and barbed wire. (NA/Heimdal.)

26 July. The 4th Infantry Division passes through La Chapelle-en-Juger, a major passing place.

1 and **2**. During the night of 25-26 July, patrols of the 4th Infantry Division had already infiltrated La Chapelle-en-Juger, a small locality at a crossroads that was almost razed to the ground by the carpet of bombs. At dawn, the 8th Infantry Regiment (4th ID) secured the crossroads, passed through the village and carried on south, eliminating a few pockets of resistance. Pictured here is an M8 armored car and a half-track arriving from the north, from Le Hommet d'Arthenay, passing in front of the ruined church choir. Today, the First World War monument pictured here has gone. A local inhabitant told us that the

4th Infantry Division

statue of the "poilu" was buried in front of the church choir, under a slab recalling the fighting in 1944…

3. A little later, an MP directs traffic near the "poilu" and in front of the large bay of the choir of the devastated church later entirely rebuilt.

4. This other photograph was taken from the crossroads, south of the chancel. The pile of rubble visible behind the Stuart tank coming from the north is the same one pictured on the right in photo 1. The large house in the background, then almost intact, is still standing today.

5 and **6.** From the church cemetery, the photographer takes the back of the statue of the "poilu". An ambulance arrives, on the left, from the north. The large house, at the bottom right, behind the wooden post, is on the edge of the road east to Hébécrevon.

(NA and D.F./Heimdal - E.G./Heimdal.)

319

**Hébecrevon
27 July 1944.**

1 and **2**. The men of the 30th Infantry Division seized the ruins of the village of Hébécrevon on the evening of 25 July. This village is on the Saint-Lô/Périers road, mostly on the south side. It was completely destroyed by the carpet of bombs. Infantry and artillerymen of Company "K" of the 120th Infantry Regiment (30th I.D.) have just passed the crossroads, in this photograph, and are advancing southwards past the destroyed church. Notice, on the right, the small house made entirely of earth, like most buildings in this marshy area where stone is hard to come by. (8888)

3 and **4**. The photographer has passed the church (which we now see on the left) and has turned round to take

these men of the division advancing southwards. Today their unit advanced very quickly through a German front that has evaporated. (8892)

5. Moving a few yards north, we again see the small earth house seen previously in photo n° **1**, and in the background, a large house built along the main highway: east to Saint-Lô on the right, and to Périers on the left. (8887)

6. Hébécrevon in 1984: this photograph was taken from the church. A solid house (on the left) has replaced the small earth house. Pictured at the bottom is the large house at the crossroads, hardly altered since 1944. (Heimdal.)

7, 8 and **9.** The cross and mutilated tombs in the cemetery. (E.G./Heimdal.)

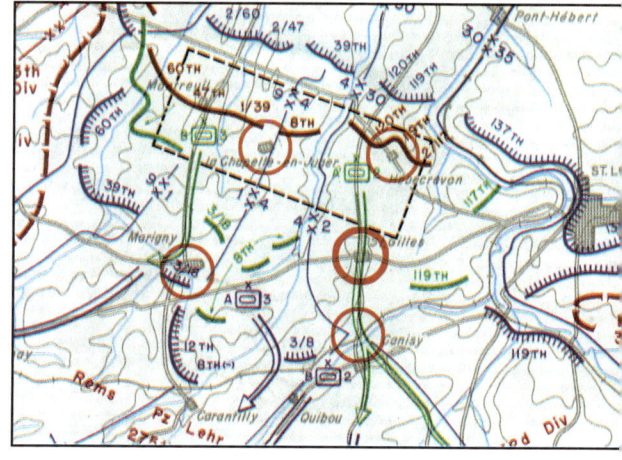

Saint-Gilles, 27 July, 30th Infantry Division, 2nd Armored Division

1. The previous day, the 30th Infantry Division advanced rapidly, taking the major crossroads at Saint-Gilles. The motorized columns of the 30th Division, followed by the 2nd Armored Division's columns of tanks, arriving from the north now pass across this strategic crossroads and the Saint-Lô/Coutances road, due south towards Canisy. Pictured here are the remains of two of the Panzer-Lehr-Division's Panzer IVs. The one on the right was blown up by heavy bombs. As the figures painted on the turret indicate, it belonged to the 3rd Troop of the 5th Company of the division's tank regiment. The wreck is still blocking the crossroads. (NA/Heimdal.)

2. In this second photograph, at almost the same spot (the ruined house at the bottom is on the right in the previous photo), we see a bulldozer clearing the crossroads. It pushed back the wreck of the 5th Company Panzer IV seen earlier and also another Panzer IV assigned to the 8th Company. (D.F./Heimdal.)

3. Most of the houses on the north side of the road were destroyed and rebuilt in local stone as shown here. The crossroads can be seen between two houses on the left. (E.G./Heimdal.)

4. A house at Saint-Gilles that survived the bombardment of 1944, with its typical architecture of clay walls (mass) on a stone base (shale), like the house in photo **2**. (E.G./Heimdal.)

5. An armored vehicle of the 2nd Armored Division passes by the big church at Saint-Gilles on the south side of the Saint-Lô/Coutances road. (NA/Heimdal.)

6. The church has been restored. (E.G./Heimdal.)

7. Commemorative plaque on one of the church's buttresses. (E.G./Heimdal.)

8. On the south side of the village, a typical house and intact section of the church steeple. (E.G./Heimdal.)

Saint-Gilles and Canisy, 27 July.

1, 2, 3. These three photographs are an addition to the reportage made at the Saint-Gilles crossroads, near the church, on 27 July, before the bulldozer cleared the junction. Again picture is the turret of the "532", notably in front of the church square.

4. Aerial photograph of Saint-Gilles taken facing north with the road on which the Americans arrived, Hébécrevon in the background on the right and La Chapelle-en-Juger in the background on the left. In this photograph, released by the SHAEF censors on 1 August 1944, the crossroads is already completely cleared.

5. An M8 armored car assigned to a recce squadron ("C" Squadron) of the 2d Armored Division enters Canisy where a house continues to burn in a blaze started by a barrage of American artillery fire launched before the troops entered the locality.

6. This aerial photograph of Canisy shows the crossroads where the armored car was.

7. A Sherman tank fitted with a hedge-cutter has slipped down a slope near Canisy. The engineers are preparing to extricate it from this predicament.

(US Army and D.F./Heimdal.)

4

5

7

6

26 July, the breakthrough.

1. Near Sainteny, observers of the 83rd Infantry Division (notice the divisional patch sewn on the sleeve of the warrant officer on the right - a black triangle and, interwoven, the letters "Ohio" in yellow) signal indications received from an outpost to a mortar battery. From left to right: 1st Lt. Robert Saettler from Clifton, New Jersey, S/Sgt E Talke from Mineral City, Ohio and S/Sgt Dick Weaver from Chambersburg, Pennsylvania. They belong to Company "D" of the 329th Infantry Regiment, 83rd Division, assigned to the VII Corps for the offensive, against the two Waffen-SS divisions in the Marchésieux sector.

2. In the center, against the Marigny sector, the artillery came in support of the front lines. Pfc Tony Andenucio loads the "50,000th shell" fired by his battery since it first opened fire on the Germans. This unit took part in the campaigns in Tunisia (where it saw action at El Guettar) and Sicily, and was among the first units to land in Normandy. It is highly likely that Tony Andenuccio's gun belongs to the one of the 9th Infantry Division's artillery battalions. It is a 105 mm howitzer and well illustrates Allied superiority in terms of artillery.

3. Again in the center (VII Corps), the 4th Infantry Division was held in reserve to come in behind 30th ID and 2d AD. Pictured here is a wireless operator carrying his portable set. The divisional badge is clearly recognizable on one of the soldiers' sleeves.

83rd ID

4th ID

326

4. A 4th Division hospital jeep passes a Sherman tank of the 2d Armored Division well camouflaged with branches.

5. A Waffen-SS tanker (probably assigned to SS-Panzer-Regiment 2 "Das Reich") is brought back a prisoner on the hood of a jeep. This tank regiment was less hard hit than the Panzer-Lehr-Division's and saved a sizable portion of its machinery.

6. A wounded infantryman with a Waffen-SS unit is treated by a medic.

(Photographs courtesy NA and D.F./Heimdal.)

26 July, the breakout.

1. Men of the 4th Infantry Division arrive from the rear base west of Le Désert to reinforce the troops already advancing satisfactorily in the front line. The roadsign points to Le Désert, Pont-Hébert and Saint-Jean-de-Daye on the left, and Le Hommet-d'Arthenay, their direction, on the right. They therefore move off the D8 road onto the D98 to their objective, La Chapelle-en-Juger.

2. Emerging from the Bocage, north of the Saint-Lô/Périers road, American infantry broke through the German front pulverized by bombs.

3. A column of the 30th Infantry Division advances on Saint-Gilles, overtaken by a First Army tank moved up to support the advance, here an M3 General Lee Medium Tank armed with a 75 mm casemated gun and a 37 mm turret gun.

4. General Eisenhower comes to congratulate the men for their action on the first day of "Cobra".

5. Lt. Gen. Collins then decided to unleash his armor. Near the Saint-Lô/Périers road, reinforcements move up towards the front, the great offensive will break out today.

6. Here Shermans of the 66th Armored Regiment, 2d Armored Division, on the eastern flank, race due south along the Saint-Gilles road. The accompanying infantry has climbed onto the vehicles. One of the GIs is wearing sunglasses.

7. Further on, more Shermans, loaded with infantry, pass by an artillery battery emplacement, notice the abandoned shell cases. This photo was transmitted to London from the front by radiotelephone, making it one of the first photographs of this offensive to reach England; the scan marks can be made out.

(US Army and NA/Heimdal.)

329

26 and 27 July 1944. "Cobra" launches its tanks across the Bocage.

1. This 4.2 inch (105 mm) mortar crew get their heads down as they fire a smoke shell, 26 July.

2. In addition to the mortars, other heavy weapons were used to support the infantry offensive. Pvt. Sam J Abbott from Chicago mans his machine-gun, 27 July.

3. T.D. M 10 tank destroyers in a field awaiting orders to come into action. They were the most dangerous enemy for the German tanks.

4. Combined operation. A half-track advances across terrain devastated in the bombardments while, overhead, two P-47 Thunderbolts come in support of this sector of the "Cobra" operation on the ground.

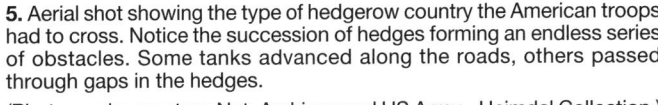

5. Aerial shot showing the type of hedgerow country the American troops had to cross. Notice the succession of hedges forming an endless series of obstacles. Some tanks advanced along the roads, others passed through gaps in the hedges.

(Photographs courtesy Nat. Archives and US Army - Heimdal Collection.)

Marigny sector, the civilians return.

1. This group of civilians fleeing the front in the Saint-Lô sector use bicycles and prams to bring along with them their meagre possessions. But they can come home now that Operation "Cobra" has burst the front wide open.

2. This couple reaches Marigny, with baggage and children loaded on their bicycles; a smile would seem to indicate that their home has maybe escaped destruction.

3. This other couple returns to Marigny, where American troops have just arrived, hoping to find their home intact. (9325)

4. Near Marigny, a GI hands out bread recovered from an abandoned German truck to civilians.

5. The battle is over, and now in the Marigny sector, they tune in to the radio to find out how the operation is progressing.

6. Civilians return with their cows and horses, passing an armored vehicle very similar to the one the captured paratroopers passed by. (9629).

7. In Marigny, on 26 July, while the day before the locality was still under bombs and shellfire, this 75 year-old woman stayed at home. She pours a glass of cider for Pvt. Edward Janick of Buffalo, New York, one of the first American soldiers to clear the locality of snipers.

(Photographs courtesy US Army and D.F./Heimdal.)

333

Pont-Hébert and Saint-Jean-de-Daye, 26 and 27 July.

1. Whereas the new offensive is launched, this M.P. directs the traffic with a crossroads near Saint-Jean-de-Daye, on 27 July.

2. Pvt. Robert J Vance, of Portland, Oregon, was a dispatch rider assigned to the 33rd Armored Regiment (see markings on the motorcycle fender). He was caught in an artillery barrage for 45 minutes on 22 July while taking a message - he was photographed at Saint-Jean-de-Daye on 26 July.

3. Aerial shot of Saint-Jean-de-Daye (from 400 feet on 27 July). The photograph was taken facing south-east towards Saint-Fromond.

4. This old woman is greatly pained to see her home has been shelled, Saint-Jean-de-Daye, 26 July.

5. Still at Saint-Jean-de-Daye on 26 July, these two old women look on with indifference at passing GIs.

6. On 27 July, GIs talking with representatives of the French authorities.

7. North-east of the front (a few kilometers north of Hébécrevon), Pont-Hébert was a major crossing point over the Vire river, with Saint-Jean-de-Daye located between it and Carentan.

(NA and D.F./Heimdal.)

90th Infantry Division

4th Armored Division

Périers, 27 and 28 July 1944

1. On 25 and 26 July, the Périers sector was defended by the 2. SS-Panzer-Division "Das Reich" here with a Dodge vehicle captured from the Americans crossing Périers devastated by the bombardments.

2. On 27 July, the locality was finally taken by men of the 359th Infantry Regiment, 90th Infantry Division, pictured advancing through Périers at the same spot, but in the opposite direction from the Germans in the previous photo … The same street also appears in photo **4.**

3. Many houses in Périers were crushed by bombs.

4. On 28 July, in a by now familiar street, the military police of the 4th Armored Division, taking over from the 90th Infantry Division, gathers up German prisoners; recognizable from their badges are Waffen-SS of the "Das Reich" Division and men belonging to KG 91. ID.

5. The day before, Pvt. Kirby Watson, a Texan with the 4th Armored Division (as his shoulder flash shows) ensured communications between the division's various units with his telephone set safely in a deep hole. ETOHQ.44 8649) (NA and D.F./Heimdal.)

Périers, 29 and 30 July 1944

1. This impressive aerial photograph taken from the north shows Périers in ruins dominated by its church with the nave and steeple badly damaged by shellfire. The vehicles of the 4th Armored Division cross the marketplace full of rubble on their southward advance.

2 and **3.** A Sherman tank of the 4th Armored Division comes out of the Rue Alfred Regnault and into the Rue de Coutances lined with debris and blazing buildings. Périers, 29 July.

4 and **5.** On this same 29 July, a column of the 4th Armored Division has stopped in the marketplace at Périers before carrying on to Coutances. Opposite is the entrance to the Rue de Carentan heading north-east.

6 and **7.** The offensive moves on towards Coutances and beyond, this GMC of the 94th Artillery Battalion, 4th Armored Division passes by the east end of the church at Périers, on this 30 July, bringing ammunition to its unit further south.

8. Infantrymen adjust the range of their mortar fire near Périers.

(Photographs courtesy Heimdal collection.)

Marchésieux, Montcuit, Saint-Sauveur-Lendelin, 28-29 July 1944

1. At the time of "Cobra", the Marchésieux sector facing the 83rd ID was held by the remnants of the 17. SS-Panzer-Grenadier-Division "Götz von Berlichingen". On this 29 July, an American unit's 105 mm HM2 howitzer mounted on a "Priest" armored gun platform passes by the grave of SS-Unterscharführer (sergeant) Josef Richtsfeld, born on 9 August 1914 and killed on 17 June 1944 near Saint-Gilles, assigned to the 9th Battery of the artillery regiment (Ss-a.r. 17) of the "Götz". His battery was commanded by Lieutenant Günther Prinz and was armed with heavy 15 cm guns. Given the place and the date, Sergeant Richtsfeld must have been killed by the fighter-bombers.

2. A GI examines a destroyed "Schwimmwagen" or amphibious vehicle. According to the "iron fist" shield stencilled on the rear left, we know that the vehicle belonged to the "Götz von Berlichingen". The tactical marking painted on the right indicates that it belonged to the HQ company of the division's engineer battalion. So it was one of the four "Schwimmwagen" of that company's reconnaissance

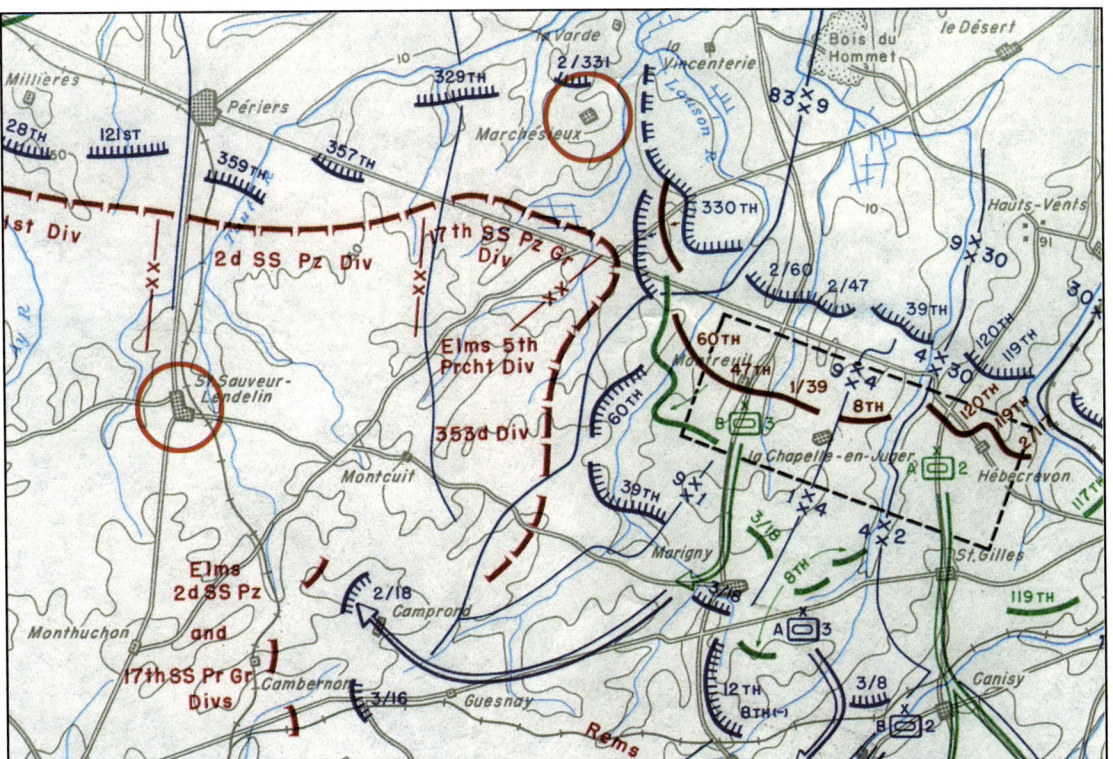

83rd Infantry Division

4th Infantry Division

squad. The company's commanding officer was Captain Müller.

3. US engineers placed metal runners across a stream at Saint-Sauveur-Lendelin to get motorized and armored columns to the other side.

4. On 28 July, men of the 331st Infantry Regiment, 83rd Infantry Division swept aside the last grenadiers of the "Götz" who had withdrawn in order to evade their impending encirclement. The GIs arrive at Montcuit in two columns on this 29 July.

5 and **6.** Moving down from Périers, the 4th Infantry Division passes through Saint-Sauveur-Lendelin on 28 July on its way to Coutances. A World War I veteran mounts guard at the entrance to his village with the French flag to greet the American columns.

(Photographs courtesy Heimdal collection.)

341

1. After the bombardment, the ground offensive was launched. A column of Sherman tanks emerges from a field where it was in position waiting to race due south along the road; notice how these tanks are camouflaged.

2. GIs of the 9th Infantry Division shelter in a ditch from sporadic German fire.

3. An armored column races due south, the destroyed tank and Jeep on the roadside were blown up by mines.

4. At the Carrefour de la Grande Pièce crossroads near Hébécrevon, MPs on traffic duty. AA half-tracks pass over the crossroads.

5. A little earlier, this Sherman passed the same crossroads raising a cloud of dust.

(Photographs courtesy NA and US Army, Heimdal collection.)

9th Infantry Division

343

Marigny sector, 28 and 29 July 1944.

1. Sergeant Bernard Newman of the 9th Infantry Division pretends for the photographer to take the sign Public Phone - No charges! at face value and tries to make a personal call. It is in fact a telephone for officers passing at 9th Division HQ. 28 July.

2. Black Americans man a 155 mm howitzer. The field artillery played a major supporting role in "Cobra". This howitzer was an excellent and highly accurate piece of equipment. Maximum range: 14,400 meters. Firing rate: 2 rounds/min.

3. A group of American soldiers belonging to the 9th Division examine a German anti-tank gun and its prime mover, destroyed and set on fire by aircraft. It was a formidable weapon: a 75 mm Pak 40 with a total weight of 1,500 kg. Maximum ground range: 7,680 m. maximum anti-tank range: 1,800 m. Barrel service life: 6,000 rounds. Photo taken on 28 July.

9th ID

4. Another fearsome enemy of the American tanks fell victim to the United States Air Force. Near Marigny on 29 July. This was the German assault gun mounted with a 75 mm gun - the type G Sturmgeschütz 40. It had the road wheels of the Panzer III. This is a Panzer-Lehr machine issued to Panzer-Jäger-Lehr-Abteilung 130 under its commander Major Joachim Barth. The three Americans who have climbed onto this assault gun and pose to their best advantage for the camera are from left to right: - Pfc Jim Ritchie of Bronx, Pvt. Carmine Calvanico of Jersey City, and S/Sgt Howard Strella of Ellsworth, Kansas. At the bottom left of the machine: Pvt. Phillip Aaron of New York State.

5. A battery of five Mk 8 Hotwitzer Carriages, a tank mounted with a 75 mm howitzer, the leading tank is fitted with a hedge-cutter. On this 28 July, elements of the "Das Reich" Division still held the high ground north-west of Marigny, firing 88 mm shells on that town. These howitzers opened fire on the German positions.

(Photographs courtesy Nat. Archives, US Army and D.F./Heimdal.)

345

Canisy, 27 July 1944.

1. Engineers of the 2d Armored Division clear a lane blocked by debris. They are wearing the "two-piece herringbone twill camouflage jungle suit". This American camouflage suit was seldom used on the European theater of operations so as to avoid confusion in action with the Waffen-SS camouflage smock. It seems that this kit was used in Normandy only by the 2d Armored Division, to which was issued in large numbers as these photographs (and others taken in August) go to show.

Pont-Brocard, 28 July.
2. GIs of CCB, the 2d Armored Division aboard a half-track are on the alert near Pont-Brocard.

3. A 57 mm anti-tank gun in position; today the Germans in the Roncey sector launched counter-attacks towards the east, against Pont-Brocard. These men await a possible attack.

4. This group of men of CCB/2, the 41st Infantry Regiment examine a German map of Europe found at Pont-Brocard.

(Photographs courtesy Nat. Arch. and US Army. Heimdal Collection.)

Pont-Brocard, 29 July 1944.

1. Infantrymen of the CCB/2, tactical grouping of the 2nd Armored Division wait in a sunken lane to progress to the west of Pont-Brocard to clear the area of isolated Germans who have escaped from the Roncey Pocket. They are recognizable by their characteristic camouflage smocks that blend in with the thick hedgerows.

2 and **3.** This 57 mm gun remains in position at Pont-Brocard to resist a possible breakout by German elements. The town was an important passing point on the Soulle river. Behind the gun crew is an abandoned German armored vehicle. There are Shermans parked in the locality. The place has remained intact, except for the corner house, which was demolished to ease the traffic.

(D.F. and E.G./Heimdal.)

4. This presentday photograph, taken in the other direction from photo 2, shows that the 57 mm gun was covering the road from Cerisy-la-Salle. (E.G./Heimdal.)

5. This other presentday photograph shows the bridge over the Soulle, in the background, and the house (far right) in front of which Pvt. De Freitos stopped.

6 and **7.** Pvt. Joseph De Freitos from Jonkers, New York state, heats up cans of rations on his small individual stove. The GIs had just about everything. On the ground there is a German water bottle. Today, the house is intact but the shutters have been removed.

(D.F. and E.G./Heimdal.)

30 July, Saint-Germain-sur-Sèves sector.

1. At first light on 22 July, the 358th Infantry Regiment of the 90th Division went onto the attack to capture "the islet of Saint-Germain-sur-Sèves". This was a village established on a long strip of slightly raised ground in the middle of a flat, marshy area. To seize this small strip turned into a strongpoint fortified by the men of 3rd Battalion of the "Der Führer" Regiment, the "Das Reich" Division, the GIs of the 358th IR had to cross a vast stretch of open ground under German fire. The men of the 90th Division sustained heavy losses and the small American bridgehead secured at St-Germain was repulsed by a German counter-attack. This German strongpoint was not taken until 27 July by the 357th IR of the 90th at the time of the German withdrawal and the general advance by VIII Corps. Pictured here is a soldier of this division, with a Browning machine-gun slung over his shoulder, crossing a stretch of water in front of the islet of Saint-Germain-sur-Sèves. He is using a ladder for a footbridge.(8977)

2. Another more general view taken of the same spot. The Germans cut down trees to improve their firing range. The photograph was taken from the old German positions.

3. Two men advance across this battle-scarred landscape.

90th ID

4. Two infantrymen pose for the photographer in the same sector. They point out to him their comrades' tragic advance here the week before. These are the same men as in the previous photo. (8976)

5. This German soldier destroyed in close combat the American tank-destroyer pictured abandoned on the roadside. The photo was taken on 30 July between Coutances and Marigny, halfway between these two localities, very near the sector where Barkmann went into action. The soldier must have been one of the Germans who tried to break through the American lines here. In this duel with the tank, he also lost his life when his legs were blown off. (9133).

(Photographs courtesy Heimdal collection.)

The armored rush, 29-31 July 1944.

1. These men of the 3rd Armored Division are resting on a farm south of Coutances. They take this chance for a quiet wash and shave, their first opportunity to do so for several days. They have closed the "Roncey Pocket" to the east. Photo taken on 31 July.

2. Sergeant Virgil Clifton of Fredonia, Kansas leads an infantry patrol south of Coutances on this 29 July. It is armed with an M3 machine-gun with a 30 cartridge magazine. Firing rate: 440 rounds/min.

3. At dawn on 29 July, these men of the 4th Armored Division under General Wood have just taken six German prisoners among rear-guard elements covering the retreat.

4. 3rd Armored Division reinforcements move on Coutances on this 31 July. They are tanks of the 32d Armored Regiment (assigned to CCA commanded by Brigadier-General Hickey). Barely visible on the left is a German signpost to the "Das Reich" Division's repair shop.

5. Men of the 2d Armored Division examine a German MP 40 machine-gun. This well-known weapon had a 32 cartridge magazine, absent here. It was taken from the captured German pictured on the left, sitting on his vehicle, a "Kübelwagen".

(Photographs courtesy US Army, Heimdal collection.)

353

29-31 July. US southward advance.

1. Notre-Dame-de-Cenilly on 29 July 1944. Men of the 8th Infantry Regiment, 4th Infantry Division supporting CCB, 2d Armored Division, examine some dead Germans (they seem to have belonged to a parachute division - notice the camouflage smocks and paratroop helmet). This photo was taken in front of the church. They are probably paratroopers who tried to escape from the Roncey Pocket; 6th Parachute Regiment commander Major von der Heydte in fact managed to break through a little to the north of this sector and the Germans launched a counter-attack at La Pinetière (south of Notre-Dame-de-Cenilly) at 4 in the morning on 29 July.

2. An exceptional photograph: two famous war correspondents are photographed here close to Pont-Brocard on 30 July 1944 as they followed the 2d Armored Division. Left to right: Life magazine photographer Robert Capa, who on 6 June took some historic pictures of Omaha Beach, the driver (Pfc Olin L Tomkins from Jamestown, Tennessee), and Ernest Hemingway, the author of "For whom the bell tolls", reporting in Normandy for "Colliers".

354

3. Corporal Paul J Watson (from Des Moines, Iowa) followed the lightning advance of his tank unit and here takes a few moments rest. 31 July.

4. Pvt. Rudy R. Stewart, armed with a Browning machine-gun, supervises a group of German prisoners at Notre-Dame-de-Cenilly on 30 July 1944.

Lessay, 28 and 29 July 1944.

1. It was on July 27 that Americans of the 315th Infantry Regiment, the 79th Division managed to take Lessay and cross the Sèves river, opening up to them the road south to Coutances. A young German belonging to one of the 243. Infanterie-Division's last strongpoints was killed at the exit from the town. He died several hours earlier and in the heat of 1944, his face is already covered with flies. (Bundesarchiv.)

2. In the center of Lessay, in the marketplace (now the Place Saint-Cloud) devastated by bombs and fires back on 8 June. On this 28 July, GIs set up a machine-gun. In the center is the Hôtel de Normandie, which burned down.

3 and **4.** Sappers of Company B of the 133rd Engineer Battalion busy clearing mines from the center of the burned out town.

5. The 6th Armored Division raced south starting on 28 July, bringing along in its wake the men of the 79th Division who passed though Lessay on their way to the new front line between Coutances and Coutainville, near the coast.

6 and **7.** Near Lessay, 29 July, an American engineer battalion throws a Bailey bridge across the Ay river to speed up the advance of vehicles southwards.

8. The abbey church at Lessay, partly destroyed in 1944, was remarkably restored.

(Photographs courtesy Heimdal collection and E.G./Heimdal.)

6th AD

5

6

8

79th ID

7

Coutances, 28-29 July 1944

1 and **2.** Coming from Périers, tank columns of the 4th Armored Division race to Coutances; the cathedral steeples can be seen in the distance.

3 and **4.** Further on, American infantry have reached the outskirts of the town, bringing a captive German NCO along with them.

5. The GIs are now entering the downtown area, an American soldier takes shelter from a German sniper's bullets.

6. An armored column of the 4th Armored Division has been halted on the Périers road (now Avenue Général Leclerc, but then Avenue Maréchal Pétain). German shells were falling on the area, the road was mined; a jeep and then a Stuart tank were blown up by mines.

7 and **8.** A few moments later, at the same spot, American stretcher-bearers bring back a casualty wounded in the explosion of the jeep or by shrapnel. This dangerous passage forced the American columns to go round the block by the east, on the Saint-Lô road.

(Photographs courtesy Heimdal collection.)

Coutances, 28 and 29 July

1. 28 July, the first American patrols cross the devastated area between the cathedral (pictured here) and the church of Saint-Pierre, as they head towards the south side of town.

2. 29 July, on the south-east corner of the square in front of Notre-Dame, in the ruins of the south side door of the cathedral, the superior and the president of the Senior Seminary of Coutances, Canons Mignot and Gazengel, fol-

lowed by two seminarists doing first-aid work. The street across the way, between the cathedral and the ruined houses, is the one leading up to the bishop's house.

3. This view taken from the cathedral's south tower on 29 July pictures the town's south-west quarter. Many houses were completely flattened during the bombardment, while certain streets were completely spared.

4. By the Croix Quillard crossroads, with the district still under fire from a German 88 mm gun, an American patrol inspects the ruins of the Carmelite chapel which was an integral part of the Maison des Œuvres. Father Cadel's office, completely destroyed by a bomb, is a few yards to the left, and off the picture here.

(Heimdal collection.)

Coutances, 29 July 1944

1. Coutances seen from the west, from the Agon-Coutainville road; an American reconnaissance vehicle has stopped.

2. An American patrol in the town (see photograph n° 2 overleaf).

3. Another general view of Coutances from the west. From left to right we see: the municipal stadium, the Senior Seminary buildings, the cathedral from the Town Hall.

4, 5 and **6.** Three photographs taken in the same Boulevard Alsace-Lorraine quarter show American vehicles racing southwards in pursuit of the Germans. All the photographs on these two pages were taken by American war correspondent Richard Boyer. (Heimdal collection.)

363

Coutances, 29 July 1944

1. General George S. Patton has arrived near Coutances to follow the progress of the current offensive. His jeep is surrounded by civilians who have come to acclaim him.

2, 3 and **4.** Scene of destruction in a small street of Coutances entirely blocked by debris. A cleared street can be seen in the background with a passing armored column (see also photograph on the preceding pages).

5 and **6.** In the square in front of cathedral, the small south door on the right has been destroyed by bombs. The "Nouvelles Galeries" store was burnt to the ground.

7 and **8.** In the Rue Tancrède, just before the church of Saint Nicolas, the Eiffel Tower has fallen off the roof of wireless

dealer M. Lemoine's house. The cathedral's impressive steeples can be seen here.

9, 10 and **11.** Coming from north, at the bottom of the Rue Saint Nicolas (the photograph was taken from further away than the previous one). An American tank crew member can be seen on the right.

(Photographs courtesy Heimdal collection.)

365

Coutances, 29 July, Boulevard Alsace-Lorraine

1. Light Stuart tanks of a reconnaisance squadron drive down the boulevard ready for the dash south on the heels of the Germans. Notice on the far right-hand side of the photograph the ruins of a garage in cement also pictured in photos **3** and **4.**

2. These Sherman tanks have stopped to let through a motorized column.

3. Vehicles and infantry advance southwards up to the front line.

4. At the same spot a Sherman tank passes with its white star removed after being painted over (likewise the tanks pictured in photos **2** and **5**).

5. At the same spot, from a different angle from photograph 2, American infantry pass alongside a stationary tank column. (DAVA/Heimdal coll.)

Coutances, 30 and 31 July

1. GIs patrolling the Place du Parvis pass by the cathedral façade.

2 and **3.** A French captain with the American army coming out of the cathedral as Canon Lepoil comes to meet him.

4 and **5.** The French captain and Canon Lepoil are now in animated discussion. During the bombardment, the Canon slept on a carpet with the foot of the cathedral's south tower.

6 and **7.** Through a window of this cathedral tower can be seen some ruined houses and the church of Saint-Pierre left almost intact by the bombs.

8 and **9.** An American soldier meditates in the beautiful Gothic cathedral.

(Photographs courtesy Heimdal collection; present-day photographs courtesy EG/Heimdal.)

Coutances, Quillard Croix crossroads

1. On its way from Périers, a light Stuart tank of the 2nd Recce Squadron, 4th Armored Division was blown up by a mine and as the Périers road had not been cleared, it was temporarily prohibited to traffic.

2 and **3.** Traffic was therefore diverted onto the road from Saint-Lô. The destroyed Stuart tank can be seen to the left of "Maison Périna" while more tanks arrive from the right along the Saint-Lô road. "Maison Périna" has since been pulled down.

4. The Boulevard Alsace-Lorraine at Coutances on 31 July, the tanks are racing south in pursuit of the retreating Germans. On the right, the road is scarred by a huge bomb crater, and a tree has been stripped of its branches. (Heimdal coll.)

5. Still on the Boulevard Alsace-Lorraine on 31 July, a self-propelled 105 mm howitzer mounted on a "Priest" belonging to "B" Company, 2nd Artillery Battalion, 4th Armored

Division passes the same spot as the Sherman tanks in photograph **4**. This angle gives a better view of the the tree with the ripped-off branches.

(Photographs courtesy Heimdal collection.)

371

Coutances, 29 to 31 July 1944

1. By the Quillard Croix crossroads, on 31 July, an armored division's medical orderlies administer first aid to a casualty hit by a time bomb. A jeep of the 20th Engineers Battalion can be seen.

2 and **3.** Further down, on the Boulevard de la Marne, the Germans had placed explosive charges against the trees in order to fell them across the road and slow the tanks' rapid advance. In this photo taken on 29 July, the charges are still in place.

4. South of the town, jeeps move up to the front line while a Stuart tank crew stops for a rest. In the foreground a 4th Armored Division staff jeep has stopped. A jeep and a truck are coming from the opposite direction.

5. The stream of 4th Armored Division vehicles continues pour down the same street: jeeps, a Stuart tank, a Sherman tank.

6. But this section is choked with debris blocking the traffic. On this 31 August 1944, a bulldozer of the 20th Engineers Battalion is pictured at work here.

(Photographs courtesy Heimdal collection.)

Roncey. 31 July-2 August, 1944.

The Roncey Pocket has been just cleared. For two days Allied aircraft bombarded and machine-gunned German vehicles piling up in this sector, destroying a great number of them.

1. At the entrance to Roncey, on 31 July, a bulldozer is at work clearing a road cluttered with Bren carriers, vehicles and howitzers.

2 and **3.** The town of Roncey was hard hit by the bombardments. The presentday photograph shows how much of it has been rebuilt. On the left the is the front of the church.

4 and **5.** The church in ruins is surrounded by destroyed German vehicles including two Marder III tank destroyers. This machine combined a Czech-built PzKpfw 38 tank chassis and a 75 mm (Pak 40) anti-tank gun. One imagines the explosions and fires that must have shaken and devastated the place two days before. An old woman returns home amid these scenes of desolation.

6 and **7.** 1 August, an American half-track crosses the main square firing an anti-tank gun. The photograph was taken facing the other way; the rears of both Marder IIIs can be seen.

8. 2 August, a bulldozer is at work clearing the streets.

(Photographs courtesy D.F. and NA/Heimdal and EG./Heimdal for the presentday photographs.)

4

5

6

7

8

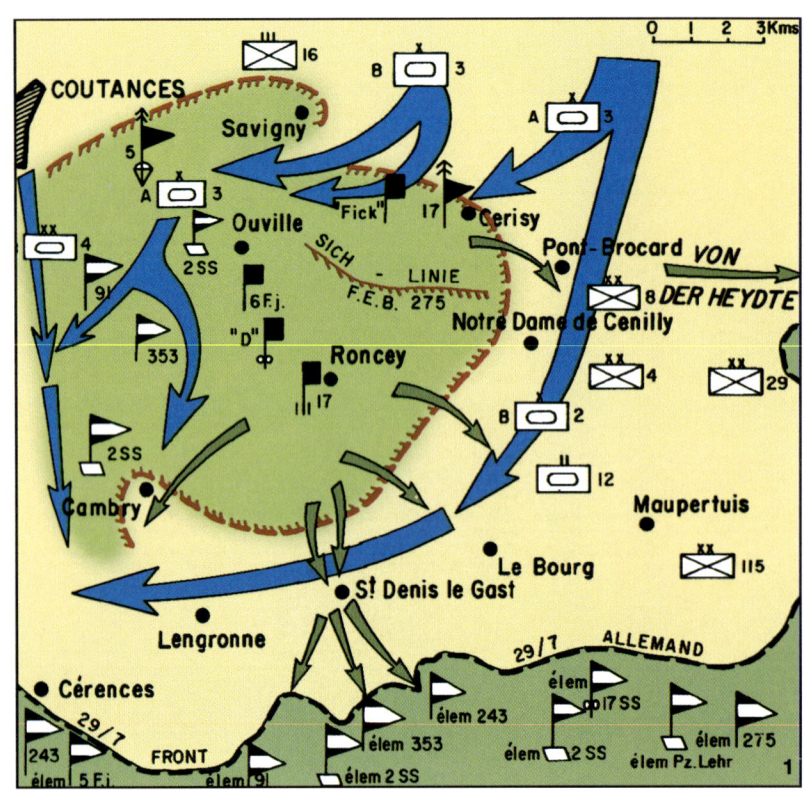

Roncey Pocket, 29-31 July.

1. This map shows the sweeping movement south-westwards by CCB, the 2d Armored Division which caught many elements of German units in the "Roncey Pocket". They include the 6th Parachute Regiment (6. F.J.R.), the 2. SS-Panzer-Division with the "Deutschland" ("D") Regiment, elements of KG 91 and KG 353 and the artillery regiment ("17") of the "Götz". Most of these were crack troops. To the north, another American armored division (the 3rd) closed the pocket from the west, along with the 4th Armored Division coming down from Coutances. By the evening of 29 July, the pocket was closed, and the 2d Armored Division had put out of action 1,500 Germans and taken another 4,000 prisoner. During the night of 29-30 July, however, many German elements forced a way out through Saint-Denis-le-Gast and fell back onto a line passing through Bréhal, Gavray, Percy, Beaucoudray, Moyon, Troisgots and Torigni-sur-Vire. (Heimdal map after Stöber.)

2. The Americans captured many Waffen-SS in this pocket, which the Germans called "der Kessel von Coutances". Most of these prisoners are wearing camouflage smocks.

3 and **4.** Fighter-bombers attacked the retreating vehicles, many brewing up after being hit. Pictured here is an artillery prime mover in the first photograph, a Peugeot 202, a Kübelwagen and a light Flak gun in the second photograph.
5. Several jeeps here pass by various destroyed tracked vehicles and an SPW belonging to one of the two SS divisions.
(NA/Heimdal.)

Roncey Pocket, Saint-Denis-le-Gast, Gavray.

1. Near Roncey, on 1 August, two men of the 3rd Armored Division (notice the badge clearly visible on the sleeve) examine a German Sturmgeschütz III model G assault gun, destroyed trying to slip out of the pocket. One of the crew members was killed while leaving the vehicle (no doubt the radio operator), the open hatches suggest that his comrades were more fortunate.

2. Another Sturmgeschütz has been knocked out and burned out near a hedge. It was also a model G, like the previous one but more recent with its "Saukopf" (the gun's "snout", round with more acute angles). Manned by a crew of four, it weighed 23.9 tons in battle order and had a range of 155 km on road and 95 km all terrain.

3. In this photograph, taken at Saint-Denis-le-Gast on 31 July, GIs examine two pieces belonging to the 1st Battery of SS-Panzer-Artillery-Regiment 2, the artillery regiment of the 2. SS-Panzer-Division "Das Reich". We recognize on the rear of the SPW the tactical marking of an artillery regiment's 1st tracked battery with, above it, stencilled in yellow, the "wolf's rune" insignia of the "Das Reich" Division. Pictured in the front is a 15 cm Pz.Haubitze auf Gw. III/IV "Hummel". This was a 150 mm (15 cm s.FH.18 L/30) howitzer mounted on a tank chassis and protected by an armor-plated crew compartment. These machines made these pieces of ordnance highly mobile. This one has the name "Clausewitz" painted on the crew compartment.

4. Pictured here is Panzer IV "831" of a tank regiment's 8th Company abandoned at Saint-Denis-le-Gast, where it was knocked out.

5 and **6.** After a tremendous battle, an American soldier comes to pray in the church at Gavray.

(D.F. and E.G./Heimdal.)

379

5. This SS grenadier was killed near Quibou on 28 July, before the pocket was closed. He is still carrying his MG's spare barrel case.

Prisoners of the Roncey Pocket, 30 July.

1. Mopping up the Roncey Pocket on 30 July, the Americans took 5,000 German prisoners, most of them assigned to crack units. This famous photograph pictures nothing but Waffen-SS officers and paratroopers (one of the latter a lieutenant-colonel, on the right). The attitude of these captured men shows just how determined they were to find a way out of the pocket.

2, 3 and **4.** A sorting camp was set up near Périers, here again withmen from crack units, nothing but Waffen-SS, recognizable mostly from the armbands worn by some of the men assigned to the "Götz von Berlichingen" (17 SS-Panzergrenadier-Division), many of them "ethnic Germans" recruited in Romania.

6. An M.P., Pvt. Gorrethon, bends over to decipher inscriptions on graves dug near Cerisy-la-Salle: SS-Grenadier Josef Heinz of the 6th Company of SS-Panzer-Grenadier-Regiment 38 ("Götz von Berlichingen" Division).

(US Army and NA/Heimdal.)

At Saint-Jean-des-Baisants, 30 July 1944

1. To the east of the American front, US V Corps (Gerow) took advantage of a German strategic withdrawal (3. Fallschirmjäger-Division by General Meindl's II Parachute Corps) to advance. The 28th Infantry Regiment, the 2nd Infantry Division captured Saint-Jean-des-Baisants on 28 July and carried on advancing south of that locality on 29 July. This is an aerial photograph of the village, with the center hit by American artillery fire.

2. Pvt. Sam Fever of Brooklyn, a member of the engineer unit of the 2nd Infantry Division (2nd Battalion), puts up a sign indicating that the road and the grass verges have been cleared of mines.

3. The division's engineers place demolition charges on an unsafe house obstructing the traffic near the ruined church of Saint-Jean-des-Baisants pictured in the background.

4. The same team of engineers at the same spot, pictured shortly before the previous shot (the demolition charges are not yet in place). Notice the divisional badge (an Indian head in a white star on a black shield) on one of the soldiers' sleeves (second on the right).

5. The bell-tower has collapsed. (D.F./Heimdal.)

6. The church as rebuilt. (E.G./Heimdal.)

31 July, 1944. Bréhal, Granville.

1. Pouring down from the Coutances area, the 6th Armored Division races to Avranches which it reached and beyond on 31 July. In the port of Granville, the docks are still burning, having been set on fire by the Germans retreating before the Americans.

8th ID

6th A.D.

3 and **4.** Men of the 28th Infantry Regiment of Maj.Gen. Stroh's 8th Infantry Division and armored vehicles pass through Bréhal past a destroyed German "Opel Blitz" truck assigned to the "Das Reich" Division's Flak battalion.

2. Another view of the port of Granville which came in for some damage. Granville was the target of a German raid by the German garrison that held out in the Channel Islands until 8 May 1945.

5 and **6.** A little further on in Bréhal, civilians watch passing columns of American vehicles of the 28th Infantry Regiment, 8th Infantry Division and tanks of the 6th Armored Division on their way to Granville and Avranches.

7 and **8.** A tank of the 6th Armored Division advances through Bréhal past the same spot. Several house fronts have come in for a facelift since 1944.

9. Pfc Joseph A. Calvello (of New York) examines the inside of a Russian tire mounted on a German 37 mm anti-tank gun abandoned at Bréhal.
(Photographs courtesy Heimdal Coll.)

Bréhal, 31 July and 2 August

1. In the Avranches sector on 31 July, a gendarme and members of the French Resistance escort into captivity some Asian soldiers in German uniform.

2. Captured Germans at Bréhal on 31 July about to bury their dead.

3, 4 and **5.** On 2 August near Bréhal, the Americans captured Russians, Georgians and Turkmens assigned to the "Buniachenko Brigade". Pictured here are some of the prisoners some of whom have very pronounced Mongolian features. They are questioned by Sergeant Armand Duval, (photo 4) from Hagerstown, Maryland. Several prisoners (photo 3) wore two jackets one on top of the other. The Russian soldier on the left in photo **4** also appears in photo **5**.

6. An American soldier visits a German military cemetery where men of various units are buried, we can read: SS-Grenadier Georg Lill, Obergefreiter Ersnt Rausch (3rd Rifle Co of 275. ID), Oberfeldwebel Werner Klein (6th Parachute Rgt), Grenadier Josef Robold, Grenadier Ernst Fassmann, Gefreiter Josef Emele, etc.

(D.F./Heimdal.)

On the road to Avranches, 30 July.

1. On the road to Avranches, abandoned German vehicles and civilian carts encumber the road and verges.

2. On 30 July, a half-track of CCB, 6th Armored Division passes through Sartilly, between Bréhal and Avranches.

3. Further on, in Sartilly, are a Stuart tank and a half-track.

4. Escorting German prisoners with their hands on their heads, GIs pass by some destroyed German vehicles on the road to Avranches.

5. Medics listening to the radio in their bivouac, in the Avranches sector. The front has started moving again at last, and they listen to the good news. (D.F./Heimdal.)

Avranches from 30 July to 3 August 1944.

1. The breakout at Avranches was the direct consequence of General Patton's Third Army's joining the front line. CCB, the 4th Armored Division reached Avranches on 30 August. That same division's CCA was in Pontaubault and Ducey by the 31st.

2. Leading elements entering Avranches pass by some burnt-out German vehicles (including a French-built Renault truck).

3. The traditional photograph of the young Frenchwoman presenting a bunch of flowers to her liberators.

4. The tanks of the 4th Armored Division pass through Avranches, a town hard hit in the bombing.

5. On 2 August, long columns of German prisoners move away to prison camps.

6. A truck of the 86th Reconnaissance Squadron, 6th Armored Division brings back German prisoners up north. They were captured in the Avranches area and here arrive at Granville on this 3 August.

(D.F./Heimdal.)

The offensive in full swing.

1. The much awaited breakout is a success. On 29 July, General Eisenhower decorates Lt. Gen. Bradley who led his First Army to victory.

2. On 31 July, at Carantilly, as the Roncey Pocket is mopped up and the tanks have already passed Avranches and about to enter Brittany, a heavy 8 inch gun is towed by a prime mover trying desperately to keep up with the front, now making very rapid progress.

3. The following day, 1 August, the corps' organic units were to the rear of the front line troops. Pictured here is Sergeant Jack Hutton of Colombus (Ohio) and Private Royce Vick, of Pitt (Texas) of the 38th Field Artillery Regiment, fraternizing with a Norman family over a copy of Esquire. On his sleeve Private Vick is wearing the insignia of the V Corps, to which this artillery unit was assigned.

4. In Granville, local traders soon adjusted to their new customers; this cafe has a notice in English advertising the sale of beer.

5. On 1 August, American units finally broke through at Pontaubault. Before continuing on to Brittany, certain HQ units made a detour via the Mont St-Michel, pictured here on 6 August.

6. South-east of Avranches and south-west of Mortain, the town of Saint-Hilaire-du-Harcouët, a strategic crossroads at the gateway to Brittany and Maine, was also hard hit. This aerial photograph was taken on 8 August. (10652).

7. South of Mortain, GIs pass through Sainte-Marie-du-Bois.

(DAVA and D.F./Heimdal.)

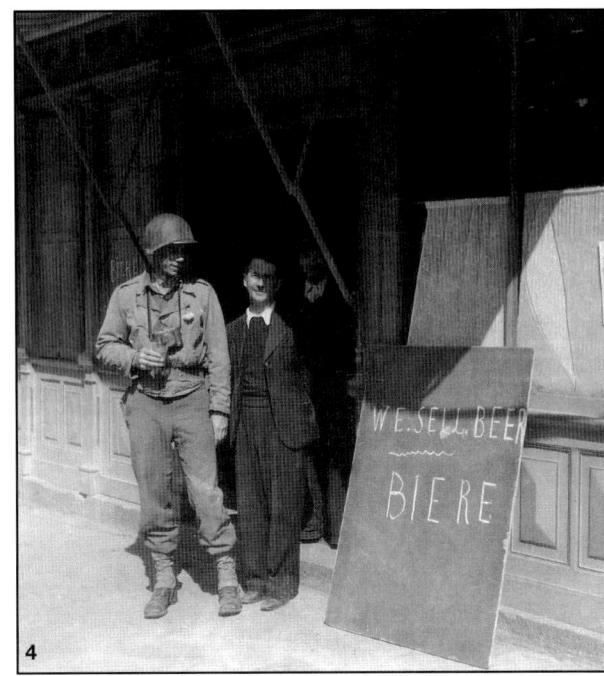

South of Saint-Lô, 30 July to 3 August 1944.

1. On 1 August, these medics try to talk with a Norman girl for the war correspondent's camera.

2. A young boy in pain is taken along in a medical unit jeep for treatment.

3. On 3 August, at Courson, these medics load a casualty onto a stretcher.

4. On 2 August, soldiers gather around a farmyard well to fill their water cans.

5. On 30 July 1944 some retreating Germans are repulsed. This squad of American infantry stays on the alert, with the cartridge belt engaged in the 30 cal. machine-gun.

(D.F. and E.G./Heimdal.)

Lison Station, 12 July to 5 August.

1 and **2.** Repair work at Lison Station (already seen on 17 June) was resumed intensively. Railroad personnel repair the damage under American supervision.

3. On 12 July, a railroad worker places a bunch of flowers on the first convoy leaving for Bayeux, this link being restored in advance of trains to Cherbourg and Caen.

8. The "walking casualties" are ready to leave on a train made up of salvaged coaches, there is even a bullet mark on the left of the photograph.

9. The command post of this hospital train which left on 5 August. From left to right, officers of the 720th Railroad Operating Battalion, Lt. Stewart St John, Lt. Jack H. Larsen, Captain Loren H. Gallup, Lieutenant-Colonel Conrad J Freeman and Lt. George H. Shavel, all from Chicago.)

(Photographs courtesy D.F. and DAVA/Heimdal.)

4. On 1 August, a member of the 720th Railway Battalion Operations, Sgt Melvin R. Holmbert of Minneapolis, Minnesota, marks up the timetable.

5, 6 and 7. By 5 August, Lison Station was very active, with trains running to the port of Cherbourg. Ambulances bring casualties to a hospital convoy of twenty coaches for stretcher cases and four coaches for "walking" casualties. The convoy's medical personnel comprised four officers, six medical orderlies and thirty-nine men. The convoy leader was Major Leon Mr. Ehrenburg of Chicago.

10

The Pursuit
(1 to 30 August)

On 1 August, a second US army, Patton's Third Army, was already in Brittany racing towards the Loire valley, reaching Mayenne and Laval by the evening of 6 August! Meantime, the First Army broadened the corridor of the Avranches breakout, advancing up to 6 August on Percy, Villedieu-les-Poêles and Saint-Sever. CCA, the 2d Armored Division was in front of Vire, the 4th Infantry Division was in the Saint-Pois sector. CCB, the 3rd Armored Division was in the Reffuveille sector and the 30th Infantry Division arrived in Mortain on 6 August.

But Hitler gave orders for a counterstroke at Mortain where the "American corridor" was at its narrowest: from Mortain towards Avranches. The objective involved completely cutting off Patton's Third Army from its bases and wiping it out with the help of the German divisions stationed in Brittany. But what had worked in the USSR was to fail in the West owing to the Allies' crushing superiority in the air. A German tank force was mustered very quickly for a counterattack: XLVII.Panzerkorps with 116. Panzer-Division, 2. Panzer-Division, 2. SS-Panzer-Division "Das Reich", 1. SS-Panzer-Division "Leibstandarte" and a Kampfgruppe assigned to 17. SS-Panzergrenadier-Division. This tank corps only had four armored divisions although Hitler wanted to commit seven. And the Allied air supremacy had two consequences: — the Germans were slowed down as they brought up their tank forces by road. — Then once in line and trying to deploy, these forces came up against all the firepower of the fighter-bombers. So was the plan suicidal? As it happened, Hitler had planned for substantial air support for his armored forces. A thousand fighters had been taken from the air force defending the Reich, but they were scattered before reaching their objective.

The tank forces moved slowly up to the front line, but given the highly volatile situation, von Kluge decided on 6 August to bring forward the launch of Operation "Lüttich" to the following day. Just 145 Panzers (less than a single full-strength Panzer-Division) went onto the attack at **dawn on 7 August**, before some of the units had even arrived. The 2. Panzer-Division, to the north of the disposition, advanced some eight kilometers west, as far as Le Mesnil-Adelée while to the south of the assault sector, the 2. SS-Panzer-Division advanced some ten kilometers west, as far as Fontenay and Milly. Above Mortain, around Hill 317, elements of the 120th Infantry Regiment (30th Division) were encircled. The "Das Reich" Division had already covered a third of the distance between Mortain and Pontaubault. But the morning mist soon cleared and from midday, fighter-bombers took massive steps to pin down the German tank force before it even reached the American tanks of the 3rd Armored Division committed in the sector. They left a grat many Panzers (about sixty) in flames, breaking the back of the assault. That evening, Maj. Gen. Collins had two armored divisions and five infantry divisions for his VII Corps, his reinforcements having been quickly mustered.

The next day, **8 August**, despite the losses of the previous day, this last-resort counter-attack was resumed. By now the US forces had the upper hand. The German assault made no headway and was kept pinned down in a stalemate lasting until 10 August. On the evening of 8 August, the Third Army and the First Army on its left flank together reached Le Mans, the starting point for the attack on Alençon.

On **10 August**, the Canadians were ten kilometers north of Falaise. In the south, the Americans (XV Corps, Third Army) were between Le Mans and Alençon, held up by elements of the 9. Panzer-Division, a newly arrived unit. **12 August** was one of the most decisive days in the later stages of the Battle of Normandy. Two armored divisions of XV Corps (Maj. Gen. Oliver's 5th Armored Division and General Leclerc 2e DB on the left flank) took **Alençon** and moved up to Argentan. A few American and French tanks of the 2e DB even entered **Argentan**, with only another twenty-three kilometers from there to Falaise! But the Canadians had not yet reached Falaise and Generals Montgomery and Bradley feared that the Americans might accidentally open fire on their Canadian allies as they moved north from Argentan to close the pocket in which a sizable portion of the German army in Normandy would be caught; accordingly, Lt. Gen. Bradley ordered Patton to stop short of Argentan. A wonderful chance was squandered! On the next day, **13 August**, the German High Command began to evacuate its forces, i.e all the units behind the lines, so important in a war where logistics were crucial. So by that evening, the 12. SS-Panzer-Division (according to the report by its chief-of-staff) had already evacuated 10,000 men east of Normandy, only keeping in the front line a battlegroup of 1,500 men with

Here we see the movement of the front from 1-6 August and the buildup of the US Third Army under General Patton. The First Army came under the command of Lt. Gen. Courtney H. Hodges in early August. The two armies were then placed under the 12th Army Group, with Lt. Gen. Bradley in command. During the six days of the Breakout, the "Avranches corridor" was widened, the Third Army deployed in Brittany and the Loire valley while the First Army widened the "Avranches corridor" to Mortain from where the Germans launched their counterstroke on 7 August. (Heimdal.)

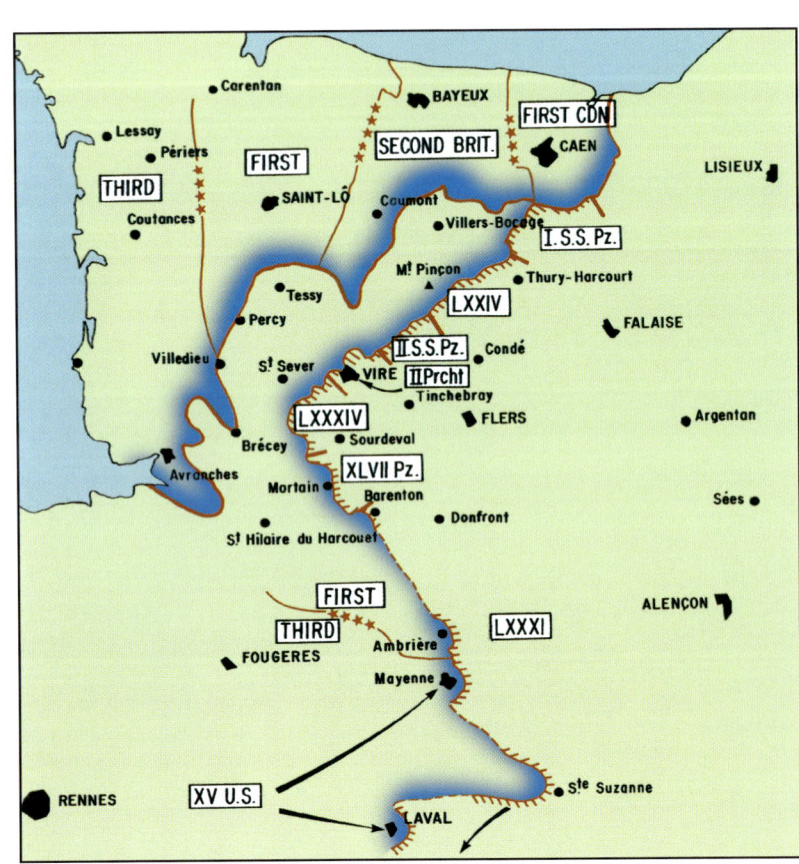

20 tanks and sixteen 88 mm guns. The same went for other units like the 17. SS-Pz.Gren.Div., the main body having already left for Lorraine! On **14 August**, General Eberbach, commander of the 5. Panzer-Armee, requested an order to withdraw so as to avoid having his troops wiped out. Meanwhile, like Montgomery, Bradley thought that the Germans had got away, and so decided to race towards the Seine River. Orders again countermanded on **15 August**, and the Canadians marched on Trun although the Americans were heading due east. On **16 August**, the XV Corps was in Dreux, the XX Corps in Chartres and the XII Corps in Orléans, after a spectacular advance, but the Falaise-Argentan Pocket had still not been closed and Hitler ordered a general retreat at 11.53 hours. Thus between 13 and 18 August, 55,000 men pulled back, or 40% of the strength of the divisions threatened with encirclement. So Bradley was not altogether wrong in thinking that the bulk of the German armies had already slipped through the net.

Finally, the Falaise Pocket now began to be closed, four days late. Montgomery had had wind of Hitler's order to withdraw and so decided to finish the job at 15.30 on 16 August, issuing orders to push ahead towards Trun, which the Canadians had just taken. But meanwhile, the Germans had already withdrawn east of Flers to the west, in an orderly retreat. On **17 August**, on the American front, only elements of the 3rd Armored Division made some slight progress east of Fromentel, with very few Germans now still west of the Orne River. Over a third of the entire pocket had been withdrawn in a single day. The next day, **18 August**, there were no more German troops west of the Orne. In the north the Canadian corps made further progress towards Trun. On the American side, the breakout was so exhilarating that the Falaise Pocket business became no more than a sideshow.

On **19 August**, the 1st Polish Armored Division linked up at Chambois with the Americans of the 90th Infantry Division. The pocket was cut off but not entirely closed. Under Allied fire, German rearguard elements attempted to break out through what came to be known as "death corridor" from Trun to Chambois. The retreating German elements had to face the Poles holding the high ground from Hill 262. On **20 August**, the Germans continued to leave the pocket under a deluge of fire; the evacuation ending during the night of 20-21 August, only two days after the pocket was closed. The Germans suffered very heavy losses, somewhere between 25,000 men (General Montgomery's estimate) and 50,000 (First Army estimate). 6,000 Germans are thought to have been killed or gone missing but they had salvaged what mattered most. The prisoners mostly came from second-rate units. And it is mostly equipment that they lost: 220 tanks, 160 guns, 700 pieces of ordnance, 130 antitank or AA guns, 130 tracked vehicles (SAW) and 500 motorized vehicles. Also 1,800 dead horses were counted; the horses endured great suffering. Of the fifteen generals commanding a division, three were captured.

On **21 August**, the Germans who had slipped out of the pocket continued to withdraw back to the Seine, which they crossed. A total of 165,800 men who had fought in Normandy thus remained available to the German High Command. That day, the Third Army commander arrived at the head of his XV Corps at the Seine River, near **Mantes**. With the Falaise Pocket an unexpected "accident", a larger-scale encirclement was now attempted: it meant crossing the Seine to cut off the bulk of the German armies retreating from Normandy. The Allies decided to dispatch divisions along the Seine, west of Mantes; but the British units were too far short of this objective and so Bradley suggested using American units on this assignment. These veered north-west, into the sector allocated to the British. Bradley, now in command of the newly formed 12th Army Group (combining the First Army and the Third Army) assigned to this operation two corps, XV Corps and XIX Corps, with five divisions. The XV Corps was to advance to Louviers and establish a bridgehead at Mantes. The XIX Corps was to advance further west, between Elbeuf and Louviers. He also gave Patton the go-ahead to commit divisions towards Melun, Fontainebleau and Sens. Fascinated by this new direction – the East and Germany – the Americans spread out their resources virtually unopposed as the Germans fell back beyond the Seine, with the Anglo-Canadian armies following slowly in their footsteps.

On **22 August**, the 5th Armored Division arrived in the eastern part of the Eure department: Pacy-sur-Eure and Saint-Aquilin-de-Pacy to the right, Evreux in the middle and Conches to the left, were all reached and left behind. Further east, starting out from Mantes, with the 79th Infantry Division pushing back the 49. Infanterie-Division, the Americans secured a bridgehead north of the Seine. They also held Vernon. Along the entire front, from Le Neubourg to Vernon, the Americans attacked with hundreds of tanks, but the Germans put up a stout defense with a few elements using delaying tactics to cover the troops crossing the Seine. On this day, the 5th AD lost 25 Shermans. Also, the French 2ᵉ DB had just been issued orders to march on Paris.

On **23 August**, Lt. Gen. Patton became conscious of the value of a "broad encirclement". He wanted to take two army corps between Melun and Montereau, and veer off north of Paris to Beauvais where the Germans would be trapped; General Bradley made no reply to this proposal. And in the Evreux sector, American gains remained small in the face of determined German rearguard action to cover the withdrawal against the British and Canadians. On **24 August**, progress was again slow in front of Elbeuf and Louviers as the 2ᵉ DB entered Paris. As of **25 August**, the Germans gradually fell back onto the bends of the Seine where most of the river crossings took place. These continued on **26, 27** and **28 August**. The operation was completed on **29 August**. The Germans left behind 4,000 vehicles, mostly destroyed by Allied fighter-bombers. But 165,000 made it across the Seine in 25,000 vehicles, which is about three quarters of the total German forces in Normandy in early August. The Battle of Normandy was over and the US armies would now forge ahead over great distances, to be confronted with refuelling problems.

Lieutenant-General Courtney Hodges, Bradley's successor as First Army commander.

Here we see the Third Army corps as they race into southern Normandy up until 16 August, the day orders were issued, partly too late, to cut off the Falaise-Argentan Pocket, with the German withdrawal already in full swing. The Battle of Normandy ended a fortnight later. (Heimdal.)

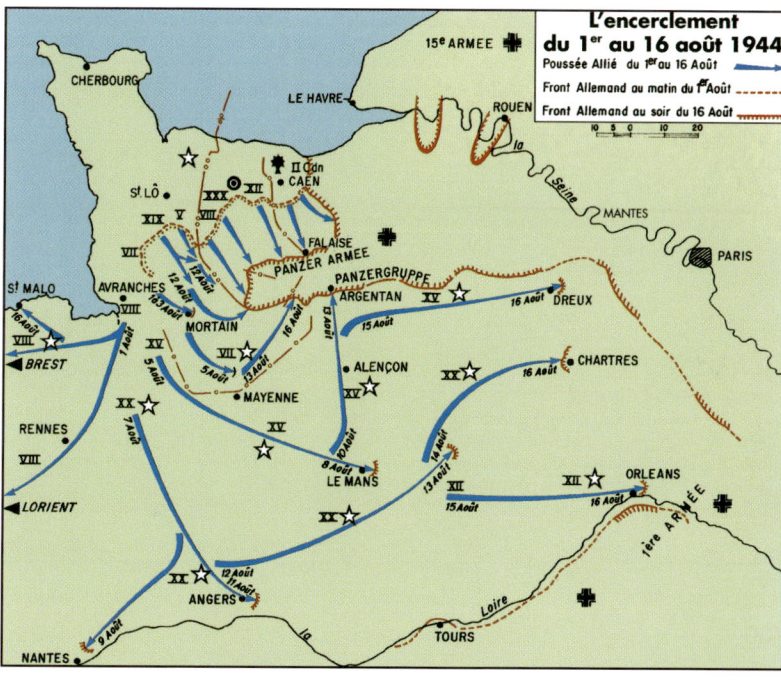

28th Infantry-Division

1 and 2 August 1944.

1. Aerial view of Percy. After the breakthrough, the front line in the XIX Corps' sector stopped in front of Percy. The sector was defended by elements of "Das Reich", "Panzer-Lehr" and 275. Infanterie-Division. The following day, the 28th Infantry ("Keystone") Division managed to break through the German front and penetrate into the hedgerow country, accompanying the movement, on its right, of the 4th Infantry Division which took Villedieu-les-Poëles. The 28th Infantry Division had only recently arrived on the Normandy front.

2. Infantrymen of the 109th Infantry-Regiment, 28th I.D. are in position in the church square at Percy, on 2 August, awaiting a possible German counter-attack.

3 and **4.** Some civilians gathered the previous day, 1 August, in front of the church porch.

5 and **6.** On 2 August, infantrymen of the 109th Infantry-Regiment, the "Keystone" Division, patrol Percy's main street, searching for isolated German soldiers.

7 and **8.** The same patrol enters an abandoned house in search of a possible sniper. The American soldier entering the house is armed with a Bar rifle.

9. 1 August, a tank-destroyer passes through Percy.

(Photos courtesy US-Army, Heimdal collection and E.G./Heimdal.)

Tessy-sur-Vire, 3-7 August 1944.

1 and **2**. South of Saint-Lô, Tessy-sur-Vire is a passing place in the Vire valley, which is here relatively deepset. This photograph was taken on 3 August at the junction of the roads to Saint-Lô (left) and Torigni (right). These two roads are controlled by a small Stuart tank and a M10 Tank-Destroyer respectively.

3 and **4.** As they advance westwards, near the town center, GIs pass by the wreck of a vehicle belonging to the 2. Panzer-Division, a Flakpanzer 38 (t) of Panzer-Regiment 3.
5. A little further on, more wrecks of this panzer division, a Pak 40 and the Bren gun carrier that towed it.
6. These GIs take a break on this 3 August, in a local storeroom among barrels of cider.
7. Four days later, on the 7th, an old woman is evacuated.
8. This monument recalls how the Americans arrived here on 2 August. (D.F. and E.G./Heimdal.)

Torigni-sur-Vire, 2-7 August.

1. As of 31 July, the town of Torigni-sur-Vire, south-east of Saint-Lô, was controlled by the 35th Division, in the V Corps' sector. Here GIs discovered a powerful heavy artillery cannon on a railtrack. It was a 24 cm Theodor Bruno Kanone, a 240 mm ALVF gun, assigned to E 722 Battery based in Cherbourg/Equeurdreville (serial numbers: 919079, 919081, 919082 and 919083). One gun was found at Vire. It was trained westwards on Coutances and the American breakthrough. The main railroad here in Torigni led onto a network of sidings originally used to load cattle, Torigni being in stock-farming country. This gun was on one of those sidings. Its home station was Berlin. Photo taken by Moran on 2 August. (9832)

Today: the disused station **(3)** which lay north of this rail junction with the ALVF gun; the wall covered with shrapnel **(4)** at the junction's terminal buffer, east of the gun; a railroad hut near this wall **(5)**; the restaurant **(6)** that was south of the junction and the gun and as it stands today **(7)**, extended; the bridge **(8)** which spanned the main line along the talweg, north-east of the junction. The gun was to be placed intermittently under this bridge.

404

2. Pfc John McDonald, of Olin in Indiana, shows Pfc John Ciesla, of Lackawana, New York State, a .45 caliber bullet found in the middle of some 240 mm shell casings. This photo was taken on 5 August. (10096)

9. On 7 August, at Torigni, a light Stuart tank is unloaded from a tank-carrier trailer.

Tessy-sur-Vire.

10 and **11.** Eight kilometers west of Torigni, the bridge over the VIre was destroyed by the withdrawing Germans. This photo was taken on 3 August. (9847). The present-day photograph pictures what remained of the destroyed building, on the far right.

(NA and D.F. and E.G./Heimdal.)

Pont-Farcy, 3 August 1944.

On the left flank of the American breakthrough, the German front south of Saint-Lô held out until 31 July. 2. Panzer-Division joined this sector on 29 July and managed to destroy 29 American tanks. It withdrew to Moyon on 1 August, then Pont-Farcy.

1. Pictured here is a Panzer IV of Panzer-Regiment 3, the 2. Panzer-Division's tank regiment, destroyed in the center of Pont-Farcy, photograph taken on 3 August.

2. This tank controlled the crossroads, now modified by the rebuilding of the ruined house (the new house in the center of the photo), the tank was on the left, with its rear to the crossroads.

3 and **4.** Then this tank, which blocked circulation, is pushed back on this site, on the other side of the crossroads.

5. Another view of this strategic crossroads, the opposite view to photograph 2.

(D.F. and E.G./Heimdal.)

Saint-Sever, 3 and 4 August.

6 and **7.** South of Pont-Farcy and east of Villedieu, the Americans were in Saint-Sever by 3 August. On the presentday photograph, the house seen on the right is the one whose gable is on the far right of the 1944 picture. The houses on the left were rebuilt.

8 and **9.** Saint-Sever station on 4 August 1944 and today.

10. A destroyed Jeep, 4 August, near Saint-Sever.

(D.F. and E.G./Heimdal.)

Villedieu-les-Poêles, 2 August 1944.

This town famous for its copperware was on the left of the breakout towards Avranches, and was still the cornerstone of the German front on the evening of 31 July. The men of the 4th Infantry Division entered the town two days later, when the Germans withdrew following the failed Mortain counter-stroke.

1 and **2.** A GI of the 4th Infantry Division makes contact with some civilians in the Rue Général Huard, on the east side of the town center.

3, 4 and **5.** GIs go round the church, heading south-west.

6. A short rest before resuming the advance.

7. Two days later, on 4 August, at Villedieu, a GI of the 12th Infantry Regiment (4th ID) also stops for a rest.

(D.F. and E.G./Heimdal.)

Saint-Pois, 3-5 August 1944.

1. Between Villedieu-les-Poêles and Mortain, the advance was now rapid. Here we see an M7 self-propelled gun in action against German units at Saint-Pois, on 3 August, west of Pérriers-en-Beauficel and Sourdeval.

2. This photo taken at Saint-Pois two days later, on 5 August, shows the result of the battle, an A type Panther tank has been destroyed, with the body of one of the crew members still lying in front of the wreckage.

3 and **4.** The front has moved and the civilians caught in the fighting can rest at last. This photograph was taken in the schoolyard at Saint-Pois.

5. The house seen behind the schoolyard.

6. The school in which civilians took shelter.

(D.F. and E.G./Heimdal.)

West of Sourdeval, 3-11 August 1944.

1, 2 and **3.** American infantry and tanks racing towards Sourdeval and Mortain. Here they are on 3 August at Champ-du-Boult where E. Lejeune's store has gone but where there is still the small zinc roof over the barn door.

4 and **5.** The next village to the south is Saint-Michel-de-Montjoie which dominates the surrounding countryside. The Americans camouflaged an M8 armored car there under some firewood.

(D.F. and E.G./Heimdal.)

6 and **7.** South-east of the above two localities, a Sherman tank passes through Pérriers-en-Beauficel, which is still as it was except for the store which again has since disappeared (house in the middle with the triangular pediment).

8. 10 August 1944, this GI notices that the store is booby-trapped.

(D.F. and E.G./Heimdal.)

Juvigny-le-Tertre, Reffuveille, 3-7 August.

Starting on 1 August, Patton's tanks broke through at Pontaubault and fanned out westwards into Brittany and eastwards into the Loire Valley.

Juvigny-le-Tertre, 3 August.

1 and **2.** West of Mortain, on the Avranches road, elements of the 4th Armored Division advance through the town of Juvigny-le-Tertre, damaged in the battle.

3 and **4.** A little further on, these houses are still smouldering.

Reffuveille, 7 August 1944.

5. We are in the same sector, near Reffuveille, still between Avranches and Mortain but west of Juvigny-le-Tertre. This day, at dawn, the Germans launched Operation Luttich, a panzer counter-attack towards Avranches to cut off the Allied breakout from its springboard. Pictured here are some Sherman tanks of I Company, 33rd Armored Regiment, 3rd Armored Division on their way through the Bocage to take on the panzers.

6. This photograph was taken on 3 August in the town of Reffuveille. It shows a captured German sniper, an NCO warrant officer, sitting on the hood of a Jeep, passing a long column of tanks of G Company of some tank regiment, probably assigned to the 4th Armored Division. The white lines on the negative indicate a realignment of the photograph.

(D.F. and E.G./Heimdal.)

415

Ger sector, from 30 July (1).

Before the start of Operation Lüttich, the German counter-attack at Mortain, infantry divisions were sent in to relieve the panzer divisions to be launched in the counter-attack. At the end of July, moving towards Normandy were six infantry divisions (84., 85., 89., 331. and 363. Infanterie-Divisionen brought in from northern France, and the 708. Infanterie-Division, from south of the Loire. 84. Infanterie-Division and 363. Infanterie-Division were assigned to the LXXXIV. Armeekorps in the sector south-west of Vire to relieve three of the panzer divisions to be used for the counter-attack. On the corps' left flank, 84. I.D. was committed from 29 July to relieve 116.Panzer-Division. PK Theobald then made this reportage, obviously on 30 July, on 84. Infanterie-Division's move up to the front line, between Beauchêne and Ger.

1 and **2.** First of all here are two infantrymen of this division heavily laden with Sten gun cartridge belts. (BA 721/388/2 and 5.)

3 and **4.** Here we are in Beauchêne, at the beginning of the reportage, as the infantry advance westwards. A farmer drives a herd of cows and calves towards Lonlay-l'Abbaye. The herd is coming in from the fields but the cart carries a white flag to avoid being machine-gunned by some Allied fighter-bomber. The place has not changed, except for the shutters and attic windows added to the house. (BA/721/388/14 and B Paich/Heimdal.)

5 and **6.** A hundred meters further on, the infantry continue their advance on Ger. The crossroads seen in the previous photographs can be seen in the background. (BA 721/388/7 and B Paich/Heimdal.)

7 and **8.** The photographer has turned round to take this shot of the same group. On the right: the road to Yvrandes and Saint-Jean-du-Bois, indicated by the signpost just visible on the right, more clearly in another picture. The present-day road has been upgraded but the surroundings are unchanged. (BA 721/388/8 and B Paich/Heimdal.)

9. Opposite the house seen in photographs **3** and **5**, this signpost was already there in 1944: to the south the D 269 road leads to Lonlay-l'Abbaye and Domfront; to the west the D 157 road leads to Ger and Saint-Jean-des-Bois. (Photo courtesy B. Paich.)

10. Grenadiers of the 84. I.D. pass by some half-tracked prime movers (3 ton Zugmaschine Hanomag) with a 75 mm gun in tow; the machine probably belongs to 116. Panzer-Division which 84. I.D. came to relieve. (BA 721/388/11.)

11 and **12.** One of these prime movers in the bend of the road where the ferns have now been mown. (BA 721/388/10 and B Paich/Heimdal.)

Ger sector, from 30 July (2)

1 and **2.** Between Beauchêne and Ger, at the place named La Haute Louverie, it seems that Allied aircraft are patrolling the skies and grenadiers of 84. Infanterie-Division have taken shelter in the ditch. The look on some of the faces testifies to the threat but others are smiling, so maybe it is a staged photograph. (BA 721/388/22.)

418

3 and **4.** Some closeups of the grenadiers taking a breather. Those in the first photograph were on the far right in photograph **1**. Those in the second photograph are drinking milk, having stopped to rest as we can see by a dairy. They include older, decorated veterans and also some very young soldiers who have not yet seen action. (BA 721/388/23 and 29.)

5 and **6.** The Belekys dairy then existed at La Haute Louverie where these soldiers are picking up supplies. The dairy has since closed, the loading quay (in the foreground) was destroyed, as was the staircase visible behind the soldiers. (BA 721/388/24 and B Paich/Heimdal.)

Ger sector, from 30 July (3)

1 and **2.** At the entrance to Ger, PK Theobald took this other shot of grenadiers of 84. Infanterie-Division moving up to the front along one of the lines of advance. This is an MG crew, with the usual cartridge belts slung over their shoulders.

3 and **4.** The same crossroads at Ger but looking towards the road which runs off to the left towards l'Essard. Very

little has changed between 1944 and today. These men are well armed. These are "tank breakers" transporting a Panzerschreck, the German bazooka and a Panzerfaust (here the model to be used at less than thirty meters range) carried by the last grenadier. He is also carrying two rockets for the Panzerschreck carried by his comrade. In front of him, another grenadier is carrying his personal weapon, the very modern assault rifle, a Sturmgewehr still only doled out to the troops in small numbers.
(BA 721/388/36 and B Paich Heimdal.)

5 and **6.** A little further on, an old Norman serves grenadiers cider from a traditional jug. These men are also heavily laden. The one on the far left, also has a Sturmgewehr. On 6 August, 84. I.D. held the Saint-Pois/Chérencé-le-Roussel/Saint-Clément line north-west of Mortain, being at the forefront, it was later trapped and destroyed in the Falaise pocket. Many of these men lost their lives. (BA 721/388/3a and 39.)

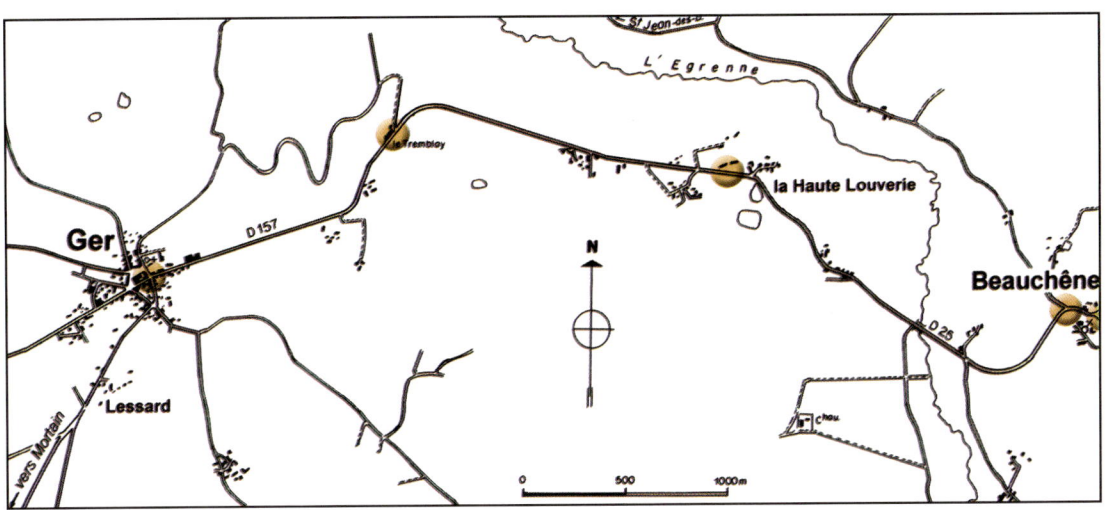

421

84. Infanterie-Division in the front line from 6 August (1).

1 and **2.** After moving up to the front line between Beauchêne and Ger starting on 30 July, 84. Infanterie-Division reached the front where it was completely in position as of Sunday 6 August. Here we are at the command post of Generalleutnant Erwin Menny, who took over command of the division in February 1944; it was raised on 2 February in northern France, the sector of the 15. Armee. It was positioned west of Rouen and later dispatched to the Sourdeval sector as we saw on the previous pages. It was then in the line against the 9th Infantry Division and, on the right (further north), against the 28th Infantry Division. (BA 722/408 - 11a and 12a.)

3. Generalleutnant Erwin Menny (1893-1949) commanded 90. Leichte Afrika-Division in Africa on 18 and 19 June 1942, then 15. Schützen-Brigade before taking over command of 84. ID.

4. The divisional staff lieutenant already seen in the preceding photographs now outlines the situation to his fellow officers. (BA 722/ 408/15a.)

5. This other lieutenant, decorated with the Iron Cross 1st Class, the Infantry Assault Badge and the Wounded Medal, is sitting by his vehicle on which is painted the divisional insignia, a lion. (BA 732/408/20a.)

6. Further on, some of the division's soldiers resting in the shelter of a hedge. (BA 722/408/30a.)

423

84. Infanterie-Division in the front line (2)

1 and **2.** The reportage by PK Theobald continues on the same film (reference 722/408). Pictured here is a slightly wounded liaison officer, helped by an NCO medical officer (a warrant officer), before boarding a medical vehicle. Then the wounded motorcyclist boards the vehicle, a Steyr 1500 DA/01 camouflaged with paint and foliage. (BA 722/408/2a and 3a.)

3. But facing the division on its right flank was the US 28th Infantry Division, which we have already seen in preceding pages on 1 and 2 August at Percy. Some soldiers of this division (with the distinguishing "Keystone" patch on their sleeves) are gathered here as prisoners. The division was not committed here against elements of 353. ID and 84. ID, until early August. This photograph was taken possibly on the 7th or the 8th, at the time of the German counter-attack. (BA 720/408/31a.)

4. In this same reportage, we see a Panzer IV passing. It belongs to either the "Das Reich" Division engaged in this sector for the counter-attack or 116. Panzer-Division. (BA 720/408/a.)

5 and **6.** Now the PK begins a new film, obviously on Tuesday 8 August, because the majority of the photographs in this film were taken during the night of 8-9 August. These are more American prisoners. They gave up their helmets then climbed aboard trucks. Will they reach a prison camp before the Allied pincer movement closes? (BA 720/329/5 and 6.)

425

Sourdeval on fire, night of 8-9 August (1).

Then PK Theobald left the front line sector of 84. Infanterie-Division down again to Sourdeval, a town north of Mortain, the vital strategic crossroads for the German counter-attack which had started less than twenty-four hours earlier, during the night of 6-7 August. It was via Sourdeval that 116. Panzer-Division launched its counter-attack Monday 7 August at dawn. Starting on Tuesday the 8th, Sourdeval came under a deluge of fire, the American artillery seeking to halt any movement by the German units. That evening, there was shellfire in the Cour Gallouin, Rue de l'Eglise, at the east end of the church. Shells continued to rain down. At around 21.00 hours, on this 8 August, a salvo landed on the choir. The fire spread throughout the town, soon turning into a blazing inferno. Sourdeval burned all night. The blaze continued through Wednesday 9th and Thursday 10th. But PK Theobald arrived at Sourdeval during the night of 8-9 August and witnessed the disaster which he recorded for History.

1 and **2.** PK Theobald arrived from the Vengeons sector by the Vire road. It was dark after 21 hours on this evening of Tuesday 8 August. In the pounding from the American artillery, a fire broke out in the Cour Gallouin, Rue de l'Eglise. It quickly spread down the street, near Saint Martin's church. This is what he saw coming off the Vire road, at the first crossroads on the way into Sourdeval, and took this photograph. (BA 720/329/17 and G.B./Heimdal.)

3 and **4.** The PK carried on westwards bypassing the town center, passing in front of the parvis which he skirted on the south side, and came to the square. He took this next picture showing the two pinnacle turrets of the south transept, on the left, and the street Rue de l'Eglise opposite, where the fire was blazing. On the photo taken in 2002, we see that all the houses in the square have been rebuilt. (BA 720/329/19 and G.B./Heimdal.)

8. The PK is now at the entrance to the Rue de l'Eglise. But he can go no further; the heat of the blaze is overpowering. Notice here the blazing beam on the house on the left, we will be using it as a landmark for other pictures.
(BA 720/329/ 27a.)

5. A German soldier observes the scene; on the right is the same signpost as in the photograph on the previous page. (BA 720/329/23.)

6 and **7**. The PK has now come to the entrance to the Rue de l'Eglise. A German motorcyclist observes the scene. The German fighters seem dazed by the fierceness of the blaze as proved by the number of the photographs taken by the PK. Notice how the fire is beginning to spread to the roof of the house on the right while the one on the left is already devastated by the flames. Now it has all been rebuilt. (BA 720/329/24 and G.B./ Heimdal.)

427

Sourdeval on fire, night of 8-9 August (2)

1. The PK also looked to his right, towards the Rue de Provence, again a blazing inferno. (BA 720/329/31.)

2. This photograph of the Rue de l'Eglise in around 1900 helps to picture the place as it then was. (H. de Prat coll.)

3. The same street in 2002. (G.B./Heimdal.)

4. This shot pictures the houses on the Cour Gallouin at the church's east end as it burns down. (BA 720/329/29.)

5. The PK steps back, the courtyard on the left is now hidden as the church's east end comes into view. (BA 720/329/32.)

6. In 2002: the pinnacle turrets that once flanked the east end are no longer there. At around 21.00 hours on 8 August 1944, the choir was hit by shellfire. The next morning, the vaults threatened to collapse, and later did so. In the background can be seen the modern constructions that replaced those seen burning in the previous photographs. (G.B./Heimdal.)

7. Another view of the entrance to the Rue de l'Eglise a little later, with the roof of the house on the right now completely ablaze. Notice our burning beam on the left. (BA 720/329/36.)

8. Map of the center of Sourdeval tracing the route taken by the PK in producing this reportage. (Heimdal.)

9. The ruined church choir in September 1944, a month after the fire. The choir was rebuilt without its pinnacle turrets; one of them is still visible here. (H. de Prat coll.)

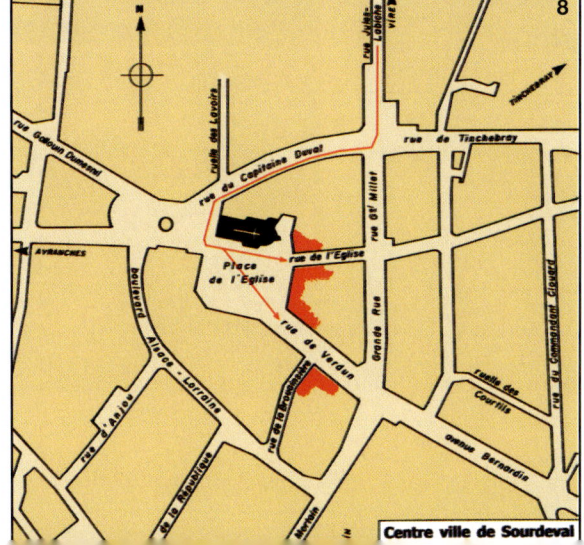

429

5. 7 August at Barenton, GIs of the 2nd Armored Division gathered round a piano. (D.F./Heimdal.)

Barenton, 7-9 August 1944.

1. American tanks have broken through. These tanks open fire on some pockets of resistance near Barenton on 9 August.

2. They were linked by wireless from a Jeep.

3. Two GIs sheltering in a foxhole camouflaged by ferns.

4. Ar Barenton, on 8 August, a German soldier has been killed by his vehicle.

28th Infantry Division

Sourdeval and Mortain sector, 9-13 August 1944.

1. Near Perriers-en-Beauficel, US observers issued with binoculars, on 10 August 1944.

2. Following the failed German counter-attack, American soldiers in two columns advance south on Sourdeval, on 13 June.

3. 13 August, near Sourdeval, three men of the 28th Infantry Division (left to right: Pvt Di Costa, Pfc Goldstein and Pfc Gagliardi) examine a saber taken from a Russian officer serving on the Germans' side.

4 and **5.** Photos taken in very thick hedgerow country near Mortain, on 9 August.

(D.F. and E.G./Heimdal.)

The Battle of Mortain.

1. This American antitank gun was east of Avranches on 31 August, just 200 yards (under 200 meters) from the German lines. In a few days, the Americans would be facing the German counterstroke.

2. American infantry advance near a house burning down in the Juvigny-le-Tertre sector, south-west of the Sourdeval salient and north-east of Mortain. (9919).

3. Norman civilians look on helplessly as a building burns in early August. Such scenes were commonplace at the time in the Sourdeval and Mortain sector.

4. On 7 August, the Germans launched their counterattack against Mortain, which was recaptured, and towards Avranches. A barrage of artillery fire then fell on the town on 8 August, and here civilian refugees have taken shelter from the bombardment in a disused mineshaft. The mineshaft was 800 feet (250 meters) long and could hold 100 people. (10930)

5. On 9 August, artillery officers have set up an observation post to control the artillery fire, near Barenton (southeast of Mortain).

6. At the HQ of the 35th Infantry Division engineer battalion at Saint-Hilaire-du-Harcouët, Major Botchin and Corporal Rajpka of the 60th Engineer Combat Battalion arrange their unit's advance. The divisional insignia is clearly visible on Corporal Rajpka's sleeve.

7 and **8.** Photos taken in Mortain on 13 August after the destruction of the town, in the same street (a multiple chimney stack served as a landmark).

9. Another view of the destruction in Mortain.

10. The 4th Infantry Division was north-west of Mortain. This is its commander, Major General Barton, kissing a civilian woman on 13 August.

(DAVA, NA and D.F./Heimdal.)

Mortain, 7-13 August

1. For several days the small town of Mortain was the hinge of a counter-attack launched towards Avranches on 7 and 8 August. Here, on 7 August, the Americans set up an anti-tank gun to face the panzer attack.

2. A little further on, medics administer first aid to the wounded.

3 and **4.** A few days later, on 13 August, GIs patrol the small town of Mortain after its evacuation by the retreating Germans.

5 and **6.** The photographer moves a few steps further into the battle-scarred town. A destroyed jeep and half-track have been pushed aside onto the sidewalk.

7. A few yards further on, this plaque recalls the role of the 3rd Armored Division.

(D.F. and E.G./Heimdal.)

436

Mortain, 12 August 1944

1. After the failure of the Mortain offensive launched on 7 August, the Americans examine German vehicles destroyed by Allied fighter-bombers near Mortain-Le Neufbourg station. This station, visible in the background, was located in the valley at the foot of the granite spur on which the small town of Mortain stands. The fighter-bombers wreaked havoc. The panzer attack was resumed on 8 August but it was pinned to the ground by the air force. There is a 2. Panzer-Division vehicle in the foreground, recognizable by the three-pronged fork painted on the wing, then a Schwimmwagen, and even a jeep, then a half-track (Kettenkrad).

2 and **3.** A little further on, a half-track and a tracked motor cycle. On the presentday picture, the trees on the left have been thinned out.

4 and **5.** The same vehicle, from the other direction, with the body of a soldier caught in bursts of gunfire from the Jabos (fighter-bombers).

6, 7 and **8.** Some shots of the now disused station still bearing Jabo bullet marks.

(D.F. and E.G./Heimdal.)

Behind the front line, 6-13 August.

1. Two American armies broke through and advanced well beyond Normandy, into Brittany and the Loire valley. The troops had difficulty keeping up as they raced ahead in these hot summer days of 1944. This GI takes a break to wash at a public fountain on 3 August.

2. In Tribehou, in the marshlands south of Carentan, where the battle raged during the first half of July, peace has now returned on this 6 August. Civilian Marc Didier shows his homemade set to two American soldiers.

3. Five days later, on 11 August, American soldiers listen to the wireless, its energy supply coming from a clever system devised by a Norman.

4. While the offensive continued, Lieutenant General Bradley remained at his headquarters at the Château de Saint-Sauveur-l'Endelin, where he is pictured here with Winston Churchill on 7 August.

5. Six days later, on 13 August, on the château steps, he is pictured with General Eisenhower.

6. Behind the front line, in August 1944, the troops take a few moments to relax at the Normandy Theater where, this evening, a world premiere is billed, Casanova Brown with Gary Cooper.
(D.F./Heimdal.)

441

The French 2d AD, 1-13 August.

1. On 1 August 1944, to the north of Utah Beach, a fresh armored division landed, a French division which fought hard in the final stages of the Battle of Normandy and during the Liberation of Paris. Pictured here is its commander, General Leclerc, coming ashore with some of his staff officers.

2. M4A2 sherman n° 20 Perthus of the 12th RCA lands from an LST on 2 August.

3. An M4A3 tank of the "1er escadron de combat du 12^e Cuir", n° 17 Grenoble, passes through Saint-Sauveur-le-Vicomte amid cheering crowds.

4. A transport vehicle passes through La Haye-du-Puits. Men of the 2^e DB and the people of Normandy are delighted to exchange a few words.

5. At Coutainville, Lieutenant Nonet-Raisin, wearing the model 43 jacket, rare at the time in the 2^e DB, is reunited with his wife (in the white jacket). He left her early in 1943

to join up with the Free French forces in North Africa. The accompanying soldier is the driver of the jeep "Saint-Lô", and he is wearing the model 41 jacket. Notice on his cap the golden navy anchor worn by French colonial troops.

6. On 8 August, men of the 2e DB enter Saint-James in a jeep. The man in the foreground is wearing a US tank crew's model 43 one-piece suit and a British cap.

7. Shortly after the Liberation of Alençon, on 13 August 1944, this corporal is reunited with his parents. Notice the Free French and divisional insignia on the back of his left-hand shirt pocket. He belongs to the RMT and on his head he is wearing the navy blue cap edged in red and bearing the golden anchor and a US M1 carbine over his shoulder.

(D.F./Heimdal.)

443

Vire from 8-13 August 1944.

This capital of the Bocage emerged forever scarred from the ordeal of the summer of 1944. As of 6 June 1944, when the local people were at table, their world came crashing down around their ears in a matter of seconds when B24 bombers dropped 200 kilo bombs on the medieval town. With the crash of the explosions, the dust, the screams and the panic, it was pandemonium. Wave after wave of aircraft came over, the horror went on all night, and the survivors fled to the outlying villages. 350 bodies were removed from the debris and 5,000 survivors took refuge in the surrounding country. The town was dead, and continued to burn for a fortnight, veiled in a huge pall of red smoke. And, from 7-15 June, there were bombardments every day. Until 1 August, the front remained firmly entrenched between Saint-Lô and Vire. It came closer on 4 August, when the Germans forced the civilian population to pull out to the south. The next day, 5 August, facing the German II Parachute Corps, the Americans of the 29th Infantry Division were at the gates of the town. Not being able to operate a frontal attack, the GIs of the 116th Infantry Regiment, who had landed on Omaha Beach, crossed Saint Martin Wood and the Vire River to reach the Rue des Cordeliers. It took them another day to reach the Rue Jean Le Houx and the church of Notre-Dame. Their advance was slowed down by the Germans and by the debris blocking the streets. They finished taking over the town on 8 August.

1. This aerial photograph, taken on 13 August below the old castle, shows us the damaged Notre-Dame church, surrounded by ruins.

2. The town was dead, having been destroyed unnecessarily.

3. GIs advance amid the ruins, photograph taken on 8 August.

(D.F./Heimdal.)

29th Infantry Division

Vire, 8 August 1944.

1 and **2.** GIs of the 116th Infantry Regiment advance through the destroyed town; progression was slow among all the rubble.

3. A bulldozer with an armored cabin was soon at work to clear the debris.

4 and **5.** A homeless family shelters in a tunnel; the GI will be getting the usual glass of cider.

(D.F./Heimdal.)

Ger and Lonlay sector, 13-16 August.

1 and **2.** North-east of Sourdeval, on this 13 August, east of Vengeons. While the Americans made rapid progress in the south, east of Mortain progress was slow against the Germans still holding out in that sector. Pictured here are infantrymen of the 28th Infantry Division passing through the tiny village of La Haute-Barre.

3. East of Sourdeval, the advance here passed through Ger then Lonlay, the way taken in the opposite direction by the 84. Infanterie-Division. We see here, on 16 August, in an American trailer, three German NCOs captured in the Ger-Lonlay sector by soldiers of the 110th Infantry Regiment, the 28th Infantry Division. The three German NCOs are wearing decorations. The wounded man is a company warrant officer, a "Spiess".

4. Pfc Louis L Hespe takes a moment's rest at the junction of the Tinchebray, Domfront and Lonlay roads, alongside signs left by the Germans. 16 August.

5. S/Sgt Teddy J Bozak of the 30th Infantry Division, advancing near Lonlay-l'Abbaye. This division was committed as part of the XIX Corps, on the 28th Division's right.

8. In Lonlay, moving around was difficult for the American armor by now. A few days earlier, a photo taken at the same spot showed 116. Panzer-Division tanks ready for the counter-attack. The abbey belltower can be seen in the background.
(DAVA and D.F./Heimdal, photo 2 courtesy H. de Prat.)

6. This aerial shot shows how badly the small town of Ger was hit.

Lonlay-l'Abbaye, 15 and 16 August.

The Germans did not begin to withdraw in the west from the Mortain sector until 16 August, which is why the Americans made little headway here.

7. This aerial shot shows the destruction in the center of Lonlay-l'Abbaye - on the right, the partly Romanesque abbey church, has been hit.

449

Domfront, 15 August.

The town of Domfront, perched on a hill, still with part of its medieval enclosure wall, was a major crossroads (to Mortain, Flers, Sées, Argentan and Mayenne); it was hit hard by the bombardments. It was now in the hands of the 30th Infantry Division.

Opposite page, from top to bottom: the aerial photograph shows that the major crossroads east of the old town came in for some precision bombing by the Allied air force, with the whole area destroyed. A view of the neighborhood at the foot of the old ramparts shows the scale of the destruction.

(Photos courtesy DAVA/Heimdal Coll.)

30th ID

Opposite: another view of the same sector, with the church bell-tower towering over the old town.

Below: two American soldiers set up a telephone line near the crossroads, in front of one of the towers of the old gate leading to the old town.

Domfront, 14 and 16 August.

1. On this 14 August, a Sherman tank of the 67th Armored Regiment, 2d Armored Division patrols in the center of Domfront old town, the only part spared by the bombs. It moves down the narrow streets passing in front of the unusual cement church dominating the town. This tank is accompanied by infantrymen of the 41st Armored Infantry Regiment, assigned to that same armored division. Notice how they are wearing the famous American camouflage smock, which was worn very little in Normandy to avoid confusion with the Waffen-SS. In fact, only the 2d Armored Division's motorized infantry units wore this uniform in Normandy.

2. Domfront Town Hall where American troops set up the "Civil Affairs" office. This photograph was taken two days later, on the 16th.

Domfront, 14 August.

3. Pictured here are some German prisoners and soldiers of the 2d Armored Division, mostly in camouflage smocks.

4. German prisoners leave Domfront to take the Mortain road but there is no more question of any offensive for them.

5. In the lower part of Domfront, coming from Ger, a 2d Armored Division half-track passes some infantrymen. (Photos courtesy DAVA/Heimdal Coll.)

6. The American engineers' machinery is now at work clearing the streets in the area razed by bombs.

(National Archives/Heimdal Coll.)

9th ID

3rd AD

From Rânes to La Ferté-Macé, 14-16 August.

1. Near Domfront, the men of an American anti-tank unit position their tank-destroyer at the foot of a roadside cross: the TD tank is camouflaged under branches.

2. East of Domfront, between La Ferté-Macé and Argentan, the small town of Rânes is invested by the 3rd Armored Division. On this 14 August, it was close to the front line, facing elements of the 2. Panzer-Division. The ruins of the houses are still smouldering.

3 and **4.** On 16 and 17 August, the Normans returned to their ruined town to salvage whatever they could of their belongings.

454

5 and **6.** Members of the 39th Infantry Regiment, 9th Infantry Division here operate a bazooka in Andaine Forest on 15 August. Notice the divisional crest stencilled on the helmet and that same division's cloth badge sewn on the sleeve. The division was committed between La Ferté-Macé and Rânes.

7. The following day, 16 August, two men from the same division clean their mortar.

8. The 3rd Armored Division advances starting from Rânes on a sector extending from Fromentel in the west to Ecouché in the east. Pfc Ray Tucker, of that division's engineer unit, examines cases of German ammunition discovered in the forest, near Fromentel.

9. On the 9th Infantry Division's left flank, La Ferté-Macé was taken on 15 August.
(NA, DAVA and D.F./Heimdal.)

From Alençon to Argentan, the closing of the Falaise-Argentan gap.

1. On 12 August, Maj. Gen. Haislip's armored divisions entered Alençon. By evening, they had reached Argentan. The closing of the pocket could have started the following day... This is an aerial shot of Alençon, the largest town in southern Normandy, located on its old border.

2. The station was especially badly hit.

3. At the entrance to Alençon, burned out vehicles on the roadside.

4. The bombardments hit the town sporadically.

5. Frenchmen of the 2nd DB pass by Notre-Dame church in Alençon town center. The 2nd DB heads off towards Argentan.

Argentan sector

6. American infantrymen advance cautiously on a farm near Argentan. Some of them have set up a mortar.

7. American soldiers pass through Argentan on their way to the Pocket. They stood outside Argentan for a week before taking the town.

8. Columns of American infantry advance along a road near Argentan.

9. They now approach the center of the Pocket.

(DAVA and NA/Heimdal.)

2. As they retreated along congested roads covered by the Allied tactical air force, the Germans sustained heavy losses in vehicles. This photograph was also taken on 13 August.

3. Pictured again here are men of the 9th Infantry Division committed on this 16 August in the south-west of the pocket, in the sector between La Ferté-Macé and Rânes. These men have climbed on a TD. One of them is wearing a German belt. They have placed a German helmet as a trophy on the front of the tank and Private Robert Dawkins is aiming his dagger at a photograph of Hitler. The divisional badge is clearly visible on the man in the foreground's sleeve.

4. Thursday 17 August in the evening, under pressure from the American armies in the south, the British armies in the west and Canadian armies in the north, the Falaise-Argentan pocket was finally closed. Some 100,000 German soldiers were caught in a zone thirty kilometers long by fifteen wide. The battle lasted five days, many German units forcing a way out to the east, and about half of those troops managed to extricate themselves from the trap. Here, on

The pursuit.

1. 13 August, at Saint-Germain-de-Tallevende, a half-track passes by an abandoned German assault gun, marked by a white flag. It was probably hit by a rocket fired with a bazooka. This is four and a half kilometers south of Vire on the left flank of the American disposition, near where it joined up with the 2nd British Army. This was difficult terrain and the advance was slow against the Germans as they withdrew into what was to become the Falaise-Argentan pocket. (10855)

incomplete victory, as about half of the encircled troops succeeded in breaking out and the German troops now retreated to the Seine. But already the American divisions were racing to further victories. On this day, the French 2nd DB, under American command, received orders to race to Paris.

7. On 25 August, the Americans and British linked up at Pacy-sur-Eure. The American motorcyclist is wearing a camouflage smock. Paris had been liberated the day before, but the Germans continued to cross south of the Seine, and retreating elements continued to hold out in the Neubourg and Louviers area. By 30 August the Germans had completed their crossing of the Seine, marking the end of the Battle of Normandy. The last action fought by the Americans was with the 79th Infantry Division in the Mantes bridgehead.

(Photos courtesy DAVA and D.F./Heimdal.)

this 17 August, at Domfront, a long line of trucks brings back German prisoners, captured on the edges of the pocket. (11414)

5. A few days later, on Monday 21 August, the number of prisoners rounded up was much higher as the rear-guard was caught in the pocket. Notice a majority of men from infantry divisions, some paratroops and, in the front half of the column, only three Waffen-SS including one tank crew member in his camouflage smock. Further on are two Heer tank crew members. There are few crack troops here. They generally managed to break out.

6. On Tuesday 22 August, tanks of the 67th Armored Regiment (2d Armored Division) opened fire in the Conches sector. The next day, they would try to press on northwards to Neubourg, only to be stopped by elements of the 116. Panzer-Division. By this morning, at 08.00, the Battle of the Falaise-Argentan pocket was over. This battle was an

Achevé d'imprimer en juillet 2004
sur les presses de Ferré Olsina
(Barcelone/Espagne)
pour le compte des Editions Heimdal